"*Couple Therapy* represents a unique, original and long-overdue contribution to the field of marriage counseling. In fact, this is indeed the most significant integrative resource for Christian couples therapy published in the twenty-first century. From theory to first steps to case studies, worksheets and handouts to specific interventions, this clearly written book is a gold mine, a library of resources in one volume, giving counselors a practical road map. It builds on a strong biblical and theological foundation, is research informed, scientifically sound, empirically validated, evidence based and therapeutically rich. Both professional and pastoral counselors will find this an invaluable resource. Jen and Ev have given us a remarkable gift. It will touch your heart, stimulate your mind, increase your confidence and encourage your practice. Simply put: if you work with couples you need to invest in this book. It will be required reading of all of my students, and it will be a resource you will refer to often."

Gary J. Oliver, executive director of The Center for Healthy Relationships and professor of psychology and practical theology at John Brown University

"Ripley and Worthington provide a text that is built on their previous work, and innovates in providing hope-filled interventions for clinicians and couples. I look forward to having my students use this book as a foundation for their training in working with couples. I also look forward to integrating these interventions into my own work with couples (and in my own marriage). Ripley and Worthington are building on the current research in attachment theory, cultural contexts impacting relationships and neurobiology. In addition, they are faithfully infusing Christian distinctiveness into these domains. What emerges is a text that assists clinicians to provide counsel based in current research, best practices and Christian virtues (e.g., Colossians 3). If you work with couples or teach graduate students how to do couples therapy, this book is a must for your clinical 'tool box.'"

David J. Van Dyke, associate professor and director of Marriage and Family Therapy Program, Wheaton College

"If you are looking for a book that integrates hope, faith and love with best practices in couple's work, this book is the one to buy. *Couple Therapy: A New Hope-Focused Approach* is an A to Z guide to successful couple treatment that is comprehensive and research based, but also filled with interventions and practical help. Worthington and Ripley have taken a good approach and made it great. Speaking as a licensed marriage and family therapist for over thirty years, this is a resource you need to add to your library today."

Linda Mintle, chair, division of behavioral health, Liberty University College of Osteopathic Medicine

"This book is a clear, organized, integrative and extremely pragmatic approach to couples counseling that helps therapists carefully tailor their treatments to couples' specific needs. Everyone from the novice to the experienced therapist can find something of great value in what these authors have to offer. Their attention to framing therapeutic tasks around couple strengths in order to better address deficits and, perhaps more importantly, give couples hope is particularly novel and thought-provoking. I found several appealing new strategies that I am looking forward to integrating into my own couples work; I am sure the reader will find many useful ideas as well."

Kristina Coop Gordon, professor of psychology and associate director of clinical training, University of Tennessee-Knoxville

COUPLE THERAPY

A NEW HOPE-FOCUSED APPROACH

Jennifer S. Ripley and
Everett L. Worthington Jr.

IVP Academic

An imprint of InterVarsity Press
Downers Grove, Illinois

InterVarsity Press
P.O. Box 1400, Downers Grove, IL 60515-1426
ivpress.com
email@ivpress.com

InterVarsity Press® is the book-publishing division of InterVarsity Christian Fellowship/USA®, a movement of students and faculty active on campus at hundreds of universities, colleges and schools of nursing in the United States of America, and a member movement of the International Fellowship of Evangelical Students. For information about local and regional activities, visit intervarsity.org.

All Scripture quotations, unless otherwise indicated, are taken from THE HOLY BIBLE, NEW INTERNATIONAL VERSION®, NIV® Copyright © 1973, 1978, 1984, 2011 by Biblica, Inc.™ Used by permission. All rights reserved worldwide.

While all stories in this book are true, some names and identifying information have been changed to protect the privacy of the individuals involved.

Cover design: Cindy Kiple
Interior design: Beth Hagenberg
Images: © bstoner/iStockphoto

ISBN 978-0-8308-2857-9 (print)
ISBN 978-0-8308-9661-5 (digital)

Printed in the United States of America ∞

Library of Congress Cataloging-in-Publication Data

Ripley, Jennifer S., 1972-
  Couple therapy : a new hope-focused approach / Jennifer S. Ripley, Everett L. Worthington,
Jr.
      pages cm
  Includes bibliographical references and index.
   ISBN 978-0-8308-2857-9 (hardcover : alk. paper)
  1. Marriage counseling. 2. Marriage--Religious aspects--Christianity. 3. Pastoral
counseling. I. Title.
   BV4012.27.R57 2014
   259'.14--dc23

                                                                                    2014013485

P   28   27   26   25   24   23   22   21   20   19   18   17   16   15   14   13   12   11   10   9

Y   38   37   36   35   34   33   32   31   30   29   28   27   26   25   24   23   22   21

To Kirby:

Happy 44th year of sharing our lives—Ev

To Jeff:

Happy 21st year of sharing our lives—Jen

Contents

List of Interventions

List of Worksheets and Handouts

Why You Need This Book

&

Perhaps you are one of the over 50,000 counselors who have used either the 1989 *Marriage Counseling: A Christian Approach for Counseling Couples* or the 1999 *Hope-Focused Marriage Counseling: A Guide to Brief Therapy* (or its 2005 revision). Or perhaps you came across the hope-focused couple approach (HFCA) to couple enrichment through the research that has made it one of four treatments evaluated as "empirically supported" (Jakubowski, Milne, Brunner & Miller, 2004). Or perhaps you are new to this approach. In any case, this book will present a theoretically grounded, strategic approach to counseling couples that we have developed with Christian principles and have practiced and studied scientifically.

We call this an "approach" because it is applicable to couple counseling and couple enrichment. In fact, even educated lay people could benefit by the many assessment tools and discussions for improving marriage. So this book might actually be a rarity in publishing—a professional book that could benefit experienced and novice psychotherapists, counselors, pastors and lay counselors, but could also benefit married couples. We believe it could give many ideas to active researchers as well. We address the book to the practicing couple counselor. Many have told us that, along with the practical interventions, it is the integrated, eclectic theoretical framework that is most friendly to combining with their own current system of couple therapy. This new book has a much deeper theory, grounded in other established theory and research in attachment and intimate bonds. We think you'll love the expanded and deepened hope-focused couple approach theory in this book.

Within these pages, you'll find over 75 new practical interventions you
have not seen before. But this book is more than simply a new bag of tricks—
although you might think that alone is enough to merit reading it. For this
reason we suggested, and InterVarsity Press agreed, that this book was not
a mere revision of *Hope-Focused Marriage Counseling* (1999, 2005). Rather
it represents its own new approach. True, it builds on the previous book, but
whether or not you are experienced with the approach described there,
you'll find this to be a strong addition to your theoretical and practical tool
kit. If you are just starting to practice the hope-focused couple approach,
you'll quickly learn the theory in its expanded form, and you'll learn many
practical interventions.

The practical interventions will enrich your counseling repertoire. *Hope-
Focused Marriage Counseling* had about 200 practical step-by-step interventions, which (along with the integrative theory) is what most readers said
they appreciated most. Perhaps the strongest portion of this present book is
the variety of new interventions we have created and couple-tested since the
publication of *Hope-Focused Marriage Counseling*. However, we also have
been discerning in what we have included from the last book. Over 15 years
of experience have accumulated since the original 1999 version was penned—
actually more, given the delay between the writing and publication of any
book. That represents a lot of clinical experience—and not just our own, but
that of the thousands whom we have trained. We have strongly tested the
original interventions and have identified many essential ones that have
worked well with countless couples. We call these the "hope-focused classics"
(and designate them with the icon $\widehat{hf}$). We include enough of them to
maintain the power of the hope-focused couple approach that inheres in
those classic interventions. When we describe them, we discuss new understandings of them based on 15 years of working with couples. We believe that
we have increased the therapeutic power of the approach by including many
new interventions and by referring you back to *Hope-Focused Marriage
Counseling* (2005) for other hope-focused classic interventions that we did
not have enough space to include.

We have also described and illustrated actual cases (disguised, of course).
This allows you to see how over 75 of these all-new and hope-focused classic
interventions are integrated into entire cases. Thus, the two books together
can form a set of about 300 practical interventions with couples, organized

within their own theoretical framework and illustrated with many cases. We also include all new assessment instruments and worksheets for couples and other resources that complement (not duplicate) *Hope-Focused Marriage Counseling*. And even if you already have a theoretical approach you are comfortable with, this book will pass the compatibility test. The interventions and cases will enrich your own theoretical approach.

Where did all of these resources come from? Many came as a result of feedback from the people who bought over 50,000 books and tried the methods with their clients. Many came from our own supervision of couple therapists or our own practice with couples. Many came from experiences gained at a community clinic that Jen established at Regent University (see hopecouples.com), including the supervision, training and research we have done there. Many came from Ev's traveling, speaking and talking to counselors and through an active research program at Virginia Commonwealth University, especially within the forgiveness and reconciliation parts. We believe that if you read one of the two previous books, you'll want this one to expand greatly your clinical acumen. We believe if you have yet to read those books, after you read this one, you'll want to go back and complete the set. We welcome you and invite you to walk with us through this new hope-focused couple approach.

Part One

A THEORY OF CHANGE

In this first part we summarize the hope-focused couple approach. This substantially updates the theoretical understanding of what causes couple problems and how to help couples address those problems. If you are familiar with the classic *Hope-Focused Marriage Counseling* (2005), you will find this a quick review but with significant new twists. If you are not already familiar with the approach, this will be a rapid primer and good theoretical base to start you toward learning new interventions, seeing new cases and getting a new slant on couple counseling.

1

Wanted: A Wise and Humble Counselor

ح

Great couple counselors are rare. There are too few wise and humble counselors who will help couples find the healthy, warm and honorable relationship that will sustain and nourish them into the future. Maybe you are a counselor who has tried couple counseling and are looking for a new and improved method to help couples. Maybe you are curious about how couple counseling works. Maybe you are reading this book because you believe couple relationships and marriages are the cornerstone of society, important to children and to God. We feel a kinship with you as readers who want excellence in your work. Couple counseling is one of the most difficult contexts for change. If you have chosen this path, then you have an important journey ahead of you.

It is difficult to become a great couple counselor or perhaps to add depth to already considerable expertise at couple counseling. Couple counseling has one of the highest incidences of dropout and recidivism of any kind of counseling (Jacobson & Addis, 1993; Owen, Duncan, Anker & Sparks, 2012). Some research reports over a 50% "failure" rate at the one-year post-therapy mark! This is not a surprise. After all, couple counseling requires two people to simultaneously make changes in order to fully achieve goals. And those goals might differ, just as understandings of the causes and solutions of the couple's problems might differ. Partners may also believe that a quick breakup or divorce will end many problems in an intimate relationship, unlike other problems such as depression or anxiety disorders. Couples you work with in counseling will interact with each other in their dysfunctional patterns all week. They likely will have only one hour a week with you. Often they do not experience the quick changes they hoped for, and they seem confused why ten hours of counseling did not change deeply set, long-standing patterns of dysfunction that took 10 or 20 years to form. Couple treatments can often feel like you have a thimble-full of water for a roaring house fire! If you have been in practice for a while, we are sure you know the feeling well. We too feel it—all too frequently.

Couple work is certainly never hum-drum. It is full of strong feelings, attachments, heartbreak, sexual dysfunctions and misbehavior. Sometimes you even find yourself in the middle of a psychological war. It requires the ability to manage strong negative emotions in the room. Research clearly shows that couple therapy without a strong plan and direction tends to end badly (Snyder, Castellani & Whisman, 2006). The alliance of the partners with each other, which you cannot control, is more important to the outcome than your own alliance with each individual (Bartle-Haring et al., 2012), which unfortunately you also cannot control. Scheduling appointments with two adults more than doubles the difficulty in finding time to meet. And just to give you one more challenge, it is often difficult to get couple counseling covered by health insurance. This is challenging work!

At times, most couple counselors feel weak in the knees or just plain tired. We could use some help. Maybe you are just desperate to find an approach that will work for you after trying different things and seeing things go wrong in your office. Or perhaps you learned an approach to couple counseling long ago and need to update your work. Maybe you have been using a secular approach in which you were trained, but some of your clients want an approach that is explicitly Christian. Maybe you have found that the approach you were trained in really did not have much evidence supporting it and you want an evidence-based practice. These are the needs this book will meet.

The new hope-focused couple approach is a simple but effective plan to help couples. It is a well-tested approach to couple work, supported by numerous empirical studies. Research began in the early 1990s demonstrating efficacy for couples in improving many aspects of their relationship (for a review, see Ripley, Maclin, Hook & Worthington, 2013). The improvements in this book are not just ideas invented in our heads and christened "wonderful" by us. They have been tested in our two clinical laboratories with couples seeking help. We have asked the couples what helped them. We have measured couples using psychometrically sound instruments, videotaped them communicating, coded every word, hooked them up to blood pressure monitors and even conducted glucocorticoid tests on their spit to assess their stress reactions. There is more. We have followed up with them for months to see whether the gains they made during counseling still work for them. We also have tried out different components of the interventions we present in this book. We have imported some methods that have been used and shown to work in other approaches. We have listened to what the couples have said to us, listened to what counselors who have used the approach have told us, and revised our approach. The result is this book.

WHERE TO START THIS JOURNEY?

We start by introducing you to a very simple and ancient idea. The most important thing to remember is that relationships improve by "faith working through love" (Gal 5:6 NKJV).[1] In the book of Galatians the apostle Paul had a problem. He was writing to people who genuinely wanted to live a good life, full of love for God and others and at peace with their neighbors. Yet they struggled with living in a society with many ideas and teachings. They were confused. In this part of the letter to the Galatians, Paul was

> *The most important thing to remember is that relationships improve by "faith working through love."*
> GALATIANS 5:6 NKJV

telling them to keep their eyes on the most important thing—faith working through love. It is the path to Christian freedom. Many other Scriptures also point to love as the cornerstone of Christian virtue and the highest calling. We think this wisdom is worth using as a navigation guide amidst the storm of couple counseling. Faith, work and love all help guide the counseling through a difficult journey. These are principles we hold on to. They steady us. And they allow us to guide the counseling to a safe destination.

    Faith. Faith is the "substance of things hoped for, the evidence of things

---

[1]J. R. Daniel Kirk, New Testament professor at Fuller Seminary, states that this is the best translation of this passage because it is the most straightforward, versus other translations that say "faith expressing itself through love" (J. R. Daniel Kirk, "Boo . . . Theologically Manipulated Translation. Boo . . ." *Storied Theology* [blog], February 19, 2010, www.jrdkirk.com/2010/02/19/boo -theologically-manipulated-translation-boo/).

not seen" (Hebrews 11:1 KJV). Faith points to hope, even hope in things that we cannot see. Spiritual hope is found in faith in God, faith in salvation, or faith in heaven and the hereafter. This principle applies to relationships. Couples hope for something. They have faith that their relationship will be full of love, care, fidelity and intimacy. Before they ever met each other, they had faith that such a relationship could happen and that they could be a part of it. This is why couples who are in serious relationship trouble are so heartbroken and despondent. They are losing their faith that love can rescue, restore and redeem their relationship.

Work. Everybody says it: "Relationships take work." It is true. The work should be positive, fun, healthy, warm and encouraging. Relationship work should not be drudgery. It should not be fending off a desire to blame or accuse the partner. It should not be parrying the thrust and blows of an adversary. It should not be digging up the psychological corpses of the past. We think the work should be like rock climbing. Rock climbing is exhilarating. It requires conditioning for strength, skills for safety and risk-taking for excitement. But the rewards at the top of the mountain are immense—a great view and a feeling of exhilaration for succeeding at climbing a mountain. Working on an intimate relationship should be similar kind of work. We also think it is no coincidence that Paul paired faith and work together here as two parts of this phrase. Some people overemphasize faith. They pray and wait or sit and hope that the partner will change. But they do no work. Other people overemphasize work. The relationship is a duty, a task, a project. Sigh. Who wants to be someone's project? Paul put the two together because it takes both to achieve what everyone wants—part three, love.

Love. Love brings life to faith and work. It is the warm bond that connects partners. Love is the nurturance that every human needs. It is the cornerstone of Christian virtues and the description of God. Psychological research on love is well developed. Social neuroscientists who have studied love have found a broad network of pathways in the brain where love has control over the parts of our brains that work our emotions, motivation, attention, memory and even self-representations (Cacioppo, Bianchi-Demicheli, Hatfield & Rapson, 2012). Social-cognitive research on love used to point to "exchange theory" or a kind of tit-for-tat explanation for love relationships. Today, research points to attachments that are biological, social and cognitive at the same time (Cacioppo, Bianchi-Demicheli, Frum,

Pfaus & Lewis, 2012). Christians would add that love is also spiritual. It is the embodied human experience of the love of God. "It always protects, always trusts, always hopes, always perseveres" (1 Cor 13:7). Love involves our whole self at its fullest.

These three concepts are a steering wheel. Hold on to them and we believe you can stick to your course of helping couples improve their relationships. Ancient Christian wisdom guides the theory of the hope-focused couple approach. We believe this wisdom is the steering wheel, but the boat is going to need more than a steering wheel to sail. This is why God gifted us with "general revelation." General revelation is knowledge about what is true about God and creation that God has revealed through nature. For example, how a bumble bee flies or how you might get good tomatoes to grow in your garden are general revelation. We learn about God by observing in nature how God made bumble bees or tomatoes. We are not going to use just any way of learning about nature. We are going to use systematic, scientifically reviewed, scrutinized and evaluated findings about how couples work and improve. Revelations from Scripture undergo a similar scrutiny by way of theological study, but one way that general revelation about couples is vetted is through psychological study. Combining the truths of Christian faith with observations of couples and couple therapy provides a rich context from which to help couples solve their problems.

WHY ARE THEY HERE?

The reason couples come to your office for counseling is that they cannot stand the idea of losing each other. They are on a journey but are often far from where they intended to be. Think of your couples as two people trying to travel together but getting repeatedly lost. They have come to your door to ask for directions. How do we stay together in this journey and find the place called a healthy, virtuous, warm and happy relationship?

Attachment theory has provided support for the idea that what motivates people to seek counseling for their relationship (an experience they are pretty sure is likely to be painful and difficult) is that they are deeply attached to one another on all levels. Attachment theory (Shaver & Mikulincer, 2010) teaches that relationship attachments are crucial to understanding people. Adult attachments are influenced by childhood experiences such that partners tend to "replay" the kind of relationship they had with their parents. There is good evidence that understanding, validation and caring are basic human responses necessary for secure attachments (Reis & Shaver, 1988). So if partners are secure, they will be confident that each partner is dependable and will respond to them when needed. Secure partners are flexible in terms of autonomy and dependency—feeling comfortable both in being independent and in depending on others. Partners who are anxious in their attachment style will worry that their partner will not be there for them when needed and easily become upset when their needs are not being met in the relationship. Partners who are avoidant in their attachment style do not seem to need their partner and do not look to their partner for needs. Those with avoidant style do not like to be depended on and do not want their partner to depend on them.

The field of attachment theory and research has grown quickly with important new findings (Shaver & Mikulincer, 2010). Anyone doing work with couples should be aware of these basic findings.

- Attachments are important throughout life. Much of the teaching on relationship attachments focused on infants or young children. Now we know that attachments help us understand people at all ages (Ainsworth, 1991).

- Cultural factors are more important than we used to think (Shaver & Mikulincer, 2010). People create relationships and attachments within a cultural context. Keep culture in mind when evaluating partner attachments. For example, socioeconomic status is a cultural variable. So someone from a low socioeconomic status is likely to have had more breaks in attachments in their lifetime due to the pressures associated with poverty.

- The biological basis of attachment is well-established now with growing research on the human brain. Coan (2008) has proposed a social baseline theory. He suggests that humans must rely on the brains of others to operate adaptively. If a human is removed from social relationships, the brain will not function properly. This has been demonstrated by orphans' poor outcomes when they are raised without validation. It also accounts for the severe physiological responses associated with grief when a particularly strong attachment is lost. There is even evidence that attachment styles relate to our autonomic nervous system (Diamond & Fegundes, 2010), the system that controls our body's involuntary actions like heart rate or sexual response. Diamond and Fegundes propose that it is possible that couples coregulate physiological responses to the world, working in tandem to respond to their environment.

All of this is important to understand because, in order to provide the most help to couples in treatment, you need to understand what is going on "under the hood" of the car that will take them to their destination of a healthier relationship. The new and improved hope-focused couple approach takes the latest in attachment theory as essential information in understanding couples *and* in understanding how a couple counselor should relate to couples as an understanding, validating and caring person for both partners.

WHAT IS THE DESTINATION?

Experts do not agree on the destination or goal of couple counseling. Most would say the goal is for the couple to be more satisfied in their relationship. That is certainly a good outcome because dysfunctional, distressed, unhealthy and immoral actions tend to lead to dissatisfaction. We believe that satisfaction, important to many clients and couple counselors, might not be the best goal. We would like to propose four other goals for couple counseling: warmth, virtue, health and happiness.

Warmth. An essential part of the destination is that it will be warm. Warm, secure bonds in a relationship are essential. All evidence (discussed earlier in our update on attachment theory) points to warm relationship as a real goal of couples. They might not come to couple counseling saying, "We are cold, we need to heat up." In fact, they may seem to you pretty heated—in a different manner of speaking—in their sessions! But what they need is less fear of the warm bond that connects them, less conflict surrounding their bond, and more of a sense of peace. They need to seek stronger and warmer relationship bonds through secure attachment. We believe there are many ways to increase the warm bond for couples.

Virtue. Couples should direct their relationship toward a destination where both partners display virtues. Virtues have new emphasis in the field of psychology (Seligman, 2012). Yet in all the cases we have seen or supervised, we have never had a single couple come in and actually say, "We want to be more virtuous in our relationship." But they drop clues of their longing for virtue. They complain bitterly if their spouse is immoral within or even outside of their relationship. They might even say they want to be "better" at being in a relationship. They long for a just or fair, enduring, self-controlled relationship between two people who know the best way to respond to each other at a given time. In classical virtue theory, these are the four cardinal virtues of justice, fortitude, temperance and prudence. Couples even long for the Christian virtues of faith, hope and love, even if they do not embrace the Christian faith.

Health. The journey should bring partners to a place of improved relational health. There should be clear and direct pathways of communication that seem validating to both partners. Patterns of intimacy and even conflict should be characterized by respect and caring. Commitments should be clearly understood and communicated. Health requires work. A human body without exercise or proper nutrition will become flabby and obese, and death can be premature. In the same way, relationships require both energy and proper nutrition. If couples do not feed the soul of the relationship and expend energy to strengthen the relationship, it will become weak, with loose bonds and lots of excess fat to carry around. Better to keep it in shape.

Happiness. The enjoyment of a loving relationship is one of the best experiences of living. As Victor Hugo wrote in *Les Misérables*, "The greatest happiness of life is the conviction that we are loved—loved for ourselves, or rather, loved in spite of ourselves." Couples need hope that happiness in love is a possibility, that it might be obtained. That hope will motivate them to take courageous risks in their journey together.

WHAT IS MY ROLE?

Couple counselors are, in a way, relationship-mechanics instructors. Our role is not to fix the vehicle of the relationship, but to teach the couple how to repair and maintain their relationship. (We acknowledge that counseling is not really mechanistic; we're just making an analogy.) The couple counselor's role is to create an environment where the couple can strengthen their bonds, create healthy and functional habits of the heart as they relate every day, and act virtuously. Our role as couple counselor is to design strategies that will help the couple to achieve the four goals for their relationship: warmth, virtue, health and happiness. These strategies should be simple and memorable enough for the couple to be able to use them every day. Couples should walk away from a counseling session saying, "Gee, this is easy. Why didn't we try this before?" The strategies should be easy enough that they help couples take responsibility for their own relationships. If they leave believing they can only relate well if you are in the room, then your counseling was not successful.

Designing simple, creative, culturally and spiritually competent interventions tailored to the couple's life stage and value system requires considerable thought and energy. The ability to accept when counseling is not going well and address the roadblocks head on requires courage and humility from you. Making yourself open and vulnerable to care for your clients requires faith and love. These goals require a good relationship between the counselor and the couple in order to maximize success (Blow, Sprenkle & Davis, 2007). In short, you are going to need a parallel process of developing warmth, virtue, health and happiness in your relationship with couples. This book will help you with that goal.

A ROADMAP

This book has six parts to help you meet your goals.

Part one is the theory of change. You will get a "behind the scenes" look at how couples relate to each other and how they improve or not in counseling. The theory is important so that you can creatively design some of your own personalized intervention strategies for couples in your office. But we will also sprinkle this part with some interventions we have used that are relevant to the concepts we are introducing.

Part two is help for the beginning of counseling. There is nothing more important than a good understanding of what is going on with the couples. This part will help you with pre-therapy information, screenings and paper questionnaires through the first intake session. It is full of ideas for how to collect and organize all the information you will discover about the couples you are seeing.

Part three is about individualized treatment planning and describes different types of couples you will encounter. A good counselor plans the treatments for couples intentionally and creatively, realizing that one size does not fit all. This part of the book will give you examples of couples and will discuss ideas for treatment that will model how to create a personalized plan for intervention with your couples. Many interventions are described, referenced by chapter and intervention number. (In earlier chapters, we will refer to interventions and cross reference them, so that if you are interested in pursuing them even before we discuss them in detail, you can easily find them.)

Part four is the heart of the book: interventions and strategies. This part is full of dozens of interventions you can use with couples to address a wide variety of goals in five broad groups. We group the interventions by chapters, and generally we also use the acrostic to refer to them (e.g., HOPE 18-6). You can choose the strategies that best fit your couples and the particular problems they have.

- HOPE (Handling Our Problems Effectively) interventions focus on improving problems through building couple skills and improving behaviors

- BOND (Bind Our Nurturing Devotion) interventions help strengthen a warm bond for the couple

- HURT (Handling Unacceptable Relationship Tears) interventions address hurts that occur in relationships that cause tears or breaks in the fabric of the relationship (and also the tears that people cry)

- FREE (Forgiving and Reconciling through Experiencing Empathy) interventions catalyze the repair of relationship hurts and bring partners back together with increased understanding and wisdom

- TRUST (Trusting Response United with Shared Trustworthiness) interventions provide ways to build reconciliation through mutually trustworthy acts

Part five offers strategies for conquering difficult counseling issues. This includes addressing roadblocks, resistances and how to avoid getting angry at couples whom you cannot help, as well as special complicating factors that need attention, such as pornography use or trauma history.

Part six concludes the book with information on ending counseling memorably and meaningfully. It helps you assess change and terminate counseling.

We sincerely hope that you enjoy this journey of learning more about couple counseling and strengthening your skills as a couple counselor. We hope that God travels with you on the journey, illuminating and bringing to your attention the things you will need as you work with couples in the future.

2

A Sensible, Tested and Effective
Approach to Helping Couples

෧

Do you often have a hard time deciding between too many good things? If you were offered chocolate cake, apple pie and homemade ice cream, would you ask whether you can have a little bit of each? You would not be alone. The same thing happens in psychological theories. There are good wisdoms found in a variety of psychological or couple counseling theories. It can be difficult to decide what theory to apply, for what client, in what setting. We need principles to decide what will help our clients. The hope-focused couple approach asks three questions to help counselors create a strategy for change:

1. Is it going to work for this couple?

2. What is the basis of the theory of change?

3. Is there evidence to support its effectiveness?

Your answers to these three questions will guide your decisions of what to include in counseling and how to strategically plan your treatment. We are not devoted to a single overarching theory of change like family systems or Bowenian theory. Theoretically, the hope-focused couple approach is (a) strategic, (b) focused on building hope and (c) committed to using "sensible" interventions that make change easy to experience but that derive from a variety of theoretical approaches. So it has a flexible but firm-at-the-boundaries theory shaping it. But from a counseling-methods perspective, the hope-focused couple approach is transtheoretical. We draw methods from many theoretical approaches. We believe there are many nuggets of wisdom found in numerous theories but that hundreds of research studies across decades have been clear that there is not an undisputed "winner" in the psychotherapeutic theory game (Barlow, 2010). Almost all theories and approaches have demonstrated some effectiveness in helping couples. Research has not demonstrated any magic bullets, essential components or necessary dynamics to change, other than general common factors (Hubble, Duncan & Miller, 1999) and some well-researched treatments for specific disorders. Thus, as an evidence-based practice in psychology, the hope-focused couple approach borrows from the most well-researched theories to tailor a strategy for change that fits the counseling situation. This pragmatic approach is more common in new couple intervention systems (such as the "Sound Marital House," Gottman, 1999). First, counselors identify their core commitments (i.e., strategy, hope and sensible interventions). Then they ask, "What will work for this couple's needs?" Third, they apply various theoretical ideas or interventions from the field of couple therapy to assist couples toward their goals. It is not a haphazard recipe, but one that is guided by principles. Let's consider in more detail our principles.

THE HOPE-FOCUSED COUPLE APPROACH IS CHRISTIAN

Most importantly, the hope-focused couple approach has always been rooted in Christian principles and traditions. Charity and Justin are seeking counseling for their relationship. Charity is a devoted Catholic woman, but Justin grew up Protestant and is now nominally Catholic after feeling disrespected by some church members. For this couple, faith is important to understanding their relationship and life. If their faith experiences are minimized or misunderstood, then the counselor has missed an important opportunity to enter into the client's world. Many counselors are uncomfortable with issues of faith, making it difficult to be comfortable in a client's experiential framework of faith. We would hope that any counselor could understand a Christian theory of couple counseling, but it is helpful for the ideas to be explicit.

The research on religion and couple therapy is recent and rather limited. Some general research on counseling that accommodates religion has demonstrated that it is equally effective as standard counseling, but may be more helpful in spiritual goals or strivings (Worthington, Hook, Davis & Mc-Daniel, 2010). Two studies on couple counseling, conducted through each of our labs, have also found no difference between Christian couple counseling and general couple counseling in relational measure (Hook, Worthington, Ripley & Davis, 2011; Ripley, Worthington & Maclin, 2011). There is a growing set of studies showing prayer to be an effective intervention in improving relationships (Lambert, Fincham, LaVallee & Brantley, 2012). While these studies represent a comparatively small amount of research, they have the same general outcomes.

Some may be shocked and dismayed to discover that Christian couple counseling is not more effective overall than secular couple counseling. We believe this lack of difference between Christian and secular counseling on relational measures is important to understand. On a spiritual level God has offered common grace to couples around the globe who may not prefer or be able to have Christian couple counseling. They can still improve their relationship even if religion is not addressed in session. That makes for a better society for everyone. Imagine a world where only Christian therapy was effective. It would be inconsistent with God's common grace in other areas of life such as medicine or education. Just like a Christian college education is unlikely to do a better job at teaching math or literature, so Christian counseling is unlikely to do a better job at improving relationships in general. Yet many people prefer to seek Christian counseling, education and medical providers. They like to include their faith in their work.

For some couples spiritual understanding, goals and strivings are an integral part of personal and relationship growth. For example, whenever a husband feels frustrated with his wife, he may focus on Christian teaching that spouses should try to be a blessing to each other. The goal of being a blessing becomes the means by which the husband is motivated to engage in positive behaviors and cognition to improve the relationship. So improvement in spirituality that comes from counseling should not be minimized or viewed as "less than" relationship satisfaction outcomes. Faith matters in living.

THE HOPE-FOCUSED COUPLE APPROACH DRAWS FROM MANY SOURCES OF CLINICAL WISDOM

The hope-focused couple approach has roots in strategic couple therapy.

Strategic therapy was developed by Jay Haley (1976). It focuses on active change, power dynamics, communication and skillful interventions used strategically to create change. Similarly, Haley's colleague Sal Minuchin (Minuchin, Lee & Simon, 2006; Minuchin, Reiter & Borda, 2014) emphasized very concrete therapeutic methods to change the structure of the couple relationship. Strategic and structural therapy theories remain overarching influences in the hope-focused approach, but other theories have had more influence in the revisions of our approach. Strategic theory helps us when thinking of goals and the big picture. Structural therapy helps us focus on concrete, sensible interventions.

Behavioral couple therapy and some of its spinoffs. Jacobson and Margolin (1979) emphasized problem solving that we still incorporate. In fact, we drew some methods from solution-focused therapy. However, as early as 1995, Jacobson and Christensen had realized that some relationships just did not yield to solving problems. They shifted to the principle of solving the problems you can and accepting what you cannot solve. This in turn gave rise to the third generation of behaviorism, acceptance and commitment therapy (ACT; Hayes, Strosahl & Wilson, 2011). We have developed a similar (but with important differences) emphasis in parallel with the evolution of these approaches. Importantly, we have focused on forgiveness more than acceptance and a Christian worldview instead of the more Buddhist worldview of ACT. In both cases, partners let go of hostility, but forgiveness replaces the hostility with an active valuing of the partners.

Emotion-focused therapy. Emotion-focused couple therapy (EFCT; Furrow & Bradley, 2011; see also Hart & May, 2003) has changed how couple therapy is done. The new hope-focused couple approach incorporates concepts from EFCT and encourages strengthening relationship bonds as a major goal of treatment and intervention. In particular, emotional softening and increasing the secure attachment between partners is necessary for full forgiveness (both decisional and emotional). EFCT emphasizes the brain biology of repeated emotional interpersonal experiences. This applies especially well to cases where a partner has been repeatedly offended in the relationship and has nursed a grudge. That brain pathway has been rehearsed well and often through rumination, creating a complex web of fear and anger-based emotional brain responses to intimate relationship. Since the grudge is simultaneously a brain event and a relational and emotional event, the change will have to involve the whole person. The couple will need to experience warm relationship events, reduce cognition about hurts and the grudge, and soothe the grudge cognitions in order for emotional forgiveness to occur.

Attachment is not only important in issues of forgiveness but also for all areas of intervention. When thinking about the work of couple counseling, the counselor should be considering how to improve the bond between the partners. An emotional bond can be improved by improving relationship skills, forgiving, increasing intimacy or a host of other interventions. A counselor should be asking why the couple is having difficulty with their emotional bond and what can be done to make their bond healthier.

Diversity matters. The influence of ethnicity and culture on couples is essential to the hope approach (McGoldrick, Giordano & Garcia-Preto, 2005). There are internal dynamics relevant to how partners perceive their own ethnic or cultural traditions: how they communicate, how they express emotions or what roles they play. Without this foundational understanding, it is difficult to effect change, particularly for couples from smaller groups that may be marginalized within society. We have long been attuned to the power of religious communities and the importance of attending to religious diversity. We thus value many dimensions on which couples can be diverse.

The case of an African American couple who were seen in the clinic is a good example of the importance of working with clients in their experience of diversity. The couple had struggles with social pressures in that the husband was underemployed. This was experienced as devaluing by the husband, causing him to "puff up" by attempting to overcontrol in the home. His wife had been hurt by men in her past, causing her to be defensive, especially when her husband would try to control her. This dynamic is influenced by the very real situation of the husband actually being devalued as an African American man. The counseling was more effective when the counselor asked about his underemployment, accepted it as a true experience, and helped the couple see the pattern of conflict. When the couple joined together with a common enemy of racism and dedicated themselves to making their home a "safe harbor," they were able to make significant gains in counseling.

Adjust for trauma. Psychologists have made strides in understanding the effects of trauma on intimate relationships. Sometimes trauma has roots in wartime experiences, a car accident, child abuse or assault. New research has explored whether relationship events such as discovery of an affair might have similarities with trauma (Baucom, Snyder & Gordon, 2009). The experienced couple counselor recognizes and adjusts treatment and techniques to issues like traumas, whether external to the relationship or internal. We strive to stay alert to cues that triggers exist and, when activated, a cascade of conscious and unconscious events might follow.

Resistance offers grist for the mill. The Borg (from *Star Trek*) stated that "resistance is futile," but any couple counselor knows that resistance to change is a major issue. After decades of conducting couple therapy and supervising doctoral students weekly I (Jen) discovered something very important. Just because you offer wonderful techniques for change does not mean the couple can benefit by the techniques. Weekly, the novice counselors came to supervision with frustrating problems of client resistance. We developed an approach to addressing resistance (further discussed in chapter 24) that is influenced by research on resistance in couple counseling (Epstein & Baucom, 2003). Couple counselors need a strategy to handle couple resistances, rabbit trails and roadblocks. With an overarching strategy, the rest of the interventions—the tactics of counseling—can be effective. We have gladly drawn on insight-oriented counseling for this important truth.

COUPLE COUNSELING SHOULD BE MEMORABLE

Coinciding with the pragmatic and transtheoretical approach, the hope-focused couple approach is designed intentionally to be memorable. Human memory and thinking is more fallible and malleable than is generally assumed. There are three facts learned through cognitive research that are very important to keep in mind when working with couples.

Memory errors are common. People tend to believe they remember their own history quite well, but when that theory is tested, we make remarkable errors (Carter, Aldridge, Page, Parker & Frith, 2009; Kahneman, 2013). You may be sure of where you were and what you were doing on important dates like September 11, 2001, but research has indicated that your memory is not as certain as you might think. Duke University researchers Jennifer Talarico and David Rubin (2003) asked a few dozen students on the day after 9/11 what they were doing when they learned about the events of the previous day and about other normal memories. They found that 32 weeks later the students had forgotten about 33% of the events from the day for both the 9/11 event and other mundane memories. Yet they were extremely confident of the 9/11 memories, which are called "flashbulb" memories—photograph-like memories that surround important events that were believed to be "seared" into our memories. This research was replicated with a larger sample by the 9/11 Memory Consortium (Hirst et al., 2009) and they found an average of 37% error of event details after one year. That is remarkable!

Not only do we have poor memories as a species but we tend to remember things that support protecting our own egos (Alicke & Sedikides, 2011). Unhappy couples often disagree about the facts of their shared history, with both partners overestimating their positive intentions and behaviors in the events. Memories tend to be shaped and changed to protect a person's ego, which can make couples vulnerable to remembering their history in self-protective ways, increasing defensiveness. Couple counselors can help couples identify traps that may be relevant to self-protective memory processes and reduce their defensiveness. Defensiveness is very hard on a relationship.

Furthermore, our memories are mood congruent. Thus if we are feeling angry, we will tend to remember injustices and offenses in our history. On the other hand, if we are feeling happy then we tend to remember happy experiences (Cahill, Gorski & Le, 2003). Experiences that cause us to feel fear are remarkably resistant to fading and the memory is often accompanied by reexperiencing the emotion (Diamantopoulou, Oitzl & Grauer, 2012). Most other experiences, such as eating a meal or even having a good sexual experience, tend to fade. Yet a fearful experience tends to be remembered throughout the brain due to the way the brain handles fear. Interestingly, research seems to indicate that our memory for details of these fearful events is no better than our poor memory for details otherwise (Dalenberg et al., 2012), so while we remember we were afraid, we may mix up the sequence or details of events.

People who are angry in a relationship tend to remember all the previous times they felt angry. This helps us see how the "kitchen sink" tends to be thrown into a fight recalling all the previous offenses. People who are discouraged or depressed in their relationship tend to easily remember the other times they felt discouraged with their spouse. They forget all those happy times and dwell on the sadness. It is easy to see why couples in negative relationships can easily test out examples of fear, anger, and sadness or discouragement. They believe that this is the way it is, the way it always has been and probably the way it will be. Mood-congruent memory is part of what makes negative relationships so difficult to turn around. It feeds depressive thinking patterns in unhappy couples. Cognitive interventions for couples can be used to help them experience more mood-congruent positive memories, which will be discussed in detail in chapter 20, "Addressing Hurts in Relationships."

POOR SOCIAL COGNITION HURTS OUR RELATIONSHIPS

I'm good, you're lucky. Perhaps sometime in your Psychology 101 course you were introduced to the concept of the fundamental attribution error (Funder, 1987) and motivational bias (Zuckerman, 1979). If we apply these cognitive errors to couple relationships, we understand why partners tend to believe that their own motivations for negative behaviors are reasonable responses to situations. However, one's partner's negative behaviors are assumed to be due to negative traits or "pure meanness." If I am speeding in my car it is because I will be late in picking up my children from school. I do not assume that I am a speed demon. If my husband is speeding in his car, I assume it is due to his speed-demon reckless nature. I know my own reasons for a negative behavior, and I tend to be pretty forgiving of myself in most situations. It is much harder to see what situations influenced other people's behaviors, so we tend to attribute their negative behavior to their dispositions. Unhappy partners often characterize their partner as possessing negative personality traits: she's lazy or he's overbearing. This makes it especially difficult to find hope for change when there is global negativity. Identifying and addressing these cognitive errors is a key to helping couples turn their perspectives around.

In response to these facts about the memory, the hope-focused couple approach uses memorable and clear interventions to effect change. For example, we encourage counselors to provide a written feedback report which can be reviewed to aid memory. Couple sculpting interventions are used to physically demonstrate the experiences of closeness. This involves the body in making stronger memories. Acronyms are used for many interventions. Such memory aids help couples overcome these universal human problems of warped memory and biased social thinking. Concrete memory aids also help to make the interventions resistant to "revisionist history." Whenever possible, hope-focused interventions are memorable and clear. For example,

HOPE intervention 18-16, the confirmation bias experiment, is a direct application of these principles for the couple to learn from this research.

COUNSELING RESEARCH IS ESSENTIAL TO QUALITY COUPLE COUNSELING

Basic research. We draw on basic research and apply it to the clinical situation in the hope-focused couple approach. Understanding how couples relate on a basic level helps the couple counselor to have the perspective needed to implement treatment effectively instead of simply using some technique in hopes that the relationship will improve. This would be akin to a mechanic changing your oil, replacing your brakes and giving you new spark plugs without understanding how a car works. The mechanic might get lucky and hit on the right solution to the problem. But without understanding, even an experienced mechanic is likely to try methods that fail, especially when there are new problems. And let's face it, people are a lot more complicated than cars, and two people with unique personalities can have many, many unique relationship problems.

Applied research. There is a line of 20 years of research on the effects of the hope-focused couple approach. Overall, the research on couple enrichment has shown that the hope-focused couple approach is an effective intervention (Jakubowski, Milne, Brunner & Miller, 2004) supported by multiple research studies in two different laboratories. Since that review, there has been a growing body of research from our labs indicating that the approach is effective for most couples seeking couple therapy in a brief format (Ripley et al., 2014). Component research has indicated that the assessment and feedback component is effective (Ripley, Maclin, Hook & Worthington, 2013) and that the communication-based interventions effect general change (Worthington, Hight, Ripley, Perrone, Kurusu & Jones, 1997) while the forgiveness-focused interventions effect change in forgiveness and quality of life (Burchard, Yarhouse, Worthington, Berry, Killian & Canter, 2003; Worthington, Mazzeo & Cantor, 2005). Finally, a study comparing a religion-accommodative version of the hope-focused couple approach to a standard nonreligious approach found no difference in relationship outcomes and a slight increase in spiritual outcomes (Ripley et al., 2014).

REFLECTING ON THIS CHAPTER
A giant river is fed by many springs and tributaries. If we want to understand

the quality of the water and how it will flow in the future, it is helpful to understand not only its current status but also its sources. From our brief review in this chapter, you can see that the hope-focused couple approach is fed by the spring of Christian faith and practice. But it also draws from commitments to be strategic, promote hope and create sensible, memorable interventions. Using those filters it incorporates decades of clinical practice from a variety of theories of couple therapy. It draws eclectically from tried-and-true interventions, all of which are selected because they bring about the principles of strategic, hope-instilling, memorable actions that are informed by research. The sources of the hope-focused couple approach are sound, and when used by sensitive personable counselors will help promote positive growth in couples.

3

Making Therapy a Positive
Growth Experience for Couples

಄

C ouples in dysfunction and dissatisfaction are miserable people. They are desperate. They often behave appallingly toward each other. Janet and Ron are a couple you might recognize. Janet complains that Ron is a "bump on a log." He never wants to have fun or engage with friends or social events. Janet goes out with friends two or three times a week and invites them over often. Ron does not seem interested. She pushes, pulls, berates and condemns him for a day or two before the events to convince him to join her. Ron does not particularly like people, other than his wife. His idea of a good time is gardening, watching basketball and reading the paper. Their disengagement has widened until Janet feels abandoned and alone. She has started flirting and texting with a man she met when out with friends. Ron is confused and deeply hurt by the disclosure of Janet's attraction to this other man. Janet hopes *this* will finally get Ron interested in her.

Many couple counselors would start counseling by trying to help Janet and Ron build their communication skills, learn to fight without berating and condemning each other, or perhaps explore their childhood wounds. Others would introduce complex concepts, language, and models of relationships to the couple. That type of counseling can easily focus on the couple's negativity, addressing the problems, going to the depth of their pain. But what if there is a different way?

Positive psychologists (Harvey & Pauwels, 2004; Seligman, 1995) have argued that most humans overcome adversity by using their strengths, as well as changing their weaknesses. Many traditional couple therapies are problem-focused and virtually ignore the strengths of the couples. What if counseling helped the couple find their strengths as a couple, and find ways around their weaknesses, perhaps not even needing to change those weaknesses? Ron and Janet need a new goal. Janet has been trying to get Ron's attention and interest in her. He's always been attending to her, but he does not express it in a way she can hear. Ron just wants to be left alone and not be pestered to act more social then he feels. He enjoys doing some things with Janet but other people stress him out. Both partners are feeling pain.

Counseling That Builds Virtue

Couples come to counseling because they are in pain, often deeply wounded. They feel defeated. Entering counseling feels like they are admitting failure. They are often asked, "What (problem) brings you to counseling?" This is a terrible beginning for them. Nearly half of partners seeking couple counseling report depression or anxiety symptoms (Beach & Gupta, 2003). We do not think that counseling is aided by forcing couples to admit defeat and go into an emotional cave. One of the most important things that must happen at the beginning of counseling is for the couple to see that it is possible to change. They must be given hope. This happens when couple therapists assess problems with wide-open eyes but exude hope of realistic change. This is not a goody-goody, Pollyannaish cheeriness. It is hard-nosed, experience-based faith both in love and in God's power to transform.

The hope-focused couple approach redirects the couple toward the strengths and virtues that they already possess with hope for the possibility that counseling can help them mature in their strengths and virtues. Couple therapists do not ignore problems. In fact, ironically, by getting people to focus on hope, they can solve or leap over those problems faster than by focusing on the problems. Often a counselor's underlying message to couples is something like, "You are terrible to each other. You have long-term intractable problems that are making you miserable. Counseling is going to be very hard. You must work to have a chance of improving." This message often sets couples up to feel pessimistic and look toward a less-work, grass-is-greener solution—divorce.

Some gifted counselors can say or do almost anything with couples and they get better. We marvel at couple-therapy magicians like Milton H.

Erickson, whose feats were chronicled by master counselor Jay Haley—himself a couple-therapy magician. We wish we were so talented. But few of us can be as successful with problem-focused counseling as Erickson or Haley. We do not need therapy magic. We need an approach that we all can do—trainees, new practitioners and counselors who have seen it all. Focus on hope, strengths and positive changes. Those emphases will help couples change. Not only that, but they are simply more fun to do as a couple counselor. They are something you can succeed with.

Let your couple counseling have this message: "You have many as yet unused or underdeveloped strengths. You have qualities and personal character strengths that you have been building most of your life that you can use for this problem. You can do this with the tools you have. Just strengthen them and use them at the right time." Counseling will help you do this.

Getting back to Ron and Janet, the counselor notes that Ron is actually quite loyal, steady, devoted and honest as a husband. This is exactly what attracted Janet to Ron to begin with, and it is a key personal character strength that holds the two of them together. Janet can count on Ron's love and devotion no matter what life storms come their way. Ron has been developing that quality all his life. In exploring how he came to develop such a strong virtue, he shared an amazing life story. There was chaos in his childhood. His unsteady mother had many bouts of depression. It was not easy to become loyal, steady, devoted and honest in that environment. Janet knew about the mother's depression but had never attributed Ron's devotion to something he developed in the midst of a "fiery furnace." The counselor said Ron could use that personal character to help with their relationship problems now. He will remain true to her, despite the hurt of her flirting. She will appreciate that. Counseling can encourage him to even further develop his virtues. This can be done through faith avenues like spiritual disciplines that focus on loyalty. Psychological avenues can also assist. He can learn to change his attributions for Janet's behavior, to forgive her, or to soften his raw emotions. But the purpose of the faith or psychological interventions is to *use personal character to repair the relationship*. Virtues are the path to relationship warmth. Many psychological goals are being met simultaneously by focusing on Ron's strengths, which can build hope.

> *Virtues are the path to relationship warmth.*

The experience of counseling is positive. The search in counseling is not for dysfunctions but for virtues. The focus is not on failures, blame and symptoms. It seeks to uncover buried or overlooked strengths, skills and virtues.

Reattribution is happening. Partners can begin to see each other as a virtuous relationship hero instead of as a villain. The power of changing the narrative from villain to hero can set off an earthquake that shakes the marriage initially and keeps rattling it with aftershocks.

The personal character of the partners is a stable and global quality. Even if Ron has "forgotten" what a steady and loyal man he is in the wake of the flirting disclosure, deep down he still sees himself that way. An angry, off-balance victim sees himself one way. A hero will act differently. People must see themselves as the hero in their own narrative in order to have hope for a future.

Anyone can understand that his or her personal character can be an avenue of change. This does not require learning a new psychological vo-cabulary, complicated relationship model or new psychological skills, or engaging in emotional backflips.

Focusing on personal character and virtues creates hope for maturing of character. Ron can become the loyal pillar of his home and community that he has always longed to be if he continues to develop his character. Janet can become the joyful and hospitable blessing to her family and everyone she comes in contact with. The current situation is a temptation to each partner and to the couple to forget their hero status and give in to a problem orientation. If they can turn away from that temptation, they can remain the heroes in their story as a couple. Who would not want that future?

We have limited resources. The field of social psychology can further add to our understanding of this process of developing relationship virtues. Roy Baumeister is a social psychologist who has for decades studied the topic of self-control. All relationship virtues require a measure of self-control to enact, especially in the face of adversity. Baumeister's research (Baumeister & Tierney, 2011) has found that self-control is a limited resource. When people must exert willpower to control their anger, disappointment or vengeful motives, that constant expectation can deplete the ability to ex-ercise self-control if one provokes the other. Similarly, lack of sleep or stress can affect the ability to exert self-control. Anyone who has attempted weight loss has experienced this self-control depletion. Early in the day, on a normal day with a good night's sleep, we can keep to our diet plan. But after using our willpower to avoid high calorie foods all day, the self-control "muscle" is worn down and the person is more likely to give in to temptation and eat a big piece of cake. This is not just something in our minds. It is physical. Neurons require energy to fire effectively, and they burn glucose. Most of the glucose burned is in our brains, not our muscles. Psychologically straining to exert self-control depletes the glucose in the brain making self-control harder. Baumeister has shown that people who drink a glass of sugar-sweetened lemonade experience rekindled willpower but people who drink lemonade sweetened with artificial sweetener do not experience rejuvenated willpower.

The application of this research is this: there are predictable times we are vulnerable to failures of self-control. It is not surprising then that couples tend to argue when they are stressed. The demands of a difficult job where people have to "hold their tongues" all day can cause a rebound effect at home after a long day of self-control. Partners can often "hold it together" after an offense for some time but then tire of being forgiving and become indignant and intolerant. Even missing sleep, coping with boredom and being on a diet can result in more arguments between partners, but the killer is the accumulations of daily hassles and little, too-small-to-mention offenses. They can build up and trigger out-of-proportion nastiness. These lapses in virtue are part of the human experience. But, be especially aware. One response is the key to maintaining the healthy relationship in the face of "losing it."

The key virtue is forgiveness. For long-term relationship health, forgiving quickly is the key. At some point in most relationships, people lose self-control. Unkind words will be said. Injustices will offend. General or specific acts of malicious wounding and suffering are common in families. Responding within the family and outside of the family with forgiveness and its related virtues of grace and humility is necessary. If we keep a short list of wrongs, we can ease the strains on our self-control so that when one person does provoke the other, our self-control has not been depleted.

Forgiveness and those related virtues need to be developed, tested and proven. These ideas are not just good ideas. They have been tested in over 2,500 research studies and in daily living. Research on forgiveness with couples has demonstrated healthier and happier relationships for those that forgive each other (Fincham, Beach & Davila, 2007; Worthington, Jennings & DiBlasio, 2010). There is even preliminary evidence that forgiveness interventions with individuals (for a meta-analysis, see Wade, Hoyt, Kidwell & Worthington, in press) and couples produce longer lasting effects in forgiveness than relationship skills-focused interventions (Ripley, Maclin, Hook & Worthington, 2013). Part four of this book has a collection of forgiveness-focused couple interventions to support building this virtue with couples. We think forgiveness is a key to lasting change for couples.

Once we introduce the principle of cultivating virtues to couples, they become more interested in growing personal relationship virtues. Orienting a couple toward making their virtues grow in their relationship is validating and rewarding.

Couples often enter counseling hoping (perhaps secretly) that their partner will do most of the changing. They are looking for validation that they can be greater spouses and partners. They are afraid they are losing the love in their relationship. The counselor can help bring out the virtues in both partners so they can be the heroes in their own narrative. As G. K. Chesterton (1905, p. 38) wrote, "We ought to be interested in that darkest and most real part of a man in which dwell not the vices that he does not display, but the virtues that he cannot." Helping the partners display their virtues feeds the secret longing of both partners that they both have valuable qualities. Unlike problem-focused approaches that seek to give the message that both partners are equally to blame for problems, the hope-focused couple approach has the message: You both have strengths. You can use them to heal. That is the key to a positive experience in this type of couple therapy.

> We ought to be interested in that darkest and most real part of a man in which dwell not the vices that he does not display, but the virtues that he cannot.
>
> G. K. CHESTERTON

Virtue-Based Interventions

Virtue or character development is deeply important to God's work of sanctification. As Colossians 3:12-14 says, "Therefore, as God's chosen people, holy and dearly loved, clothe yourselves with compassion, kindness, humility, gentleness and patience. Bear with each other and forgive one another if any of you has a grievance against someone. Forgive as the Lord forgave you. And over all these virtues put on love, which binds them all together in perfect unity." Those counselors that work in pastoral settings or Christian counseling centers may find that Christian virtue development resonates well with your goals and work in counseling. Those in secular settings should also find that character development themes can fit their clients' needs, whether or not they are religious.

The use of virtues can be a context for understanding and intervention. Worthington and Berry (2005) discuss three themes that might be helpful in thinking about virtues-based interventions with couples. First, there are two classic themes in virtues: passion and reason. Couples can have difficulty in virtues both in too little warmth or passion and in too little reason. Virtue development may target broadly those two classes of virtues. Second, the couple and counselor should be aware of the role of relationships in their lives. Often relationships serve unstated needs, even if dysfunctional and full of vice. There are also other relationships that intersect with intimate relationships, such as children, in-laws, community and friends who may rely on the couple. Third, the couple and counselor should consider who is responsible for the couple's virtue development. Is it up to each partner to be virtuous individually? Is it a joint responsibility? Is it their church's or God's work? At times the counselor can assume that the partners individually carry some responsibility for their virtue development, as is often assumed in these interventions. Yet the couple may not see things that way. They may assume a collectivist perspective of communal responsibility, or even the responsibility of their religious group or church. These assumptions might need to be brought to light to fully inform the virtues-related interventions.

Some couples may need to adjust their attitudes, beliefs or goals to engage in these interventions. Couples who are engaged in spiritual sanctification of some type may find that these interventions fit nicely with their personal goals and strivings. For couples that do not have life goals that include virtue development, the counselor may need to go slowly and discuss whether the partners would like to develop their virtuous characters individually and collectively as a couple. Part of the assessment process should be an assessment not only of their own personal character strengths and partner's strengths, but also of their successes and failures in attempting to live virtuous lives. Some partners may feel disempowered or discouraged. This may look like resistance or reluctance to engage in virtue development. Yet it may reflect a need to contextualize the interventions to the capacity and developmental stage of each partner and their relationship. Some interventions may be more easily engaged in with those who are discouraged, such as prayer (3-3), self-care (3-8) or building a new strength (3-7).

In addition, counselors should be careful to work with the virtues that are important to the couple. Many couples, especially those from different religious traditions than the therapist, may have different ideas about what makes a virtuous husband or wife. Respecting the autonomy of the partners in virtue development is paramount to success.

INTERVENTION 3-1: ASSESSING PERSONAL CHARACTER

Instructions: In one of the first few sessions photocopy and give the couple the Personal Traits in Relationships Assessment. Have couples identify the top three to five strengths for themselves and their partner. Create a list of strengths for each person. If even one of them identified something as a top strength and the other does not seriously disagree, then include it. Each list should have three to ten strengths on it. Discuss those with the couple and talk about how those strengths are now the avenue to use for improving their relationship. Ask for examples to help you understand the strength. If the couple has some insight and ability to glimpse a goal for their future, you could ask whether they see any way these strengths might help them face their problems. If they struggle with that idea, state that struggle is normal and that you will help them with that.

INTERVENTION 3-2: PERSONAL NARRATIVE OF SELF AS "HERO"

The counselor can ask the couple to describe the adversities and temptations of life that they have faced and overcome. People with low self-esteem or couples caught in negative attribution cycles may have difficulty with this task and require active support. In discussions of the narratives, the counselor characterizes the adversities of their past as temptations. Efforts to overcome the temptations are taken as evidence of ability to overcome their current adversity. Each partner contributes a narrative. The narrative may be about individual adversity, relationship adversity they overcame, or outside adversities they overcame together. This narrative intervention

Personal Traits in Relationships Assessment

To what extent do you think that you and your partner possess the following personal strengths in your relationship? Most people have three to five top strengths for themselves and three to five for their partner. Circle three to five for yourself and three to five for your partner.

Table 3.1

Personal trait or character quality	Me	You
Staying committed to the relationship, despite difficulties	A top strength	A top strength
Showing love and affection	A top strength	A top strength
Being friends with each other	A top strength	A top strength
Using faith or religion to improve our relationship	A top strength	A top strength
Showing kindness	A top strength	A top strength
Communicating positively	A top strength	A top strength
Forgiving when I am wrong or have offended	A top strength	A top strength
Being gracious for faults or weaknesses	A top strength	A top strength
Showing compassion when the other is suffering or struggling	A top strength	A top strength
Trusting	A top strength	A top strength
Retaining perspective even in overwhelming situations	A top strength	A top strength
Being willing to take risks for the relationship when needed	A top strength	A top strength
Persevering with goals for our relationship despite obstacles	A top strength	A top strength
Listening to the other	A top strength	A top strength
Being aware and attuned to the other	A top strength	A top strength
Acting as a team together	A top strength	A top strength
Showing gratitude for the good things in our life	A top strength	A top strength
Refraining from acting when it is unwise or unwanted	A top strength	A top strength
Controlling emotions or desires when needed	A top strength	A top strength
Using positive humor	A top strength	A top strength
Treating the other with fairness	A top strength	A top strength
Staying humble, not arrogant or self-righteous	A top strength	A top strength
Other?	A top strength	A top strength

within session can be strengthened by having them write out the narrative at home as homework.

Christian couples might resonate with the addition of discussing how their personal narrative fits into the grand narrative of God's intent for humans, and especially for marriages. Couples may benefit from spending time thinking about God's grand narrative for marriages with their pastor or with readings recommended by their church leader. Writing their narrative of their own ways of overcoming temptations and facing adversity in the larger picture of God's work in the world as a homework assignment can provide a hopeful and encouraging intervention for partners.

INTERVENTION 3-3: PRAYER FOR A HOPE AND A FUTURE

For couples that are interested in using their faith in counseling, prayer can be an effective tool. It must be used ethically. It is important to let the couple lead the way in the use of prayer because there are many styles of prayer even in the Christian traditions. Counselors should inform couples that they can pray together or on their own. Time spent in prayer should not take away from the time needed for counseling. A proper assessment of the couple's history and traditions of prayer is important before engaging in prayer. One couple may want to read from the *Book of Common Prayer* but another may want to pray in tongues. We have included a couple prayer journal with suggested topics of prayer at hopecouples.com.

Partners can use prayer for blessing each other and the relationship. Or partners may want to pray to God for guidance in their relationship or for their counseling. Pair any spiritual interventions with relationship interventions so that couples understand that both are necessary to see the results they are looking for. A couple's faith can be damaged if their faith and works do not coincide. Counselors should not step into the role of pastor-shepherd (unless they are officially in that role) because they can create potential conflicts with ministry leaders who are providing spiritual care for the couple. Any doctrinal or faith tradition questions can be referred to their minister as the authority. Avoid getting triangulated in their disagreements over doctrinal points.

For the development of virtues, it may be helpful to pray with the couple and ask God to provide guidance, or a vision, about how God made each partner virtuous. While in prayer, counselors should be vigilant for partners who may experience God negatively. Many people experience God as a task-master, or as harsh and unforgiving when they have not been virtuous in the past. Bringing observations about these experiences to light can develop spiritual maturity and help couples to build spiritual intimacy, a goal for many religious couples.

One well-developed research program has shown that counselors can help couples by having them pray together during counseling or on their own. Frank Fincham and Steven Beach have developed this research for years. One study (Lambert, Fincham, LaVallee & Brantley, 2012) found that couples who prayed together had increased trust after four weeks of praying for and with each other. That was better than couples who discussed positive topics together for the same amount of time. So when partners pray together, something special bonds them. We haven't tested this, but we expect it might be the Holy Spirit.

Beach, Hurt, Fincham, Franklin, Kameron, McNair and Stanley (2011) studied 393 African American couples. They compared PREP, a widely used and empirically validated couple enrichment intervention, with PREP with focused prayer. They found that wives in the PREP with focused prayer program did better than in the standard PREP condition. This is remarkable. It is very difficult to find interventions for couples that are better than the PREP program, though several seem equal to it. Prayer can provide an additive effect to couple interventions when it is done ethically and appropriately.

INTERVENTION 3-4: USE OF TIME-OUT TO DEVELOP THE "MUSCLE" OF SELF-CONTROL

For couples in high conflict, use time-out as an important early intervention. This allows self-control or willpower to replenish (Baumeister & Tierney, 2011). This can be done positively by using personal character qualities. Couples high in conflict may seem weak in self-control, blowing up at each other easily. Relative to others that may be true. But the focus can still be on how the partners have used and can use self-control. Encourage them to continue to develop it.

In this intervention the counselor and couple have identified strong conflicts as an area that needs quick response. Not much time is spent identifying the problem. Problems tend to be dramatically obvious anyway. The couple instead identifies any time they were able to stop an argument, had to or decided to call a time-out or walk away. The counselor emphasizes that they were *able* to stop the argument at least once before. The counselor is looking for positive exceptions to build hope and empower the couple with a sense of ability. With that fuel of willpower, the counselor then suggests an avenue for change, the time-out.

The goal for a time-out is for the couple to calm down, cool off and control themselves. Afterward, they can use more effective strategies to deal with their difficulties. Most of the time in these situations, emotions tend to "flood" the couple's minds to such a degree that they cannot think straight and they "fly off the handle." They have lost their reason-related virtues. The goal of time-out is for the couple to preventing *flooding, flying* and *fighting*.

Set up the rules of the intervention by telling the couple that either of them can call a time-out when they feel emotionally flooded, feeling they might fly off the handle or run away, or become afraid they might get aggressive. Follow these steps:

1. Ask the couple to role play calling a time-out to ensure they understand how to do it. They should develop a "script" of what to say when calling a time-out. It should be unique to their personal style.

2. They specify the amount of time that the time-out is being called for. Unless violence is imminent, partners calling the time-out for themselves should state "Time-out for 1 hour" or "Time-out until after the kids are in bed." Typically, time-out should be 1 to 24 hours.

3. The counselor coaches the couple about what to do *during* the time-out. Their job is to cool down, not rehearse their "comeback." This may require supportive emotion-coaching for partners who are easily flooded with negative emotions. They should identify soothing strategies, whether distraction, self-talk, exercise, reading, doing chores or surfing the net.

4. The counselor asks the couple how they would like to come back together after a time-out. What things would help them? Some conflicts should just be forgotten. After a time-out, some fights make both partners think, "What were we fighting about that for anyway?" Some issues may be chronic. For those, acceptance-based or grace-based interventions would pair nicely with a timeout. Other issues are solvable and conflict-resolution interventions should be paired with time-out as the next step in treatment.

For more help, a worksheet for time-out for couples can be found at hopecouples.com.

INTERVENTION 3-5: INTERVIEW A SUPPORTIVE CHILDHOOD FRIEND OR MENTOR

The couple might interview people who knew them as children or adolescents to ask about strengths in childhood. The person interviewed should be carefully selected, not someone who will focus on weakness or problems but someone who was supportive and caring in their history. The couple should do the interviews together. If the person lives far away they can use a three-way phone call or Skype. The couple asks the person, (a) What good characteristics or qualities did you notice about me as a child/teen? (b) How did I overcome challenges or problems that I faced when I was a child/teen? (c) What did you think would be in my future when I grew up?

INTERVENTION 3-6: CREATIVE BUILDING OF PERSONAL STRENGTHS

If the positive psychology movement is correct, then emphasizing personal strengths in character and virtue will produce rewards. The counselor can return to the Personal Traits in Relationships Assessment worksheet (see intervention 3-1) and discuss ideas the couple might have to actually increase their strengths. The couple can also use the Ideas to Create Personal Growth handout. When the ideas for improving the relationship are created around personal strengths, the partners will likely see the plans for improvement as feasible, and even enjoyable, because they already have developed that characteristic.

INTERVENTION 3-7: BUILDING A NEW STRENGTH

Partners select a positive character trait that they feel they sometimes can achieve and would like to show more often. The counselor can encourage them in personal growth. Discuss what has kept them from showing this trait in the past and what things in their life now will be obstacles to showing this trait more often. They should identify what support they will need from each other, God, workplace, church, community organizations and friends or family to see real progress in the coming months. They should identify behavioral indications of when the goal is being met. For instance, if a husband is working to improve his ability to have self-control of negative

Ideas to Create Personal Growth

Below are some thoughts to inspire you to form your own ideas about how to grow your personal strengths.

"And over all these virtues put on love, which binds them all together in perfect unity" (Col 3:14).

Table 3.2. Personal Strengths

Personal strength	Idea to build the strength
Staying committed to the relationship, despite difficulties	Write vows of commitment and give to partner.
Showing love and affection	Plan a romantic evening together.
Being friends with each other	Bring up topics of mutual interest to talk about like news, sports or community activities.
Using faith or religion to improve our relationship	Read a book about relationships and faith and share the ideas you learned there with your partner.
Showing kindness	Do five acts of random kindness for your mate this week; make them surprises if you can.
Communicating positively	Open up discussion about plans for the future as a couple while listening well.
Forgiving when I am wrong or have offended	When any offense happens this week be the first to offer forgiveness for it.
Being gracious for faults or weaknesses	When your partner is preoccupied or "stressed" this week, do not dwell on it, just let it go.
Showing compassion when the other is suffering or struggling	Tell your partner you admire him or her for holding up so well in the midst of so much responsibility and difficulty he or she is facing in life.
Trusting	Write a letter reminding your mate why you trust him or her.
Retaining perspective even in overwhelming situations	Identify the time during the week that tends to be the most stressful. Focus on remaining level-headed in that time.

Personal strength	Idea to build the strength
Being willing to take risks for the relationship when needed	Plan a "grand romantic gesture" such as a public declaration of your love or a big gift (it does not have to be from a store) that will be appreciated by your partner.
Persevering with goals for our relationship despite obstacles	Identify a goal for your relationship, perhaps one you are focused on through counseling. Tell your partner you will never give up on it. Then do something that shows you are working on that goal this week.
Listening to the other	Tell your partner that you would like to sit down and hear about his or her hopes, dreams, plans or struggles sometime this week. Make a date to listen.
Being aware and attuned to the other	Write down for your partner all the "little things" you notice. They may be positive traits, actions, qualities, current events or physical attributes.
Acting as a team together	Ask your partner whether you can plan a team project to do something together—perhaps home improvement, community volunteering or a hobby.
Showing gratitude for the good things in our life	Create artwork that communicates your gratitude to your mate and to God for what is good in your life.
Refraining from acting when it is unwise or unwanted	Promise your partner that even if he or she says something rude or unkind in the future, you will not say anything unkind in return.
Controlling emotions or desires when needed	Offer to prioritize a goal or desire of your mate's as first in line to complete before one of your own goals or desires.
Using positive humor	See if you can cheer your partner up. Try to make your mate laugh at least once a day.
Treating the other with fairness	Offer to divide up the work as equally as you can when planning a joint task.
Staying humble, not arrogant or self-righteous	Tell your partner that you know there are things about you that are hard to live with. Thank your partner for loving you anyway.
Staying humble through admitting wrongdoing	Be first to admit any offensive or hurtful behavior you did. Don't wait for your partner to bring it up.

emotions during stressful times, he would state that he would try to increase the time per week that he edits out hurtful statements said in anger. He can keep track of when he edits and even create a chart (if he is a bit OCD!). He can even apply the change in other areas of his life besides the couple relationship, such as parenting, extended family and workplace. Similar to a fitness coach that might help a person achieve fitness goals, the counselor can support the partners in their virtue development goals.

INTERVENTION 3-8: SELF-CARE INTERVENTIONS

Many people take on too much in their lives to handle practically or with positive emotion. At times, the adversity faced is genuinely stressful. If the response is to simply "hunker down" and try harder, a partner is unlikely to see gains. The counselor will help the partners identify ways they can take care of their personal needs, which may free up resources to get back on track for their goals. Self-care can take the form of increasing sleep, ensuring good nutrition, engaging in exercise, getting a massage or haircut, saying no to a new responsibility, cutting back at work, canceling unnecessary activities, or getting extra help with responsibilities such as hiring someone to clean their house. The important thing about this simple adversity planning is to frame it as freeing up resources to allow the couple to devote energy to their relationship and virtue goals.

INTERVENTION 3-9: INSIGHT-ORIENTED INTERVENTIONS

When progress and efforts slow, insight into the problem can help to reactivate motivation. Talk with the couple about how they might need to stop and see whether there is something they do not understand that is preventing them from moving forward in their goals. Understanding is one of the keys to a secure attachment to one's partner, so it is worth developing insight and understanding in couple relationships.

Insight-oriented interventions are especially helpful for times when there has been an apparent setback in progress, or no improvement. Their counselor uses this "setback" to help the couple better understand what has happened. For example, one couple readily identified a sleepless night as a major cause of the problem. They were both emotionally depleted. Next, the wife was able to disclose that she felt lonely and unappreciated in her role as stay-at-home mother. The counselor asked the husband to explain what he *understood* about her experience at this stage of her life and asked whether he could use his strength of being a good listener to increase his insight into his wife. The husband also shared that he really does not like it when his wife storms out of an argument. Apparently this was not the first time this had happened and it caused him to feel a great deal of distress. The counselor wondered with him what exactly it was that was most distressing—perhaps her anger, or feeling alone, or worry she would leave him, or something else? The husband stated that her anger was overwhelming to him—he just froze in response to it usually. The counselor took the opportunity to further explore the husband's experiences with anger to help him see patterns in his life. This helped to motivate him to return to cultivating his ability to tolerate strong emotions like anger, and to use his typical strength of kindness as an antidote to relationship anger.

INTERVENTION 3-10: PARTNER-ASSISTED INTERVENTION (PAI)

In one tradition of couple treatment, one partner assists the other partner with an individual problem such as substance abuse or depression. A couple counselor could further explore this type of treatment through a number of resources (Snyder & Whisman, 2003). Yet PAI can be used for any kind of issue—whether helping a partner with low self-esteem or even helping one's partner build strengths. Two important principles from PAI can be used when the couple faces adversity:

- *Empathy.* First, some partners have a tendency not to understand why the adversity is so difficult for their mate. This causes him or her to respond unhelpfully. Criticisms increase in an attempt to assist or change the partner. To prevent this negative pattern, the counselor can help the partner who is giving aid (criticizing) to more deeply understand what makes the adversity so difficult. Coach the partner trying to give aid to respond with empathy instead of criticism. Empathy is more likely to achieve the goals without damaging their relationship.

- *Understanding.* The second important principle is for the partner to realize his or her own role in the problem. Most of the time partners have created a kind of "dance" where they each contribute to the problem. The classic example is the spouse of an alcoholic who calls in a work excuse. In this dance the pain felt by the partner is responded to with defense. This can be obvious, such as responding to hurt by putting down one's spouse. A subtle way might be a partner inadvertently undermining the spouse's attempts to change by using humor to lighten the situation. Another common inadvertent defense is not responding when the partner says, "Thank you" or "I love you." Even though it seems mechanical to say, "You're welcome" or "I love you too," these responses are important and, when they are omitted, they are deadly.

When the counselor can coach the couple to respond to their partner's problems with empathy and understanding of their role in the problem, this can loosen juggernauts of conflict and help the partners assist each other in individual life problems instead of criticizing or ignoring each other.

INTERVENTION 3-11: DEVELOPING WISDOM

Wisdom is a master virtue. Wisdom is the ability to know the best response to various situations. Often when faced with temptations or adversity, people feel unsure what avenues they can use to escape or avoid adversity. They lack wisdom. A counselor can help the couple by offering many of the common wisdoms of psychotherapy to help them. For example, in the case where the wife stormed off after a fight, the counselor can help the wife consider how to avoid the temptation of running off when she faces strong feelings of anger. She could consider other avenues she might have to respond. A role play in the office of what else she might have said or done can help the couple practice a wiser action. Role plays from the wisdom of behavioral therapy can often help to make the intervention more memorable.

Locating the Warmth Virtues in My Relationships

Think of three important relationships in your life. One would be your relationship with your partner, one with Jesus and one with another important person in your life. Then also think about how you are in relationship with others. Make a checkmark for which of the following is your experience of those relationships in the last month. If a yes or no checkmark is too difficult, you can write in how often you experience each of these things in the relationship with a percent. For example, if half the time you felt valued by Jesus, then you would write in 50%.

Table 3.3

Experience in the relationship in the last month	Partner	Jesus	Other
1. I felt valued, treated as important			
2. I felt loved			
3. We are deeply connected and emotionally bonded			
4. I was treated with kindness and compassion			
5. This person was forgiving and merciful toward me			
6. I am sure this person is passionate or excited about me			
7. I felt trusted			
8. I knew our relationship is committed, steadfast and solid			
9. I felt safe and protected			
10. I felt understood, listened to and cared about			

INTERVENTION 3-12: LOCATING THE WARMTH VIRTUES IN MY RELATIONSHIPS (WORKSHEET)

After completing the worksheet, discuss the following questions with your counselor and with each other.

1. When have you had these warm relationship experiences in the past? Discuss which of these experiences you most want, or long for, in your relationship with each other, with Jesus and with important others in your life. These ten things are warmth-based relationship virtues. They are the hallmarks of a healthy warm relationship. Even if you are doing "all the right things" in terms of relationship skills, healthy living and being faithful, if the relationship does not have these qualities, it will feel hollow and may not meet your deepest needs.

2. Where do you get your needs met in these three relationships? The relationship with God should be one where you can have all your needs met. Yet it is important to develop your relationship with God and invest in it to fully experience God meeting needs. God is infinitely capable of being present, available, warm and giving in relationship with you. Your partner is not always able to provide all that you need. Others, such as family members or friends, are also not able to provide everything we need.

3. Do you sometimes look to others or your partner to be like God in your life and meet all of your needs? (If you have been looking to your partner to be like God in your relationship, you just might be frustrated.)

4. Was this exercise hard for you? How so? If you found this questionnaire difficult, or if your experience of these warmth-based relationship virtues is lacking, then discuss with your counselor what is blocking you. Three common roadblocks for people in these areas are that they (a) did not experience warm virtues in their family growing up, (b) are losing hope that they are possible today, or (c) have cut off parts of themselves in an effort to survive difficult things in life. Consider what might be your roadblock. It might be one of these or something else entirely.

4

Addressing the Couple's Context

ð

Effective couple therapy requires a strong understanding of the contexts, culture and traditions of the couple. Consider the case of Carlos and Grace.

A Case Study Illustrating Cultural Sensitivity

Carlos and Grace are a couple in their forties. They have two sons in middle school, one of whom has a learning disability. Carlos grew up in Chile with his family and immigrated to America when he was ten years old. Grace is Caucasian and from a poor rural community in Kentucky. They now live in a white, middle-class neighborhood, where Carlos is a police officer and serves in the Air Force reserves, and Grace teaches high school English. Grace had a problem with substance abuse when she was in her twenties. They are somewhat disillusioned with their Pentecostal church but continue to attend regularly because they have many friends there.

What if a couple counselor missed some of the contextual information in the case of Carlos and Grace? Most counselors today have been trained in issues of culture and context or have upgraded their understanding through continuing education required by licensure. However, it is easy to miss the importance of these factors in a busy day's work. It is also common to find that couples minimize the influence of all of these contexts on their own relationship problems and strengths. Understanding the influence of context on problems can help couples conceptualize their problems and find best solutions. For example, Carlos feels pressure to earn money and is frustrated at not being promoted in his job. That pressure is creating frustration that he expresses at home. The pressure to provide financially is related to his experience as a child immigrant, his being a minority in a community, and his understanding of traditional gender roles influenced by his faith. Grace does not have the same experiences. Despite growing up in a poor community, she does not have Carlos's deep-seated fears about finances. Grace and Carlos reported that understanding this about each other was one of the most important things they discovered in counseling.

CULTURAL DIVERSITY

Cultural diversity is such an important aspect of context that we think we need to address it directly. The central Scripture of the hope-focused couple approach is Galatians 5:6, which speaks of "faith working through love" (NKJV). But it is not a coincidence that this chapter of Scripture is focused on freedom in Christ. Paul is teaching the readers to focus on faith working through love and not blindly adhere to cultural traditions like circumcision (the hot topic of their time). Jews and Gentiles came from different cultural perspectives. Paul was saying, "Understand the other side's culture but value your relationship more than your cultural tradition." Especially in hot-button, culturally loaded topics, conflict will be heated! Show your love by not insisting blindly on your own way. But at times we must conform out of love, sacrifice for the relationship, or think of the other person and value him or her more than we value our own needs in a particular conflict.

It is important to understand the cultural context in order to address what might be underlying redemptive truths in the context. For example, in the case of Carlos and Grace the fear of not being able to provide for their family is a principle they can understand, can support each other in and not turn on each other. They can pray together and trust in God to be faithful to their family. They can focus on the lessons of humility, a simple life and rejecting materialism as redemptive aspects of having fewer resources. This transforms the fear into a redemptive, joining experience as a family. And importantly, understanding their cultural roots reduces their conflict and makes them more likely to make a loving sacrifice. It does not minimize either Carlos's experience of immigration or Grace's experience growing up in a poor community.

Christians within cultures. In almost every culture, many Christians have shaped and reshaped the traditions of the faith to work within that culture. There is an important lesson: eternal truths can work in every culture. It is important to discern what is an eternal truth and what is an adjustable cultural tradition. Christians believe there are eternal truths— such as "love one another." It is good for a family to love each other. But how they express that love might differ widely to fit their culture, language, gender, age and personality. This freedom gives counselors the ability to work within any culture, any tradition, any diversity of experience, with redemptive purposes.

The counselor's attitude of humility. The master clinician holds an attitude of cultural humility toward contextual issues. These contextual religious issues discussed in this chapter are but one aspect of a couple's context. Many couples seek help for a troubled second marriage, have various struggles due to their minority status, are cohabiting, live in low socio-economic situations where survival trumps relationship health, have varying concepts of gender roles, have same-sex attraction issues, or wrestle with decisions about what is best for elderly parents while also caring for their children. The clinician's response is one of humility.

Cultural humility. Cultural humility is a concept used in many helping professions that emphasizes taking a "learner" role for issues of culture. It advocates having the client teach the counselor about cultural values, norms and expectations (Hook, Davis, Owen, Worthington & Utsey, 2013; Tervalon & Murray-Garcia, 1998). Consider the following case.

A CASE STUDY ILLUSTRATING CULTURAL HUMILITY

A cohabiting couple comes to see you. They have just moved to your area from rural Oklahoma. They are in survival mode; in fact, the man's brother is paying for counseling because the couple lost their home and are living with him, looking for work after six months of being unemployed. The long-time cohabiting couple's children are struggling with the move. Their 14-year-old child has a strong negative reaction to the move, blaming the parents for failure to care for the family. The conflicts with the 14-year-old are eclipsed only by their negativity toward each other. The wife is considering leaving the relationship. The husband's drinking has increased. They are in financial crisis. Where to start?

We propose that the first place to begin is with the virtue of counselor cultural humility. Cultural humility focuses on the counselor's own self-examination and self-critique. The culturally humble counselor would know her own limitations due to her own cultural perspective. A lack of cultural humility may result in a counselor who wants to fix a client's situation, give advice or answers to their problems, and guide them through the crisis. The humble counselor instead responds by having them teach her what life has been like in their shoes. To return to our cohabiting Oklahoma couple, they can teach the counselor about their reluctance to marry, despite 15 years of cohabitation. The counselor can learn about the reasons for the unemployment stress on the family. The man can explain his reasons for drinking heavily. Following the virtue of humility will open the door for future transformational change in the couple's life. Giving the couple all the "right answers" is the opposite of transformational humility.

Cultural humility has another, often overlooked, aspect as well. An experienced counselor learns a lot about the cultures that house most of his or her clients. It is easy to become so sure we understand the culture—whether fundamentalist or Pentecostal, whether Mexican American or Korean American—that we might stop listening to our clients (Hook et al., 2013). When that happens, problems will soon arise. Cultural humility takes an attitude of "teach me about your context" and avoids problems involved in making assumptions.

FAITH CONTEXT AS DIVERSITY

Sacred meaning. Faith, community and Christian teachings can create a context of strengths for a couple. The teachings of many couples' faith traditions will strongly encourage them to love each other, be patient, show kindness and love mercy. When both partners are Christians, the counselor can help the couple find ways to draw from these beliefs applications to their relationship problems. Christian couples exist within a Christian community where there can be role models of virtuous marriage, peer support and pastoral care. They often treat marriage as a covenant (Ripley, Worthington, Bromley & Kemper, 2005), which is sacred or ordained by God (Demaris, Mahoney & Pargament, 2010). This meaning making in marriage helps protect the relationship. Ideas like marriage-as-covenant draw the couple together for the good for the relationship. Marriage becomes a priority for living a good life. Seeing marriage as sacred or ordained by God reminds the couple that they answer to a higher authority in the way they treat each other. Both protective and restorative processes are inherent in the Christian faith for the benefit of marriages.

Violation of the sacred. There is a dark side to the Christian meaning of marriage. When a person feels that the sacred bond of marriage has been violated, the negative response can be amplified. If any loving marriage is violated, whether a minor offense like unkind words or major offense like infidelity, there is a negative emotional response. Unkind words are usually followed by anger, sadness or shock. However, if the marriage is not only a loving marriage where partners are bonded to each other but also a sacred covenant that is ordained by God, the emotional response can be felt much more deeply. It can be perceived as a desecration of the sacred (Pargament, Magyar, Benore & Mahoney, 2005). This can make it much more difficult for partners to respond kindly when faced with adversity, because the adversity may be perceived more negatively. The client may say, "He's a Christian. How can he have used pornography like that?" Or he might say, "She's the one God intended for me. How can God have allowed her to fall into alcohol abuse?" This demand to cope with a desecration can deplete resources needed to face adversity and can be a particularly hard-to-forgive transgression (Davis, Hook & Worthington, 2008). For highly religious couples a marital problem can set off both a negative response in the marriage and a spiritual crisis.

When warmth virtues are lacking. Another important contextual understanding of Christian meaning in marriage is religious attempts to improve a relationship. If a couple is highly religious, then they often will use religious activity to try to improve their relationship. If they use religious activity such as prayer, reading Scripture or seeking spiritual care, as well as relational activity such as increasing positivity, softly sharing concerns or resolving conflicts, then the outcomes are likely enhanced by using both avenues for change.

Couples who come to our labs and the Regent clinic often are highly religious but not applying Christian warmth virtues such as love or compassion. They are faithful in their practice of the faith, but are unaware or find it difficult to be warm in their relationships. They are often highly committed to their faith and confused about why their faithful practice is not rewarded with a loving relationship. In a distressed relationship, their prayers can often be something along the lines of, "Lord, please fix this man! He is so messed up!" Prayers like this are often not answered positively or quickly by God. This can lead to a loss of faith, because the prayers were not answered. The couple then enter counseling with two problems. First, their often immature faith has been damaged. Second, they have not tried to change their relationship—just prayed that God would fix it. They have made no real attempt at change in a relational way. The counselor's response must be empathic. He or she should try to be an exemplar of warm relational virtues. The couple can be empowered to apply warmth virtues to their relationship. If you have couples like this, consider using the Locating the Warmth Virtues in My Relationships worksheet (see intervention 3-12).

CONCLUSIONS

There are many important contexts to consider when working with couples in the hope-focused couple approach. There are two we consider crucial to effective practice. First, a full understanding of the context that a couple lives within is necessary for good treatment. We have especially focused on religion or faith and on ethnicity. Most counselors today receive education on ethnic diversity, but we believe many people do not have adequate training in religious diversity. Surveys of clinical or counseling training directors (Worthington et al., 2008) and directors of programs that handle the education of student psychotherapists bear this out. Yet other aspects of diversity such as gender, culture, language and sexual orientation are all important to understanding the couple's perspectives. Second, we believe an attitude of relational cultural humility is necessary to address issues of diversity of contexts and for general good therapeutic stance. We invite you to do intervention 4-1 to assess your own cultural humility.

INTERVENTION 4-1: COUNSELOR CULTURAL HUMILITY DEVELOPMENT

Explore cultural humility as a counselor. The field of healthcare broadly has begun to discuss the concept of cultural humility. Many of these concepts are built into the fabric of mental healthcare. Yet it is worthwhile to take time to explore for yourself where you can grow in cultural humility.

- Where have you been in the past in terms of understanding issues of culture and diversity?

- Critique yourself. What areas do you still need to grow in for serving various cultures and diverse people? What is limiting you?

- What gaps in knowledge of diverse people groups do you need to fill in?

- In what ways is your own culture's perspective limited? In what ways do you and people from your cultural group have common assumptions or prejudices?

- What skills or abilities do you need to enhance to better serve diverse people?

- What could you do to redress the inherent power imbalance that exists between you and your patients or clients?

- In what way can you advocate for the people you serve in your job, community or nationally in terms of empowering them?

- Do you think you understand well the culture of most of the clients you see? Are you still listening to each person?

Want to learn more? Search for cultural humility in the medical literature on the internet. It is growing. Consider the following free cultural competency training from the medical field that includes a module on cultural humility: www.uniteforsight.org/cultural-competency. A YouTube video on cultural humility can be found at www.youtube.com/watch?v=SaSHLbS1V4w. Internet resources do disappear over time. If you check and these are gone, we are confident you will find other recent references and resources.

Part One Summary

You should now have a good sense of the principles of hope-focused couple counseling. In *Hope-Focused Marriage Counseling* (2005), I (Ev) described the basics as (1) promoting hope, (2) developing the strategy of faith working through love, (3) locating the areas in which problems mostly exist and (4) intervening. There I described over 100 interventions that we do not cover in the present book. As you have seen here in part one, while the basic structure of the hope-focused couple approach is the same as in the first book, there are important additional considerations in the present approach.

- The sources from which we have drawn are supplemented by considering positive psychology and much new research that has occurred within the last ten years.

- The strategy of faith working through love strongly emphasizes (a) more focus on identifying and using strengths and promoting virtue and (b) the emotional bond. In the 2005 book, I (Ev) oriented readers toward building, maintaining, strengthening and repairing the emotional bond. But in this book we get to the nitty-gritty of how to do that.

- Many interventions are all new and include worksheets and practical assistance for counselors.

- We are even more concerned with making every intervention memorable for partners.

- We have added cases to aid in your application of this learning. We believe that extra benefit can be gained if you see how change occurred in real cases of couple counseling. We describe many for you.

- For counselors, cultural humility is vital to understanding clients. These days, professional training in counseling emphasizes understanding different cultures. Because we pay so much attention to cultural sensitivity, the opposite side of cultural knowledge can rear its head. We can get so confident that we understand other cultures that we forget to listen to the clients. We must listen carefully to what couples share with an attitude of humility.

Armed with these formative basic and new or updated principles, you are ready to take the plunge. Let's get into the nuts and bolts of beginning counseling.

Part Two

BEGINNING COUNSELING

There is nothing more important than beginning couple counseling well. The beginning phase of working with a couple involves multiple simultaneous goals:

- Instilling hope for their relationship
- Creating a positive relationship with both partners
- Assessing the relationship and individuals
- Determining possible diagnoses (if appropriate)
- Considering cultural, spiritual and developmental needs of the couple
- Helping the couple reflect on their own needs and goals
- Creating norms of safety by containing conflict and various client agendas

The first few sessions of couple counseling are a complex task. If you have been doing couple counseling for a while you may remember feeling overwhelmed by the many tasks of the couple intake session. Whatever your experience, this part will help you review your plans for the initial stage of counseling with a couple and see if there are new things you can add to your repertoire.

5

Pre-counseling Interventions

જ⁀

Put yourself in the shoes of your client. You have had it with your relationship. There has been another stressful situation or discussion. Things have been going the wrong way for months (or years). All you can see is negativity in the relationship. You are trying to decide what to do. You have talked to your minister and asked for prayer support but the problems still persist. You wonder whether God has abandoned you. You have talked with friends who offer good and well-meaning advice, but it has not worked. You realize you need a specialist, a counselor who knows how to do good couple counseling. You take a chance and ask your minister for a referral, hoping not to offend for asking for the referral instead of more pastoral care. You do not want the minister to think that the prayer and good advice did not work! Your spouse is withdrawn and does not respond to your suggestion for counseling. You seriously consider just calling a divorce lawyer to find out more information about what it might be like if you were to separate. But in your heart you just cannot do it. You still know there is some love left for each other, and you do not want to put your family through a divorce. You are not even sure that anything will work. After all, you have tried so many things. You search the internet for the counselor and see that the person seems to look okay. You take the number, give the office a call and . . .

Now, from your vantage point as the counselor who has been contacted, what happens next? For many offices, it is just setting an appointment with the front desk staff on your calendar and starting the intervention when the couple arrive at the door, if they both come. Perhaps you and your office do more. The hope-focused couple approach includes serious consideration of what happens between the initial contact for services and the first appointment. There are two good reasons to capitalize on this time period.

First, the motivation for change may never be higher than it is when the person calls for an appointment. Research on motivation indicates that the highest degree of motivation for many clients is at the beginning of psychotherapy (Irving et al., 2004). Even a week is a long time when facing relationship distress. You want to get them started down the path of improvement at that point when they were at least enthusiastic enough to phone you.

Second, clients generally expect counseling to last less than ten sessions. This is especially true in couple counseling. In individual counseling, if the person does not improve in ten sessions, he or she will likely still continue if there is any chance of help. There is the sunk cost, of course, but also the person knows that if he or she does not get over the depression or anxiety, he or she will just have to live with it. And the person tried dealing with it on their own before. Dr. Phil McGraw's well-known words easily come to mind: "How'd that work for you when you tried it before?" The couple seeking counseling do have another option. They are more willing to drop out if they do not feel they are making enough progress because, unlike the depressed client, they do not think they have to live with the problem (whom they usually think is the spouse).

Therefore, if you begin new cases with the assumption that you may only get eight to ten sessions with the couple, then every single session counts for helping effective change happen. It is important to use the valuable time in the initial sessions efficiently by transferring as much likelihood of change as possible to the pre-therapy stage of treatment.

There are several things that you can do *before* the first meeting. First, the client can receive information about you, your practice and your approach to helping couples. Those will help acclimate the clients and save valuable time in the first session. Second, you can introduce some general terminology and conceptualizations. A better educated client can use counseling more effectively. This makes initial treatment more efficient, and thus more likely to be effective. Third, you can receive information about your client efficiently. If you use screenings or assessments and they are not received until the second or third session, then there is considerable time spent before you as the counselor have an informed understanding of the couple and their problems. We offer ideas in this chapter to maximize your work with couples by using the pre-therapy stage of treatment effectively.

Your Web Presence

First contact with you as the counselor is likely to be a Google search that coughs up your webpage. Counselors should regularly Google themselves to ensure their web presence is favorable and professional.

Often the people looking at your website are in the contemplate stage of change (Norcross, Krebs & Prochaska, 2011). Your website should move people from contemplation to action. People in contemplation stage are weighing the pros and cons of action. They often doubt their ability to make changes with the resources they have. They need to think about the barriers to changing their life and see reasonable pathways around, over and through those barriers. The goal of your website is to answer questions for clients, give them confidence that they can receive help, and move them from contemplating coming to counseling to acting to make that appointment. For example, you can offer a measure such as the Couples Stage of Change Questionnaire (C-SCQ; Bradford, 2012) so that the couple can assess for themselves where they are in terms of readiness for change.

Pre-counseling Intervention 5-1: Creating a Video or Webcast and Having a Web Presence

There is nothing that makes counselors more nervous than thinking of themselves talking about relationships on camera or demonstrating counseling. They worry that they are not going to come across as competent, likeable and helpful. But the reality is that creating a video or webcast will increase your web presence and connection with your clients. If clients can begin to get to know you before they enter your office, they (and you) can save time once counseling begins. Trust can begin even before they ever see you. Many people, especially in modern cultures, learn best from visual learning formats such as video. Video can ensure that some of the information you want to communicate about counseling can be done in the same way as clients experience you—personally. You can communicate your voice tone, emotional expression, care and concern, and nonverbal behavior much more effectively using a brief YouTube clip than you can with a flood of written words. Make your YouTube entries interesting and educational. Teach about couple relationships—what makes them flourish, where they sometimes go wrong, how to get them back on track. Students in a film production high school or college group might be able to assist you—while they earn course credit for doing a project. Professional productions can range in cost, but often are less than other marketing costs for a product that is helpful not only for marketing but also for clinical intervention.

PRE-COUNSELING INTERVENTION 5-2: WRITTEN MATERIALS

Many clinics provide considerable written materials to clients. You might have received such information from a doctor. Think about how you react. If you are anxious and uncertain, you probably read most of the information. More information usually gives some sense of control. But sometimes, you look at the wall of words and just carry the printed material home and toss it. Or leave it in the doctor's office. So, when you write informative handouts, make them user friendly. Use bullets. Use pictures. Include information that people do not know and would fascinate them. Tell them what is going to happen if they attend counseling. People always want to know that.

Creating information that gives psychoeducation to clients should include information relevant to their relationship. If you create written information, then consider who is reading the information. Many readers are in contemplation stage of change, so materials should be tailored to the issues relevant to that stage of change also. Other readers are already in therapy and have made substantial changes but are attempting to avoid relapse. So tailor materials to the client. Consider posting written materials on your website to make them readily available to clients or potential clients.

PRE-COUNSELING INTERVENTION 5-3: CAPTURING ESSENTIAL ASSESSMENT MATERIALS BEFORE THE FIRST VISIT

The flow of relationship information in the pre-therapy stage should be bi-directional. The client should learn a great deal about you, how you conduct therapy, what you will be like to work with and what you have to offer. You as the counselor should also obtain information about your client before the first visit. The hope-focused couple approach has encouraged counselors to obtain some information about couples *before* the first session.

In the Regent University lab, we require partners to complete an online secure screening about their relationship before an appointment is scheduled. There are numerous online vendors who provide secure online survey options. The benefits of an online assessment are numerous.

1. If both partners are unwilling to complete a brief online questionnaire, then that might indicate that their ability to use couple therapy effectively may be too low. So this might screen out some couples who simply will be wasting their time. They are probably thinking of couple therapy as having the counselor "quick fix" them.

2. This small investment in completing an assessment is a first step for them to make a change. It starts them down the road to making their relationship better. It is a first small commitment to change.

3. It also helps to reduce the no-show rate for intakes.

4. In group practices the counselor can be selected from a group of clinicians based on the information obtained in the online screening. If you work in a group practice and a group of clinicians invests together in the screening, then the clinician who specializes in domestic violence or substance abuse issues can pick up cases that screen with those issues. In our clinic more novice students are often also protected from seeing couples with more complex problems. This benefits both the counselor and couple. So, if your counseling center has trainees, novice clinicians or those that have less experience in couple counseling, it can be helpful to screen.

5. The clinician starts the first session with valuable information about the couple. The intake meeting can be focused on the particular areas of the couple's concern and on doing further assessment of particularly troublesome problem areas instead of collecting basic information.

An ideal screening lasts no more than 20 minutes and can be easily accessed. An alternative paper version of your initial screening assessment should be available for people without good internet access. For ethical purposes, we recommend consulting with the fast-changing ethics in online screening for mental health issues within your disciplinary area. For instance, we do not screen online for suicidality. The reason for this is that the online screen is likely not immediately viewed by a counselor, so it is possible that a potential client might respond that he or she is suicidal and then act on the suicidal intention before the counselor could reasonably contact the person. Counselors should realize these types of risks.

PRE-COUNSELING INTERVENTION 5-4: ONLINE OR PAPER SCREENING ITEMS[1]

1. What would you say is the most important thing you want to see change during couple counseling?

2. What is one main strength for the two of you as a couple?

3. Have any of these things happened in your relationship? (indicate which ones)

a. Physical pushing, shoving, pinning or hitting	Yes, this happened in the past year	Never	Not in the past year
b. Not letting me do things I wanted to do (see friends, go on a trip, individual activities . . .)	Yes, this happened in the past year	Never	Not in the past year
c. Being jealous of relationships	Yes, this happened in the past year	Never	Not in the past year
d. Using a weapon, knife, gun or threatening violence	Yes, this happened in the past year	Never	Not in the past year
e. Yelling, screaming, cursing or verbal attack	Yes, this happened in the past year	Never	Not in the past year

4. Is there any history of infidelity in your relationship?

   ❑ No infidelity   Explain:

   ❑ Emotional infidelity

   ❑ Physical infidelity

   ❑ Internet type of infidelity

5. Have you used any illegal substances in the past year (marijuana, cocaine, LSD, drugs you were not prescribed, etc? This information is confidential).

   YES   NO   If yes, please explain,

   Concerning alcohol. Do you drink alcohol?   NO   YES

   (If yes, complete questions)

---

[1]A downloadable version of this screening is available at www.hopecouples.com.

SMAST 13

Please circle the appropriate answer.

Do you feel you are a normal drinker?	Yes	No
Do your spouse or parents worry or complain about your drinking?	Yes	No
Do you ever feel bad about your drinking?	Yes	No
Do friends or relatives think you are a normal drinker?	Yes	No
Are you always able to stop drinking when you want to?	Yes	No
Have you ever attended a meeting of Alcoholics Anonymous?	Yes	No
Has drinking ever created problems between you and your spouse?	Yes	No
Have you ever gotten into trouble at work because of drinking?	Yes	No
Have you ever neglected your obligations, your family, or your work for 2 or more days in a row because you were drinking?	Yes	No
Have you ever gone to anyone for help about your drinking?	Yes	No
Have you ever been in the hospital because of drinking?	Yes	No
Have you ever been arrested even for a few hours because of drinking?	Yes	No
Have you ever been arrested for drunk driving or driving after drinking?	Yes	No

Clinical Couples Assessment of Relationship Elements (CARE)

Please rate your relationship on the following seven areas from 1 = *could not be worse* to 7 = *could not be better*. Rate your relationship over *the last 2 weeks*.

	Could not be worse	Not bad not good				Could not be better
Communication	1	2	3	4	5	6	7
Resolution of differences	1	2	3	4	5	6	7
Freedom from blaming your partner when things go wrong	1	2	3	4	5	6	7
Willingness to admit to having hurt your partner and ask your partner for forgiveness	1	2	3	4	5	6	7
Ability to forgive your partner after a hurt	1	2	3	4	5	6	7
Intimacy and closeness	1	2	3	4	5	6	7
Central values and priorities of what is important in life	1	2	3	4	5	6	7
My thoughts about our relationship being positive and hopeful	1	2	3	4	5	6	7
Commitment to my partner for the long term	1	2	3	4	5	6	7
Sexual relationship	1	2	3	4	5	6	7

Created by Worthington et al. (1997) & Ripley (2009)

Relationship Efficacy Measure

How do you feel about your ability to handle problems in your relationship?
Please answer each.

	Strongly Disagree						Strongly Agree
I have little control over the conflicts that occur between my partner and me.	1	2	3	4	5	6	7
There is no way I can solve some of the problems in my relationship.	1	2	3	4	5	6	7
When I put my mind to it, I can resolve just about any disagreement that comes up between my partner and me.	1	2	3	4	5	6	7
I often feel helpless in dealing with the problems that come up in my relationship.	1	2	3	4	5	6	7
Sometimes I feel that I have no say over issues that cause conflict between us.	1	2	3	4	5	6	7
I am able to do the things needed to settle our conflicts.	1	2	3	4	5	6	7
There is little I can do to resolve many of the important conflicts between my partner and me.	1	2	3	4	5	6	7

Created by Frank Fincham. Available at www.fincham.info/measures/marital-efficacy.htm.

Parenting Alliance Screen

1. How often do you and your partner disagree about how to parent your children? (skip if no children at home)

Always Disagree	Almost always disagree	Sometimes disagree	Agree	Always Agree

Created by Hope Project.

CES-D10

Below is a list of the ways you might have felt or behaved. Please tell me how often you have felt this way during *the past 2 weeks.*

	Rarely or none of the time (less than one day)	Some or a little of the time (1-2 days)	Occasionally or a moderate amount of time (3-4 days)	Most or all of the time (5-7 days)
I was bothered by things that usually do not bother me.	1	2	3	4
I had trouble keeping my mind on what I was doing.	1	2	3	4
I felt depressed.	1	2	3	4
I felt that everything I did was an effort.	1	2	3	4
I felt hopeful about the future.	4	3	2	1
I felt fearful.	1	2	3	4
My sleep was restless.	1	2	3	4
I was happy.	4	3	2	1
I felt lonely.	1	2	3	4
I could not get "going."	1	2	3	4

Created by Kohout, Berkman, Evans & Cornoni Huntley (1993).

GUIDANCE FOR SCORING THE COUPLE SCREENINGS

Violence screen. Any positive answer to this should be followed up in *individual* interview to determine the context, frequency and severity. Asking for the most recent violent situation entailed is a good start. This screen does not include many of the more severe violent behaviors. A Conflict Tactics Scale 2 (Newton, Connelly & Landsverk, 2001), or similar full measure of domestic violence, should be used for a more complete assessment. The screen created by Ripley for clinical use and included in this book has not been tested for psychometric validity. It is intended for clinical screening use only.

Infidelity screen. If there has been any type of infidelity, this should be followed up in *individual* interview. Frequency, situation, perception and current relevancy of the infidelity should be further assessed. The Gordon-Baucom forgiveness measure (Gordon & Baucom, 2003) is a more complete measure of the stage of response to the infidelity for each individual.

Drug use screen. Any positive response should be followed within an *individual* interview.

The Short Michigan Alcohol Screening Test. This screen is commonly used in a variety of settings to gain information helpful in determining whether there might be a problem with alcohol. Be aware that research has indicated about a 10% rate of incorrect diagnosis based on this screening. So, it is important that a good assessment for alcohol problems is done as well as a screening. To score the S-MAST, each "yes" answer earns one point, except for questions 1, 4 and 5, where each "no" earns one point. Two points total indicates a possible problem. Three points or more indicates a probable problem with alcohol.

Couple Assessment of Relationship Elements (CARE). This screen (Worthington et al., 1997) focuses the clinician into areas that the couple deem to be strengths or weaknesses in their relationship. If the client scores less than five in any area, it is worth exploring further. In addition, if the client reports a global high score, then possible precontemplation stage-of-change or just-seeking-enrichment interventions would be explored.

The Relationship Efficacy Measure (REM). This screen (Fincham, Harold & Gano-Phillips, 2000) measures a sense of personal agency, which is an important aspect of hope. A low score on the REM indicates a low sense of agency and hope for the relationship, which may need further attention during initial phases of treatment.

Parenting Alliance Screen (PAS). This single-item screen created and used at Regent University assesses whether issues of parenting are likely to be important in treatment of the couple. We consider it only ethical to address issues of parenting when working with couples who are currently raising children. Any indicator of disagreement on this screen warrants further discussion in the interview with the couple.

Center for Epidemiological Studies Depression Screen (10-item version). Because depression is the most commonly related disorder to relationship distress, a depression screen is given. The CES-D (Kohout, Berkman, Evans & Cornoni-Huntley, 1993; Olino et al., 2012) is a widely used and publicly available depression screening instrument. Questions five and eight are reverse scored. A cutoff score of 11 indicates significant or mild depression. Scores approaching 11 should be further explored in the interview. Other depression screens could be used, such as the 20-item version of the CES-D or the Beck Depression Inventory.

6

The Intake

&

The hope-focused couple approach has a long history of concentrated time and effort in the intake phase of treatment. We believe that if you can get a good conceptualization of what is going on with the couple, then the treatment phase will be more effective and efficient. Thus investing time in in-depth assessment is worthwhile. By spending effort on assessment, counseling can be briefer. We want to focus counseling on what is important as quickly as is reasonable, and not spend four or five sessions trying to understand what the needs are before beginning intervention. Also, the intake is actually an effective intervention with layers of clinical benefit.

1. The couple reflects on and increases their understanding of their relationship.

2. They create a relationship with you so they can trust you.

3. They should increase in hope, especially increasing their sense of agency. Thus they will be more able to find their path to a better relationship.

4. They begin to understand the social norms, behaviors and language that characterize couple counseling.

A major goal for the intake is to develop therapeutic alliance with the partners. The research in common factors (Sprenkle, Davis & Lebow, 2009) has taught us that the alliance between the partners and the counselor is an essential component of successful counseling. It is like the gasoline needed for the journey. Without a strong alliance of the partners with each other, and each partner with the therapist, it is difficult to reach goals. But it can be difficult for a couple who are seeking counseling to have a sense that they are working together for the good of their relationship, and that their counselor is "with them" in that goal. It is important for the counselor to attend to strained alliance relationships.

DYADIC INTAKE SESSION

Goals of the intake session. One of the main goals of this initial treatment session is to gain information that will assist in the conceptualization and treatment of the couple. Sometimes you might conclude that couple treatment is not indicated. It is crucial to assess accurately whether the couple should be seen as a couple. However, there other critical goals for the intake session. The counselor aims to build a strong rapport with the couple and instill hope in them that their relationship can be better. This latter goal is particularly important—after all, this is the *hope-focused*

Goals of Intake
1. *Gain necessary information*
2. *Build strong rapport*
3. *Instill hope for change*
4. *Set counseling norms*

---

couple approach! Consistent infusions of hope and positive effort are needed to cultivate and sustain the couple's motivation to work on their relationship. Without such motivation, they probably will not work hard enough to change their relationship permanently. You, the counselor,

serve as a wellspring of that hope, not just in the initial treatment session, but throughout the entire hope-focused couple approach process.

INTERVENTION 6-1: BEGINNING THE DYADIC INTAKE SESSION

Welcome the couple warmly and address issues relevant to them or to the setting (e.g., informed consent forms). Be sure to see whether there are any questions they might have from the pre-therapy information and screening assessments before moving forward.

The dyadic intake session is designed to help you capture information about important aspects of the couple's relationship. The classic approach to hope-focused couple assessment intake involves a semistructured oral interview (30-45 minutes) and a video-recorded communication assessment (20 minutes), which we consider a "hope-focused classic." If possible, we now recommend that you also conduct brief individual intakes on the same day or soon thereafter. Finally, you will spend 10 to 20 minutes processing the results of the interview and the screening information with the couple. You also will explain their homework to them. Between the first and second sessions, you will synthesize the information you have gleaned into a concise written feedback report, which you will give to each partner at the next joint session, when you will go over it. Keep in mind how you will use the information you gain during the initial treatment session so you can gather information accordingly.

There are two potential paths for intake. We recommend you complete the entire intake in one long two-hour assessment session. This concise assessment engages the couple in treatment more quickly and allows for complete intake procedures. The other path is two one-hour sessions.

INTERVENTION 6-2: DYADIC SEMISTRUCTURED ORAL INTERVIEW

For the semistructured oral interview, counselors should move through the core questions (see table 6.1) without referring to notes in order to demonstrate competency to clients. Both partners should be engaged in answering each question. Each of these areas of inquiry may involve several related follow-up questions. But as any good counselor knows, an intake session should not consist of just questions and answers; it should also be a good reflection of content and emotions.

Table 6.1

Question	What the counselor is listening for
1. Why did you decide to seek couple counseling at this time? Follow-up: What caused you to call for an appointment now?	Here you are trying to get an idea of their motives, readiness for change and presenting problems.
2. What are the most positive things about your marriage/relationship? What are your strengths as a couple? What are the things that are hardest for you?	Difficulty in remembering strengths is not a good sign. Look to see if there is any fondness or admiration left in the relationship. See if their description of what is hard for them triggers them to blame, put down or be negative toward each other or if they take responsibility for their own contribution to the problems.
3. Tell me a little bit about how you met and give me a general history of your relationship.	You should look for a negative history narrative. That might indicate that the partners have already decided on the inevitability of divorce. Follow up on negative narrative in individual intake.

Question	What the counselor is listening for
4. Imagine you went to bed tonight and while you were sleeping, a miracle occurred. You woke up, and to your amazement, everything about your relationship was suddenly perfect—just like you've always hoped it would be. If that kind of miracle happened, what would your relationship look like? Be as specific and concrete as you can.	Here the couple may need a lot of coaching. You need them to be very specific, detailing behaviors, cognition and relational dynamics that have changed. You may have to ask follow up questions, like "How would you know things had changed for the better?" and "What specific things would be different?" "What would it look like if it were better?" Have them frame the changes in terms of what they do want—not what they do not want.
4b. Christian enrichment: For those couples seeking explicitly Christian counseling, the counselor could ask the "miracle question" using Christian language (e.g., "If God answered all your prayers for your relationship and performed a miracle . . .").	
5. I noticed in your assessments that (neither of you, one of you, both of you) rated spirituality and religion as very important to you or central to your life. Does that seem correct?[a]	Here you are looking to see how much religion or faith might be part of counseling for this couple.
5b. If there is an interest in faith ask: How does faith play a part in the problems in your relationship? How might your faith play a part in the solutions to your relationship struggles? When both partners are highly religious ask: We can address issues of faith as they relate to your relationship and I will follow your lead in what issues you need to discuss about this part of your lives. Were you expecting to include practices from your faith like prayer or discussing Scripture as part of this counseling?	Be sensitive to how similar or different the partners are on religion. You can spend time in counseling with the couple teasing out this issue of faith and life meaning/values and how their differences affect their marriage.
6. Address any other issues of diversity here—race, age/family life stage, culture, language, disability, economic situation, sexual orientation, etc. You can ask this in a question like "Is there anything about ____ that we should discuss as part of your treatment?"	Some of this will be applicable or not, based on their answers to diversity questions in your assessment. Consider how the couple might need alterations or additions to treatment to address diversity issues that affect their relationship. Here the counselor takes an attitude of humility, asking the couple to teach him or her about their experiences related to diversity.
7. In the surveys you filled out [online], you indicated _____. Could you tell me a little more about that?	Here you are following up on any issues that may indicate: (1) clinical unsuitability for couple therapy and/or the hope-focused couple approach (e.g., one or both partners are seriously contemplating divorce/separation), and (2) the need for possible further assistance (e.g., individual counseling in cases of clinical depression, emergency treatment in cases of suicide risk, crisis management in cases of domestic violence).

[a]**Ethics**: Counselors must obtain consent and discuss what using religious practices would mean for the couple. Matching the couple's practices and not expecting them to be more than they are is very important—or else the couple may not internally change. See intervention 3-3 on use of prayer in counseling.

INTERVENTION 6-3: VIDEO ASSESSMENT (hf)

The partners discuss a difficult topic with each other for eight to ten minutes on a recording. Then they will watch the tape and evaluate themselves and their partner in terms of how positive versus negative their communication style was.

As you introduce the couple to this exercise, say something like this: "How you communicate with each other is a very important part of couple counseling. I want to be able to see how you communicate, particularly about difficult topics. I also want you to be able to observe yourselves communicating to get your own ideas to improve communication. I'm going to ask you to discuss a topic that is sometimes difficult for you to navigate in your relationship—something you sometimes, maybe often, disagree about. But it should not be something that you're likely to become completely flooded with anger or resentment over either. Talk with each other for about eight to ten minutes. I'll video record your interaction. Then we'll watch the recording together, and I'll ask you about what you see. Is it okay if we create this recording?"

Answer any questions they may have. Then ask, "So, what difficult topic would you like to talk about on the video?" Again, try to strike a balance between a topic that would cause them to completely flood with emotion and not be able to talk, and a topic that will not engage their emotions at all.

As the couple is talking, be as unobtrusive as possible. Do not interrupt the couple unless they appear to be getting violent or dangerously emotionally swamped. Require them to complete at least eight minutes but not more than ten minutes.

As they comment on their own video, watch for emotional flooding and for comments on the video that are very negative or hostile. If they only point out negative things, attempt to introduce something positive that happened in the video and see if the partners can acknowledge positivity. Their responses are important to your treatment planning. If they are globally negative, then you will need to spend much time early in counseling building positive interactions and helping the couple notice those positive interactions. The video provides a wealth of information about their attachment, communication styles, patterns of relating, nonverbals and more. After the couple has discussed the video, introduce a couple of hopeful things that you noticed. Assure them that any negative patterns can be turned around with effort. However, importantly, do not discourage the couple with many negative observations. The more negative they are, the more you must attend to promoting hope (without appearing unrealistically Pollyannaish) to counter their hopelessness.

INTERVENTION 6-4: THEIR FIRST HOMEWORK: OUR FOUR BEST IDEAS

Homework each week is a crucial part of the hope-focused couple approach. In fact, if we could require it of all clients using the approach, we would! Homework is the key to change for the couple. They will only be in your office about one hour a week (typically) and then will go back to their daily routine for the other 167 hours of their week. So getting partners to take the ideas home and make them work for them is key to reaching their goals.

You should assign some sort of homework the first week. Typical homework interventions for the first week increase the positive energy in the relationship to fuel the work of counseling and increase hope. Here are some common initial homework interventions we use.

1. Invite them to go on a date together, just the two of them. Ask them not to talk about their relationship problems and concerns. If they cannot seem to be together without arguing, ask them to choose to do something that does not involve much talking, like a movie or a bike ride. Try to have the couple come up with their own ideas for their date night. If they are having a lot of trouble, step in and help them brainstorm ways to overcome obstacles. The most important thing about this assignment is getting them to make their specific plans for the date night—including activity, day, place and time—before they leave your office.

2. Have them create a daily list of things they are grateful for or appreciate about their partner. You can encourage them to share the lists with each other if you think they can do so without conflict. Or they can share their gratitude list in counseling the next meeting.

3. Have them complete a "love bank" type of exercise (Harley, 2001). This classic hope-focused intervention considers loving acts as depositing love dollars and relationship-destructive acts as withdrawing love dollars. The intent is to keep a positive love bank balance. Partners each write down things that they appreciate their partner doing to better their

relationship. Those might include things like helping with household chores, hugging or showing affection, writing a love note, planning a vacation together, or listening to their favorite music when driving. These things tend to be idiosyncratic to each person, so once the partner lists their deposits, the spouses know clearly what they can each do to bless the partner. Ask whether each partner will commit to try to make some lovebank deposits this week. Ask them how many things they think they can do this week. Then ask them to watch and see whether they can guess when their partner is depositing love. Tell them that you'll get them to report back next session on what they saw.

4. Have them do a self-designed intervention. Sometimes couples have already begun to take some action toward improving their relationship. In the positive hope-focused couple approach, it is important to capitalize on that strength if it exists. Encourage it strongly. Ask them to increase their effort in that area if it is working for them.

It is vital that you ask about and process the homework at the beginning of the second session. This is true even if they come in with a very emotional issue. First attend to the emotional issue, but then get to the homework. If you do not process it the week after the first assignment, you will likely not get any cooperation with homework assignments after that time.

INTERVENTION 6-5: CLIENT FEEDBACK ON THE INTAKE SESSION

Considerable research shows that creating a continual feedback loop in counseling will increase the efficacy of the couple's work (Irving et al., 2004). Requesting feedback from the couple usually increases client perception of your credibility as a counselor, which is a good predictor of outcome. It also helps locate anything you might be doing in counseling that is distracting or difficult for clients. Unique to couple counseling, the alliance between the partners may be more important to success than the alliance with the counselor (Friedlander, Escudero, Heatherington & Diamond, 2011). Therefore, specific attention should be paid to creating a regular feedback loop in counseling. We recommend that feedback take two forms: first written and then a discussion within the session. We include in chapter 23 a one-minute one-page measure that you might find useful. The measure was created specifically for the hope-focused couple approach. Note also that Barry Duncan

(Owen, Duncan, Anker & Sparks, 2012) has also created a simple and well-studied system for client feedback that counselors may want to investigate further for training in using client feedback within counseling (see heartand soulofchange.com/content/measures/login.php). The primary goal of the feedback measure we use is to spark discussion about whether counseling is meeting each partner's needs and to empower them to ask for what they need.

INTERVENTION 6-6: INDIVIDUAL INTAKE SESSIONS

Not every couple counselor does individual intake sessions. In the previous version of the hope-focused couple approach, individual sessions were not included as part of the approach. However, after a decade of seeing couples in our clinics we have noticed that many more couples seem to present with significant issues of psychopathology, violence, substance abuse, infidelity or other problems that require changes to previous versions of the approach. We now believe that most couple counselors should plan for individual intake sessions. After meeting with the couple, a counselor might not include individual sessions if the couple were clearly seeking enrichment and had no indicators or red flags for counseling. However, today many couples whose problems have progressed to the point where they are seeking couple therapy do have red flags that should be queried individually. Usually the counselor should expect that individual sessions will be needed within that extended initial session.

At the beginning of each individual session, the counselor should remind the partner of his or her policy on sharing information disclosed by each individual partner. We usually suggest that all information shared by each partner individually be treated as shared information, unless safety is an issue. However, it is up to the counselor to decide on a policy and communicate it clearly to each partner, both verbally and in writing. Your policy about sharing information should conform to the ethical guidelines and standards for your discipline and the relevant laws and regulations in your state. It should be made in consultation with an experienced colleague or attorney, and written in your practice information for clients.

In the hope-focused couple approach, an individual session should be primarily used to assess for individual psychopathology and other red flags that may indicate the couple is able unsuitable for couple therapy or the hope-focused couple approach. Possible red flags may include any of the following: depression, untreated substance abuse, ongoing or recent infidelity, domestic violence, untreated or active trauma symptoms, divorce or separation intent, cognitive deficit issues, or low motivation for change. In particular, depression has high comorbidity with marital distress, so you should always be alert to whether one or both partners are depressed. The individual session is also a good time to address any complicating life situations that may affect treatment, such as work stress, financial problems, other family issues (like child rearing or elder care), or health concerns.

Use your clinical judgment to determine whether the hope-focused couple approach is indicated for the couple. In the following chapter, we discuss several conditions that contraindicate couple therapy. If couple therapy is not indicated, then refer the couple to more appropriate sources of help. If the hope-focused couple approach does not seem like a fitting approach to use with the couple, modify the treatment appropriately.

7

After the Intake

❧

The couple exit the office and perhaps there is hardly a break before your next appointment, or perhaps you must leave immediately for home. Sometime later you find space to think about the couple's intake you completed. What treatment would be best for them? What do they need? How can issues and diversity factors specific to them help create the best treatment fit? Great couple counselors take time to consider the couple's needs as they make treatment decisions. The hope-focused couple approach provides four questions you should ask yourself about any new couple. Then you will construct a written report to offer them. The answers to these questions will direct the entire course of treatment.

Four Questions: AFTR

A: Appropriate for couple therapy?

F: Fit for hope-focused approach?

T: Typical treatment or not?

R: Relevant to couple's needs?

Here we examine the most common issues associated with each of the four questions, which we remember with the acronym AFTR: appropriate, fit, typical and relevant.

QUESTION 1: IS COUPLE COUNSELING APPROPRIATE FOR THIS COUPLE?

Empirical research, clinical lore and theoretical discussions have generally agreed that couple counseling is contraindicated in some cases. Some situations clearly suggest that counseling not be started. For others, indications are suggestive, but the counselor must weigh the decision and might decide to move ahead with the hope-focused couple approach but adjust it to the couple's special needs.

Situations that are clearly contraindicated. *Is one or both of the partners intent on divorce?* If one partner is intent on divorce, regardless of the outcome of couple counseling, the prognosis for the relationship is poor. The counselor can ask whether partners are willing to put aside plans to separate in order to work on the relationship for a few months. An appeal to their investment of time and of their shared memories might lead some to give counseling at least a reluctant chance of success. But if one or both partners refuse, the clinician should refer the couple for court mediation services to facilitate as amicable a separation as possible.

Is one or both of the partners involved in ongoing extramarital infidelity? There is widespread agreement that conducting couple counseling when one or both of the partners are concurrently engaged in ongoing extramarital infidelity is likely an act of futility. Here the clinician should refer the partners to individual counseling until the affair is terminated and contact with the extramarital partner stops.

What constitutes "infidelity" is often unclear. The counselor will have to use his or her judgment on issues like emotional infidelity, internet-only infidelity, or even addiction to pornography. However, the principle of the matter is that partners cannot maintain and develop other romantic relationships outside of their relationship and fully engage in couple counseling at the same time.

Is one or both of the partners engaging in moderate to severe domestic violence toward the other partner? Couple counseling is contraindicated with couples where there is ongoing moderate to severe domestic violence. We define this as violence that has left marks, has resulted in significant physical or emotional harm, or has led to fear or trauma. Treating couples who report this kind of violence is considered unethical.

However, couple counseling may be helpful if a couple has had moderate to severe abuse in the past but have not engaged in any violence for at least one year, and if neither partner is abusing substances. Likewise, couple counseling may be indicated for couples who are experiencing only mild domestic violence. Mild domestic violence is defined as (1) neither partner has been physically harmed, (2) neither partner has a fear of being harmed, and (3) the violence is relatively mild—such as pushing, pinning or throwing nondangerous objects. Mild domestic violence also assumes that neither partner is abusing substances. Substance abuse might disinhibit violence.

If you decide to provide couple counseling to a couple engaged in some domestic violence, then the focus of treatment should initially be on promoting healthy conflict resolution, such as the use of time-outs. You should also use weekly assessment of violent behaviors to insure partners' safety. If the couple cannot engage in time-outs and positive conflict resolution soon after couple therapy is begun, then couple therapy should be halted. At that point, the clinician should refer the couple for individual treatment until the point that safety is adequately developed and maintained. Be aware that many couples are ashamed of violence in their relationship and will minimize it or simply not report it.

Is one or both of the partners engaged in substance abuse and unwilling to give it up? If a partner is abusing some substance and is unwilling or unable to give it up, then couple therapy becomes contraindicated until the substance abuse can be effectively addressed. However, if the abusing partner is willing to give up their substance abuse and engage in treatment for it, then couple counseling can be beneficial. Substance abuse focused couple counseling is particularly beneficial as an adjunct to substance abuse treatment (O'Farrell & Schein, 2011). In such cases it can help support the goals of the substance abuse treatment (e.g., relapse prevention) of the treated individual, and it can assist the changing dynamics of the family or dyadic system as treatment goals are increasingly met. However, the course of treatment using the hope-focused couple approach would need to be significantly altered to address the patterns relevant to substance abuse and provide support for sobriety. The hope-focused couple approach is not designed for this purpose, but it might be adapted.

Situations that are possibly contraindicated. *Is one or both of the partners engaging in repeated moderate to severe destructive behaviors?* If one or both partners are engaged in moderate to severe destructive behaviors regularly (e.g., deceitfulness, substance use, gambling, problematic use of pornography, emotional abuse, extremely irresponsible financial decisions, etc.), then couple counseling might be contraindicated. If the couple did engage in couple treatment, the destructive behavior would probably consume most of the couple's counseling attention and focus. Until the destructive behavior is effectively addressed, further progress as a couple might be unlikely. We might (or might not) recommend simultaneous individual (with another counselor) and couple therapy that focuses on the problematic behavior. But the hope-focused couple approach alone is unlikely to be adequate for this goal and for relationship improvement.

Is one of the partners struggling with significant psychopathology? Couple counseling can be quite effective in the treatment of various mood disorders when the root of the problem is the relationship distress. However, if a partner has a significant psychopathology with issues like hallucinations, delusions, extreme mood symptoms or a personality disorder, then the couple is unlikely to make much relationship progress if there isn't simultaneous amelioration of the psychopathology. In particular, couple therapists should consider screening for depression with all couple cases, since the comorbidity of depression with relationship distress is high. If the relationship is the major cause of mild to moderate depression, then couple counseling is likely the best treatment. Otherwise the therapist should discuss with the couple whether simultaneous individual or medication treatment is needed, or if couple therapy may need to wait for improvements through other treatments first. If a partner is unlikely to be able to engage in couple treatment due to psychopathology, then other initial treatment is warranted.

QUESTION 2: IS THE HOPE-FOCUSED COUPLE APPROACH A GOOD FIT FOR THIS COUPLE?

Even if the couple needs couple counseling, the hope-focused couple approach might not be the treatment of choice. Like any theoretical approach or treatment modality, the hope-focused couple approach is not a good fit for every couple. It is up to the clinician to determine what treatment approach is likely to result in the most benefit for the couple and to use that approach. Ultimately such a decision depends on the practitioner's clinical judgment. There are a few guidelines for this decision from our experience. The hope-focused couple approach is a general approach to couple problems. It is not designed for every type of problem. Nor is it designed for crises. The types of couples that would likely benefit from other types of couple therapy are shown in table 7.1 (although this is not an exhaustive list).

Table 7.1

Those seriously considering divorce or separation	May need to explore that decision before engaging in counseling
Those with primarily parenting concerns	Should receive a parenting intervention that may include issues of parenting alliance as a couple
Those with primarily sexual concerns	Should receive a medical evaluation and certified sex therapy, or be referred to someone who is qualified to address the relevant sexual issues
Those with primarily psychopathology of one person	May benefit from the hope-focused couple approach but the pathology needs to also be assessed with concurrent treatment of the psychopathology as this approach does not directly address individual psychopathology
Those reconciling after a separation, affair or major offense	May be able to use forgiveness and reconciliation portions of the hope-focused couple approach but will likely need much more time and tailoring of treatment than this approach is designed for managing reconciliation. We recommend the approach developed by Don Baucom, Douglas Snyder and Kristi Coop-Gordon (Baucom et al., 2009) which has been published broadly in numerous venues and includes forgiveness. The two approaches would likely be able to be blended together creatively if a counselor were able to apply them both to a couple.

QUESTION 3: DOES A TYPICAL COURSE OF COUNSELING NEED TO BE ALTERED FOR THIS COUPLE?

One of the most important things you can do for the couple entering your office is to tailor the treatment to their particular style, needs and values. Here we discuss some common issues faced in the first stage of counseling that we have observed with couples in our practices.

A highly unmotivated partner. In couple work, there often is one partner who is more motivated to engage in treatment than the other partner. However, sometimes a partner can be so unmotivated that it becomes a serious obstacle to treatment. In such a case, the treatment may need to be altered. For this type of couple, we suggest that the clinician allow time at the beginning of treatment to address the reluctant partner's concerns and resistances. However, it is also true that seeing is believing. If the partner is willing to experiment with some intervention or homework to see whether it might make things even "a little bit" better, this approach is often effective with reluctant spouses as well.

A partner who has difficult characterological issues. In the initial stage of treatment, the clinician might discover that one partner has characterological issues that may make treatment difficult. Because the hope-focused couple approach does not specify personality change as a treatment goal, clinicians using it must find ways to work around personality issues. This will likely require blending with other modalities of treating long-term characterological types of problems.

A partner or couple who has difficulties with forgiveness. Sometimes one or both partners will have marked difficulties with forgiveness. Sometimes partners have had bad experiences with forgiveness in their past—such as having been coerced to forgive or having been mistakenly told that forgiveness means reconciling with an abusive person—causing them to resist the idea. In such cases, the standard hope-focused couple approach treatment protocol for HURT and FREE (see chapters 20-21) might need to be altered to slow down and address the concerns around forgiveness. Often the concerns are fears based on previous negative experiences with offenses and forgiveness. Those concerns will need to be understood before engaging in any interventions.

A partner or couple who has marked difficulty engaging in empathy and compassion. If one or both of the partners has difficulty with empathy and compassion, you might need to alter or remove from treatment some of the interventions that incorporate empathy. Instead, treatment for this type of couple is likely to focus more on behaviors and creating behavioral changes in the relationship instead of directly seeking to promote emotional connection between the partners. We believe that emotional connection is the key to successful couple relationships, but there are many paths to that connection, and some people simply cannot deal with empathy and emotions directly.

A partner or partners who have a trauma history. If one or both of the partners have a trauma history, their trauma needs to be attended to in treatment. Trauma can cause difficulties in the couple's intimacy and in their cognitions (e.g., attributions). Trauma-focused treatment (Hecker, 2011) can take place in dyadic or individual counseling. But it is important to attend to the symptoms and needs relevant to the trauma history. The hope-focused couple approach would be altered to address the needs relevant to the trauma for the couple. In chapter 26, we provide some guidance for working with couples where at least one partner has a trauma history.

In all of these difficulties, the hope-focused couple approach might well succeed. But substantial adjustments might also be needed. Some interventions might need extra time, focus or effort before the remainder of the hope-focused couple approach can be implemented.

QUESTION 4: IS THE APPROACH RELEVANT TO THE COUPLE'S PERCEIVED NEED?

Couple counselors consider dozens of pieces of information during the initial stage of counseling. Sometimes the couple's concerns or desires can be lost or ignored. Even if the couple counselor believes the couple is not assessing their relationship needs accurately, it is important to use their ideas regarding their needs and not simply ignore them. This empowers the couple to find solutions to their own problems, to become their own healers in collaboration with God (and you). The hope-focused couple approach strongly encourages client autonomy as a key to improvement. Addressing *their* primary concerns is essential.

> *It is important to be relevant to the couple's concerns and needs.*

INTERVENTION 7-1: WRITING THE INTAKE REPORT AND TREATMENT PLAN (hf)

If you can answer yes to these four questions about the couple, then you are ready to create a plan of action. You may find the chapters on the different typologies of couples (chapters 8-16) useful in developing a creative and helpful plan for the couple. It is easy to get lost in all of the information. One technique to handle this overload of information is to take a blank piece of paper during intake meetings and write down keywords of things that are important or difficult to remember. Then after the intake you can add more information. Consider the four questions (AFTR) and any unique information from their written assessments and add this to your preparation.

Mutual agreement. "A whole couple report? *Really?* Do you know how busy I am?" One of the most important aspects of the hope-focused couple approach is for the couple and the clinician to come to a mutual agreement on the course of treatment—and (oh dear) to put it in writing. Typically, when there is such an agreement, the treatment process is more grounded and the treatment outcomes are favorable. With agreement there can be clear goals and clearly defined strategies for reaching each of these goals.

In contrast, when there is not a mutual agreement on the course of treatment, treatment progress often seems elusive. Goals never seem to be clear, or the partners and the counselor might have three different sets of goals. Positive outcomes are usually minimal at best.

The couple report has demonstrated consistent significant outcome results in component research in both of our research labs (Ripley, Maclin, Hook & Worthington, 2013; Worthington et al., 1997). Yet when people in the field are new to the hope-focused couple approach, the couple report seems to be the part that counselors struggle with the most. They are too busy, too stressed. They think, *this is just another piece of paperwork to suck up my time*. They think, *it will not be worth the hassle*. Often they simply ignore this part of treatment. But those who have used the report in their practice—especially if they did not utilize initial assessments and feedback in prior couple counseling—tells us often and repeatedly how they are amazed at how important it is to effective counseling.

Finding the time. If you are serving in an outpatient counseling center or clinic, then sessions are how you receive payment, and reports are generally not part of the payment schedule. If you are in that setting, then we encourage you to consider two options. One is to simply regard it as part of effective practice, just as high-quality medical doctors' offices create medical reports for patients. The other option is to build the time on the report within the intake fee schedule requiring clients to pay for the time in assessment and reports, noting that it is often not covered by insurance. Some insurance situations may allow for this fee schedule, and others may not be aware of your ethical contractual obligations. If you are serving in a capitated system or pastoral care setting, then the issue of income for hours is not of such concern. However, demands on your time can still be intense. In either situation it is crucial that your reports be created quickly. We have developed several tactics to create reports efficiently.

1. *Use templates*. We have used numerous templates that help clinicians create personalized reports but with some information repeated. We have made these templates available in the "Counselors" section of hopecouples.com. Having clear headings, graphics and easily understood tables help make sense of the relationship information. If you look at the sample report in this book you will find simple graphics that can be used with any couple. The graphics in the sample report in this book were created by using an average of the Couples Assessment of Relationship Elements (CARE) measure as the primary guide, and then shifting the bar right or left on the guide based on the counselor's judgment. Couples find this helpful as they decide what aspect of their relationship they should work on first.

2. *Obsession is your enemy.* Remember that the goals of the report are to focus on the most important aspects of the couple's problem, help them feel understood and create a record of the relationship assessment for them to use in the future. If you write about a lot of details, you will confuse the couple. Make a few of the most relevant and important points in the report.

3. *Work on the report quickly and quietly.* If you are able to work on the report within 24 hours of the intake, then your memory is still fresh and writing is much easier. Interruptions while you are thinking about the couple or writing the report may be inevitable. You'll finish faster, though, if you can complete it in one sitting and do not have to re-review the information on your brainstorm sheet.

4. *Run a readability statistic.* Counselors are often surprised at how "educated" their language is in written reports. The typical newspaper is written at a sixth to eighth grade level to make it accessible to the general population. Most word processing programs will run an automatic readability statistic. Based on vocabulary and sentence structure, it will give you an estimated grade level for the writing. This is a good check on your writing. Consider whether any words better communicate the idea than a "college" psychological word. Also look for ways to keep sentences as short as possible. Because you are writing to a specific couple, you likely know their education level. Yet even with college-educated couples it is important that the language you use in the report is readable and understandable to someone outside of the profession. The concepts are emotionally laden, so it is important not to distract the couple from the important emotional content. You want the couple to read the report and have a solid idea of the status of their relationship, the realistic chances of change and your proposed recommendations for treatment. An easily understood report facilitates buy-in by the partners, which is usually needed for their active participation, faithful attendance and positive outcomes.

How long does it take to write a great report? In our experience, if you use these principles, you can write a report in 30 minutes, less if you do them often and have many templates.

SAMPLE COUPLE REPORT

Couple: Darnell and Gloria (names and other identifying information, as always, have been changed for confidentiality)

Assessment made by: Tamara Erspamer, M.A.

Date: March 14, 2013

PERSONAL HISTORY

Darnell and Gloria have been married for two years. They sought counseling to improve their relationship and learn new ways to communicate with one another. After being together for several years, this couple wants to develop new patterns of conflict resolution and increase the sense of emotional intimacy, forgiveness and trust.

RELATIONSHIP HISTORY

Darnell and Gloria met at a local church in the spring of 2008 through mutual friends. They dated for a year, lived together for three years, and then married in 2012. Due to difficulty with finding work, the couple lived apart their second year of marriage. Currently the couple live together. Darnell reported that he has one child from a past marriage but the child lives with his mother. Despite current difficulties, they say they are committed to finding ways to better their marriage.

PRIMARY RELATIONSHIP CONCERNS: RESOLVING DIFFERENCES AND INTIMACY

The hope-focused couple approach looks at seven major areas of relationships to see where the main concerns are in your marriage. This is what your tests indicated (see figure 7.1).

Overall, your relationship is fairly similar to other couples who come for couple counseling. Couples tend to score around 4 on most areas. Your main concerns appear to be in the areas of conflict resolution (called "resolving differences" in the table) and intimacy and closeness.

Regarding conflict resolution, you often disagree. There are several recurring conflicts in your marriage, especially about employment and finances. Both of you are hesitant to address the conflicts. What's more, even though you both want to resolve conflicts, it seems hard for you to see the other's perspective.

In intimacy, you say that you have trouble being close and vulnerable with each other. Because of hurts from the past and continued challenges today, you both seem to have trouble creating and holding on to a close and forgiving marriage.

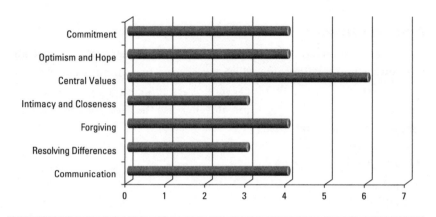

Figure 7.1

Also, it seems that you both struggle with feeling optimistic and hopeful about your marriage. You love each other (this is important!), but due to long-standing difficulties in your relationship, you seem unsure whether you have the ability to create the kind of marriage you hope for.

RELATIONSHIP STRENGTHS: VALUES

Darnell and Gloria, your primary relationship strength is your shared values. You both report having God at the center of your marriage. You stated that his grace has kept you together through some very challenging times. Also, you both agree on the areas for change in your marriage. You both recognize that it is important to work to improve ineffective communication and problem-solving patterns. Two other strengths of your marriage are your commitment to work on your relationship and to engage in counseling. Your willingness to seek counseling is a sign that you have hope for a better marriage and for more intimacy with one another. These are great strengths to build on.

PATHWAYS TO CHANGE: FAITH, WORK AND LOVE

The good news is that your relationship can change. There are three pathways to change your relationship that we will work on (see figure 7.2).

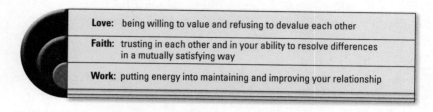

Love:	being willing to value and refusing to devalue each other
Faith:	trusting in each other and in your ability to resolve differences in a mutually satisfying way
Work:	putting energy into maintaining and improving your relationship

Figure 7.2

The conflict-resolution and intimacy issues you are unhappy about can improve with new experiences, skills and insights. You can learn to use these when difficult issues arise. You both admit you use unhealthy patterns that ultimately hurt each of you and your marriage. It seems that often your fears take over and drown out your love for each other. The love is there, but you seem to be putting each other down and not understanding each other. In counseling, we will work on changing these patterns so that you can develop a healthier marriage.

Your work: Darnell and Gloria, I ask that you focus one work week (about 40 hours) of effort on your marriage while you are participating in this counseling over the next 8-10 weeks. That will be about 8-12 additional hours of counseling (beyond what you've already invested in this evaluation) and another 25-30 hours of spending positive "homework" time together working to improve your marriage.

Your goals: When asked how you would know that a miracle happened in your marriage, you shared that you would have more stability, consistent communication and loving interactions with each other. These goals are a great match for the hope-focused approach, which will focus on helping you value each other and your relationship more often. All of the experiences and skills shared in counseling can strengthen your relationship and take it to the next level in meaning and intimacy.

SUMMARY

Darnell and Gloria, you have a special relationship and show commitment to each other. You are also both willing to work to improve your relationship. Your primary strength is reflected in your shared values and commitment to God. The difficulties that you identified within your relationship can begin to be restored if you are willing to work hard on your relationship.

TREATMENT PLAN

I propose that, subject to your agreement, we begin with reviewing your goals and vision for your marriage for the coming years. Then we work on creating better communication that will allow you to resolve conflict better. After you get better at resolving your conflicts, we will focus on forgiveness to begin to put the hurts you've both experienced safely in the past. Finally, to strengthen your bond with each other, we will focus on improving intimacy. I believe this will take about twelve counseling sessions, as long as we do not hit large unexpected roadblocks. This means counseling will last from March 14 to the end of May or beginning of June if you do not miss sessions. I think if you work hard this spring, you will find many positive changes in your relationship by summer.

Part Three

CASE STUDIES IN TREATMENT PLANNING

We have been training doctoral students and other professionals in couple therapy for a long time. I (Ev) have heard from many people regarding *Hope-Focused Marriage Counseling*, originally published in 1999 and revised in 2005. What Jen and I have heard repeatedly is that the techniques and approach were very helpful. I actually had many people tell me that they had never had a psychotherapy book that was so practical and yet solidly theoretical. Jen and I have sought to give you an even more practical and theoretically grounded book. Couple therapists, students of couple counseling and couples seeking to improve their relationships have asked for more help in creating strategies that they could tailor to fit precise problems. They have asked how the treatment would be shifted and adjusted for various types of couple concerns. They have also asked repeatedly for more case examples.

In addition, psychotherapy and couple therapy have gotten increasingly more focused. No longer does one size fit all. General theories of treatment are passé. Laser-targeted therapy is not only the wave of the future, it is the wave of the present.

We want to be responsive—to clients, to counselors and to the professional standards. This part of this book was the result of that responsiveness.

We created this part of the book to offer exemplar couple cases with strategies for treatment aimed at each case. These are common types of couples to enter couple counseling. If you are new to couple counseling, we hope this will help you think through the important factors in couples when you are making treatment decisions. If you are an experienced clinician, we hope this part of the book provides some new avenues to explore in conceptualizing and treating your couples. These cases are exemplars. But no case will ever perfectly fit the "textbook" example. Rarely should treatment plans be implemented exactly as suggested for these cases. Each case is unique and needs individualized planning. This is similar to the way that medical treatment is moving to individualized treatment. It is just as necessary in helping couples. We hope these examples will provide some templates that you can revise for your own cases.

8

The Wounded but Hopeful Couple

Janet and Doug were a middle-aged, middle-class Caucasian couple seeking couple counseling for the first time. They scored fairly low in their relationship measures, with Janet scoring lower than Doug.

Janet and Doug with Tabitha

- Built up hurts
- Anger and withdrawal
- Low in faith
- Treatment focuses on increasing emotional understanding followed by forgiveness interventions

---

In the intake session Doug complained that Janet is critical and negative toward him. He was perceptive. It was obvious to Tabitha, their counselor, that Janet had a cool attitude toward him. Janet complained that Doug had hurt her so many times she did not know what else to do.

Doug looked down.

Janet then told how he took large amounts of money for "get rich quick" schemes. In fact, Doug had lost over $50,000 of their money in the past five years. She said that's almost a year's income for them! She said she could have gotten over that but that he began hiding money and lying to her about money the past two years. She felt betrayed and deeply wounded.

Doug countered with his own narrative about the home improvement business he works hard to run and the down economy. He argued that each of the things she called "schemes" were real business opportunities. They just never worked out because of the recession. He said that her criticism of him had gotten so constant and shrill that he decided just not to worry her. So he kept some of his earnings aside for his investment ideas. She really was responsible for their problems. Doug was quick to point out that he does not do irresponsible things like his alcoholic father does.

Janet was not so sure. And she worried that if he keeps headed down the road he's been on, he could end up like his father. Janet felt extremely insecure about their future. She worried that his financial decisions will affect her career because she works for a bank. She hoped to move up in rank once their children were headed to college. She also came from a "dirt-poor" family that had to rely on public assistance just to live. She worried they would end up with no retirement fund. That possibility brought her great anxiety. Her beliefs about marriage, and her loyal and steady personality, meant that she refused to consider divorce. Yet she was extremely distressed about their situation. She had some mild depressive symptoms with difficulty sleeping, recent loss of weight and crying easily.

The counselor, Tabitha, saw the main problem, and here is how she conceptualized it. Using the "faith working through love" motif, she saw that the couple is low in faith. They love each other, although Janet is at risk of becoming cool in her love over the long term. The partners are actually working on their relationship. They have gone on date nights and attended church marriage retreats to keep the marital heart pumping. Yet these repeated offenses by each of them have been difficult on their faith. Janet is even struggling with her faith in God because it seems to her that the prayers for her marriage and her husband have not been answered. Faith is the key principle that needs attention.

The couple has had severe or repeated moderate offenses in their relationship. They are low in faith in the relationship (or God). They also lack forgiveness. As Christians, Doug and Janet have made decisions to forgive each other but their decisions have not extended to emotional forgiveness. Doug sometimes denies responsibility for the offenses but other times feels ashamed or guilty. They want to repair the emotional bond between them but feel inadequate to do so. They need an avenue for change.

Tabitha asked them to commit to 40 hours of work on their relationship: 10 hours of therapy and 3 hours of positive and healthy time together each week with homework they would create together. Tabitha wrote an intake report and treatment plan for the couple (see intervention 7-1).

COURSE OF TREATMENT

Demonstrable hope. The first stage of treatment for a couple like Janet and Doug was to increase their hope quickly. To do that, they needed demonstrable quick change. Tabitha first focused the couple on their first goals for treatment. She returned to the miracle question (see intervention 6-2), which she had asked in their intake phase, and she asked them to expand on their primary goals.

Tabitha said, "Behind the requests and bids for things in an argument is often an unmet need for security, belonging, recognition or control. Is that happening for you?"

Doug said, "I would like to feel respected again. I don't feel I get any credit for what I do for the family." Tabitha suspected that this need may predate his relationship with Janet because Doug always described his childhood as, "I raised myself."

After some exploration, Janet decided that her goal was to feel safe and secure in Doug's love and care for her. Janet said, "I feel very insecure about our future because of the financial crisis."

As their understanding of what was missing in their marriage—faith in each other and in God—grew, both partners began to feel more hope for change.

Janet said to Doug, "I need to make a confession. I've been complaining about you on the phone when I talk with my sister. This isn't fair to you or our relationship because it just makes me angrier. I'm going to tell Nancy that I won't complain about you to her anymore and that I was wrong to do that."

Doug realized that he had lost Janet's trust. He asked her how he can regain it. Doug said, "I need to earn your trust again. I will order a complete financial record of everything with my business and personal accounts. I feel a little ashamed to have to do this, but I know it's important for you." He says, "It is worth it if it will help rebuild trust."

Tabitha felt like this was a good start for this couple to address the wounds they have both inflicted in their relationship. This successful early session was a good sign that the couple could change. The counselor encouraged them to consider asking for pastoral care (see intervention 28-2) from their small group leaders at their church. This long-term friendship with an older couple was a valuable resource for this couple, and they both thought the leaders were understanding and encouraging to them.

Emotional understanding intervention. When the couple began counseling after the intake phase, they felt a general sense of movement toward what they hope for their relationship. Janet had already talked with their small group leader about her commitment to value Doug more and not speak negatively about him to her sister. Doug had an appointment for breakfast with the male leader in a few days. Doug also had shown Janet a full financial accounting. There were only a few small expenses she was not aware of on their financial records, which was reassuring.

Tabitha introduced soft emotional sharing to the couple as an intervention. They agreed. They said they have many feelings about their problems that they keep to themselves. Janet was better able to access her feelings than Doug was. Janet was struggling with loss and fear. Doug was still struggling with not wanting to feel he did anything wrong. Tabitha introduced the concept of intent versus impact to help Doug with this block. He may not have intended to hurt Janet, Tabitha explained, but when asked what the impact of his financial decisions was on Janet, he was able to "own" that he had an impact he did not intend. His hurts had led to her feeling afraid and overwhelmed about debt. This helped Doug keep moving in treatment.

The apology intervention. After some softening and insight through the empty chair intervention (BOND 19-2), Doug said, "I feel alone when you are not encouraging me. I feel like I did when I was a kid and no one cared what I did." At the end of this emotional session, Tabitha suggested that they write letters of apology to each other. They reflected on it and began to apologize for all the things they could remember from the past years where they had hurt each other, intentionally or not. They felt a little overwhelmed when they realized the extent of hurtfulness each had inflicted over the years. However, Tabitha encouraged them to just focus on what came to mind and to pray and ask God for help in writing their letter. She also gave them a Seven Tips for a Good Apology handout to help them (intervention 8-1).

This apology intervention has been part of the hope-focused couple approach since its inception. In fact, the apology was one of the first creative interventions of Don Danser and Ev Worthington when Don, a student then (and now a therapist with almost thirty years of experience), faced a particularly difficult case in the 1980s. For a Christian couple like Doug and Janet, apology and the forgiveness that often follows are usually readily understood and already valued. Other couples may need more discussion to describe a good apology and to address fears regarding apologies. There is often a sense of vulnerability.

The good apology session. This was a good session for this couple because they fully engaged with this intervention. They read their apology letters to each other in the next session, and both were tearful and sincere during that session. Tabitha ended the session by predicting for the couple that something might happen in the coming week or two that would cause them to wonder about the apology. She suggested that perhaps a harsh word, or something that triggered a past hurt for them, might make them doubt the sincerity of the other person's apology. She said not to be surprised if that were to happen. Rather, she encouraged them to treat it as an opportunity to take all that they have learned so far and try and use it "in the moment" at home. Little did she know.

Beauty from ashes. The plan for the next session was to introduce the REACH forgiveness model (see FREE 21-4; see also Worthington, 2003 for full explanation of this model or "bibliotherapy" for couples). But when Tabitha invited the couple in at the beginning of the session, she noticed that the tone between the partners was not good. They were both visibly upset.

Tabitha asked, "It seems like something negative has happened. There seems to be a bad feeling between you." They agreed. "Do you think we might be able to have a helpful discussion about the problem this hour?" They consented.

Janet said, "I had a disastrous week. I found out that I had been passed over for a promotion at work. I have to say I was devastated. Still am. I told Doug about it when I came home. He just was not there for me. He was preoccupied. He was self-absorbed. He was nowhere near as understanding as I needed. Well, I guess I just unloaded on him. I said it was the stress in our marriage that is mainly responsible for why I have not been able to do as well at work. Then I said, 'First, you steal from us for your lame-brain business ideas, and now all *your* problems keep me from getting promoted too! You just drain the life out of me!'"

"Whew. What then?" asked Tabitha.

"I just stormed off for the evening," admitted Janet.

"What's your perception of this, Doug?" asked Tabitha.

"For the last two months," Doug said, "I have only tried to improve things in our marriage. I've busted my buns. I've done everything 'right.' Did it matter? No, it did *not*. She was still disrespecting and devaluing me. Why even try to change if this is what I get?"

Silence stretched out. Tabitha wisely did not answer that question. She asked the couple if they had come back together and improved things any since that big fight. They said they returned to their normal routine the next day but had not talked about it in the last three days.

Tabitha had seen this kind of pattern before. She knew that learning how to recover from a big fight would be a key to improving their relationship. This fight was a disguised gift. It presented an opportunity to work on deepening their forgiveness as a couple with a real and pressing issue.

She said, "You both seem very wounded by this situation. I wonder whether the situation might have activated each of your needs that you've been working on in counseling?" Tabitha pulled out a worksheet on patterns (see intervention 8-2) to help focus the discussion and to highlight the couple's pattern. Tabitha tried to help the partners gain some insight. This could refocus the couple on something other than their injury and thus let the emotional flood recede. In turn, this would likely increase their insight into their patterns.

Janet definitely saw how the loss of the promotion would cause her fear about their financial future to "skyrocket." Doug said "I felt deeply wounded by Janet's explosion of condemning words just when I had gotten my hopes up that I was regaining her respect."

Tabitha noted that this was a difficult situation. "I wonder," she said, "if you are able, right now, to repeat what you did, but here and now try to turn the situation around."

"I'm not sure how I can forgive Doug emotionally," Janet said. "I think my feelings of unforgiveness were the reasons I overreacted and blamed Doug for my job problem."

Tabitha said, "You both might be ready for an emotional-forgiving intervention. The session is about over, so I do not want to start it now. But this week I wonder if you both can let your emotions calm down. I think it will help if you can each take personal responsibility for trying to do things to improve some positive feelings toward each other. Can you do that? Next week we can talk about forgiving."

REACH forgiveness. Tabitha noted that the couple continued to recover from "the big fight" in the subsequent week and restabilize their relationship. This was a good sign of readiness to address emotional forgiveness. The five-step REACH forgiveness model (see FREE 21-4) has steps to help people forgive—*recall* the hurt; emotionally replace negative with positive emotions through *empathy; altruistic* gift of forgiveness; *commit* to forgiveness; and *hold on* to forgiveness during doubts. REACH forgiveness was introduced to Janet and Doug. Tabitha placed special emphasis on the *empathy* and *altruism* aspects of the intervention as pathways to improving their emotional forgiveness. Tabitha had them first focus on forgiving someone else besides their spouse to understand the concepts and "see if it will work for you."

In the midst of that discussion, a pivotal moment of empathy and humility developed. Tabitha said, "Doug, I think it might be especially hard for you to have a humble attitude about your money. You have expressed a lot of pride in creating a much better life for your family than your father did for your family. Yet you also are well aware that you have these problems managing money."

There was silence. Then tears began to stream down Doug's cheek.

"I do not want to be like him," he choked out. "I always feel like he was a failure. I do not want to fail like that." The tears began to tumble onto his shirt.

Janet reached over and took his hand. They looked with soft eyes at each other.

Tabitha asked them both to rate their emotional forgiveness on a scale of 1 to 100. Their intake paperwork had indicated that their emotional forgiveness was extremely low. They had said that only around 25% of the resentments toward each other had been fully forgiven, and that on the two hot-button issues of money and Janet's critical spirit, even less had been forgiven. They both now rated their emotional forgiveness at about 75%.

Tabitha congratulated them. "I know you must be happy with this," she said. "Dealing with these hurts is both difficult and emotional work. Doug, you faced the giant just now and it did not slay you. In fact, you showed a lot of courage. And Janet, you also did not resort to a single critical statement or nonverbal expression. You just stood by Doug. What a great moment. I hope you'll burn this moment into your memories because it is by moments like these that you as a couple will triumph over these difficult times."

Holding on to forgiveness. They both were concerned, however, that another "blow up" might occur in the future. Such caution is typical when people have failed repeatedly at forgiving and then have a breakthrough. They do not want to get their hopes sky-high only to have them body-slammed. Tabitha wisely did not try to push back against their resistance to accepting the forgiveness as a meaningful part of their relationship. Instead, she went with the resistance. "Yes, there surely will be other bad days," she said. "Let me ask you, though, what will you do to minimize the damage when that inevitably happens?"

Both of them said they wanted to focus on "the present problem" and not throw the proverbial kitchen sink at each other in disagreements. This was going to be more difficult for Janet whose disposition was more reactive and emotionally expressive than Doug's.

Tabitha then had the couple focus on ways to "hold on" to forgiveness with reconciliation and trust-building interventions (see TRUST 22-2). The couple learned to recognize triggers that might cause them to lose their emotional forgiveness and move away from each other.

Considering termination. At this point, counseling had reached ten sessions, the original agreement for intervention. Tabitha reminded the couple of this. She asked what they thought they should do at this point. They said that although they would really like to do some more counseling, their sons' sports schedules were increasing. With a new season just starting, they were feeling overcommitted. "Plus," Doug said, "we agree that we need to be there for our sons."

Tabitha framed the decision as a choice between continuing to improve using counseling or improving using other avenues in their life. They discussed an upcoming money management class at their church as something that might be helpful to their needs. Because it was offered on Sunday mornings, they could fit it in their busy lives. Because they both liked reading marriage books, Tabitha suggested Ev's *Forgiving and Reconciling: Bridges to Reconciliation and Hope.* She noted that many of the ideas they had used in counseling on forgiveness, which they had found especially helpful, were the core of that self-help book. They decided to get the book so they could reinforce and explore both forgiveness and reconciliation more deeply. They agreed to meet the following week for a final session.

In their final meeting with Tabitha, they completed a Joshua memorial exercise (see intervention 28-1), in which they created a physical memorial to help them remember the gains they had made throughout counseling. They also scheduled a follow-up meeting in five months to serve as a "checkup" and to create accountability to continue working on their relationship. Tabitha made herself available to appointments if needed but predicted that they had turned a corner in their relationship and would find things would not be the same again.

Prognosis. The couple were better but fragile. They had not made dramatic long-term structural changes or solidified those changes in their relationship, yet they had experienced new ways of handling their anger, hurts and issues with trust. Five or six additional sessions would likely help to solidify their work and allow them to face another "bad day" or two and work through those experiences so they could grow as a couple. Nevertheless, it seemed to them that they had made a fundamental change of direction in their marriage. It was as if they had been aimed at driving west from Virginia Beach to West Virginia, but during counseling they had begun driving south toward Florida instead. It seemed to them that they had changed highways, and although they were still on the outskirts of Virginia Beach, they were headed in a radically different direction toward a sunnier destination.

It is not unusual for other pressure demands to pull a couple out of counseling before they have solidified their gains. Janet and Doug had considerable support, good motivation for change and abilities to change. Their prognosis for continued change was good.

Follow-up. At the follow-up meeting six months later the couple were essentially on the same road that they were traveling at the end of counseling—still headed for sunny skies. They had created additional strategies for money management due to the financial planning course they had enrolled in, which created rules and structures to help them feel more competent and safe about their use of money. They still had some bad days. But time had begun to heal some of Janet's wounds regarding Doug's money management.

In a final assessment, the couple were in the nonclinical range on the Revised Dyadic Adjustment Scale and the CARE measure. Tabitha again offered to meet with the couple as needed in the future, but did not expect to see them.

Principles for Treating the Wounded but Hopeful Couple

1. Wounded couples often need some kind of intentional, memorable and fresh intervention to help them gain enough hope for the hard work of healing wounds in their relationship.

2. Forgiveness interventions need to move with caution to ensure the couple is ready for the intervention. Setbacks and "bad days" are normal—they should be predicted to help lessen their impact on the couple as they try to reconcile, reattach and rebuild trust in their relationship.

3. Once forward movement is happening, the counselor should capitalize on the couple's ability to move forward. This is a good time to help the couple learn about and forgive each other for the wounds in their relationship.

4. Forgiveness work can take time to fully work. For reasons of limited time or finances, the couple may need either to space out treatment or end before it is "complete" in order to address other needs in their lives.

Intervention 8-1: Seven Tips for a Good Apology

Confessing our mistakes is a vital part of healing hurts in relationships. Below there are seven principles that make for a good confession. Discuss these with your partner. Talk about what confessions are like in your relationship currently and what, if anything, you would like to work to change. Use these principles the next time you know you need to confess to your partner.

Timing

1. Confessing before you are caught or asked to apologize will make it easier.

What to say

2. Remind your partner of your commitment to the relationship, your love and care for him or her.

3. Make a clear direct confession, without explaining circumstances or situations that contributed to your offense.

4. Take responsibility for any sins or problems that may have contributed

to hurting the other (such as being overly busy, preoccupied, or being focused only on your own needs).

5. Use tenderness and touch throughout the process if accepted.

After the confession

6. Immediately do something to show your change of heart and repentance. For example, if you were not paying enough attention, then plan some time together just to attend to each other. Or if you said something mean, write a love letter full of kind and encouraging words. Be generous in showing your change of heart. If you can, choose something that relates to how you hurt your partner.

7. Remember the importance of accumulating trustworthy post-hurt events. Repairs rebuild trust. If you repeat the same hurt soon after a confession, it makes you seem insincere.

Application of these principles. Write a journal entry confessing some marital offense that has happened. It could be something common like getting caught up in your own issues and not paying attention to your partner's needs, or it could be something more difficult. All relationships have some offenses. You can confess this offense to God as well. Later, when the timing is right, read or give the letter to your partner.

INTERVENTION 8-2: EXEMPLAR RELATIONSHIP PATTERNS OR PROCESSES

One of the most important things that couples receive from couple therapy is learning how to identify their relationship patterns, especially the patterns that bring them distress. All relationships have them. She wants help in the kitchen, he makes himself scarce, she feels rejected and complains, he is fearful of her criticism and withdraws further, she calls her mother and complains about him, he is offended by her complaining to her mother and goes out with his friends for the night. They never talk about it, and the pattern of complain-withdrawal continues. For most couples, their dysfunctional patterns become so predictable they hardly need to say anything; they know how their partner will react next, how they will respond and how the whole process will end.

This worksheet is intended to help with the process of discussing the relationship pattern. The one here is the emotional pattern that applies to many relationship situations. The couple you are working with might fit exactly with this exemplar pattern. Or you may adjust this and create a revised pattern with the help of the couple. Once identified and clearly understood, as the pattern repeats, either in counseling sessions or in stories of conflicts between sessions, you can take out the pattern worksheet again and ask whether this conflict has a similar pattern. After some repetitions, many couples begin to see their pattern and can work more effectively with their counselor to find ways to break the pattern.

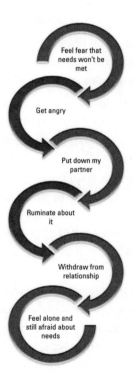

Figure 8.1

9

The Cool Virtues Couple

୧ଈ

Worthington and Berry (2005) discussed relational virtues as having two broad categories—warm and cool. The cool, or conscientiousness-based, virtues are justice-based types like commitment, diligence, right-living, perseverance, purity and self-sacrifice. They involve conscientiousness and self-control. These virtues are agent-based, meaning they rely on inhibiting temptations toward vice. They can be self-regarding virtues, but do not have to be. Many people are oriented toward the cool virtues because they are simply conscientious by basic personality or because they are seeking to please God out of gratitude for divine love. Plato theorized that virtue is based on the power of the soul, so his definition of virtue would be focused on cool justice-based types.

Anthony and Tiana with Ana

- Low in warm attachment but high in conscientiousness
- Low in valuing love
- Interventions to improve attachment are indirect: communication skills and confession/forgiveness are the avenue for improving valuing love and attachment

---

In contrast, warm virtues are relational, for instance, benevolence, empathy, sympathy, compassion, love and altruism. From a psychological perspective, they are rooted in altruism and attachment. They are demonstrated in acts of altruism. They often result in improved attachment between people.

Both types of virtues are Christian and can be motivated by a sincere heart toward the love of Christ. However, as in human nature, both types of virtues can be destructive and can be warped toward self-interest rather than toward promoting love of God and others. Typically God wants people to exercise both the warm and cool virtues. When there is imbalance, there can be problems. We suggest that there can be couples that are too heavily focused on cool virtues to the detriment of warm virtues.

TIANA AND ANTHONY

Anthony and Tiana are a young African American couple referred to a counselor, Ana, by their minister. They have been seeing their minister for counseling for two months and the relationship does not seem to be improving. Anthony is in training to become ordained in their local independent Pentecostal church. He works as a construction foreman during the week. Tiana takes her role as a ministry leader seriously, leading both women's and children's ministries, as well as being employed as an administrative assistant within the church.

The couple met at their church. They have been married for three years. They stated in the intake meeting that the problem is that they fight often. The subject of the fights seemed to change frequently, but they say that the process is usually the same. Tiana gets mad about some situation and withdraws. Anthony says that Tiana is not being a good wife. He puts her down. Tiana either agrees or avoids him. Both partners agree that Tiana is the problem because she is "selfish." It is very important to Anthony that they do the right thing as a couple and follow their understanding of biblical standards for marriage. He is not harsh with her in this, but he has some indicators of rigid and concrete thinking about how the principles of a "biblical marriage" are applied.

ANA'S CASE CONCEPTUALIZATION

The couple is highly focused on the virtues of justice, righteousness, diligence and commitment. However, they are low on compassion, grace, forgiveness and love. The primary problem in their relationship is that they are low in valuing love.

This is very confusing to the couple. They feel they are doing "the right thing" in their relationship on a daily basis. They are good people. They serve in the church, pray multiple times a day, read their Bibles. Yet they fight and feel unloved. They have developed a joint conceptualization to understand the problem—it must be due to Tiana's lack of "self-sacrifice." This matches their interpersonal styles. Anthony tends to be "in charge, a leader and highly moral." Tiana is familiar with the one-down position in relationships and has low self-esteem.

The marriage problems have affected their faith as well. They repeatedly confess their sins (especially Tiana's), yet they find no relief and no improvement in their relationships with God or each other. They wonder why God is not answering their prayers. Anthony believes perhaps there is a spiritual attack on their marriage due to their ministry work. He has redoubled his efforts toward righteousness. Tiana feels that she can never live up to Anthony's or God's expectations for righteousness. She is a fount of guilt and shame. She has become depressed in both her emotions and her spiritual life.

Their dysfunctional pattern starts with brief spats. Then Tiana withdraws from the relationship for some days. She left their home for several days to stay with her sister after their last fight. That fight had prompted them to begin counseling with the senior minister at their church. They recognize that they are at risk for divorce, and this is also a risk for their ministry goals.

INITIAL PHASE OF COUNSELING

Ana's first intervention with the couple is creating a vision of what their ideal future relationship would look like. She listened closely for anything indicative of warmth, attachment or love in their descriptions. She especially focused on one statement by Anthony.

"I really want better listening in our marriage."

Ana tentatively said, "It sounds from that statement that you really want to feel understood, and you also want for you and Tiana to be a team together."

"Yeah, you got it."

Tiana said, "I want us to be a team, too. But not just in our ministry, also in our marriage. I want to feel more love between us."

"So," said Ana. "Both of you sense a failure to be joined in that one flesh that the Bible describes. You feel joined under God in marriage, but not joined in living out the teamwork and closeness between you." After they agreed, they created a treatment plan together to address their lack of closeness and failure to act as a team.

Ana quickly saw it. A warm bond was lacking in this couple. However, she was experienced as a couple counselor and knew that taking on that aspect of the relationship directly can often increase fears in couples who do not sense that bond. Many people who lack closeness in their relationship have underlying fears of intimacy or even fears of being known. So they have an interpersonal style that keeps others at a distance. This is not always the case. Some people merely get too busy with life and let their bonds grow cold. However, both Tiana and Anthony seemed to Ana to have interpersonal styles that kept others at a distance. Even their way of taking ministry leadership roles separated them from relationships with peers in their church.

Because a "frontal assault" is not typically suggested for this problem, Ana started counseling with some communication exercises. The goal of the communication exercise is not to teach them to become great listeners. They are capable of listening. They are just gun-shy about being vulnerable with each other. So to ease them into it, Ana had the couple create their own communication "rules" (see intervention 13-1) and to practice listening (see HOPE 18-1). This took a couple of sessions. Ana was wise. She met the couple where they were. They were focused on "right living" at this early stage of treatment. So Ana entered through the open doorway.

As the couple created the rules, Ana gently seized the reins.

"So," she began, "you have a lot of really great communication rules. I was wondering what will happen if one of you does not follow the rules." This was the most important part of the intervention.

Anthony said, "Well, we will probably stop talking and Tiana will withdraw. I'll probably keep pushing, maybe criticize her for withdrawing."

Ana said, "Hmm. Sounds like the same pattern. Can you think of something that would be different—something scriptural, even at the heart of Scripture itself—as a way of dealing with failure, even if it is sin?"

"Well, forgiveness. I could encourage Tiana to seek forgiveness."

"What about you? What if it is you who breaks the communication rules?" said Tiana. "I'm not the only one who messes up."

This was the first time in counseling that the mousy Tiana had asserted herself. Anthony gave a quick withering look at Tiana. It was easy for Ana to see how she could come to feel that she was always the one who was violating rules.

"Yes, of course, I would seek forgiveness too."

Ana said, "What about the fallout between the two of you. If you hurt or disappoint the other person, it leaves a lingering wound. Are we not supposed to forgive each other? Doesn't Jesus say something about that?"

Anthony said, "Yes, right after the Lord's Prayer, Jesus says that receiving forgiveness from God depends on our forgiving each other."

"So, are you saying that a scriptural response to breaking the rules is both seeking forgiveness from God and seeking forgiveness from your partner? We have a gracious God, and we know that God will forgive us. That is what our faith is all about, and I'm sure you both rely on God's gracious and merciful forgiveness." She paused. "I guess the really hard question, though, is whether we can be gracious with each other. Can we really forgive each other instead of blaming?"

Ana thus introduced the idea of being gracious (see HURT 20-5), or forgiving, when they did not follow the rules. The couple struggled a bit with this idea. Ana asked about their experiences with forgiveness or grace (see FREE 21-2).

COURSE OF TREATMENT

This forgiveness idea is new. Neither Anthony nor Tiana had any significant human relationships that were characterized as forgiving or gracious. They could say that people do not have to earn grace or mercy from God, but their emotional experience was that they did have to "earn" relationships from family members and friends.

Anthony told an especially moving story of how his grandfather had told him he would never be anything unless he "straightened up." Anthony had many friends who had taken self-destructive paths in life, but he had avoided the major risks for a black adolescent young man, such as drugs or gangs. Yet he felt that he could never please his grandfather. Even when he got good grades, entered into a competitive apprenticeship program for construction leadership, and married Tiana, his grandfather had never shown him warmth and appreciation. Anthony's pain was obvious in his hard face as he told the story of his grandfather's death the previous year. They had never reconciled this strain between them. Anthony said he had forgiven his grandfather after he died, because God had told him to. But it had been hard to do. "Sometimes," he said, "I just do not feel I have the strength to forgive."

Ana asked the couple if they sometimes did not feel forgiven by God either. Tiana's eyes welled up. She wondered how God could forgive her so often because she seemed to "screw up" all the time. Unlike Anthony, Tiana had been involved in drugs when she was a teenager. Her parents had worked hard to create a middle class life for Tiana and her siblings. So she had carried a sense of shame in "ruining my parents' lives" for several years while she was involved with drugs. Tiana had suddenly stopped using when a friend died from an overdose. Tiana was at the party when the overdose occurred and carried a sense of responsibility for her friend. She had never talked about or addressed the drugs or her friend's death—even with Anthony. The sense of guilt had grown inside of her. Tiana had completely turned her life around and become a successful young woman, yet she continued to feel like a failure with others and God. The FREE 21-1 intervention was useful for helping Tiana focus on receiving forgiveness from God.

Working through their emotional experience of God became a crucial aspect of learning warm relationship virtues for this couple. Anthony and Tiana decided to read a spiritual book on forgiveness together that they had on their shelf but had never gotten around to reading, *The Bait of Satan* by John Bevere. This homework became an important part of their relationship change. More important than whether the book was or was not the best book ever written on forgiveness was that it was one the couple had selected themselves. So it was effective. There were slow but real shifts in their understanding of their faith in terms of warmth, forgiveness and love instead of only righteousness and justice.

As the couple began to reconceptualize their problems, the deadlock in the relationship began to weaken. Their feelings began to soften. Interventions in the office included creating and practicing saying "words of grace" to each other. This helped them practice applying the principle of grace and love in their life. This is similar to a gratitude intervention (TRUST 22-1) where partners express their gratitude for each other and their relationship. It created a positive experience in counseling.

Turning Points

A key intervention for a couple like this is a "safe sanctuary" conversation, similar to an empty chair intervention (BOND 19-2).

Ana began, "Imagine a safe sanctuary. It might be a church, garden or building. The key is that there is a sense of safety. Can you imagine a place like that? Tell me about it."

"I would be in the upper prayer room at our church," said Anthony. "Oh, I agree, that's a great safe place," said Tiana.

"Okay. So let's imagine we are there. It's quiet and still. There is a sense of God's presence in the room. Now, let's talk about the difficulties with forgiving," said Ana.

The counselor checked in a few times in the session to ensure they felt safe with each other and the counselor. The goal of the session was to increase the couple's closeness by exploring strong emotions in other attachment relationships together and moving toward forgiveness in those relationships. This softens their emotions toward each other, increasing empathy without asking them to engage, at that point, in the very difficult task of forgiving each other.

Anthony expressed frustration that he continued to have such strong feelings even though he had decided to forgive his grandfather after his death a year earlier. He said, "I just feel so indignant about my grandfather even though I've forgiven him, and he passed away. I should be over this by now."

The counselor said gently, "I wonder if perhaps your heart has not caught up to your decision yet."

The rest of the session explored roadblocks and avenues to increase Anthony's sense of emotional release. He decided to write a letter of forgiveness to his grandfather and to read the letter to one of his brothers, who also struggled with this problem. Anthony thought that his brother would understand. Ana encouraged Anthony to read the letter to Tiana first. He agreed that was a good idea.

After the good experiential sessions where the couple softened toward each other, Ana suggested they begin to address some of the unforgiveness they felt toward each other.

Tiana began by sharing, "I don't feel good enough for you. It is kind of like you felt toward your grandfather," she said.

Her analogy simply blew Anthony away. Ana stepped in and helped coach Tiana in how to discuss her unmet needs and hurts with Anthony. She had strong fears about sharing these needs, so she was being too blunt and negative in how she delivered them.

Ana asked, "Did you intend for Anthony to be surprised and step back?"
"That's the opposite of what I want. I want him to understand me."

Ana had the couple stand up and physically position themselves in the
room to represent how close they felt with each other in the moment (see
BOND 19-11). Anthony stood fairly far away from Tiana, who stood in the
middle of the room. Ana asked Tiana whether she thought she could talk
with Anthony about her needs and stay connected as a couple. Tiana re-
stated her needs more softly, and at Ana's urging, Anthony took a small step
forward in response, which represented that he felt closer to her. Given how
new this skill was, Ana redirected the couple to the soft start-up intervention
(HURT 20-6) for the rest of the session.

Tiana responded well to Ana's teaching about using soft voice tone and
asking with a direct but uncritical request for something she wanted or
needed from Anthony.

"I like the idea of talking about this and not making Anthony upset. I
guess I'm too worried about upsetting him, and so I do not really ask for
things I want or need. Then I think he ought to read my mind, and when he
does not, I get really mad that he does not give me what he ought to know
that I want. Like I say, it seems like a 'big duh' when I think about it. But it
does not seem as obvious at the time. I am just afraid of making him upset."

Anthony jumped in. "I do know when she is angry but I'm always confused about what it is all about. That does not seem fair. It doesn't help to be
understanding with her. So I'm glad she's learning to ask for the things she
needs. I love her and am willing to lay down my life for her, but I just need
to know what she wants."

The following session, Ana asked the couple to return to forgiving and
reconciling as a couple. They both offered some heartfelt apologies for patterns of communicating in the past. These apologies were difficult for both of
them, so they reduced the injustice gap (see FREE 21-5). Tiana offered to make
a special meal for the couple's date night that week as an expression of her
apology and to reduce their injustice gap even further. Anthony offered to fix
a door in their home that he had broken when he slammed it after a fight.

Tiana burst into tears.

"Wow," said Ana. She waited.

"Repairing that broken door is the most meaningful thing I think Anthony has ever done," she said. He vowed not to fix it. He said it was my

fault and if I wanted it fixed, I should fix it. I was too stubborn. So it hung there. It was kind of a symbol for how hung-up our marriage was. So," she looked at Anthony, "I really appreciate your being willing to take the initiative and fix it."

Ana emphasized how they had increased their compassionate empathy for each other already, making the forgiveness process much easier for them now. The warm virtue of compassion was discussed as a key for the emotional experience of forgiveness.

TERMINATION AND FOLLOW-UP

The couple had now completed ten sessions of counseling and the Christmas holiday was approaching. They discussed finishing counseling before Christmas. Ana recommended they schedule one more meeting for termination and then a follow-up meeting in May as a checkup.

For termination Ana suggested the couple create a Joshua memorial (see intervention 28-1). The memorial that they selected was to jointly create a song about their relationship. The couple was musically gifted. Anthony was the instrumentalist, and Tiana was the lead voice with Anthony singing harmony. Their song included things they had learned in counseling such as experiencing grace, intent versus impact of things they say, concepts from the forgiveness book they read on their own, being soft toward each other, and following the listening rules they created. The couple even brought a guitar to the termination session and sang the song for Ana. Experienced counselor that she was—and having seen many Joshua memorial—she still cried like a baby. "That was one of my most moving moments ever in counseling," Ana said later.

At the follow-up meeting in the spring, Ana found that the couple had continued to maintain most of their gains from counseling. Tiana had decided to get a different job because she felt that working for the church kept putting her in a position where she could not say no or stand up for her needs. So she found a job as a receptionist at a local business. She still served in women's ministries at the church. She said she still struggled with asking Anthony for what she needed, but she was getting better. She felt the new job had helped her overcome some of her relationship patterns. Anthony had become ordained as a minister in the church. He had given his first sermon the previous week. He was in a very positive time in his life. However, Anthony had the last word in the counseling. Just before the end, he said, "I'm in a good place today, but I truly believe that if our marriage had fallen apart a half a year ago, I would not be whole, either as a man or spiritually." He then thanked Ana, and he also, significantly, thanked Tiara.

PRINCIPLES FOR TREATING THE COOL VIRTUES COUPLE

1. Direct interventions to increase closeness often do not work if either partner is nervous about being vulnerable or close in relationships.

2. Tailored Christian interventions using the virtues that the couple held as strengths and needed to develop were matched to the couple's values and worldview. If the couple had not matched that approach, then the counselor would have used more psychological language about growth, personal development and relationship health. The counselor needs to meet the couple where they are at in their life.

3. Experiential interventions that provide support in improving the warmth and closeness in the relationship are effective. Key interventions we often use with couples include "sanctuary" or "empty chair" types.

4. Exploring previous hurts and distant relationships with people other than the partner can help decrease anxiety about vulnerability or closeness. Partners should be involved to be supportive through the process. If either partner is undermining the closeness in the session, then explore with him or her whether his or her discomfort with strong emotions is common. Also explore what the person might be able to learn from that.

5. Interventions designed for other aspects of the relationship (communication, confession and forgiveness in this case) might be helpful in reaching the ultimate goal of increasing closeness. This is especially important if an indirect approach to improving the couple's bond is needed.

10

The Enrichment Couple

❧

The enrichment couple can be an enjoyable change of pace in a practice. They might be engaged and looking for some skills. They might be a married couple convinced that it is good to invest time in enriching their relationship. Either way they tend to have "normal" problems of living but are eager to improve their relationship.

Identifying this type of couple in the assessment process is not always easy. Occasionally, what appears to be an enrichment couple at first actually is a much more complex case with factors, like psychopathology, violence or significant relationship dysfunction, that the couple is minimizing. The counselor has to balance trust in the couple's self-portrayal with factually based assessments of the couple's strengths and weaknesses. It is important to have a good assessment of all couples, even those that appear to be enrichment focused.

Rhoda and Joe with Justin

- Everyday relationship problems using brief intervention
- Couple is low in work
- Focus on increasing work in relationship through any means that fit the couple's style

Rhoda and Joe

Rhoda and Joe have been married for two years. They are deeply in love, having met and married in midlife. Rhoda is 35 and Joe is 40. Both of them are strongly committed. He works hard at a position in a hospital where he is an administrator in aftercare for surgeons. Rhoda is a counselor in a local group practice. They decided to seek couple enrichment from a local psychologist, Justin, because they want to maintain a healthy marriage across time. They heard about the hope-focused couple approach from a friend who had good results with Justin in repairing their marriage.

This couple's dynamic is fairly healthy overall. Both partners are emotionally mature and even-tempered, so they tended to work out differences without much damage. The recent passing of Joe's father had been hard on them both, and it was coupled with a miscarriage. The two losses on top of each other made for a difficult summer for the pair. By fall they had re-engaged their life routines and felt their marriage had not been damaged.

Justin did a thorough assessment of the couple to ensure there were not dynamics that needed attention. It was clear that any issues they had were "normal" types of problems.

Justin's Case Conceptualization

One of the risks in providing counseling to this couple was that they were very busy without a high need for change. They had many responsibilities. Both had engaging professional jobs. They had their home to care for, and they were primary caregivers for Rhoda's elderly mother living next door. Justin discussed this with the couple up front.

He said, "It seems you are motivated to attend to your marriage despite a busy life with many responsibilities. However, it seems that there is not something going on right now that just *has* to be fixed. Also, your schedules are going to make meeting with me difficult. What kind of investment in couple enrichment were you thinking would work for you?"

After a brief discussion, they all agreed on a brief four-week intervention (after the intake). They wanted 90-minute double sessions to meet their time constraints and match the enrichment focus of counseling.

Justin then explained that he would like to make sure they had a good assessment with a focus on strengths as the first step of counseling. They had already started that step. Then he explained to them that the hope-focused couple approach could address various areas of their relationship. In four weeks of intervention, they would likely benefit most from focusing on perhaps just one or two areas of the relationship at this time. So Justin pulled out a "menu" of typical types of interventions within the hope-focused couple approach and asked the couple to talk through the different ideas with him. (We have included an exemplar menu at hopecouples.com.) They decided to focus primarily on increasing intimacy and communication.

In terms of the hope-focused couple approach areas of faith, love and work, Rhoda and Joe were especially high in love and faith. They had a good bond. They had faith in each other, supreme faith in God, and confidence that the psychologist could help them enrich their relationship. Their weakest area of the relationship was their work on the marriage. Rhoda often worked evenings and some Saturdays with her clients. Joe had regular office hours, but often more than 40 a week. So they rarely had meals together, and they tended to spend their time together doing errands or housework on weekends. They had date nights their first year of marriage but had not picked up the habit again after the difficult summer of losses.

COURSE OF TREATMENT

Instead of focusing on the weakest area of the relationship, Justin wanted to use the couple's strengths as the means to relationship enrichment. In the assessment, Justin used the CARE (Worthington et al., 1997) to assess the major areas of their marriage, the relationship strengths measure to examine virtues, and a set of screenings he typically used (for substance abuse, violence, depression, separation intent and current or recent affair) to ensure important issues were not missed. The CARE indicated that communication and commitment were strengths for the couple. A review of their virtues in an assessment (Furnham & Lester, 2012) indicated that Joe was high in perseverance, self-control, dedication and humility. Rhoda was high in positive listening, gratitude, humor and teamwork.

In the second session, Justin reviewed a hope-focused couple approach report with the couple. He identified their strengths and suggested they consider ways to improve these within the marriage relationship. The couple had wanted to learn a communication technique that Justin was known for in the community as he worked with couples—the TANGO technique (see HOPE 18-4). Rhoda, a counselor in town, was aware of his reputation for helping couples. Justin explained that the technique could allow them to look at how they communicate and pull out principles or rules for communication. The couple used the TANGO to communicate their feelings about the miscarriage.

Because the couple had good communication skills, they were easily able to engage in the TANGO intervention. Rhoda was not sure she had wanted to have children. The pregnancy was a surprise. So, after the miscarriage, her struggle was more that she felt she "should" feel loss and sadness than that she actually felt sadness. Joe had been looking forward to having a child for the few weeks they knew they were pregnant. The pregnancy coincided with the time his father passed. It had given him something positive to tell his father in his final days. But the miscarriage occurred only days after his father's death. For Joe, the two losses were linked in his experience. The couple listened to each other attentively. They were generally caring to each other in their responses.

Given that there was substantial time with the double session, Justin asked them to double back on the intervention and look at how their strengths played out in the communication. Justin asked them what made their communication "work" for them. Joe thought that Rhoda's ability to listen to him was reassuring. He felt that her listening validated that his experience was important. And given that nothing could change what had happened, that was the most important thing to him. Justin emphasized that their positive traits were helping them to address things in their relationship.

If Joe remembered to stay steady and dependable during difficult conversations, this would be helpful to their relationship. Rhoda felt that if she could keep using her good listening ability and throw a dash of humor into their difficult communication times, those strengths would help them understand each other.

The second session focused on improving closeness. The couple brainstormed times and things they did that helped them feel closer. They created a good list and committed to reinstituting their date night. The counselor also encouraged them to talk about what it was like to share a life together after living as singles for many adult years. They both said that they had always liked their alone time and still enjoyed some time apart from each other. They had been afraid they would lose that when they married. However, they both enthusiastically affirmed that gaining each other's love and care was worth the price.

The third session returned to the topic of closeness to check in on how their date night had gone and to further their discussion of control and adjustment to married life. The couple's independent style was obvious in this session. They had difficulty finding time for a date night because they had each scheduled time for personal hobbies over the weekend. So grocery shopping had become their date because they had run out of time for a "real" date. Justin wondered with them what might be going on in their relationship. They discussed how surprised they were that they wanted to do couple enrichment but then could not make time for having a date. They both explored patterns from previous important relationships where they acted independently.

Rhoda said, "This will have to be something we schedule because we don't have an internal need to spend a lot of time together."

Joe said, "I'm committed to arranging time together, though, because if we ignore our relationship then it can hurt us over time."

The final session focused on looking again at their strengths. They brainstormed ideas for how to keep their relationship close.

Rhoda said, "I think that perhaps I might not really need to work so many evenings and Saturdays anymore." She wanted to use her teamwork and humor traits to show how she was willing to give up something for the relationship and to shift her schedule to work fewer nights and weekends.

Joe reflected, "My style will work best if we pick a particular time each week to spend together. I think we benefit by picking a time for sex and then other times to focus on friendship."

Rhoda thought this was a good idea that would work for them. The rest of the session was spent reviewing what they had learned in their brief intervention. Justin encouraged them to seek couple enrichment opportunities in the future to maintain their relationship and keep "the fires alive."

PRINCIPLES FOR TREATING THE ENRICHMENT COUPLE

1. During the assessment, ensure that the couple has "normal" problems and are not minimizing relationship issues.

2. Some enrichment couples are not highly motivated to make changes to their relationship because it is already positive. It is important to work with the couple's level of motivation for work or change at the level that

they are able and willing to engage in. This may require some creative formats such as weekend-intensive or double sessions across a brief period of time.

3. It is best to focus on a few things that the couple would like to improve than to try to squeeze in too many interventions. Even if they are capable of doing interventions well, it is important not to overload them with information and techniques.

4. Enrichment couples are especially good candidates for using strengths to maintain or improve the relationship. By identifying enduring traits and relationship styles, the couple can often find readily available means to better their relationship.

5. If the couple seem to lack skills in conflict resolution or communication, then a stronger focus on skills would be a good emphasis for enrichment. What is important in many interventions for conflict resolution or communication is not the specific technique but the principles behind it. For instance, it is important to slow down difficult or conflict-empowered conversations, to have boundaries that will not be crossed in terms of disrespecting each other, to work to understand the other person's perspective, and to fully communicate one's own perspective in a caring way.

11

The "Should We Marry?" Couple

❧

The "should we marry?" couple is engaged or considering engagement. These days they are often cohabiting. Unless you work in an unusual setting, you will see cohabiting couples seeking help in deciding if they should continue to cohabit or marry. Most couples now cohabit before marriage (Rhoades, Stanley & Markman, 2012), so it is important to be ready to help them.

It is common for cohabiting couples to have already faced considerable adversity. Scott Stanley (Rhoades et al., 2012) has proposed that in cohabiting, partners "begin the clock" of their relationship that in previous generations began when couples married. Cohabiting speeds up the formation of emotional bonds felt by both partners, but it also increases the chances that they will face life's struggles or adversity. They often share some financial resources—like bank accounts or joint cell phone plans. They might share rent or buy a home together. They have increased chances of pregnancy due to regular sex, and their individual life stressors affect their relationship more deeply. Unfortunately, cohabiting couples typically lack the level of commitment that is protective of married couples. They can be in the difficult position of going through the tests of their relationship common to early married couples, but one or both partners may lack a long-term commitment to the relationship. The issue of when and whether to marry can be distressing to them due to the increased bond but low commitment. Or the decision to marry might actually never really be a decision. They might just *slide* into marriage, says Stanley.

> **Gail and Stephen with Liz**
>
> - Cohabiting couple low in faith, love and work
> - Counselor-client religious differences addressed
> - Address commitment concerns, communication skills, their bond and forgiveness

STEVEN AND GAIL

Steven and Gail sought couple counseling because they found that they were often fighting, felt alone and were concerned about the future of the relationship. They were concerned even though they were planning a wedding for six months from then and had a one-year-old child together. They were both Caucasian. They had been living together in rural Colorado for four years. They met through mutual friends and dated for five months. Steven had been living with his parents while working as a mechanic, and he wanted to get a place of his own. Gail was a nurse at a local nursing home and had just purchased her first home, a townhouse near her family's home. Steven moved in and the couple felt that the relationship was going well. Gail's family was concerned about the cohabitation because they were more traditional, but the families soon adjusted to the couple's decision.

About two years into the cohabitation Gail discovered she was pregnant. This was a crisis for the couple. Steven enjoyed the relationship with Gail, but he had not considered marriage or a family with her. Gail was keenly aware of this and felt very insecure. She began looking into moving back in with her parents. At that point, Gail's father sat down with Steven and talked with him about responsibility and the direction he wanted his life to go. Steven responded to this talk and told Gail he wanted to be there to raise his child. He asked her to marry him.

There had been some major difficulties. Steven was laid off from work for five months and Gail's mother was undergoing treatment for cancer. The couple felt it was not the right time to marry. This only reinforced their level of concern about marrying in general. Both of them felt unsure about marrying. Yet as the baby girl arrived the pressure from family and friends increased. So they set a date and planned a wedding.

LIZ'S CASE CONCEPTUALIZATION

The counselor has an issue. Liz was a theologically conservative Christian counselor practicing in a local Christian counseling center in rural Colorado. Gail and Steven arrived at her door because the minister who was marrying them suggested they seek further help beyond his premarital counseling. As a new counselor, Liz found that seeing the couple brought out feelings and (she was ashamed to admit) even judgment about cohabitation. She was not sure how she would handle the couple who had different values about relationships and sexuality than she did. She consulted with a more experienced Christian counselor in the community about the issue. The experienced counselor, Marla, had a long talk with her. The main part of the conversation went like this.

Marla asked Liz, "Are there any other clients you are seeing that have unrepentant sins in their life?"

"Yes," Liz readily admitted.

"What kinds?" asked Marla.

"The whole range, I guess," said Liz. "Pride, gossip, and even embezzlement. Pretty much all the sins."

"So what is it about this particular sin is difficult for you?" asked Marla.

"Well, I feel like I'm aiding and abetting them in their sin when I provide counseling for this cohabiting couple."

"So, can you think that there might be in other couples different sins that you might be aiding and abetting?"

Liz thought, and then said, "When I counsel someone who has a problem with pride, I sometimes feel guilty about not confronting that. In fact, when they solve other problems in counseling, I can sometimes see that their pride actually increases. When someone is depressed but judgmental, I help them with the depression, but rarely confront the person's judgmental acts, unless the person is asking for direct help at not judging."

"So what do you think your role is in the couple's life?"

"Counselor, of course," said Liz.

Marla said, "Then you are similar to a doctor, pharmacist or other healthcare professional. You provide care for people."

"Yes."

"If the couple seek your help for spiritual direction, it seems that you would be honor bound to help them straighten their path toward God. But if a couple come to you with relationship problems, then even though they are communicating sinfully many times a day, you do not have to straighten out their spiritual lives. You just work on a better relationship, and you leave the confrontation to the Holy Spirit. Right?"

"Right."

"Of course, all analogies break down at extremes," said Marla. "If you find that a person is planning a crime, you have a moral responsibility to intervene. But we make judgments continually about what to address and what not to treat as a focus of counseling. Those are hard judgments, and you are right to think through them outside of your counseling with the couple."

"I suppose it is like providing secular counseling. I would not dream of imposing my Christian values on a couple who aren't Christians. I might not even bring up the issue. I suppose that this might be similar. This Christian couple does not seem to believe that cohabitation is incongruent with their spiritual lives. I think it is likely to be harmful, but so are a thousand other sins that they are committing—and if I'm honest, that I'm committing too. I guess I should not impose my Christian beliefs on them either. Counseling might help them parent their daughter together better. I suppose I should leave the questions of the morality of cohabitation in the hands of the minister who is marrying them—unless they ask me directly." This helped Liz to redefine her role with the couple.

We recognize that different settings (like counseling in a church counseling center versus in a secular counseling center) and individual beliefs (of counselors and clients) will result in different approaches to counseling with couples who are cohabiting. These differences in settings and individuals will not affect the counselor's beliefs about what is biblically consistent. But they will affect what the counselor says and does with the client. We believe there are professional and religious reasons for counselors to enter into the world of their clients and attempt to help them where they are. Helping is about joining the client where the client is, not demanding that the client come to where the counselor is.

Professionally, all mental health providers uphold the ethics of client autonomy. If mental health professionals everywhere were to promote their own personal values with clients instead of joining clients where they are, then the profession would suffer. Vulnerable and needy people would have a difficult time obtaining help for mental health needs if counselors were constantly stating their own values and implying that clients should adjust their values to conform to the counselor's values. This is especially true for people who are in minority groups and already feel disempowered.

In addition, Christianity upholds freedom of choice as a principle of Christian living. If people are not free to make choices regarding their life and how they interpret Scripture and church teachings, then there is no such thing as Christian liberty. Historically most Christians have affirmed that Jesus is Lord of the conscience. So we allow people to attend to their own conscience, and we trust that if a course correction is in order, it will be Jesus who prompts the client. Mature people must make choices about sexual morality. There can be caveats to this freedom. For instance, individuals in a society must weigh the costs of their choices and refrain from acts that lead to negative outcomes for others, such as diseases or unwanted pregnancies. *Yet Christians must uphold the principle of autonomy and freedom because God upholds it.*

COURSE OF TREATMENT

After settling into the case, Liz felt ready to help the couple address some of their questions. The typical hope-focused couple approach was altered to spend some time up front discussing what this major commitment of marriage meant for Steven and Gail and their doubts about it. They both expressed doubts about their ability to have a healthy marriage, but they felt motivated because they loved their daughter. Liz supported them. She observed how they had already weathered several difficult challenges in their relationship. The couple explored some of their doubts about the relationship in individual intake meetings with Liz.

Steven was having a hard time seeing himself as a married man with a family. He felt that he was not going to be able to fulfill those roles for Gail and the baby. He struggled with negative self-esteem.

Gail felt unsure that Steven was going to stay with them long-term. She tended to do things in the relationship that undermined his role due to that fear. She never left Steven to care for the baby. She took on almost all childcare responsibilities. Liz challenged Gail's decision saying that it seemed that Steven was capable of caring for the baby. She suggested that leaving him with the baby while Gail went to work or out with a friend would increase Steven's confidence and competence—and help him form a stronger bond with the child. Gail agreed that there was no reason to be concerned about Steven's ability to watch the baby. She was ready to try it this week. Liz also encouraged the couple to go on a date that week because they were not enjoying their engagement and wedding planning due to all their responsibilities. They readily agreed.

This is a couple who are somewhat low in each dimension of the hope theory—faith, work and love—but especially in faith. They love each other but they are not sure what they need to do to improve their relationship, or even whether they will be able to improve the relationship. They are motivated to work on the relationship. However, they don't have an idea of how to change things (no "waypower"), and they lack wisdom in how to change.

Liz sat down to write the couple report. She thought about the treatment plan for this couple. First, she felt that getting them to cement their commitment to counseling was important because they were struggling with commitment overall. She planned to use the "Promote a Commitment to Therapy" intervention from *Hope-Focused Marriage Counseling* (Worthington, 2005) as the first intervention after the couple feedback.

She felt they needed another commitment intervention. She designed a new intervention where the couple begin to create (in counseling) a narrative of what their life would be like in the future if they were to stay together and work on a realistic but good relationship. They then would finish that exercise by writing down the joint vision together as homework with as many details of what their future life together would look like. The couple agreed this would be helpful to them.

TURNING POINTS

After Steven and Gail completed the narrative exercise, Liz asked if they were open to moving forward in counseling with the assumption that this narrative they wrote down and discussed together will be what they are working toward, instead of deciding whether to stay together. The couple agreed. Liz then moved the couple into a simple intervention in communication.

Leveling and editing (see HOPE 18-2) was used as the first and simplest intervention to help create some guidelines to reign in some of the couple's negative communication.

Steven said, "I tend to shut down when the discussion is tense, so being 'on the level' is the more difficult for me."

Gail was astonished. "I didn't know you felt that way. I feel like that too. I just want to walk away when things are tense. I guess we both do that."

Liz had the couple practice bringing up something they needed to communicate about in session and being "on the level" with each other. After talking for a while, Liz had the couple double back and reflect on what made the conversation go better than past conversations. They had some difficulty thinking of why, but they were able to notice that they were listening to each other and trying to solve a problem together. Also, Gail was being more honest.

For the next session Liz brought in a video recording device to make a video of the couple (see HOPE 18-14). Gail and Steven also had their baby with them. Gail's parents were not available to babysit that night because they had the flu. So the couple had brought the baby. Because the couple were already at the office, Liz decided to go ahead with the video, but she noted that it would be difficult to do as much work because the baby's needs had to be attended to as well during the session.

Liz had the couple communicate with each other for ten minutes while she recorded their conversation. She set up the conversation saying that they should choose something that they sometimes had difficulty talking about, but not something likely to cause them to flood with emotions and want to run from the room. The couple decided to talk about their in-laws. In watching their own video they had the opportunity to get a third-person perspective on their communication by asking Liz what she thought. The couple were surprised by how much Gail would turn her back to Steven to pay attention to the baby. They agreed that having serious conversations with the baby present was difficult to do.

Steven suddenly shared something that seemed to surprise even him. "I sometimes feel," he said, "that I just am not as important to Gail as the baby is. It is really a scary feeling."

It was obvious that he was in the grip of some uncomfortable emotions. Gail reached over and stroked his back. She murmured how important he was without coaching from Liz. This seemed to be an important moment in counseling.

Liz decided to repeat the video intervention with the couple for another two weeks, these times without the baby, to punctuate their growth and change as a couple. She reinforced and emphasized how many good interac-

tions Steven and Gail were having as they watched the video, which increased the couple's confidence.

The next module of counseling consisted of several sessions addressing
forgiveness. There had been hurts in the relationship so far that they had not
discussed. Steven felt like he was not important to Gail. Gail felt insecure with
Steven. She often wondered whether he *really* wanted to marry her. Given the
couple's interpersonal style of withdrawing during difficult conversations, Liz
proposed that the couple go through the process of apology and forgiveness
for these hurts (FREE 21-1, 21-3). Steven especially felt like this was important
because he wanted to get rid of his feelings of hurt in the relationship.

Liz's approach to forgiveness with the couple combined some of the
REACH forgiveness model (FREE 21-4) and reconciliation work (TRUST
22-1, 22-2). This was important because the couple wanted to work on forgiveness for a long-term pattern of relationship hurts instead of for a specific
hurt. So it would be important to emphasize empathy and grace and to deal
with post-forgiveness hurts and rebuilding trust. Liz thought it would be
good to plan for one week per concept for the couple.

Empathy was the first component of intervention. Gail demonstrated
empathy when she said, "I see how much you don't want to lose me and the
baby. I guess you do really want us in your life."

The couple listened closely and tried and put themselves in their partner's
shoes. There was some discussion of the personal experiences and vulnerabilities that made them susceptible to these offenses. Liz prepared them for
the next session which would focus on grace, suggesting that they both
benefitted from extending some grace to each other in difficult times.

The grace-focused session (HURT 20-5) first defined what grace meant
in a relationship. The concept was completely foreign to Steven, who said he
had heard the word but never knew what it meant. Gail had a grandmother
who had taken her to church and taught her about grace within the Christian
context, so she had some understanding. The couple responded to the idea
that they could offer each other undeserved kindness in the face of something negative to protect their relationship. They developed an example that
worked for them.

Steven said, "If one of us were upset and pulling away from the other,
instead of getting angry, we could just let the other off the hook and say, 'I
love you. Talk when you are ready.'"

They saw this as a potential powerful protection for their relationship. Both of these partners were keenly aware of and willing to admit their vulnerabilities, so this made the possibility of grace more readily available to them. The couple practiced offering grace in a session with each other. Spontaneously, the couple engaged in apology and offered forgiveness to each other at the end of this session.

They recognized that some of their patterns and vulnerabilities were not just going to go away because they focused on them. Liz was now thinking about ensuring that the counseling work she did with the couple was being primarily led by the couple, instead of depending on her. Thus she asked them, "There are going to be hurts in the future. What are your ideas on how to deal with post-forgiveness hurts?"

The couple did well with a discussion about apologizing again, even if it is for something that happens often. Steve suggested, "We should offer to do something nice for each other to help fix things in the relationship."

Gail suggested, "We should also try to just keep going with our routines with the baby too. Even if we get hurt, we shouldn't leave the house or make things worse."

The session ended with preparation for the final session and the assignment of homework to create a graduation memorial of their time in counseling (intervention 28-1). For their graduation memorial, the couple created a collage of words and pictures that reminded them of their counseling. There was a picture of them as a couple, and one of the baby. There were words like *grace* and *trust*. They had decided to frame the collage and put it in their bedroom to remind them of what they had learned. Liz said she was available to meet with them in the future if they needed it. She wished them all the best with their wedding, which was now only a couple of months away.

FOLLOW-UP

At follow-up, this couple reported some continued difficulties with trust in the relationship. Steven had returned to some withdrawal behaviors and was drinking heavily. It is not unusual for couple treatment to involve some relapse back into old patterns. The follow-up intervention is intended to help assist with addressing relapse. Liz asked whether they wanted to do some additional "booster" sessions of counseling to refresh and refocus on their relationship. They agreed and engaged in treatment again.

PRINCIPLES FOR TREATING THE "SHOULD WE MARRY?" COUPLE

1. Some cohabiting couples have stressors and difficulties in their relationship similar to those of couples who have been married for some time, but often with less commitment to the relationship long-term.

2. Working with a couple with purely secular goals for counseling is an ethical decision in which counselors need to consider the needs and autonomy of the client, the role of the counselor, and the counselor's ability to work in diverse frameworks in making decisions about how to help couples with values that are different from his or her own.

3. The couple presented in this case did not have any factors—such as violence, infidelity, psychopathology or drug abuse—that might cause a counselor to encourage the couple to delay the decision to marry. If such factors are present, then couple counseling is generally contraindicated (regardless of the status of the relationship as married or cohabiting). Individual counseling would likely meet the needs of the couple more readily in these cases.

Most of the interventions created within the hope-focused couple approach are readily adaptable to the secular counseling situation by revising the interventions to address issues from a relationship-health perspective instead of a Christian perspective.

INTERVENTION 11-1: NARRATIVE OF A BETTER FUTURE

Step 1: Each partner individually writes down the history of the couple in the form of a story that proceeds all the way to the present. Some couples may benefit from parameters, such as a limit of no more than a couple of pages. They can focus on how they met, when they knew they would be a couple, when they felt they had fallen in love, how their courtship proceeded, and when they decided to marry. They are to write about their happy times. Then they should describe their first difficulty and any significant events in their recent history. This account will differ based on how long the couple has been together. (Instruct them to spend most of the time on the positive aspects of the history rather allowing this to become a narrative of problems.) The couple then brings their stories to the counseling session.

Step 2: In session the couple discusses what the future would look like if their relationship were to turn a corner now and improve. The couple should brainstorm ideas of what would make the future look more positive and loving.

Step 3: At home each partner writes a narrative describing a realistic but positive future for them as a couple. They should try to be specific and tell a story of an event or situation that illustrates how things might change their life as a couple and how they would act, given that they have been through a difficult period. What could they learn from this period that would provide a source of strength in the positive future? What enduring positive virtues could carry them through difficult times?

Step 4: The partners share their narratives with each other. If the couple has been relatively healthy, then they might do this on their own time. Couples with more conflict, or those who are expected to struggle with a positive future, can share their narratives in session so that the counselor can address any concerns.

This intervention is inspired by narrative therapy treatment modality (Madigan, 2010).

12

The Complicating Factor Couple

෨

The complicating factor couple is generally depleted on all fronts due to stressful circumstances. They may have just had their first child, have been out of work for an extended time, be struggling with health problems in the family, or caring for a disabled family member. Due to excessive stress, this type of couple tends to have few resources to give to their relationship—and usually they are the couples that most need to work on their relationship. A Christian couple in this situation may need to rebuild trust in God or even increase feelings of trust in God if they feel angry or disappointed with God.

Treatment plans for couples with complicating factors begin with stabilization and problem solving regarding the stressful circumstances. This is followed by rebuilding the bond and finally by forgiving each other for hurts that happened during the stressful period (and perhaps before that). Roadblocks and resistances are common for couples with significant or chronic complicating factors due to depletion of energy for the relationship.

Carlos and Rosalie with Seth

- Couple is low in work
- Address crisis stabilization
- Garner energy for relationship building
- Increase their bond, forgiveness, grace and trust

ROSALIE AND CARLOS

Carlos and Rosalie sought counseling to help them with multiple stressors. They were the caregivers for Rosalie's parents, both of whom had advanced Alzheimer's disease. Rosalie's mother was still living with the couple, and her father had just recently been admitted to an Alzheimer's unit. Their 25-year-old son Jorge had multiple problems, including addiction to heroin. Jorge and his girlfriend Carlita had recently lost custody of their one-year-old son due to both Carlita's and Jorge's multiple arrests for heroin possession. The child was in the care of the couple's other son Raphael and his wife. In addition, Rosalie had a breast cancer diagnosis last year. She had recently finished all her treatments, but the experience left her depleted of energy. Carlos was preparing for an early retirement from the police force where he had served as a local precinct captain. Rosalie retired from teaching when she was diagnosed with cancer, but she missed having an active career. The couple sought counseling because they felt like they were losing their relationship amidst all their other stressors. The couple said they wanted to "be there" for each other but found that they felt alone. Occasionally, they had a spat over their drug-abusing son, but typically they were quietly living separate lives. They said this was a new experience for them in their 30 years of marriage. They were depleted of energy and their relationship was suffering.

Seth was the psychologist who picked up the case. The initial meeting consisted of supportive listening as the couple explained the many stressors and complications in their life. Seth was warm and available to the couple so they decided that they would continue counseling.

The first thing Seth assessed was their energy and motivation to change. The couple was so depleted of energy that it was difficult to see where they would find any to invest in their relationship on a daily or even weekly basis. Rosalie had participated in some psychotherapy after her cancer diagnosis and found it extremely helpful. That counselor had retired. Given that the couple were insisting that they were ready to make changes in the amount of energy they put into their relationship, Seth talked with them about the pace of treatment. If the couple had seemed ambivalent, then he was going to offer two choices to them, one of which was a "full-meal-deal" type of counseling that fully addressed issues of their relationship in a straight-forward way using the hope-focused couple approach, and the other would simply provide a supportive environment for them to just talk with each other and reconnect weekly.

At the feedback session, Seth reviewed their options for counseling, stating that the "full-meal deal" version of counseling would likely produce more change quickly for them but would require investing considerable energy in their relationship at home despite ongoing stressors in their lives. They insisted they wanted to fully invest in counseling. Now that cancer treatment was done and their grandchild was in a safe environment, they felt that they had room to breathe. Seth assigned them to have a weekly date night, plus "mini-dates" with each other for five minutes at least once a day (intervention 12-1). Seth then reviewed the highlights of their intake as-sessment, emphasizing that they were a couple with good skills and abilities in relationships, but were depleted in the necessary work of marriage. Their positive virtues of commitment and self-sacrifice were going to help them reengage in their relationship in order to move toward the warm relationship they needed. They had faith, and they had love for each other, but they were not expressing it in action.

INITIAL PHASE OF TREATMENT

Given that the couple were still in the preparation stage of change, the written assessment was an important tool in helping them shift gears and move from preparation into the action stage of change. Seth thought it was important to spend considerable time discussing the roadblocks and bar-riers to improving their relationship and how they planned to remove them.

The next session Seth checked in on the couple's dates, which were going well. He then asked the couple to help make a list on the left side of a sheet of paper of all the roadblocks to a healthy, more intimate relationship. Their first idea was to deal with the disagreements about what to do with their son who abuses drugs. Rosalie wanted to demonstrate tough love with him and refuse to help him with legal expenses. Carlos felt that they should help with his legal defense. Seth reframed the issue as a disagreement about parenting and money. He suggested that he wanted to list at least a few things before addressing any one of them.

Carlos said that Rosalie's mother living with them was often a problem because the Alzheimer's Disease had progressed to where she would not respond to social cues. The couple had to go to their room and lock the door to have time alone together, which he said was often very inconvenient.

Rosalie also stated that her own health was sometimes a roadblock to a better marriage. She said that she was often tired, less interested in sex since her mastectomy, and having difficulty putting energy into the relationship in general. "I'm just not well," she said.

Seth wrote down three barriers for the couple: (1) disagreements about parenting/money, (2) Rosalie's mother's needs and (3) Rosalie's health. The session was spent exploring the history of these three barriers and what they meant to each partner, and discussing the fact that since they could not actually make changes to these situations right now, they would have to learn how to live with this set of problems. As a Christian couple they decided that prayer for grace could be a good response to these situations.

COURSE OF TREATMENT

Three sessions focused on grace followed. These three sessions were experiential. The couple reflected on times in their life when they had experienced grace. As Christians they were both readily able to reflect on their faith in terms of grace. The couple shared their personal experiences with grace. Carlos grew up in a Mexican-Catholic family that did not emphasize grace, so when he was introduced to the idea and experienced it as a young adult at church, he had been deeply moved. Carlos described himself as a nontraditional Christian who was grateful that he had been spared some of the negative things his son is experiencing now. He had smoked marijuana in the 1960s, and even distributed it for part of a year, but never faced legal consequences or violence. Rosalie had significant personal strengths in the virtues of grace and humility. She said that she "took after her mom" who had always been generous, gracious and humble in nature. Carlos praised his wife for this, and it was a positive moment in counseling for them as a couple.

The next session they were asked to demonstrate gratitude for the grace from God and others in their life. Carlos said, "Rosalie is so good with expressing her gratitude in her art. She created these paintings that are memories of things God did for her when she was sick with cancer. They even put them up at the hospital for a month."

This led to a discussion about how he was being gracious and expressing gratitude (HOPE 18-10) in that moment. Part of the struggle was that Carlos would sometimes get upset when Rosalie got behind in household responsibilities. His mother had been a traditional Mexican woman who had always cooked, cleaned and taken care of all home responsibilities. Prior to her illness Rosalie had also done most of the housework, or they had hired help. Carlos said he had a hard time accepting their situation now and having grace for Rosalie in her weakness. This characterization did not sit well with Rosalie. She said she did not like to think of herself as weak.

TURNING POINTS

Seth stopped the conversation. "This might be a good time for you to demonstrate grace with each other around tender issues in your lives."

"You know I love you very much," said Carlos. "I was not trying to put you down by saying you were weak. In fact, you are enormously strong, and you are dealing with ten times as much as a superwoman might crumble under. I was just saying that I am also under stress, and sometimes I get stressed and easily aggravated—at work as well as at home. So when I am stressed out it seems like I have to be careful how I treat you, and yet it is a struggle."

"Thank you, honey. I do know you've been under a lot of stress too. I feel guilty because I seem to be always tired. I know you are used to a clean house, and it frustrates me that I see myself failing. I'm sorry that I got defensive."

Seth stopped the couple. "That was a beautiful thing. You are loving toward each other, and you are both carrying heavy loads. I am so encouraged because you have the ability to step back when you hurt each other's feelings and offer the gift of acceptance and grace. That is a terrific strength."

The third session focused on grace brought the couple further into talking about their areas of weakness or struggle in life. Seth asked whether each of them would be willing to share their most difficult struggles with each other in session and have the other partner offer grace in response. In particular, Seth encouraged them to share struggles that affected the other person and made things difficult for him or her. Carlos started by stating that he struggled when Rosalie was actively battling her cancer. He had "held it in" and been strong through the process. "But," he told Rosalie, "inside I was terrified of losing you."

Seth asked how Carlos thought that his "holding it in" had affected Rosalie. "I'm not sure if it did."

Rosalie said that she had felt alone in her cancer sometimes because Carlos was always trying to be upbeat. She said, "I wished you could have cried with me when we went for prayer with church leaders. And other times too. But while I wept, you just seemed quiet and withdrawn. I felt so alone."

Carlos said, "It makes perfect sense now. But at the time, I thought that what would help you the most was for me to stay strong for you."

Seth asked what would be a gracious response now, and Carlos spontaneously apologized for his withdrawal from her and his voice was heavy with emotion. Rosalie leaned over and hugged him, and the hug lasted a minute or more. She said, "I knew it was just as hard on you emotionally as it was on me."

The session was drawing to a close, and Seth asked what they got out of this. Carlos was quick to respond, "I learned that I should not assume that I know what Rosalie wants. I should ask."

Rosalie said, "I learned that if I had told him then that I was feeling alone, he could have met my needs. So, really, I cannot blame Carlos. I have only myself to blame, not for feeling alone, but for allowing that feeling to torture me for a long period."

Seth warned the couple that after such a powerful session sometimes people have a tendency to step back from the emotional intensity of it. "Do not be surprised if you experience some sense of withdrawal this week at home."

Seth thought about this couple after this session. They had been through a lot and had a tendency to isolate themselves in times of crisis—both justifying it by thinking it was for the sake of the other person. Their intent was to meet the needs of the marriage, or the partner, but their style of meeting those needs was self-protective. Seth wondered whether the couple might further emotionally bond with each other by talking about their fears more directly. That might change their dynamic of withdrawal to "protect" the other. The following week would be full of opportunity for the couple.

During the week, the couple's younger son Raphael was taken to jail. Raphael and his wife had been caring for their infant nephew during his mother Carlita's incarceration. When Carlita was released, she accused Raphael of physically abusing the child.

Carlos and Rosalie felt sure that the arresting officer had profiled Raphael, who had a darker complexion as a Mexican American and had retained a Spanish accent. Raphael also had been angry toward the officer when questioned. He was incensed at the accusation. The child had been bruised when he fell down a few steps a day before Carlita had visitation, shortly after making bail from her own incarceration. Carlita was already on edge. She had used the situation to regain sympathy from her family of origin and distract from her own drug and legal problems.

Raphael's lawyer felt certain that the charges would be thrown out in two weeks when brought before a judge. A neighbor had witnessed the child's fall but had not been interviewed by the arresting officer.

However, the incident had caused a financial crisis for Carlos and Rosalie. There was no money for bail for Raphael due to having used their available money as security and payment for their other son Jorge's bail bond. Carlos and Rosalie had another spat over finances (whether they should put their cars up for bond security) and the degree of responsibility they should take toward their children. The couple had withdrawn from each other after the argument.

Seth sympathetically listened to the couple as they shared their complex struggles that week. He realized that he had the opportunity to demonstrate humility and grace toward the couple himself in how he interacted with them around this situation. Seth asked them to teach him what they needed in the session. They said they had no idea. He asked whether it was helpful to tell the story to him and have someone listen. They both agreed that it was. Then he asked if it might be possible for the two of them to support and turn toward each other in times of struggle. The couple stopped.

A pregnant pause ensued. Rosalie stepped into the void. "I guess I do not know whether Carlos will actually be there for me if I ask for him to listen to me. I feel terrible about saying that. It seems, uh, irrational. After all, Carlos has been listening to me and has been helpful in our mini-dates for weeks. But, well, I just am not sure whether it will work that way in the harder topics. After all, we did not listen to each other this week during out argument."

Carlos confessed, "I am not really a natural at listening to Rosalie's problems. I felt so strongly about the problems. Especially the problems with our sons—which never seem to end—and, of course, Rosalie's sickness."

Seth encouraged Carlos to tell Rosalie that directly. They then doubled back to reflect on what had just happened in the session and how they might repeat the supportive stance with each other's struggles at home.

The couple continued down this route of counseling for several weeks. They would come to Seth to discuss their struggles, and they did so sensitively. They showed that they had exceptional patterns of communication.

However, they continued not to go directly to each other with their problems. After weeks of gentle challenges and reflecting on that process, Seth asked whether he could have a stronger intervention with them. He felt that the couple needed to have faith in each other and in God that they could weather the difficulties they might face as a family.

Seth integrated in some cognitive interventions into treatment. He explored the underlying beliefs behind their thoughts on their son's situation. Both partners' underlying belief was that they were failures as parents and as Christians because they had a son with a drug problem. They had lost faith in themselves and in each other after years of struggling.

Seth asked them whether they were ready for a change. He repeatedly asked them for permission for interventions to increase their motivation for change. Seth asked the couple if they had sought out any information or support from groups like Al-Anon or even other parents in similar situations who had children with drug problems. No, they said. They had kept isolated out of embarrassment. So Seth encouraged them to seek information about the issue that week.

At this point, it was important to return to the goals of counseling for this couple because their complicating issues were likely to pull them into additional crises in the future. Seth also was aware that the couple had developed a dependency on counseling. They kept looking to him for guidance or at least for permission to talk safely with each other.

So in the next session Seth asked about the homework of seeking information for parents of drug abusers. They had "not gotten around to it" that week. Seth spent about 30 minutes reviewing with the couple in a supportive, gentle but firm way that they seemed to be losing energy toward improving things in their relationship. The couple agreed that the initial crisis that drove them into counseling had resolved itself in the previous six weeks and so they had less motivation, and the new crisis of Raphael's legal struggles had depleted them.

Seth laid out two pathways for counseling at this point. One path was to review what they had learned so far, create a plan for independent change, and plan for termination within a week. The other path was to decide to use counseling on a regular basis for several months to make more changes in their relationship. Seth explained his concern that they not depend on him too much because he was not able to be with them all the time. The couple decided to stick with counseling for several more months and double down on doing the work at home themselves.

The rest of their time in counseling blended the hope-focused couple approach with other interventions—improving and empowering communication, increasing intimacy, learning the REACH forgiveness intervention, and learning some interventions for parents of drug addicts. The hope-focused couple approach interventions that were used included the TANGO (HOPE 18-4) for communication, the LOVE intervention (HOPE 18-5) to resolve conflicts, and the REACH model of forgiveness (FREE 21-4) for them to both forgive each other for hurts during this time of crisis in their relationship, as well as find forgiveness for their son Jorge and his girlfriend.

Seth also brought in psychoeducation about parents of drug addicts and about family dynamics he observed that appeared to be related to substance abuse. He supported them as they attempted to minimize the impact on their relationship of any crises created by their son.

After five months of counseling, the couple seemed to have stabilized. It appeared to them (and also to Seth) that they had improved greatly from when they entered counseling. They felt they were ready to terminate.

The termination session was particularly moving for Seth as the couple faced yet another crisis with Jorge, their drug-abusing son, that week. Jorge had lost his home and car in one week. He was going to be homeless. Carlos and Rosalie had decided to offer to care for the baby for a few weeks to prevent him from being sent to foster care. However, they also had decided that they could not take in Jorge and Carlita. It was unclear how much they were still using substances. However, Carlos and Rosalie had been able to keep from allowing the crisis to pull them apart. They had turned to each other for support (rather than withdrawing into themselves). They also had kept calm in the midst of the crisis. They decided to terminate counseling as a sign to themselves that they trusted in God and each other to be able to use what they had learned on their own now.

PRINCIPLES FOR TREATING THE COMPLICATING FACTOR COUPLE

1. Counseling often begins with stabilization of current or recent crisis, trauma or stressful event. Throughout that phase, the counselor can integrate minimal hope-focused couple approach interventions. However, interventions to promote change are secondary to stabilization.

2. Resistance and roadblocks are more common than not. This is especially true for the couple with too much on their plate. It is difficult for them to find the energy and time to invest in their relationship when there are other problems. A supportive, understanding but firm stance that mirrors back to the couple the roadblocks they seem to be facing and allows them to decide how to handle them is best. If a couple is almost totally blocked, then reflecting on the reasons, history and experience of the roadblock often helps dislodge them.

3. The path of treatment may differ depending on whether the complicating factor is internal or external to the couple. If the problem is internal to the couple (e.g., financial crisis, health change or moderate trust violation) there may be more energy for relationship change. However, in that case they would likely need more relationship repair. For couples with external complicating factors, their focus can easily be directed toward the person or situation that is calling for attention, with less energy available for their relationship. Self-care and pacing may be needed. In some cases, couples in a "survival" psychological state may need to delay couple intervention until the crisis passes. They can focus on their relationship later. In that case, typical couple interventions would be delayed in favor of crisis management.

4. Most couples with some complicating factor benefit from integrating some psychoeducation, such as the education about Al-Anon in this case. Adding the psychoeducation to the typical hope-focused couple approach tailors the intervention to their needs.

INTERVENTION 12-1: THE FIVE-MINUTE DATE (JEN'S FAVORITE HOMEWORK)

One of the more important things a couple does is to stay connected to each other on a daily basis. It is not possible for most couples to have a "date" with each other every day. But most couples can plan to have "five-minute dates" daily. The five-minute date occurs when the couple step away from all other responsibilities to focus on connecting with the daily life of their partner. It is recommended that couples who are repairing their relationship plan to have *two* five-minute dates daily. Couples who are maintaining a healthy relationship plan at least *one* five-minute date each day. In addition, one longer (more than two-hour) weekly date is recommended for couples who are repairing their relationship. For couples in maintenance, dates at least twice a month are recommended.

Goal: Keep a connection with your partner. Keep up a mental map of your partner's daily life. Do not lose track of what is important to your partner. Know what is going on so you can be responsive and caring.

Virtues: Kindness, love, compassion and other warm relationship virtues are helpful. Commitment, steadfastness, self-control and temperance are also helpful to maintain the schedule and discipline of a daily five-minute date.

Setting: Anywhere you are unlikely to be interrupted. Step onto the back porch, or take the dog for a walk together. Commute to work together or sit down to a meal together. Talk while getting ready for bed. It can be a scheduled phone call if needed. The setting should allow you to focus on each other for an uninterrupted period of five minutes. Ideally eye contact and tender touch can be used.

Activity: Check in briefly with each other about what is going on in your lives. Think about the things in your partner's life right now. What is going on at work? How are things with the children or parents? How is your partner's health today? What stress is your partner facing today? Ask about it. It is okay if the discussion is "mundane"—turning to such things as what to plan for dinner, or discussing a disagreement your partner had with his brother. But it is good to reach for more existential issues like long-term hopes and dreams for life. Questions to ask during the mini-date might include:

- What is going on in your life today?
- What's the best thing going on for you today? The worst thing?
- If you could do anything at all today, what would you do?
- How are things going with (that stressful thing you told me about before)?
- Let me guess, are you feeling (tired, happy, relaxed, deflated—pick an emotion) today?
- What would you like to talk about today?

More five-minute date questions and discussion ideas can be found at hope couples.com.

What not to do: This is not the time to complain, to criticize each other, to be defensive or to withdraw from interaction. The goal is not to try to fix each other or to solve your partner's problems. Focus on staying connected by just listening and understanding what is going on with your partner today.

13

The Couple with a Psychological Disorder

?☙

Couples often present for therapy where there is an identified patient with a psychological problem. This type of couple may also have the characteristics of one or more of the other couple typologies discussed in this part of the book. The most common type of psychological diagnosis related to relationship distress is depression. But anxiety disorders, substance abuse, personality disorders and even schizophrenia spectrum disorders will sometimes bring a couple to treatment together.

If you decide to see them as a couple, the treatment should integrate empirically supported treatments for the individual psychopathology (for descriptions of many evidence-based practices in Christian counseling, see Worthington, Johnson, Hook & Aten, 2013). This may include additional partner-assisted therapy or adjunctive treatment for the psychological disorder (by counselor, referral, psychiatric care, etc.) with the nondiagnosed spouse acting as support. The counselor would integrate a hope-focused

---

John and Danika with Brittany

- Depression of one partner leading to low valuing of love and work
- Blend effective treatment for disorder with couple work and community assistance
- Couple treatment focused on conflict-resolution skills and forgiveness

couple approach treatment plan with additional modules from other treatment manuals, such as substance abuse couple treatment to assist with issues of codependency.

JOHN AND DANIKA

John and Danika had enjoyed a full life together. After 20 years of raising four children and a life of service in the Navy, they thought that life has been good to them. John had just retired as a master chief a few months earlier and had already taken a Department of Defense position in Washington, D.C. Two of their children were leaving for college that fall and the other two had settled into high school. Danika had struggled with anxiety attacks when she was in her twenties, but the couple had been able to weather them with a combination of supportive short-term counseling at the base clinic and anxiolytics. Back then she had been a mother of four young children, living on base in Japan with a husband who was deployed half of the time. She had been overwhelmed. Recently, her anxiety was back. She felt confused about what was overwhelming her now. She made an appointment with a local psychologist, Brittany, known to work with military families.

Brittany saw Danika for an individual intake and noticed that almost all of the discussion focused on her husband and the retirement. She asked whether couple counseling might be worth trying. Danika had not considered it but readily agreed that it would be helpful if John came with her. After meeting John, Brittany thought she knew what might be going on. John seemed depressed. He was having difficulty sleeping and eating. He was withdrawn and sluggish in the meeting. John's depression was making Danika anxious, although not to the point of panic attack.

This couple seemed to be having great difficulty adjusting to civilian life after a full career in the Navy. Brittany gave John a diagnosis of adjustment disorder with depression, due to the magnitude of their recent life changes. Danika was subclinical for an adjustment disorder with anxiety. However, Brittany thought that John was at risk of a full-blown major depressive episode. He had called in sick to work eight days in the past month, was tearful even in the intake session and was drinking heavily on the weekends. The couple were either ignoring each other or fighting daily. John was sleeping on the couch most evenings. In the past, they had handled their problems by focusing on the next deployment, which gave them space from each other. Now, however, there were no more deployments. The relationship was suffering and they did not seem to have the relationship skills to deal with the pain.

BRITTANY'S CASE CONCEPTUALIZATION

Brittany considered referring John for individual therapy for his depression but because the likely diagnosis from most psychotherapists would be adjustment disorder, and because Danika was also affected, Brittany decided that the couple relationship was a better environment for change. They both had significant motivation to improve their relationship. Brittany referred John to his physician to discuss the depression and consider medication if things did not improve quickly. Danika had more energy for ensuring that they would attend counseling sessions. John was less motivated. No doubt the depressive symptoms contributed to his reduced motivation, but the armed-forces lifestyle, which often denigrated counseling, also affected this former master chief. They could benefit from addressing both the psychopathology and the relationship.

After intakes, Brittany gave the couple a hope-focused couple approach report which included a structured treatment plan. She explained that the plan would likely be altered as needs changed across time. However, the report seemed to her a necessity to motivate and obtain buy in for treatment from this highly structured military couple. Because both partners had strengths in areas of structure, tasks and commitments, Brittany tailored their treatment to their personal character strengths. The plan was as follows.

- Week 1: Couple intake and assessments
- Week 2: Review relationship report, discuss goal for counseling and medication
- Week 3: Introduce depressive cognitive distortions with CBT workbook
- Week 4: Communication intervention for peace at home; psychoeducation on military retirement
- Week 5: Conflict Resolution—LOVE
- Week 6: Review CBT concepts; explore cognitive distortion playing out in the relationship
- Week 7: Connecting as a couple, understanding your pasts
- Week 8: The history of cognition for each partner

- Week 9: Apologizing and forgiving
- Week 10: Forgiving and moving forward in life and love
- Week 11: Irrational fears about moving forward
- Week 12: Termination

Brittany explained to John and Danika that this plan would almost definitely change as they moved forward—"Like any plan during a combat mission, huh, Chief?"—she said.

John said, "Yeah, I like a plan though. I don't want to just sit here and talk about our feelings."

Brittany asked, "Would these kinds of active interventions be helpful to your relationship and to you individually?"

They liked the structure and the ability to put the meetings and the plan on their calendars. This helped to increase their hope. John agreed to go to the Veterans Administration Medical Center for a medication evaluation for an antidepressant.

Brittany conceptualized this couple as being depleted in faith, work and love due to the life change and psychological disorder. John had been showing depressive symptoms for several months, and it was progressively getting worse. They were not religious so faith in God for change was not a factor in their lives. And they were not putting work into their relationship since moving and retiring eight months earlier.

Blending multiple goals for treatment into a limited amount of time is a challenging aspect of this case. Brittany knew that John would start the medication and likely improve in his mood within a few weeks. Until then his energy for working toward change might be low.

She leaned more heavily on Danika for the first weeks to lead the discussions in counseling. Once the medication kicked in for John (by about session three), Brittany expected that John would become more engaged in treatment.

COURSE OF TREATMENT

The couple did not have much support in the transition from enlisted to Veteran status. Their final assignment had been in rural West Virginia to a small base with a single social worker providing all mental health care and transition training for troops. After retirement and moving to D.C., the couple had not taken voluntary advantage of the transitions opportunities. Brittany requested information from the local VAMC on transition programs. She found many resources for couples in John and Danika's situation. The couple attended a few classes about the transition to retirement. The couple also stated that they had been surprised how much their four children had been affected by the retirement when one of the kids had found two books the couple were reading and wanted to read them as well. As the whole family became better informed, their situation improved.

The hope-focused couple approach interventions that Brittany selected were classic key interventions for most couples. The character-development focus was particularly helpful with John, who had appreciated the character-development aspects of his life in the Navy. His current position focused exclusively on management for military bases. He no longer had the other personnel development aspects of military life such as physical training, social support, or character and leadership development. John talked about how much he missed that aspect of his former career. When John discussed things he missed about military life, Danika was quick to step in and try to refocus him. She would say things like, "But isn't it nice to settle in and not have to move anymore?"

Brittany was concerned that this might result in John feeling misunderstood. "Danika," she said, "I was wondering what you were feeling when John was talking about the losses he has felt in retiring?"

"I guess I just felt that he would get himself into one of his depressed moods if he kept heading down that road. Also, it is one of those things that, as they say, 'is what it is.' We cannot undo the retirement, so it is better, I think, not to dwell on it."

"So what effect do you think it has on John when you change the topic abruptly like that?"

"I don't really know. I guess he might feel grateful that I kept him from dwelling on the past."

"Hmm," said Danika. "What if you asked him about the impact it had on him?"

Danika looked at John. "So how did you react when I tried to get you thinking about the positive future instead of the long-gone past?"

"I don't know," said John. "I mean, of course, I know I cannot go back, but it's hard to readjust my whole way of thinking. I guess it seemed like you were not really interested in seeing how I was trying to deal with the retirement."

"Wow. That kind of backfired," said Danika.

John later made a good direct request to Danika to allow for space in times of struggle. He said he felt crowded, as if she were pushing into his office and moving his personal effects around. She agreed to try not to be as intrusive. Even though he had struggled with depression, she thought she could hold her anxieties in check rather than intrusively trying to protect him. Brittany reinforced the positive interactions.

They used an additional session that was not on the original schedule to discuss their couple communication rules (intervention 13-1). This helped reduce distress in the relationship.

Cognitive behavioral therapy (CBT) interventions were helpful to them, since both partners were struggling with mood. Early in treatment, Brittany taught some basic concepts in handling irrational thinking and links among cognition, behaviors and emotions. Then she had the couple work through a CBT workbook (Knaus & Ellis, 2012) as homework. They discussed something from it in most sessions. Because the psychological disorder was related both to relationship problems and to adjustment to retirement from the military, it was important to address both problems in counseling. The couple were seen as a couple throughout treatment, even in sessions primarily focused on retirement issues. John's beliefs about retirement were affecting the family, and the family was affecting John.

Brittany identified a relationship dynamic where Danika tended to give directives to John. She saw it in session. Danika said to John as they entered the therapist office: "You share this time. You need to talk this week."

This pattern was identified as a contributor to John's feeling of inadequacy. Danika expressed her own anxiety—"I feel we will fail in this relationship. The more scared I feel, the more directive I get." This was a predictable pattern that led to more feelings of inadequacy from John, which triggered more inadequacy feelings from Danika. It was a catch-22 situation. The couple then used their CBT workbooks to work on their individual fears. They encouraged each other in managing emotions and trying new behaviors associated with the fears.

The forgiveness module was used next to help the couple repair and protect their relationship so that it would be stronger in the future. John's transition to becoming a veteran was the most stressful life transition for the couple, but they were also facing other chronic difficulties. Their interpersonal stressors were unlikely to magically disappear. There were two children planning to move away to college in a few months, which was something Danika worried about. And two teenage children in high school added their own life stresses to the family. Most couples at least partially fall back into dysfunctional patterns in times of stress. The chances they would return to dysfunctional patterns were high. The goal of the forgiveness interventions was to help them accept the inevitability of hurts in relationships, recognize when they needed to come back together after hurts and repair the relationship, and to protect them long-term.

Turning Points

The couple especially responded well to the apology intervention (FREE 21-3). They focused on skills in making an apology. John was reluctant to apologize for harsh words he said to Danika or negative emotions directed toward Danika.

John said, "My father, a captain of a ship, often said 'never explain, never complain.' So we never apologized in my family. I don't know. I like you and all Brit, but why would it help us?"

Brittany slowed down the intervention and focused on their definitions of forgiveness (FREE 21-2). At this point in counseling, John was beginning to trust the counselor. He moved from a precontemplation stage in terms of the importance of apologizing for wrongs to contemplating whether it might be helpful in their relationship. Danika was excited about this change. She had long complained that John did not own his mistakes. The couple practiced some apologies in subsequent weeks and began to apologize more often.

The final part of the forgiveness module focused on repairing their relationship and coming back together when inevitable hurts occurred. The couple had fought that week over a parenting decision with their youngest child. Brittany was able to use that fight as grist for the mill.

She asked, "Would you be willing to apologize and talk about coming back together as a pair?" The couple paused, looked at each other, and saw what Brittany was doing. It was one of the better moments in counseling. Both Danika and John had been emotionally expressive, apologized and reconnected after the fight.

Danika said, "I don't think I really got what you were talking about in apologizing until today. I mean I know it's simple, but it helps us stay close."

The planned intervention about fear of moving on was dropped from treatment because both partners felt they had been addressing that with their CBT workbooks and discussions in counseling. They also felt it was no longer a key problem they were facing. So it was time to plan for termination.

Termination included a graduation memorial (intervention 28-1) where the couple brought in a picture of a tree they planted in the backyard of their new home. They talked about how the tree symbolized their relationship in being strong but always needing to grow and renew itself. And it symbolized their putting down roots in their life after the navy.

Brittany encouraged them to discuss what they wanted to keep from the time they had spent in counseling and what they wanted to continue working on in the future. The couple believed that going to classes at the VAMC and reading more information on the transition to civilian life was helpful in normalizing their experiences.

John thought the antidepressant he had been taking was working well. He thought that he might be ready to stop taking it after the holidays in a couple of months. Brittany encouraged him to talk with his doctor before stopping his medication. She gave him information about problems arising from stopping medication improperly.

In the final wrap-up, Danika said she especially appreciated the forgiveness module of intervention and thought that would be helpful "because hurting each other at least a little is inevitable." John liked the rules for communication that they created as part of the listening skills training early in counseling.

Finally, Brittany had the couple take brief measures of depression (Dozois, Dobson & Ahnberg, 1998) and anxiety (De Ayala, Vonderharr-Carlson & Kim, 2005), which indicated they both were in the normal range with improved symptoms. Brittany made herself available should they need her in the future and said goodbye to the couple.

FOLLOW-UP

At follow-up Brittany was amazed at how much Danika and John had maintained and improved their relationship. John had taken on a role in a local Veteran's social group doing community outreach and this provided many of the things he missed from his military days. Danika had also found a job she enjoyed and was focused more on varied parts of her life than John.

Their assessments and self-reports indicated that they had found their own natural ways to improve their family life after the boost of couple therapy with Brittany.

PRINCIPLES FOR TREATING THE COUPLE WITH A PSYCHOLOGICAL DISORDER

1. Assessment of the psychological disorder, contributing factors and the role of the relationship in the disorder help to determine whether couple counseling is appropriate. If the partner can help support improvement, or if the relationship problems are a major contributor to the disorder, then couple therapy may be the best and most efficient modality of treatment.

2. The typical hope-focused couple approach may need to be augmented with interventions from the empirically supported treatment literature for the presenting disorder in order to provide the range of care needed for the client. Counselors should provide full disclosure and discussion with the client in the first sessions to discuss which should have priority in counseling—the relationship problem or the individual problem. However, these problems are typically not distinct and unrelated, so understanding the clients' priorities can help with deciding how the intervention will be conducted.

3. There are advantages and disadvantages to the structured version of treatment planning that Brittany provided in this case. Advantages include the couple's higher awareness of the full course and direction of counseling, their increased commitment because there are specific dates of treatment that are communicated, and the decreased likelihood that counseling will lose direction and momentum. Disadvantages occur because some counselors or couples are not flexible with the treatment plan when flexibility is needed throughout treatment as new issues and understandings evolve over the course of treatment. Client needs, personalities and style should also factor in to whether a structured or flexible treatment plan is used with a couple.

4. Some Christian couples may need to explore what mental health means to them because some Christian churches have direct teachings that deny or minimize mental health diagnoses. It is important to meet the

couple where they are in terms of faith issues. However, it is also important to balance this with facts and information about mental health diagnoses, treatment and processes.

INTERVENTION 13-1: OUR COMMUNICATION RULES

Couple communication is like horse racing. It can be exhilarating and enjoyable to communicate with your partner and find your understanding and connection racing ahead. But when it goes badly someone can be injured.

Couples need to create rules, boundaries and expectations for communication in their relationship. This is particularly true when the discussion becomes heated or difficult. If feelings of anger, righteous indignation or sadness rise up during a conversation, then it is more likely that the rules of the game will be broken and injuries occur.

Think of communication rules for your relationship and write them down. Many couples have never articulated what they need when they are having a difficult conversation. Try to use "I" statements, make direct and respectful requests for rules, and work together as a couple in rulemaking. In this way, you are practicing good communication at the same time that you are discussing the topic of communication.

Questions you might ask include, "What do you need to happen in communication to help things go well?" and "What do you need both of you to avoid doing to prevent the conversation from going awry?"

How this intervention can go wrong: Things go badly when you veer toward the "kitchen sink" conversation, reminding each other of all of the negative things done in previous fights. Couples with high conflict may struggle with this intervention and need more support and active intervention on the part of the counselor. If things are heading that direction, your counselor can coach you toward good communication by asking you to observe how the current conversation is going. Notice each other's nonverbal responses and voice tone, and discuss your intent in the conversation.

One advantage of creating your own rules is that it is difficult to break your own rules. For many couples, there is a "win at all costs" mentality in conflict or difficult communication. Sometimes just creating the rules will bring that attitude to light, allow both of you to reflect on it and make more intentional choices about your communication.

14

The High Conflict Couple

ₑ❧

The high conflict couple has conflict characterized by emotional flooding, severe negative behaviors and possibly mild violence. They are usually low in valuing love and high in devaluing each other. They are difficult for counselors to work with due to the anger that permeates the couple's relationship.

Treatment might begin with a thorough assessment, a time-out conflict-resolution intervention, and then behavioral-based changes in conflict and communication to increase safety and create boundaries for relating as a couple. The counselor must frequently reassess for safety in relationship. For progress, the counselor must often assess the couple's readiness to move forward with increasing their bond, explore histories of broken bonds in family of origin as needed, and promote forgiveness. If partners are able to improve, it is not uncommon for such cases to involve longer term treatment of 15 to 25 or more sessions.

Yvonne and Jack with Lisa

- Couple with high emotional conflict
- Use of time-out, behavioral interventions for conflict, then improving bond and forgiveness
- Increase insight into patterns of broken bonds

YVONNE AND JACK

Jack and Yvonne were in their late twenties. They had been married for three years and had lived together for five years before marriage. Jack and Yvonne were from a rural county characterized by poverty. Jack was from a relatively wealthy family that owned several stores; Yvonne was from a family that struggled to put food on the table. The two fell in love when they were in high school where Jack was a football hero and Yvonne was a beautiful, academically focused teen who was ready to leave their small town. The couple moved to a nearby big city after high school for college and then moved in together after college. The couple had fairly high conflict throughout their history. Twice the conflict had overflowed to violence when Jack pinned Yvonne down and she kicked him. Their fights were often accompanied by throwing objects, yelling, cursing and rage-filled verbal putdowns. They would then come back together as a couple relatively quickly with a dramatic show of love and affection.

The conflict subsided when the couple finished college and obtained good jobs. However, when Yvonne had discovered she was pregnant five months ago, their conflict suddenly increased. They had planned to wait several more years before having children, and Yvonne felt considerable stress because she was about to be promoted to manager at work. She was afraid that her pregnancy would derail the promotion. Jack had withdrawn from the relationship since the pregnancy by spending more time with friends at a local bar. Yvonne wondered if he had been unfaithful one night when he did not come home. He denied any sexual involvement, saying he had too much to drink to drive home, so he had slept it off on a friend's couch. Yvonne's uncle was gay and she wondered if Jack might be attracted to men. There was no reason to believe this, but she kept ruminating about his friendship with other men at the bar. Their conflict had escalated to the point where the couple decided to seek counseling on the recommendation of Yvonne's obstetrician. Neither of them had been in counseling before. They were unsure of the process or whether it would help.

Lisa is a psychologist practicing in a medically integrated setting within an obstetrician's office. Most of her practice is with women or couples dealing with infertility, loss of pregnancy or relationship issues. Yvonne stopped by for 15 minutes after her appointment with her obstetrician. Lisa recommended that Jack join her in counseling. Lisa gave Yvonne a packet of assessments including the Dyadic Adjustment Scale (Carey, Spector, Lantinga & Krauss, 1993), Conflict Tactics Scale-2 (Newton, Connelly & Landsverk, 2001), the Personal Traits in Relationships Assessment (see intervention 3-1), the CARE (Worthington et al., 1997), the MAST to screen for alcohol abuse (Fagbemi, 2011), and some open-ended questions about their concerns and goals for counseling.

Yvonne and Jack returned the next week for the meeting. They had completed the questionnaires, and Lisa spent an hour with them trying to understand their needs and goals for counseling. The assessments indicated that there was mild "common couples" type of violence (throwing nondangerous things, a few incidents of pinning, that mostly Yvonne was the one who was violent in their arguments), very low satisfaction globally for Yvonne in particular and an elevated score on the MAST for Jack. Further assessment in individual meetings with each of them helped to identify the issues. Jack did not drink during the week but did binge drink on Friday evenings particularly when he met with guy friends at a local bar. That was when most of the couple's arguments occurred. Yvonne used to go to the bar as well but since being pregnant she did not drink and was tired, so she would leave early. Jack had a DUI on his record from six years earlier.

LISA'S CASE CONCEPTUALIZATION

The couple were distressed about the conflict between them but seemed to follow a cycle of aggression and conflict. Tension would build between them. Jack would say angry and hurtful things and Yvonne would try and keep him calm. Then some kind of emotional outburst would occur where both of them would unload on each other. Jack would call Yvonne names and Yvonne had lately been accusing Jack of being gay. This infuriated him. Eventually they would make up, typically with Jack minimizing the incident. Then they would go to a calm period of feeling positive toward each other. Then tension would begin to build again. The cycle had sped up since the pregnancy.

Should they be seen together in counseling? Generally, couples with violence are not seen in a dyadic format. However, because (1) Jack and Yvonne were not afraid of each other, (2) neither had ever physically hurt the other, (3) Jack's alcohol use was problematic but did not rise to the level of a disorder, and (4) Jack did not engage in any concerning controlling behaviors, they seemed to be good candidates for couple intervention. There was some risk in seeing the couple together, yet they were intent on couple treatment and the risk factors were relatively low. Lisa conducted individual intake assessments (see intervention 6-6) with both partners to fully assess their symptoms, violence and alcohol use. At that point she felt sure that Yvonne's worry about Jack's attraction to men was relevant to her insecurities about their sex life during pregnancy, rather than based on any actual relationship or attractions.[1]

In Lisa's written report for the couple, she focused on giving the couple a realistic but hopeful picture of the patterns in their relationship. They were especially low in love. They repeatedly devalued each other. Their faith was actually fairly good. They tried to work on their relationship but were not necessarily effective. They wanted things to be better—they had willpower to change—but they did not have "waypower" to get there. Their virtue strengths included teamwork, dedication, humor and perseverance for Yvonne; and friendship, trust in Yvonne and taking risks for the relationship for Jack.

Their treatment plan would begin with using time-out (see intervention 14-2) and other conflict-resolution interventions to help them find new ways to handle their conflict and break the cycle of violence. Following that, the couple would work through a course of forgiveness interventions to help them learn healthier ways to come back together after inevitable hurts and disagreements. Lisa would watch for any negative and distorted cognition about the relationship throughout counseling. The pregnancy and its effect on the partners was also expected to be a theme throughout treatment as well.

INITIAL PHASE OF TREATMENT

Jack and Yvonne responded well to a no-violence contract (see intervention 14-1). They generated many ideas for what signaled escalation of anger with them, and they also had practical ideas about what to do during the time-out to cool down. Lisa stressed the importance of cooling down during the time-out period (see intervention 14-2) and not ruminating about the argument or working on their "come back" speech. Lisa also created a rule for the couple that they would not even start an argument if either of them had too much to drink. That intervention alone should help reduce the risk of aggression.

---

[1]The work of the Institute for the Study of Sexual Identity can help guide couple therapists in addressing same-sex attraction issues. See www.sexualidentityinstitute.org.

During the second session, the couple began berating each other and interrupting when the other was trying to talk. Lisa stopped them.

"Excuse me," she said. "I don't mean to be rude, but I was wondering whether this is how you normally act toward each other at home."

"Yes," they said almost in unison.

"I hate to sound like Dr. Phil, but how's that been working for you?"

"Not too well," said Yvonne.

"While we are in here, I think it would be good to practice a new way of relating to each other. I'd like to ask you to try not to talk to each other in devaluing ways or to interrupt the other person. If you catch yourself interrupting or devaluing your partner, just stop. But if I notice it I'd like to hold up my hand in this stop-sign like gesture. This would serve as your cue to stop talking or to begin talking in more valuing ways. As counseling proceeds, though, I expect that you'll recognize the pattern earlier and interrupt yourselves more quickly. Is it okay if I do this?" They agreed.

Lisa also encouraged the couple to use "I" language and for each person to only speak for himself or herself rather than speaking for the other person. Lisa then used a simple "love busters" intervention (see HOPE 18-3) to help the couple identify things that set each other off and devalue each other.

COURSE OF TREATMENT

The LOVE intervention (HOPE 18-5) was used to help the couple find a better way to handle disagreements or conflicts. The LOVE intervention is a conflict-management intervention used in most of the research conducted on the hope-focused couple approach (Worthington & Ripley, 2009). The couple readily had conflictual topics to discuss. For example, during the previous week, they prepared the nursery for the new baby. Yvonne thought that Jack was withdrawing from preparing for the baby. Yvonne was getting nervous about being unprepared.

Lisa had the couple tell each other what was going on with them and listen (the L in LOVE) to each other. The couple had difficulty with sharing talk time so Lisa took out a large paperclip from her drawer and asked them to use the paperclip as a reminder of whose turn it was to speak. This increased the structure for the couple. With a few prompts, they were able to take turns talking and were coached to reflect back what they heard.

Lisa had them stop and observe (the O in LOVE) what was going on between them. This was obviously new for both of them. They were not sure what she meant by "observe." Lisa described her observations of their behavior—their voice tone, eye contact, word choice, proximity, volume of speech, or how they were turning toward each other or pulling away in the conversation. The session was over at that point and, given their continued level of disagreements (but no violence), Lisa recommended they have a positive date night that week that did not involve much interaction. With high-conflict couples, it is important not to increase their intimacy until they are ready because conflict is often partially related to fear of intimacy.

The following week Lisa had the couple discuss the *V* from the LOVE intervention—valuing each other. Lisa helped the couple dig a little deeper to understand that they tended to devalue each other because they had such a long history of devaluing relationships. Yvonne had experienced devaluing all of her life. "My family struggled in all aspects of living. My mom was always critical. Her revolving boyfriends were always more important than I was." Yvonne was crying and having trouble getting the story out coherently.

"Jack," said Lisa, "I notice that you don't seem to be tracking fully with Yvonne's story."

"Well, this is a new story to you, but I've heard it fifty times before. She is always critical of her mother—not without good reason. But it still is hard to listen to the same story again and again. I think it would be good if she could move on with life and not keep living in the past."

"Is that what you think I'm doing? Living in the past?" Yvonne's voice was rising and becoming more shrill.

Lisa held up her hand. They both stopped talking. "Yvonne, I think I need to work with Jack for a few moments."

Lisa worked with Jack to uncover his fears about when Yvonne gets upset and about emotions in general.

"My family was pretty much a perfect family," he said.

"Yeah, except for that little inconvenience about your mother's drinking problem, which occasionally slips your mind," inserted Yvonne.

Lisa said, "Let's take stock a minute. Can I ask you to observe how your conversation is going in terms of listening and valuing each other?" They both looked down, recognizing their difficulty. Lisa continued, "I have a hypothesis. It is very tenuous. I wonder whether the roadblock in this area might be due to something unknown, something that makes you feel vulnerable as a couple."

Surprisingly, Jack jumped in to say that, yes, he felt touchy about their past, and he did not like to discuss it. The counselor decided to watch for this topic for several weeks of intervention.

Next, Lisa decided to introduce the *E* of the LOVE intervention. Despite the fact that the couple was limited in their ability to fully integrate the concepts discussed in counseling, Lisa felt it was important to keep moving because the process of change was more important than any particular intervention. The *E* stands for "evaluate common interests." Lisa asked them to focus on their core interests and needs in their relationship. In their best-selling book *Getting to Yes*, Roger Fisher, William Ury and Bruce Patton (2011) argue that resolving conflicts depends on both parties identifying their common interests and trying to meet both people's interests instead of locking in to opposing positions. Fisher and Ury identify four basic human needs: security, belonging, recognition and control. Lisa introduced the couple to these four needs and asked them what they needed in terms of preparing for the baby. She directed Yvonne to start first because she was more capable of discussing her need for security and recognition.

Then Jack shared his need for security and control. Lisa had the couple double back to the discussion about their past. She asked whether they had experienced unmet needs in these areas of their life prior to preparing for the baby. She encouraged them in their personal strengths to help them with this roadblock they were facing with conflict. This seemed to help break up the roadblock for them.

The next module of treatment dealt with apologies and forgiveness. Lisa had to work with the couple's concerns about apologies and forgiveness for a session because they were not sure how it would be valuable for them (see FREE 21-1, 21-2). They felt they were "too good" at apologies because they tended to fight and then apologize so frequently. Lisa gave the couple some information to read about reconciliation and building trust after an offense. Then, after a particularly frustrating week, they practiced apologies.

Yvonne complained, "This is really difficult because we get so angry. I don't feel we really know how to apologize when are so angry. You called it 'flooded' before—that is just how it feels to me. I'm trying to swim in a flood and now you want me to apologize. It seems crazy."

Lisa said, "I wonder if it would be helpful for you to learn a practice called self-soothing. It might help you calm down when the floods hit, so you have a chance to apologize more often" (see intervention 14-3). Practicing self-soothing helped them lower their anger and allowed them to talk about their need to learn to make better apologies. They decided to focus on that next week.

After practicing self-soothing at home and in the office, the couple spent two weeks addressing apologies (see FREE 21-3). Their pattern of using apologies to minimize their angry and sometimes physically hurtful behaviors was especially important to address. There were several disagreements during those weeks to process together. This helped the growth process for the couple who were improving in deescalating their conflicts and apologizing more effectively. Overall, there was a softening of the couple. Lisa had them complete the CARE and other relationship measures again. They showed continued improvement in the relationship, especially Jack.

The forgiveness intervention was coupled with trust building. There was an emphasis on acting in trustworthy ways and offering small trustworthy acts as gifts (see TRUST 22-2). The couple were recognizing that they had used apologies and forgiveness in the past as part of a negative pattern.

Jack struggled the most with the humility aspect of offering the gift of forgiveness. He felt a strong blow to his role and masculine identity when Yvonne had kicked him a year earlier in an argument. He processed how much this offended him. Lisa had to engage in considerable coaching to help Yvonne see Jack's perspective on the kick because both partners had been aggressive that day. Lisa directed them to take responsibility for the harm they had done that day and apologize for their own behavior. There was some movement on this past offense for the couple, but there continued to be lingering resistance in moving forward. For homework, Lisa asked the couple to write down in a letter all of the things they wanted to apologize for and take responsibility for in hurting their relationship.

TURNING POINTS

The next session Lisa asked the couple if they were ready to read their letters. They turned toward each other and were coached to look at each other and listen well. There were many tears. The heartfelt confession by both partners was, they said in their last session, one of the best moments of counseling.

Jack took a risk and was able to admit to the harm he caused by yelling, throwing things and pinning Yvonne. Yvonne took responsibility for her own cursing, kicking, punching and putdowns.

Lisa pointed out that this seemed different than previous times they apologized in their dysfunctional conflict cycle. They agreed. Yvonne was not walking on egg shells or minimizing Jack's offenses. Jack was clearly stating what he did and that it was wrong. They both felt a great sense of relief.

The final few sessions were focused on rebuilding trust as a couple. Lisa emphasized the importance of post-hurt trustworthy behaviors to build up a healthy relationship (see TRUST 22-2, 22-3). There was a good deal of reflecting back on what they had been learning in sessions and Lisa knew that they were beginning to be ready to move forward.

The couple decided to have a Joshua memorial (intervention 28-1) session to show gratitude for the changes in their lives as they sensed the end of the time in counseling. The couple created a mirror with tiles as a craft project for their memorial. On the tiles, they had painted some words and pictures to remind them of what they had learned. They said that the mirror symbolized how they looked at themselves more clearly now.

FOLLOW-UP

Three months later at the follow-up visit the couple was maintaining the gains they had found in counseling. There had been some stress two weeks after the baby arrived when the baby spiked a high fever. Yvonne called her sister who had taken her to the hospital, but did not call Jack until after they had seen the doctor. This upset Jack, who felt deeply injured that he had not been consulted first. Yvonne used some of the apology skills she remembered, and Jack forgave her. This had helped, but the couple continued to struggle with acting independently and not working as a team. Lisa asked if they thought they needed to return to counseling to address the concern and they declined.

The couple did return to counseling nine months later. Lisa was able to help them make more progress toward a healthier relationship in another course of counseling. Becoming parents had significantly matured both of them. This time they were better able to use counseling to help them more quickly. They also addressed more of the longstanding dynamics in their relationship. Lisa blended the hope-focused couple approach with emotion-focused couple therapy (Johnson & Woolley, 2008) in their second course of counseling.

Principles for Treating High Conflict Couples

1. Manage countertransference reactions to couples. High conflict couples can pull the counselor into behavior that is not therapeutic. It is easy to become judgmental, critical, frustrated, angry or helpless in the face of the strong emotions and volatility of this type of couple. Relapse seems to be a way of life for this mercurial relationship. A solid conceptualization of the clients' needs and issues will help with most countertransference. At times, a consultation or supervision session may be needed. Counselors may have to work harder to maintain empathy for a couple with high conflict. Finally, the counselor needs to be aware of their own experiences that may influence their response to high conflict couples.

2. Never let them see you sweat. Couples with high conflict need a counselor who is a "solid object," to borrow a term from object-relations theory. The solid object is a counselor who is consistent, steady, self-assured, and warm but authoritative, and has reasonably positive expectations of the couple. The counselor must operate by a rule that emotions are good but toxic behaviors will not be allowed in the office. When tested, the counselor must call toxic behaviors "on the carpet" with a sense of a caring authority. If a counselor with a high conflict couple changes the approach, is passive, lacks authority, or seems unsure of how to handle the couple's high emotions, then the counselor will unlikely be able to create a kind of "containment field" in the therapy room that will show the couple they can be safe. Any challenge to this goal should be processed with the couple.

3. Effective time-out or cool-down interventions are the first response to common couple violence. There is some research that mild common couple violence responds well to dyadic treatment (Stith, McCollum & Rosen, 2011). However, it is important to stop even mild violence patterns. A time-out intervention is a key way to do that.

4. Build conflict-resolution skills with the couple. The couple will need additional tools for conflict resolution beyond the standard toolkit. Depending on their psychological abilities, those skills might lean toward

behavioral or cognitive behavioral intervention. Or if the couple is more mature, they may be able to handle experiential or emotion-focused interventions for conflict. Regardless, research seems to support the importance of changing schemas and beliefs around conflicts as a key to lasting change (Fincham, Harold & Gano-Phillips, 2000; Gordon & Christman, 2008).

5. The higher the conflict, the more pessimistic is the couple's prognosis. It is important to be hopeful but realistic with couples who come to therapy with high conflict. There are often long-standing psychological needs being met through the conflict, often for control. They are getting something from the conflict and will need a new way to have their needs met. However, this may be difficult to accomplish in short-term counseling. Interventions with this type of couple may require more time, more attention to reducing resistance to change, and more intensity. Essentially the dosage usually needs to be high for the intervention to work.

6. Be a good model. One of the most important things that a counselor can do with a couple who have high conflict and low resources is to be a role model in conflict resolution. Look for opportunities in the room when the couple has conflict to model and coach more healthy conflict patterns. Our experience suggests that those will usually not take much searching. If the counselor is feeling frustrated with client behaviors (e.g., being late to sessions), then clearly, firmly but warmly communicating the concern or frustration can demonstrate how to challenge someone. There are a myriad of ways to engage in the couple's dysfunctional patterns of conflict and help them try new behaviors, experience new emotions and reflect on the change.

INTERVENTION 14-1: THE COOL DOWN CONTRACT

During times of conflict escalation, I agree to do the following:

1. *Self-watch.* I will watch for cues that I am building up tension and negativity. List some "cues" of build-up in terms of emotions, behaviors and thoughts:

2. *Signal.* I will signal my partner with a word, phrase or sign that I am escalating and need to take a time-out. Our signal will be:

3. *Respond.* If either of us requests a time-out, I will acknowledge that and agree.

4. *Separate.* I will go and cool down. To cool down, I will . . . (e.g., distraction tasks, working off energy, changing thinking, changing mood).

5. *Reconnect.* I will return to discuss things when things are calm between us. I will not avoid the discussion if either of us needs to have it. If too difficult, we will discuss it in counseling. I will take responsibility for my part of the conflict.

A written contract worksheet can be found at hopecouples.com

INTERVENTION 14-2: TIME-OUT

Remember the 4 Cs:

Clues. Discuss clues that would signal when a time-out is needed.

For instance, if one partner feels a sense of fear, feels emotionally flooded or wants to be aggressive or display violence, then a time-out is needed.

You can talk specifically about times in the past when a time-out would have been helpful and plan to use it in similar situations in the future.

It may be helpful to have a neutral, nonblaming signal to cue the other person a time-out is needed.

Commit. Commit to take the time-out when either person asks for it. Set an agreed on length of time for the time-out.

Cool down. Plan to engage in cooling down, self-soothing or distracting activities during the time-out.

Typical time-out activities include exercising, watching television, surfing the web, writing in a journal (*if* it can be positive), cooking a meal, taking a soothing bath or running an errand. This is a crucial part of the time-out.

If one person ruminates about the partner or the conflict during the time-out or plans new strategies to win the argument, then the conflict will only escalate, causing further damage to the relationship and to you as individuals.

The primary goal of the time-out is to decrease emotionally negative "flooding" so you can reengage with each other about the issue effectively.

Come back. It is important to come back together after the time-out to apologize for offenses committed before the time-out; take responsibility for your actions within the conflict; reconcile; agree, or agree to disagree; and try to make any decisions that are necessary.

Typically time-outs need to be long enough to allow for physiological flooding to stop (blood pressure to come down, heart rate to slow, blaming or condemning thoughts to return to normal), which on average is about an hour.

INTERVENTION 14-3: WAYS TO SOOTHE IN DIFFICULT INTERACTIONS WITH A MATE

In the midst of a difficult conversation it can be difficult to stop emotions from escalating. Yet difficult conversations in life are inevitable. It will be important to be able to discuss difficult things as a couple. If the emotions are flooding either of you, then you might need to declare a time-out. But for other difficult conversations, see which of the following might be helpful to you. Check off the ones that you think are worth trying. It is important to practice soothing yourself regularly, first with your counselor's help, then in a time that is not too tense, and finally during a more tense moment.

Perspective Taking

❑ Think about the long-term perspective on the issue at hand. Is it that important? Will it matter years from now?

❑ Remember it is more important to be loving than to be right or get your way.

❑ Give yourself permission to give up control of a situation and just see where things will take you.

❑ Say something valuing and nurturing about your relationship as a couple, how important it is and how much you appreciate the relationship.

❑ Say something you are grateful for within the difficult conversation. For example, perhaps you are grateful that there is no swearing or yelling.

❑ Ask yourself, "How old am I?" By doing this, you remember you are an adult and capable of handling difficult conversations.

❑ Say something valuing about yourself. Be valuing and nurturing to yourself by thinking something positive about yourself.

Body Awareness and Calming

❑ Attend to tense body cues like raised shoulders, tense belly, wrinkled brow, pulled down facial muscles, fidgeting hands or legs, uncomfortable body position or others. Relax the tense body part.

❑ Take a slow, deep breath and slowly blow out your anxiety, frustration or sadness.

❑ Lay down in a comfortable position if you can. If you are at home, you may find getting on the couch or bed in a comfortable position is helpful to calm your body.

Refocusing

❑ Stop and pray together as a couple asking for wisdom for the difficult situation.

❑ Change the topic to something more positive if the discussion is not an important one. Ask your partner if it is okay to talk about something else for a while.

❑ Stop and consider what would be the wise course of action here. Ask yourself how someone whom you know to be wise might act in this situation.

Scenery Change

❑ Go for a walk together as a couple and discuss the issue outside.

❑ Have the difficult conversation in a public place to increase the constraints on extreme negative behavior.

❑ Take a mini-break from the conversation and then return to talk. This can often prevent escalation. For example, even a trip to the restroom or a quick check on the kids can bring down tension.

❑ Light a candle or fireplace. The fire has a calming effect.

❑ Turn on beautiful music.

❑ Eat or drink something delicious while you talk. (Avoid more than a minimum of alcohol. Alcohol can lower inhibitions too much and is often associated with aggressive behavior.)

❑ Have the talk naked if it tends to make your more generous with each other.

15

The "Accept the Things
I Cannot Change" Couple

੨ঌ

The famous serenity prayer asks God to help a person accept the things they cannot change, the courage to change the things they can, and the wisdom to know the difference. For many couples there are biological, characterological or situational problems that are highly unlikely to change. It may be due to chronic health or mental health problems, severe history of abuse, or a persistent attachment style that is difficult for the couple. This couple could be low in love, faith, work or all three. Christian couples in this situation may have compounded problems with a struggle in their faith. They may hope for a miracle, have prayed for years for change and feel confused as to why they continue to face this intractable problem. Commonly couples do not consider "accepting the things they cannot change" as a good option in their relationship. It seems like simply admitting defeat.

A treatment plan for this couple would avoid typical skills-focused treatments. The goal is not to activate false hope for change. Instead counselors focus on psychoeducation around the historical problem, map out ways to increase closeness that are effective and realistic, improve emotional regulation, and decrease the worst of their conflict with more effective conflict-resolution skills. Some couples may need some allowance for grieving the dream of what they thought marriage would be like and adopting a new meaningful dream. Overall, an acceptance and forgiveness-based approach is adopted, with reduced attempts at influencing change in the identified problem.

Carl and Mariel with Aleksandra

- A couple with problems that are unlikely to change
- Promote grace, forgiveness, emotional understanding and regulation
- Focus on BOND and FREE interventions and avoid most relationship-skill change

CARL AND MARIEL

Carl and Mariel, a couple in their forties, came to counseling with many serious problems. Carl and Mariel met in California when Carl was serving a short-term enlistment in the military. Mariel was a recent immigrant from the Philippines with her family. They were a young couple who entered into marriage just a few months after meeting. Mariel had experienced physical and sexual abuse as an early adolescent and was timid and insecure interpersonally. She had suffered from some PTSD symptoms (subclinical) and chronic depression through most of her adulthood and had been treated with antidepressants and CBT for her depression in early adulthood. The treatments helped her fight off the more severe symptoms she had as a teen, but she had struggled with depression several times a year since then. She was not currently depressed.

Carl could be blustery and insensitive, but he met her need for a sense of protection in a new country. He was a high school teacher and wrestling coach. The two had teenage daughters who were doing fairly well in life. The couple's struggles were primarily in sexual intimacy and chronic avoidance of conflicts. They were discouraged. Their friend had tried to help them with a PREP (Braithwaite & Fincham, 2009) marriage retreat weekend and encouraged some pastoral counseling. Their long-standing problems, however, had proven to resist change, so the referral had been made.

ALEKSANDRA'S CASE CONCEPTUALIZATION

Aleksandra recognized that this couple might have very different needs than the other couples she saw using the hope-focused couple approach. Given that Mariel had tried psychiatric and psychological treatment, it appeared that the PTSD symptoms and depression were chronic. Carl's interpersonal insensitivity, low level of empathy, and task-focus were also unlikely to change. Carl and Mariel had a poor prognosis for change.

The treatment approach then was to look for strengths they could use to handle the weaknesses that seemed unlikely to change. Mariel's character strengths were self-control, ability to create friendship, Christian faith and gracious style of relating to others. Mariel was pleasant and likeable. Carl's character strengths were his hope, sense of belonging with Mariel, and trusting and forgiving nature. Although blustery, Carl never complained about Mariel's symptoms. He quickly forgave offenses and moved forward. Aleksandra thought she could likely work with their character strengths to help the couple find "work-arounds" for their most pressing problems.

The couple were low in faith and work, but high in love for each other. They had lost their willpower for change and were not sure how to improve things. This had led them to not work on the relationship for a long time. Yet they were relatively kind to each other and did not devalue each other.

INITIAL PHASE OF TREATMENT

Aleksandra used a thorough assessment, which included screening for depression as well as a collection of relationship measures: Locke-Wallace, the CARE, the Dyadic Trust Measure, screening for violence, affairs and substance abuse. Aleksandra held back on the couple report until she had a conversation with the couple about their goals for counseling in individual intakes. Both partners were unsure what could be gained in couple counseling. After unsuccessful couple enrichment and pastoral counseling, they wondered whether their marriage could be improved. Aleksandra used that opportunity to introduce the "accept the things I cannot change" concept to the couple.

Acceptance theory has been steadily influential in couple's treatment (Lawrence, Eldridge, Christensen & Jacobson, 1999). The theory essentially teaches that more damage is done when partners keep trying to change each other when emotional acceptance of their differences is more appropriate. Acceptance does not include accepting clearly unhealthy offenses such as violence or affairs. Rather, spouses accept the partner's personality, interpersonal style and weaknesses. It is helpful to present acceptance as a positive skill requiring active effort, rather than allowing the couple to default to the incorrect conclusion that acceptance is nothing but a surrender flag. Importantly, from a Christian perspective, acceptance is the extension of grace in the relationship. The other person does not "deserve" to be accepted and loved despite their weaknesses, but is extended grace. When introduced to this concept framed as an effortful application of grace, the couple readily agreed that this approach might be helpful for them.

The couple report focused on increasing the bond of the couple and on forgiveness. By drawing from the BOND and forgiveness interventions, their treatment would avoid skills-oriented treatment that might exacerbate their situation. The treatment plan Aleksandra introduced to them was as follows.

- Week 1: Client feedback; focus on virtues (interventions 6-5, 7-1, 18-9)

- Week 2: Sharing needs card sort (BOND 19-6)

- Week 3: Understanding hurts from the past (BOND 19-7); accepting what has happened

- Week 4: Understanding hurts from the past (continued); mourning losses together

- Week 5: Spiritual intimacy to increase the bond (BOND 19-8)

- Week 6: Healthy ways to get needs met (BOND 19-14)

- Week 7: Apologies and forgiveness habits to protect the relationship (FREE 21-2, 21-3; psychoeducation on forgiveness)

- Week 8: Making amends to rebuild trust (FREE 21-5)

- Week 9: Accepting emotional forgiveness from God and each other (FREE 21-1)

- Week 10: Vow making termination (BOND 19-16)

COURSE OF TREATMENT

Deviations from the treatment plan erupted at session three. Mariel was too threatened by the idea of delving into her past, which was filled with trauma and abuse. She refused to attend the session. Aleksandra reassured the couple of their control—that Aleksandra would not *force* or *coerce* either partner to talk about anything that he or she didn't want to discuss. After that, the couple did come a week later. However, after discussing the fears, Mariel decided to pursue individual psychotherapy with another therapist to focus on her trauma history in parallel with the couple therapy.

Carl and Mariel found many things they needed to accept about each other when dealing with their different needs for spiritual and emotional intimacy. When they began to work on forgiveness, the subject of Carl's use of the internet to access pornography derailed the course of treatment for a few weeks, but Aleksandra emphasized the employment of grace, which made a big impression on both Carl and Mariel. When Carl poured out his frequent struggles to stay away from porn, Aleksandra at one point spontaneously said, "Isn't it hard to be human?" That became an oft-repeated tagline for both Carl and Mariel as they tried to be vehicles of grace for each other. Forgiveness intervention helped solidify those gains. For example, the couple read some stories about grace from *What's So Amazing About Grace?* by Philip Yancey, and Aleksandra had them watch the movie *Les Misérables* for experiential intervention.

Near the end of their originally planned ten weeks of treatment (plus two for assessment), Aleksandra brought to their attention that they were approaching the time they had planned to terminate. Both partners felt that they were not ready to finish counseling yet. Together they decided to move to a monthly format for maintenance of gains as a couple. They decided to come monthly for the following six months to reinforce what they had learned across the 12 weeks of counseling. At the end of that time, they engaged in a vow-making session (BOND 19-16), which they both found to be moving and meaningful.

TURNING POINTS

Three significant turning points occurred in treating Carl and Mariel. The first occurred when the couple attended session three, the week after Mariel refused to come to couple therapy to deal with hurts in the past. When the couple came in, Mariel began to cry almost as she sat down. After Aleksandra calmed her down a bit, she was still crying, but with more controlled tears than the uncontrolled weeping at the outset of the session.

"What do you think has brought this on?" Aleksandra asked Mariel.

"It has always been like this."

"Always?" said Aleksandra.

"Since the abuse. About as long as I remember. It is almost like there was not any past before the abuse. And since then, it has been like a pivotal point for my life, looking back instead of forward."

"It is, it seems, like the balance point of a see-saw, both sides looking toward that common point."

"I think crying is kind of—what do you psychologists call it?—a defensiveness mechanism. If I cried, my abusive uncle did not like it. He'd hit me and yell at me to stop, but when I cried, he did not keep abusing me long. The pig wanted me to like his sex. Maybe when I did not, when I cried, it made him feel impotent, or angry, or irritated. Anyway, pretty soon after I would start crying, he'd get frustrated and hit me a couple of times and leave. I did not cry on purpose, but as I look back now, it seems like my tears protected me."

"I had no idea!" said Carl. "Man, does this explain some things! Always when we have disagreements, Mariel cries. I feel so bad. She's so helpless. I feel like a brute just asking for anything. It is frustrating for me and makes me feel bad about myself. Now, I almost feel worse because I must have triggered some of those horrible memories of when her uncle abused her."

Aleksandra helped them better understand the impact of the history of abuse on their relationship and change their attributions for Mariel's tears to more positive attributions.

The second turning point dealt with their efforts to improve spiritual intimacy. Mariel was just beginning to open up about her past in her individual counseling and it left her feeling vulnerable. By sharing their sense of spiritual growth and change with each other in the session and homework, the couple felt "shored up," which increased their ability to take risks. The perspective taking allowed by this exercise was especially helpful to them. By looking at their long-term existential purposes they gained resources for addressing their current problems.

The third key point in their treatment was an acceptance of their interpersonal needs. Carl had relied too heavily on Mariel for friendship types of needs, having no other friends in his life. He resolved to get involved in a food pantry outreach at his church to increase his friendships with other people. Mariel leaned too heavily on Carl for emotional support when her symptoms of depression arose. She recognized that Carl was not a "warm fuzzy" guy, and she needed to accept that about him. She decided that she needed to go to God in prayer, her friends from church, and her own

counselor when she had symptoms. Aleksandra encouraged her to let Carl
know she was struggling with symptoms and perhaps ask him for prayer
to gain support. But she would disengage from attempting to get him to
be her "counselor." Changing this process appeared to be a key intervention for the couple.

Principles for Treating the "Accept the Things I Cannot Change" Couple

1. Counselors should avoid attempts to "rescue" or "fix" this couple. Their
   problems are chronic. An attitude of acceptance might be a healthier
   response to their issues. Counselor narcissism—in which the counselor
   thinks that he or she can fix a couple's problems when previous attempts
   were ineffective—might be damaging here.

2. Accurate assessment of the problems as chronic issues is vital to proper
   treatment. Indicators of chronicity are that (a) problems are long-
   standing issues, (b) meaningful attempts at change in the past have not
   been fruitful, and (c) there are no pressures or forces in their life to
   predict change.

3. It is important for counselors to model grace with couples like this. The
   resistance of the couple's problems is likely to cause the counselor to have
   negative feelings toward the clients if the counselor has unrealistic goals
   for the couple. Feelings of tenderness, care and grace are good indicators
   that the counselor has a therapeutic attitude toward the couple.

16

The Kitchen Sink Couple

ॐ

A counselor does not have to see very many clients before he or she realizes that couples tend to have layers of problems. The "kitchen sink" couple seems to have all the problems except the kitchen sink—and sometimes the counselor might check to see if the office sink is missing. These partners may be wounded, have a weak bond, lack confidence, have complicating factors, live with psychological disorders and experience high conflict. The difficulty with real couples is they never look like the couples in the textbook. The counselor's task is to integrate the previously discussed treatment plans as well as other treatment options. Typically the moderately severe kitchen sink couple will require a long treatment plan (15 or more sessions).

When couples have many problems, our general strategy is to begin with behavioral types of interventions to help establish stability and safety. Next, we employ bond-focused interventions for couples who are ready to increase their bond. Finally, forgiveness and trust interventions are used for couples who need to learn how to repair their relationship after an offense.

Nancy and Dave with Jon

- Couple often comes with difficulties in multiple areas
- Craft an intervention that combines couple work with specific interventions for most pressing problems
- Focus more time on fewer goals

DAVE AND NANCY

Dave and Nancy had been married for 18 years. They had three children and lived in a rural area sharing property with several of Nancy's family members. Dave commuted an hour to a suburb where he owned a real estate business that specialized in high-priced homes. Nancy home-schooled their children.

The couple had chronic marital problems from the beginning. Nancy was socially awkward with low empathy, poor social skills and negative self-esteem. She was usually flat emotionally. Their counselor, Jon, wondered whether she might have Asperger's disorder, but further exploration indicated that she was more emotionally restricted and flat in personality style rather than someone on the autism spectrum. Dave was extremely social, a real "glad hand." He dressed a bit too nicely for their community, which was due to his underlying weak ego and narcissism. He tended not to respect boundaries with others and became very upset about perceived abandonment. Jon eventually diagnosed him with elements of borderline and narcissistic personality disorders.

The couple had burned through several churches in the community where they would seek help for their marriage and parenting from the leadership, then have numerous crises which drained those leaders. The family would then move to another church. They had a similar pattern with three previous counselors. Their crises generally were just arguments. Their adolescent son had just been convicted of his second DUI and spent three weeks in jail, and his suspended license necessitated the family's help in transporting him to and from his job. He was causing great distress for the family with his burgeoning substance-abuse problem.

JON'S CASE CONCEPTUALIZATION

Jon was like most clinicians when assessment reveals a couple like this. He took a deep breath, uttered a short prayer for wisdom, and reminded himself that he was there to help people with problems. To plan how to help the couple, Jon asked himself important questions after the intake.

What can and cannot they do? He felt that he could help with crisis management and behavioral change because they were motivated at present. He also thought he might help stabilize the couple. He was unsure whether they could successfully manage their emotions, benefit by experiential treatments, or even improve their emotional bond. Their long-standing issues limited them. He elected to start with behaviorally oriented interventions.

What is motivating this couple now? The primary motivation was the son's DUI. The son was already in counseling with a good substance-abuse counselor, who had referred the couple for couple counseling. Jon anticipated that issues of co-parenting might be a primary topic of discussion in treatment.

What is the prognosis? This couple's prognosis was not positive. Their history of multiple helpers who had been unable to help the couple was discouraging. They reported what Jon concluded to have a "push-pull" relationship with help-givers. Jon knew he needed to be steady and reliable in the sessions and to exhibit unflappable compassion and self-control at expected provocations.

Jon thought that the couple was low in faith, work and love. They had some willpower but little "waypower" or wisdom for change. They insisted that there were no real strengths in each other, which Jon thought was diagnostic. However, he wanted to return to character strengths later in treatment as an avenue for growth.

TREATMENT PLAN

- Intervention 1: Feedback report (intervention 7-1); psychoeducation about adolescent substance abuse

- Interventions 2-4: Communication skills for co-parenting; leveling and editing (HOPE 18-2); TANGO intervention (HOPE 18-4)

- Interventions 5-7: Create family conflict boundaries (drawn from substance-abuse literature); stopping negative reciprocity (HOPE 18-15)

- Interventions 8-10: Conflict resolution: LOVE (HOPE 18-5)

- Interventions 11-14: Parenting adolescents program focused on parental monitoring of substance abuse and behavioral interventions for behavioral problems (drawn from substance abuse literature)

- Interventions 15-17: Forgiveness interventions, apologies (FREE 21-3); repair after offenses (FREE 21-5)

- Interventions 18-19: Consolidation of gains; rehearsal of principles learned; prepare for termination return to topics as needed

- Intervention 20: Termination or reassessment for continued treatment (interventions 28-1 and 28-4)

Given the nature of the situation with the family, Jon decided to give this couple a modified hope-focused couple approach report. He typically mapped out for families what the weekly course of counseling would look like. But given the barriers to progress and this couple's history with counseling, he instead used the report to motivate them to invest in counseling differently this time. He gave them a general concept of what would be addressed in counseling strategically. He encouraged them to take an active part in shaping what happened each session, especially given their difficulty in working with helpers. He used weekly feedback to help short-circuit some of their pattern of resistances (see chapter 23). Jon also implemented a weekly parenting check-in page to ensure that there was a focus on behavioral progress in parenting.

COURSE OF TREATMENT

Perhaps not surprisingly, the resistance to change started almost immediately with this couple. The wife was late for counseling by 20 minutes for both first and second sessions. Jon processed this with her. She had a poor view of counseling, blaming previous counselors who were humanistic, listening-focused clinicians with whom she grew frustrated. Dave chimed in that he preferred insight-oriented counseling similar to what they had before though he admitted that it had not worked for them. Jon thought that as counselor, he could be flexible with them but wondered if they could be flexible with each other. They agreed to focus primarily on behavioral change and structured interventions, with occasional "stopping" to develop insight.

They were on time the next week and Jon launched into a high-structure intervention, the TANGO (HOPE 18-4). The couple used the principles from the communication intervention to address parenting their children. However, disagreements erupted about the lack of insight-orientation of the approach. Over the next few weeks, small crises—like their son being arrested for public alcohol consumption at the local mall—"prevented" their using the communication methods at home, but Jon was able to help them use the methods in counseling instead of allowing them to derail counseling with small crises and fights.

The next set of weeks would be focused on handling strong emotions and setting boundaries. Their substance-abusing son in particular was getting his need for attention met in the family by acting out. His behavior was becoming increasingly the target of the couple's arguments and explosive angry outbursts (especially Dave's). This was used as the basis for change—for the couple to become role models for handling anger in the family. Some simple communication rules, such as using "I" statements and time-outs, were the initial family-level interventions. Handling strong emotions had not been addressed as much as Jon would have liked, so he asked the couple about this in the next few sessions. They engaged in self-soothing training (intervention 14-3) and learned how to begin difficult conversations using soft start-up (HURT 20-6).

They began to work on conflict resolution, but Nancy was agitated in the first two sessions though did not share what her agitation was concerning. She then brought out that someone from their conservative Baptist church had criticized their use of psychotherapy with a "nonbiblical" counselor, and this had made her wonder whether they should stop counseling. Dave flew off the handle, and a conflict erupted, with the couple declaring a time-out and ending the session 20 minutes early. But by the next appointment things had settled down, and there were three weeks of calm. Dave and Nancy made good progress on the LOVE intervention, which helped them move toward some resolution of long-existing conflicts over care of Nancy's mother, and parenting interventions drawn from behavioral parenting paradigms and portions of the adolescent STEP (Systematic Training for Effective Parenting) program (Dinkmeyer, McKay & Dinkmeyer, 2007).

The final intervention module for the couple was forgiveness and relationship repair, which lasted four weeks. This started with helping them identify what emotional skills they needed to be able to stop dysfunctional behaviors in their relationship and family. They made attempts to repair the relationship. Most of the session was focused on the kinds of things they have tried to do to repair the relationship in the past. Their conclusion was that most of what they tried has not worked due to lack of reciprocity. One partner would attempt to apologize or act kindly, but the other person would reject the act. Jon had the couple think a good deal of about that process, the costs of that in their family, how their children had picked up on that pattern in relationships, and what might be blocking them from relationship repair. Then Jon spent three sessions helping the couple practice offering an effective apology and accepting it. They explored that pattern in light of earlier insights into their relationship dynamics. This moved them to where they could benefit by a variety of forgiveness interventions (see chapter 21).

The psychotherapy for this family had now lasted for six months. Considering the barriers, there had been good progress overall. There continued to be problems with anger expression and some ineffective parenting practices. Yet the gains from counseling were unlikely to improve the family much more at this point. Jon spent two weeks with the couple reflecting on changes. They talked about accessing community resources to continue their growth (intervention 28-2).

Dave struggled with ending therapy, given his difficulty with perceived abandonment. However, the termination was assisted with Jon continuing his tradition of giving the couple the control of how they would end counseling. At the end, they told Jon they wanted to give him the gift, so they wrote him a moving goodbye letter.

Their oldest son's substance abuse problem had improved considerably. He still had anger issues but had been sober for three months. The couple's conflict had significantly improved according to their weekly self-evaluation. Jon expected they would have further difficulty, due to characterological issues, but they had made meaningful improvement on their family life.

KEY INTERVENTIONS

The first key intervention in helping Nancy and Dave came when their son's arrest at the mall threatened to derail their work on communication. They already had failed to do homework because of crises, so Jon believed that if they allowed the sessions also to be diverted, then the couple's chances of success were miniscule.

After a few minutes of empathic listening Jon said, "You said at the beginning of counseling that you wanted to have high structure and behavioral plans for change in the family. We could spend your time today talking about your son's charges but that would mean we will not move forward on our plans for communication work. Would you like to instead practice your TANGO communication with the topic of the charges?" The directive nature of Jon's statement helped add structure. There was some improvement when the couple used the technique.

Later in counseling, when the church member had criticized their counseling, Dave had lost control of his emotions and the partners had declared a time-out, ending the session early. Jon saw this as the same pattern of behavior that had beset the couple previous times in counseling and in the interruption of the earlier TANGO intervention. He decided to confront the pattern at the beginning of the following session. After checking in with the couple, he found that the week had actually been quite uneventful. Jon dived in.

"I wanted to talk about the session last week."

"Shoot," said Dave.

"We seemed to be making a bit of progress in counseling, and suddenly, a crisis erupted."

"Yeah, I was pretty put-out with being criticized," said Dave.

"Instead of getting into the issue again, I wanted to ask you both to reflect on whether you've seen that pattern before."

For at least a minute and a half, silence stretched out. Its pressure was palpable. Nancy finally said, "I guess it was like the time when our son got arrested in the mall."

"Yeah," Dave jumped in. "That crisis threatened to interrupt our work on communication."

Jon said, "How did that turn out?"

"We decided that we would keep working on the communication but communicate about the arrest. We kind of compromised."

Jon said, "So you are saying that we were making progress and then you got side-tracked from the progress by a crisis."

"Almost. We almost got side-tracked."

"And how did you get back on track?" asked Jon.

"We did not let the crisis actually reroute us," said Dave. "You helped us see that we could keep our focus and still pay attention to the crisis."

"What happened last week?"

Dave answered again. "We used one of the methods you've taught us, the time-out, and it kept us from getting into a shouting match."

Nancy said, "But we did let the crisis get us off-track and we left the session early."

"Hmm," said Jon.

Dave said thoughtfully, "I guess even though I was proud about the time-out, we did get side-tracked. That probably was not an all-good solution."

"We've done this with other counselors too," said Nancy.

"Tell me about those," said Jon. The couple recounted three other incidences when crises had changed their focus away from making gains in their relationship. They drew a conclusion.

"I think," said Dave, "that we are always going to have crises. They seem to have stalked us for years. But we need to keep our eye on the ball a bit more if we want to get better as a couple.

FINAL NOTE

The prognosis for this type of couple at intake phase of treatment is poor. This case included a full treatment plan across a considerable amount of time. Many kitchen sink couples would not be able to engage in the level of treatment they need for change to occur. This type of couple is truly a case of the poor becoming poorer with high risk for persistent dysfunction and dissolution of the relationship.

Clinicians should monitor their own counselor narcissism with couples like this so that they do not become discouraged when these couples cancel sessions or withdraw early from treatment. Predicting that the couple may have difficulty with the things that will make counseling effective (consistent attendance, being vulnerable in meetings, trying new things, trusting the counselor or finding space in their life to do work at home) can help but is no guarantee of success. The Christian counselor can trust that God has a plan for every life and act out of an abundance of grace toward the kitchen sink couple. They truly are "the least of these."

PRINCIPLES FOR TREATING THE KITCHEN SINK COUPLE

1. Couples with multiple chronic problems tend to need longer-term treatment, but often have difficulty committing to a longer course of counseling. Don't take it personally if dropout rates are high.

2. Counseling may need to integrate other empirically supported treatment modalities along with the hope-focused couple approach. This case used the example of parenting issues and substance abuse, but other cases may have additional issues that would respond well to integrated treatment. If a counselor lacks the background or training to conduct this kind of treatment, then a referral for additional counseling may be needed.

3. This type of couple will often have traits of other types of couples and be high in resistances and roadblocks. A creative plan for the couple is helpful. However, beginning with basic, simple, behavioral interventions is often necessary to match the couple's level of need. The inclusion of more difficult skills such as BOND or forgiveness interventions would be predicated on some success with simple interventions.

4. This type of couple often has traits that cause a counselor to have negative feelings toward the partners. See chapter 25, which deals with negative reactions to clients and offers some principles to assist when this problem arises.

Part Four

INTERVENTIONS WITHIN THE SESSIONS

This section is the heart of the book. The following chapters describe many interventions (many of which have multiple steps, each of which might even be considered another intervention itself). We have described each intervention, giving enough theory for you to understand why we are doing what we do, but focusing on exactly how to do each step of the intervention. Most of these interventions are new to this book, but updated essentials (labeled *HF Classic* (*hf*)) from *Hope-Focused Marriage Counseling* (Worthington, 2005) are also included. Whereas we believe you can be greatly enriched by the previous book (and we recommend it to you), we also want to make sure you know that the present book can live and thrive on its own. With both books in hand, you are truly well-armed to intervene with many couples.

17

Session Management

҉

This chapter describes a typical session using the hope-focused couple approach. Sessions will typically have four components. To help with our memory, we use the mnemonic device RILY: *review, intervention, lack of fit* and *your plan.*

The typical hope-focused couple approach counseling session involves an in-depth assessment period at the beginning of counseling involving written assessments and dyadic and individual meetings. A report is written and reviewed with the couple to focus counseling on the areas of the relationship and interventions that are the best match for their needs. At this point, the counseling sessions should follow a rhythm of change that helps the couple know what to expect and to emphasize the important keys to change.

Session Management: RILY
Review. Review the week, repair any damage to the relationship and request their homework.
Intervention. Implement the planned intervention.
Lack of fit. Check to ensure there is a fit between the intervention and goals. If not fitting, explore why and adjust interventions.
Your plan. Say yes to homework for the coming week.

REVIEW

Should we take a detour? The session opens with greeting the couple and checking in on their week. Some counselors do this verbally, but many use a paper questionnaire at the beginning of each session when couples check in at the front desk. The questions ask for a general relationship "temperature" for the past week and whether the couple has engaged in any relationship-improvement actions through homework or under their initiative. An example of a form specific to the hope-focused couple approach is provided in chapter 23.

There is a very real possibility that relationship or life stressors might have detoured the carefully constructed plans for improving the couple's relationship that you and they devised in collaboration during the previous session. Life happens. And it happens more to some couples than others. What should the counselor do?

Making the decision. Deciding whether to take a side-trail in the journey of counseling is not easy. For some couples, staying on track with plans for the relationship is the healthier decision. In other cases, you have to deal with the legitimate crisis. In still other cases, crises are an indication that the plan you are pursuing needs to be jettisoned and you need to refocus.

All detours should be discussed with the couple, giving them primary control over their treatment. For example, it may be that the detour reflects an assumption by one or both partners that counseling will not be effective. The couple might have deep underlying fears about facing issues in counseling that cause them to throw up defenses by "tanking" the counseling session. The counselor needs to dig deep and address the couple with compassion. The fears must be profound.

When a flood of conflict arrives in the office. Another common detour occurs when a couple has an argument that spills over into the counseling session. The counselor in that situation would be wise to help the couple review their history of arguments to see whether there is a pattern behind these "floods" in their relationship. If the couple is flooded in the session then it may be difficult even to have this conversation. In this case the counselor has little choice but to help the couple "swim for shore" and bring down the flood of negative emotions. Occasionally a couple is so flooded with negative emotions in the session that it must be cancelled. This should be avoided if the partners are even minimally willing to stick with the counselor through the session. The emotional flooding in session can be reframed as an opportunity to practice self-soothing. However, if the couple is intent on hurting and offending each other, then a time-out may be needed, even if it means canceling the session.

Written report and treatment plan to the rescue. On a practical level, the treatment plan designed at the beginning of counseling can help couples decide how to proceed with any possible detour. The counselor can pull out the treatment plan and ask the couple whether they would like to address the detour today instead of going with the plan, or ask whether they would like to add an extra session either that week or later to the plan. This gives the couple an informed choice. It lets them see the consequences of taking detours in counseling. Even a few detours can turn short-term counseling into longer-term counseling or shift counseling far from its original destination.

Review of homework and effort to improve the relationship. After the check in, the counselor should ask the couple what they did that week at home to improve their relationship. The counselor should ask "What did your partner do this week to improve your relationship?" "What did you do?" By asking a broad question, it allows the couple to reflect on their and their partner's efforts.

The improvement may have been in planned homework, or they might have done additional things. It is crucial to reinforce any efforts they are making to improve their relationship. It is common in troubled couples for partners not to notice when their partner is making efforts to change. Thus the discussion also helps to highlight this for each partner. For couples for whom the counselor is using basic or behavioral approaches to treatment, it might be useful to create a weekly journal or log of change efforts.

The discussion can then focus more specifically on whether they did any homework that had been agreed on during the previous session. For many counselors this is their least favorite moment of the session because it often seems that couples do not do planned homework more often than they actually do it.

Homework is more important than sessions. When couples do not do the homework, some counselors make a general statement like, "It would be good to do that homework this week. It is really important." After that cursory admonishment, they move on to the intervention planned for the week. We liken this to a physician who has a patient with diabetes. The patient says, "No, I did not take my insulin as you told me to this week." What is the physician to do? It would not be sufficient to say, "Well, make sure you start using it correctly now." The chances that the diabetic patient will change without a medical emergency are small.

This permissive message is actually just saying, "Taking your medication [or doing your homework] is not *that* important." Instead, it is crucial that the counselor is convinced that what happens in the homework is actually *more* important than what happens in the session. This can be hard to conceive for a psychotherapist who has been trained in psychoanalytically informed or interpersonal psychotherapies. Those therapies see in-session counselor behaviors as reparenting, providing corrective emotional experiences, or making unanticipated social responses that dislodge a person from rigid behaviors.

We believe this is erroneous thinking especially when it is applied to couple counseling. It suggests somehow that the relationship with the counselor based on one hour a week for a time-limited contract will somehow outweigh the importance of the relationship with the spouse or partner with whom one might be spending the rest of one's life. In couple counseling, this overinflates the role of the counselor. It simultaneously disempowers the couple's activity in finding solutions to their own problems. What the couple does at home in those 167 hours not in the counselor's office each week is where the action is.

Why aren't they doing the homework? Counselors should review the plan for the homework to determine whether the problem is due to a lack of *willpower, waypower* or *wisdom*. Lack of "waypower" is the simplest problem. This means that the couple did not understand *how* to do the homework. Perhaps the ideas were reviewed too quickly or not at a level of understanding that the couple could grasp. The couple and counselor should explore whether this was the reason that the couple did not do the agreed-on homework.

Lack of willpower is likely the most difficult problem. This suggests that the couple did not have the motivation to carry out the homework. Why? Usually because the rewards seemed insufficient. Many couples early in counseling still lack willpower because their hope for change is minimal. If this is the case with a couple, then it is important to talk about their concerns. The discussion must focus on their barriers for relationship change and concerns over whether counseling can help them. Barriers for change are as varied as couples—over-busy lives; emotional fears; energy expended for other problems like family issues; psychopathology; health problems. Some barriers to change, such as one partner's psychopathology, might need separate interventions. Some barriers might require a sacrifice such as cutting back work hours or hiring a sitter for date nights. Other barriers will simply need to be discussed, brought out into the open for the couple to find a strategy to not allow it to stop them from reaching their goals. These barriers boil down to two simple questions that the counselor should ask: (1) "What was not perceived to be rewarding about the homework, or what was perceived to be costly about it? (2) "What attractive and competing behavior was more rewarding or less costly?"

Some couples are not sure whether counseling will be able to help them. For these couples, a frequent discussion should take place about what is working for them in counseling and what else they need. The counselor must be humble and open-minded about shifting the approach to meet the needs of the couple.

Finally, lack of *wisdom* can be the source of the problem on two levels. *Practical wisdom* is the ability to know what to do in a situation. The first problem is that a couple may not be matching what they are learning in sessions with the problems they are facing at home. It is common for a couple to have a breakdown in communication at home and forget to apply the communication principles they have learned and practiced in sessions. Counselors can help couples with this by not blaming the couple for the failure but simply helping the couple develop specific plans for using the principles the next time they face a problem at home.

The second problem with wisdom is a failure in the *wisdom of patience* in response to their problems. At times the couple's expectation for change needs to be adjusted. Counseling is effective. However, many couples expect the counselor "fix" them or their spouse in three easy sessions or change 30-year patterns of dysfunction in ten one-hour sessions—both without much effort on their part. They think of counseling as a magic pill or miracle cure. Instead, the counselor can address the expectations with metaphors for change like diet, exercise, physical therapy for injury, going to college to obtain education, or engaging in spiritual practices and disciplines. Couple counseling is similar to those processes—it is limited in its effects, takes time and requires the active participation of the couple. Without awareness that counseling is not a cure-all and that it takes time and requires effort, couples will not succeed in making their relationships better.

The couple who do not do their homework—whether from failure in waypower, willpower or wisdom—might actually be in the contemplation stage of change (Bradford, 2012), weighing the costs and benefits of engaging in the work. This could be discussed in sessions. Within the discussion, the counselor should express compassion for both partners' feelings about the amount of work necessary to see real change. The counselor should take an unbiased stance on change. The couple can choose not to work on their relationship and maintain things as they are or to work on their relationship and improve things. It is up to them. This allows the couple to make the leap to the preparation or action stage of change without feeling coerced.

INTERVENTION

The hope-focused couple approach has responded to research on couple counseling that indicates that a more structured and somewhat directive approach to counseling predicts better outcomes (Owen, Duncan, Anker & Sparks, 2012; M. J. Scheel, 2010). Couple counseling that utilizes only good listening techniques is usually ineffective, and at best inefficient, in helping couples change their relationship. Couple problems are often extensive and persistent, and have multiple causes. A ready source exists to blame for lack of progress— the partner. So an active counselor with a plan of action that the couple buy into is a key to best possible outcomes. Thus it is important to select interventions that will help to make the work of counseling clear, memorable and undeniable.

Introduce the intervention. Describing the intervention to the couple in a way that matches their experience in counseling is important. Couples that are new to the role of client and have not had much exposure to psychology in general will need more concrete explanation of interventions. They will likely need even a demonstration if possible.

The counselor's role during interventions is that of coach. The couple is supposed to be doing the work of using the intervention to improve their relationship. Like a coach, the counselor helps explain, motivate, demonstrate and evaluate how well the intervention is working. Like a coach, the counselor does not rush onto the playing field and start playing the game. A typical script for a counselor introducing a new intervention might sound something like this:

> Today we are going to try a new intervention to help with the sense of disconnect that you said you wanted to work on in counseling. Is that something

you would be okay with working on today? [If they agree, move forward.]

> So what we're going to do is use the room here as a metaphor for how close you feel to each other. We're all going to stand up to do this. If you feel very distant from each other, then you will stand far apart from each other in the room. If you feel very warm and close, then you will stand right next to each other in the middle of the room. Do you understand what I am saying? [If they agree, move forward, or answer questions.] So we'll start with you just doing that right now. Move to the degree of separation or closeness that indicates how close or far apart you feel from each other at this moment. Would you do that now?

Translate the closeness or distance onto a number scale. For example, you might say,

> So if this room represented a scale from 0 closeness, with each of your backs to the wall, to 10 as perfect closeness, with you hugging in the center, you look like you have placed yourself at about a . . . ? [Pause and wait for the couple to fill in a number.]

Implement and reflect on the intervention. The intervention would move forward from that point. In the case of the illustration above, you would talk with the couple about events, behaviors, words and actions that cause them to feel closer to each other or further apart. As you sense that their feelings of closeness or distance are changing, you would ask them to reposition themselves. This is just one example of an intervention, but this book is full of possible interventions that would be used in session.

LACK OF FIT?

At the end of the intervention, you would ask them to sit down and talk about what just happened. Ask them to reflect on what they experienced and were learning in the exercise. It is important to check in on whether the intervention was helpful to them and whether they can think of an adjustment to it that might make it more helpful. To sharpen the point, end the exercise with a brief summary like, "So you have found that you each have the power to affect how close or distant you feel toward each other based on what you choose to do or talk about."

Reflect on their progress. We recommend a weekly evaluation of the couple's progress. In physical therapy for an injury, the physical therapist checks in weekly on the pain, mobility and muscle strength of the patient. In a weight loss program, weight is taken weekly. For a couple in counseling, check on how well their relationship is doing overall and on specific goals.

A reflection on what is or is not working in counseling is also crucial. There is considerable evidence that the process of review and evaluation of the counseling will actually improve the efficacy of counseling (Owen et al., 2012). Clients need to be empowered to voice their needs repeatedly in sessions. By voicing their needs, they become more active participants in their treatment. They also have more buy in. Many common issues of power and control are diffused. An effective counselor may say something like, "You are the expert in your life and experiences. I have expertise in helping people in general. Let's see how we're doing together as a team."

If the homework plans and reflection time are handled effectively, then problems with enacting change outside of the session can be minimized. It does not mean there won't still be roadblocks within sessions. But the odds begin to favor the couple meeting their goals.

Your Plan

Couples often have difficulty transferring what they learn in session to home. So the counselor should spend time considering how they might continue to work on this goal at home using the principles they learned or other creative ideas. Some interventions can readily be implemented just the same at home as they were in session. Other interventions do not easily translate to the home environment. In that case, discuss the underlying principles of the intervention. Talk with the couple to help create things they can do at home to put work into improving their relationship. To make it clear, it is best to write down what they plan to do. You can use either a form you create or, if simple, the back of the appointment card.

Is the intervention used at home? Those clients not yet in the action stage of change and those with many roadblocks and detours will need simple plans for intervention. They also need more practice. In contrast, other couples can implement even complex interventions. It is wise to discuss time utilization with the couple. They usually want to use the time (which is generally expensive for them) effectively—and sometimes they think this means cursory exposure to many interventions—even though they never use the interventions at home. Instead of operating on a "more is better" principle, clinicians must maintain that an intervention not used at home is not helpful.

Progress. Counseling is more like Daniel Boone exploring the wilderness than taking a wagon train on a clearly marked trail. Exploration has a plan, but the terrain might necessitate retracing steps, skirting blockages, and moving in fits and starts. It is important not to be too rigid with the schedule because detours can sometimes turn out to be the most significant experiences.

18

HOPE Interventions

≈♠

The hope-focused couple approach has historically had two strategies for change (Worthington, 2005). The two approaches are HOPE (Handling Our Problems Effectively), covered in this chapter, and FREE (Forgiveness and Reconciliation through Experiencing Empathy), which is covered in chapter twenty-one. The HOPE interventions generally offer skills or behavior-based interventions. We retain skills and behavioral interventions because:

1. Many couples need higher structure and direction in the first stages of intervention.

2. These interventions tend to produce the obvious "quick" change that helps to promote hope in couples that counseling will be effective for them.

3. Many couples come to counseling saying that "communication" is the problem in their relationship, and these interventions help with communication in some way.

4. Some couples have few internal resources available for counseling and will need behavioral-oriented treatment for best outcomes.

Starting counseling with skills and behavioral types of interventions allows the counselor to continue to assess the couple's abilities, how quickly they are changing, and what resistances and roadblocks they will face.

HOPE interventions focus on behaviors, which may appear to be highly congruent with Christian beliefs. However, what God seeks in his creation is much bigger than correct behaviors. He desires a heart, mind and body that follow hard after him. For example, in Acts 13:22 David is described as a man after God's own heart because his internal orientation and emotions were bonded to God, even if many of his behaviors were not righteous. The behavior is what we as humans can understand, because we can see it. We can see the couple who stop to listen, attempt to show their love with a gift, or pray for their marriage. Only God can see the heart bond and hidden intentions behind the behaviors. Even the partners might have difficulty understanding the ever-changing nature of their own intentions in their relationship. On the other hand, behaviors are not unimportant. Behaviors are also all that partners see when they are trying to understand each other, cooperate and show their love. It can be helpful for the counselor with a Christian couple to point out that the internal heart bond can be strong even if there are lapses in good relationship behaviors at times. The biblical example of David can be helpful. (Note, though, that sometimes couples are threatened by infidelity as one of King David's behavioral failings.)

The biblical truth that the internal heart bond is very important is reflected in research on behavioral interventions. There is some consensus now in recent literature that skills and behavioral-oriented interventions for couples help people; however, they help because they improve people's attachment or bond, not because they teach couples something they did not know previously (Furrow & Bradley, 2011; Furrow, Edwards, Choi & Bradley, 2012). We can think of skills and behavioral-oriented interventions as practicing free throws in basketball. Every practice one might shoot 100 free throws. This essentially "burns" deep memory grooves in the brain and body so that shooting free throws is automatic. The great basketball player can simply think, "free throw" and the body and brain do their work, putting the ball in the hoop most of the time. This is true even when the championship is on the line.

Learning relationship skills in session and practicing them in the context of the couple's unique relationship at home is similar to learning any skill or developing any virtue. However, just like a basketball player, the couple need to practice the skills frequently and consistently before they can be used effortlessly. Most couples do not often practice good relationship skills. Given that reality, it is important that the skills they are practicing are simple enough to benefit them even by less-than-perfect practice. Also, they must be able to implement the skills at the right time. Many of the HOPE interventions in this chapter are intentionally simple. Couples can practice them repeatedly in a session and at home. In working with communication and conflict-resolution skills, the counselor should always keep in mind they are a *means to an end* of improving the bond for the couple. Think of these HOPE exercises—and indeed all of the exercises in the following chapters— as drills that will become useful in the "game" of a couple's life together.

HOPE Intervention 18-1: Simple Listen and Repeat

This intervention is the most simple communication skill. It is useful when there is limited time or when the couple has limited abilities. It can be the building block for more complex skills.

This exercise works best if the counselor helps the couple select a manageable topic. Something they feel "hot" about should be avoided so that they can learn the skills. (Just as you would not try to learn to shoot and play defense against LeBron James!) In fact, this works best if the topic is some stressor, concern or decision relevant to a part of their life *other than their relationship,* such as stress at work.

Speaker. Designate one person as the speaker and one person as the listener. The speaker talks about something he or she wants the partner to know about him or her. The talking should be between one and two minutes. There are some rules for the speaker. Sometimes, if you have partners create their own rules, the rule making process can be an effective intervention itself. Couples can even make a reminder card of their rules with a simple piece of cut cardstock and a magnet to keep on their fridge. Creating the magnet significantly helps the rules be more "sticky" or memorable for the couple during the week and into the future.

Listener. The listener's job is to listen for what the partner is really trying to say to them. Then they repeat or reflect back what they hear, like a mirror. If sharing talk time is difficult for the couple, then an object can be held by the listener and exchanged as they change roles (e.g., the rules card, a stress ball or anything handy that would not cause damage if thrown!).

Virtues: self-control, perseverance, gentleness, patience, risk taking

Goal: To improve the bond between the partners by increasing their understanding and respect in communication and by decreasing negativity.

Example rules for the speaker: Speak the truth in love. Whatever is said should be both true and loving. No criticizing, no refusing to talk, no blaming, no putting the other person down and no yelling.

Example rules for the listener: Be slow to speak and quick to listen. Do not interrupt, no nonverbal negativity, look at the person and try to understand their way of seeing things.

HOPE INTERVENTION 18-2: SIMPLE LEVELING AND EDITING (hf)

This intervention teaches couples when to be "on the level" in divulging their heart's desires to each other, and when to "edit" or hold back putting their thoughts into words in communication. The couple can use personal strengths and virtues to help them work through this skill.

The couple should first discuss when in their communication they should "level" and when they should "edit" their conversation. Understanding this can be more powerful if they bring up a communication breakdown that occurred recently and are able to apply the principle to the specific case.

Generally the couple will then have a conversation together and apply the leveling and editing principle with the counselor coaching them. To kick the experience up a notch the counselor could videotape the couple in their communication and have them review the tape with an eye toward how well they were on the level or editing.

Many couples—especially conflicted couples—struggle more with editing than with leveling. They may have an underlying belief that they should tell their partner everything they think, even if it is hurtful to them. Sensitivity, restraint, choosing words wisely and love (i.e., valuing and not devaluing the partner) fall by the wayside. The counselor can help a couple think through the positive and negative consequences of the "completely honest" rule. For Christian couples, the Scripture that urges believers to "speak the truth in love" (Eph 4:15) can be a guiding principle for communication with this technique.

Virtues: self-control, wisdom/prudence, compassion, love, gentleness, honesty

Principle: Help couples identify circumstances where leveling or editing are needed in their communication. Provide a relational boundary against hurtful conversations or withdrawal from communication.

HOPE INTERVENTION 18-3: LOVE BUSTERS (hf)

The "love busters" intervention teaches couples to identify negative triggers in their relationship. Common examples are: "You always ignore me," "You're selfish, just like your father," "I'm leaving you," or simply refusing to talk or stone-walling. The concept of love busters was developed by Willard

Harley (2008). If this is a particular area of focus for counseling, the couple might want to read the book to support the counseling work.

After identifying love busters, the couple work to create a strategy to avoid them. Just identifying triggers can be an important skill for a couple to develop. This technique works best for couples who are either early in their relationship or not entrenched in high-octane negative reciprocity. It may seem that doing love busters with high conflict couples would match their needs. However, the counselor should be cautious. Partners who have trouble controlling the emotional conflict often use what they learn through this exercise as ammunition for their next battle. A good assessment of the couple regarding their ability to "edit" themselves is important before deciding to use this intervention. A number of virtues can be used as a resource to help the couple as they learn this skill. Reminding them of their personal strengths and virtues can assist in improving motivation.

Step 1: Identify "love busters" that have occurred. This should be done gently and when the couple is calm. If they appear to become activated with anger at the memories then the counselor should stop and process with the partners. It is not necessary to list every "bust" in their relationship, just some that are relevant.

Step 2: Talk about what was happening in the context of the "love bust." Were there circumstances that helped contribute to the offensive act? Was the time especially stressful? Identifying the circumstances or context is important to helping the couple identify high risk times, situations or topics in their relationship.

Step 3: Discuss how to avoid offending each other with love busts. Generally couples should be discussing times when they might want to stop a bust. It's helpful to examine what nonverbal or verbal cues would indicate when a redirect or a time-out might be needed. The couple can be creative and develop their own strategy for handling love busts.

Step 4: When the inevitable love bust happens the couple need to discuss ways to repair the damage. This step may be paired in time with an apology or forgiveness intervention (chapters 20-21) if the couple needs the support. Some couples will be able to find natural ways of repairing their relationship after a love bust.

Virtues: gentleness, love, forbearance, temperance, humility, self-control
Principle: Couples identifying love-busting as a problem in their rela-

tionship will reduce their attacks and putdowns. Couples then discuss strategies for refraining from love-busting.

HOPE INTERVENTION 18-4: TANGO COMMUNICATION SKILLS

This communication skills exercise involves a speaker-listener technique to improve communication. It is one step up in complexity from the simple listen and repeat (HOPE 18-1) in that it gives directives on what the speaker and listener should say. This intervention was originally inspired by the Communication Wheel (Jakubowski, Milne, Brunner & Miller, 2004; Miller, Wackman & Nunnally, 1983), which also inspired the STEPS intervention in the 2005 hope-focused book. TANGO has been researched as a part of the hope-focused couple approach in clinical studies and has been reported on an exit questionnaire to be the most well-liked intervention (Ripley et al., 2013). In qualitative follow-up interviews, some couples reported that they continue using the actual five steps of the TANGO; however, most work to incorporate the principles of the technique more naturally.

The TANGO is a method of teaching communication skills that helps people understand each other's meanings. It teaches couples to use a script for good communication to guide what to say. However, *the specific steps for the intervention are not the important part of the intervention.* What is important is that the couple learn the principles for good communication. Therefore, clinicians should not concern themselves with the couple being good at following each step, but in being able to incorporate the principles naturally into their relationship. Personal virtues can be used to help the couple focus on positive interactions and behaviors.

Step 1: Review the "rules" for TANGO. These are actually principles for good communication:

- Take turns talking
- Really listen to your partner, and do not just think of the next thing you'll say
- Slow down the conversation
- Infuse difficult conversations with loving statements
- Do not make assumptions; make sure you understand each other

Step 2: Coach them through the steps. To coach them through the technique, everyone should stand up, which involves gross body movement rather than merely talking. People retain more when more modalities are employed. We have found that many couples need the clinician to role play how to do the TANGO parts of the exercise so they can succeed at it in a brief training time.

Help the couple choose a topic. It should be a topic that is something they really do need to communicate about but not something that will cause them to emotionally flood. The selection of the topic is very important and can cause the exercise to be effective if selected well or ineffective if too "hot."

As a coach, the counselor should:

- Step in and assist but not be controlling or ever put the couple down for their difficulty learning to communicate
- Encourage them to state things simply and with care in their voices and nonverbal behaviors
- Ask them how they feel when they are listened to
- See if this feels better for them than their usual communication at home. Ask them what, in the TANGO, helps them communicate well
- Say that this is to help them learn the elements of good communication. Emphasize that once they are comfortable with the method, they will just employ the principles, not the artificial elements of the method

Step 3: Once coached, have the couple practice communicating using the TANGO on their own for eight to ten minutes. Video record them if you can. Then stop them and review how well they felt they did the skill. It is often helpful to have a printed card or magnet to give them with the five steps and five rules from the TANGO (see figure 18.1). A copy of this card can be downloaded and printed from hopecouples.com.

Step 4: Context. Discuss times in their relationship when they might need to use the TANGO in all of its detail. Typically this might be when there is going to be a difficult conversation, something that has been hurtful in the past, or if they are feeling disconnected from each other. They can reflect on how the exercise of doing the TANGO created a situation where they were able to communicate with each other better than they had in the past.

Step 5: Homework. Encourage the couple to practice the TANGO daily at home for 10-15 minutes. Help them consider times and places where it might be convenient to use it—for example, on a car ride, over a meal, or during a quiet moment in the evening.

TANGO— *for communication*

* **Tell what happened**—*directly and briefly.*

* **Affected me**—*it affected me . . .(feelings)*

* **Nurturing and valuing statement.**

* **Get it?** *Reflect what heard to make sure you understood.*

* **Observe** *how this conversation is affecting you both right now.*

THE RULES

1. Take turns being the leader of this dance. Only one speaker (**TAN**) and listener (**GO**) at a time.

2. Be brief when you're the speaker.

3. Don't try to solve the problem. Just work to understand the other person's perspective, feelings and hopes for the issue.

4. If either of you feel emotionally flooded, take a break and cool down.

5. Affection, valuing statements and tender touch is needed. Being positive will make the conversation go well.

Figure 18.1

Virtues: temperance, compassion, love, gentleness, honesty, self-control, prudence/wisdom

Principle: Communication principles can be learned through an exercise that creates a strong situation that promotes good communication. Creating the situation of good communication with rehearsal and reflection allows the couple to build skills with hope that they can improve their relationship.

Jen's video demonstration of the TANGO intervention can be viewed at hopecouples.com.

HOPE INTERVENTION 18-5: LOVE (hf)

LOVE is an exercise that teaches principles of healthy conflict resolution. This is one of the classic and well-researched components of the hope-focused couple approach (Worthington, Ripley, Hook & Miller, 2007). *L* stands for *listen and repeat; O* stands for *observe effects; V* stands for *value your partner;* and *E* stands for *evaluate common interests.* A reminder card is available to print from hopecouples.com (see figure 18.2).

LOVE— *for problem solving*

- **Listen and repeat**—*keep it brief and repeat to show you understand.*

- **Observe effects**—*how is this conversation affecting you both right now?*

- **Value Partner**—*tell your partner what you value, love, and admire about them.*

- **Evaluate common interests**—*what goals and motives do you both share?*

Figure 18.2

The *E* portion of the intervention is built on principles from the Harvard Negotiation Project (Fisher, Ury & Patton, 2011). This intervention has not changed much since *Hope-Focused Marriage Counseling*, so we will only highlight key components of it here.

As Christians, we believe that the LOVE intervention is an extension of grace in the midst of conflict. Neither partner deserves the grace, it is offered out of the love and compassion of the one giving it. Jim Sells (Sells, Beckenbach & Patrick, 2009) has proposed that grace is the necessary ingredient to help couples traverse through conflict without harming their relationship. The LOVE intervention is a practical means to achieve grace in conflict.

Step 1: Discuss conflicts as having two categories: solvable and perpetual. Perpetual problems are issues that have come up repeatedly in the relationship, often from early on. It may be something that never seems to lead to solutions. Couples can also tell it is a perpetual issue because as they discuss it more, they become more committed to their personal point of view rather than moving toward understanding and compromise. Solvable problems are issues on which partners have a good chance of coming to a resolution. Have the partners discuss this concept, applying it to things in their experience.

Examples of solvable problems: where to go on vacation, whether to take a new job, how to be more affectionate in their relationship, how to divide housework.

Examples of (often) perpetual problems: Having an introverted personality, health problems, being messy, wanting to have independence in the relationship. Many personal chronic problems, like chronic depression, are perpetual. There may also be conflicts in the relationship—such as who has power over which decisions—that have become perpetual. It is helpful for partners to understand that conflict *resolution* may not be an effective intervention for perpetual problems. Rather, they may need to work on acceptance for perpetual problems (see HURT 20-1).

Step 2: Review the LOVE principles. LOVE is really four interventions packaged together as one.

L stands for *listen,* which is HOPE intervention 18-1 from the present chapter.

O stands for *observe your effects.* The couple is directed to pay attention to verbal and nonverbal indicators that the discussion is or is not going in the preferred direction. The counselor can discuss with the couple what cues warn them that they need to slow down the conversation, use more positivity or take a time-out.

V stands for *value your partner.* Partners discuss how they can value, respect and show love or compassion for their partner in the middle of a disagreement or conflict. This is the opposite of a discussion about love busters.

E stands for *evaluate common interests.* Whenever there is a disagreement between two people, there are usually common interests. Positions might be staked out, which each person believes is the best or only way to meet his or her interests. Positions often disagree, but there might still be common interests that can be met in win-win agreements. A position might be something like "I want to go to the Bahamas for our vacation," while an interest would be something like "I want to spend relaxing, enjoyable and warm time together to increase the bonds of our family." A win-win solution could easily be agreed on if the partners identified their interests.

The most powerful interests are basic human needs (Fisher, Ury & Patton, 2011):

- Security (economic and psychological well-being)

- Belonging (bonds, guidance)
- Recognition (attention, valuing)
- Control (freedom to make decisions)

Look for basic human needs as the interests behind the positions. Share these four needs with the couple and see whether they can identify what needs might be behind their stance on a conflict.

For example, if a couple is disagreeing about how much time the wife should spend working, then there are interests behind their positions. If the husband wants the wife to work fewer hours, then perhaps his interests include her having enough time and energy for household responsibilities (security), not seeing his wife stressed out (belonging), and feeling important to her (recognition). If the wife wants to work more hours, then perhaps her interests include providing for the family (security) and performing well at her job (recognition). If the couple can *softly* share their interests, they may find they agree on the interests—or at least that their interests are compatible.

Step 3: Coach the couple through the LOVE acronym with a real life problem. If there is time, ask whether they want to discuss an issue using the LOVE principles on their own without your involvement. Videoing this discussion and having the couple view it is optional.

Step 4: Discuss how the LOVE intervention went for them. Here are four questions you might use.

1. Did you feel like you listened to your partner?
2. Were you able to observe what was going on during the conversation?
3. Did you express yourself in a valuing way to your partner?
4. Did you feel like you engaged in finding solutions that would meet both of your real interests in the situation?

Any "no" to these questions is simply an opportunity for growth and change. So be sure to use positive frames and language to help the couple learn new skills for problem solving.

Step 5: Discuss how to apply the intervention at home. The couple may need to have a conversation about how the LOVE principles can be used naturally at home. They may alter the intervention. That is okay as long as the principles of LOVE are used.

Virtues: prudence/wisdom, courage, love, humility, gentleness, honesty

Principle: Resolving conflicts uses the following principles: distinguishing perpetual versus solvable problems (with solvable problems responding better to conflict-resolution intervention), listening well, observing the effects of the conflict and attempts at resolution, valuing each other, and understanding underlying interests in conflicts.

HOPE INTERVENTION 18-6: TANGO-E

This alternative intervention blends the principles of communication skills and conflict resolution into a more complex single exercise. This intervention is often used when a couple has more capacity to move quickly, so can handle addressing more principles at once. Other couples who have done both TANGO and LOVE often find that time to put the principles of communication and conflict resolution together are helpful to them. To implement TANGO-E, the counselor uses the same intervention as the TANGO but adds the "evaluate common interests" step of LOVE for an intervention that incorporates communication and conflict-resolution skills together.

HOPE INTERVENTION 18-7: PRAYER INTERVENTIONS

There is a line of research indicating that couple prayer can be enriching and protective to couples as an intervention (Lambert, Fincham, LaVallee & Brantley, 2012). However, clinicians should be wise in the implementation of something as powerful as prayer because there are relational and spiritual implications. Virtue intervention 3-3 described using prayer for the couple's wisdom and virtues to provide what they need for changing their relationship. This intervention more broadly includes prayer for any issue for the couple.

Informed consent. Deciding whether and how to pray for a couple has ethical and practical implications all counselors should be aware of. Some counseling roles, such as pastoral counselor, may assume that religious practices like prayer will be a part of counseling. But not all couples will be aware of this. So, in order to be ethical, we recommend an *informed consent* from both partners that they agree to use prayer in their treatment.

Counselors who use prayer often may want to add a statement to their informed consent form such as this:

> At times, clients want to use religious or spiritual practices alongside their counseling work. This is called "spiritually integrated" counseling. I can offer spiritually integrated counseling if you would like that. For me to be ethical,

it is important that you clearly communicate to me your practices, beliefs and spiritual needs. I want to support your desires to the extent I am able. If you both wish for us to spiritually integrate your counseling, I will work with your traditions and practices as much as I can.

If a couple or partner presents for counseling with a different religious tradition than the therapist, there are some ethical issues. For counselors in church or ministry roles, they would likely discuss their position and role in ministry, offering to support the couple's goals and discuss how they might pray in their faith tradition on their own. There might be religious leaders that can provide spiritual care for the couple specific to the issue of prayer. For licensed therapists there are some ethical considerations including whether the couple can obtain counseling from someone in their tradition in the local area. The couple's needs and autonomy are respected as they pursue the faith of their choosing. Even so, counselors are not expected to pray to a God they don't believe in or practice a faith that is not their own.

Heterogeneous couples. If one partner is not religious, or if the partners embrace different religions, then the couple and counselor should work together to support each of their beliefs about God. However, there will simply be things that not all participants agree to, and those should be avoided if possible.

Match their spiritual development. Our experience is that partners who identify as Christian or religious but do not practice prayer on their own will often consent to prayer. However, they might then seem lost or disconnected from prayer interventions. So a good assessment of the partners' experiences and prayer practices should help the counselor tailor the language and interventions to the spiritual development and style of the partners. Common problems we have seen include the couple using prayer practices that are surprising or foreign to the counselor (e.g., a Pentecostal couple praying in tongues), a partner engaging in partner-bashing within a prayer, or poor time boundaries in prayers. If any of these things seem likely, then either direct instructions to avoid negative behavior or significant controls on the prayers may be needed.

Consider the spiritual authorities in their life. If a couple is involved in a religious group or church, then they likely understand their priest or pastor to hold some spiritual authority. It is important for a counselor not to assume the role of spiritual authority but to work alongside those in that role. That can be done by consulting with their minister or referring them to ask for spiritual support from their minister. This is an important boundary to respect.

Use your prayer as a blessing. It is important for the counselor to have courage in prayers. Prayers by the counselor should never state things that have not been said in the session. Prayers should not be used to correct or reproach the couple. Prayers should bless and encourage them. All prayers should be guided by love for the couple and should be both spiritually and psychologically healthy words.

Prayer worksheets and a couple's prayer journal with guidelines and an exemplar prayer can be downloaded from hopecouples.com.

HOPE INTERVENTION 18-8: FOCUS ON CHRISTIAN VIRTUES

N. T. Wright begins his book *After You Believe* (2010) by recounting the story of U.S. Airways Flight 1549 on January 15, 2009, at 3:46 p.m. EST, bound from LaGuardia to Charlotte. The pilot, Chesley Sullenberger III (Sully), had to react when birds spoiled the engine and the plane was going down in New York City. Sully landed the plane in the Hudson River—an extremely dangerous and delicate operation. Yet he did it successfully without any death or injury to the citizens of New York or to his crew or passengers. Why? Because he had practiced staying calm in emergencies. He had practiced doing mundane landings repeatedly. He had practiced and rehearsed what might happen if . . . And when the test came, he met it and passed it. He behaved with virtue when the test came because he had practiced virtue. He had built virtue within and practiced accessing the right virtues in times of trial (Worthington, 2013).

According to its official catechism, the Roman Catholic Church's definition of virtue is "an habitual and firm disposition to do the good" (Church, 2003). The word *habitual* stands out as the key to virtue development. Developing a character strength or virtue is just like developing a good habit. There are a myriad of spiritual disciplines and personal spiritual practices that can help partners develop virtues. This is something that is encouraged by churches, Sunday school teachers and even the public school system. But virtues are not often considered by counselors. We think they should be, and this is consonant with the thinking of many positive psychologists. We suggest that there have been three emphases in positive psychology—positive emotions, happiness and character strengths. A virtue orientation is in line with that third emphasis.

For this intervention, have each partner consider what virtues they want to develop that will aid in reaching their relationship goals. Intervention 3-1 is an assessment of personal character strengths that might be the basis of creating goals. Partners might consider actually working to strengthen goals they are already strong in. This might be counterintuitive but positive psychology research posits that people make significant gains in life by excelling in a few virtues instead of trying to capture all virtues. But the partners can set their own goals for their own relational purposes. If the partners can be supportive in the development of virtues, that is an added bonus of relationship attachment.

The counselor can prime the pump by offering ideas to develop virtue:

- Read books on the virtue
- Create a playlist of songs about that virtue
- Find inspirational quotes about the virtue and post them in the car, bathroom mirror, etc.
- Ask God for strength to grow in virtue
- Engage in good deeds, random acts of kindness or other relevant virtuous acts
- Log opportunities in practicing the virtue whether realized fully or not
- Identify times when it is difficult to express the virtue, and consider ways to avoid them
- Accept that growth in virtue takes time to develop and so accept grace from God and others in failures
- Seek spiritual direction from a ministry leader in the development of that virtue
- Create a list of shades of the emotion of joy derived from the virtue when the habit is realized

Virtues: Development of all virtues requires discipline.

Principle: Growth in virtues will focus the couple toward positive actions instead of their own hurts and negative thoughts. This is also an individual activity and so does not require the partner's cooperation in order to effect change.

HOPE INTERVENTION 18-9: POSITIVE ACTIVE RESPONDING (PAR)

This communication principle involves responding to one's partner's life triumphs or struggles. A partner is coached to respond to a discussion involving the partner's personal triumph or experience of some positive experience—like a promotion at work—with positive style (in a supportive, caring way) and actively (with active nonverbals and emotional expression). The objective is to help the partner savor the positive experience.

Many couples in difficult personal or relationship times will tend to withdraw and drift apart. If a couple seem to be disengaged from each other, positive active responding (PAR) can help. One advantage of the PAR intervention is that it encourages good understanding and listening to each other for things other than relationship problems. By increasing their attachment to each other with PAR, the couple can have a stronger footing to address more difficult topics in the future. The counselor should consider whether character-building or virtues would help the couple have a long-term perspective on their goal for learning PAR skills.

Step 1: Tell the couple about positive active responding. Say something like:

> One of the things you wanted to work on was being supportive and understanding in your communication with each other. This intervention helps you to connect with your partner's life dreams, triumphs or struggles. I will ask each of you to talk with your partner about a life dream, triumph or good experience for you. This intervention is not about dealing with the negative but supporting and helping each other experience and savor the positive. Generally this will not focus on your relationship, but on your life otherwise. Your job is to really listen and try to understand your partner's experience. Then I'll ask the listener to check out that they understood what was said by summarizing it. Does this make sense to you? Do you want to do this today?

Step 2: Coach one partner to talk about his or her life dreams, triumphs or positive experiences. The more personal and emotional, the better. If the partner is staying on the surface of the topic, then help him or her reach deeper for emotions, meaning and relational impact of the experience.

Step 3: Coach the other partner to keep responding and encouraging the talking partner to expand on the positive experience. After the talking partner has "run down," have the listener summarize what they think their partner was saying and what positive meaning it had for the partner. A typical summary might be something like, "You are very excited that your boss

noticed your work. This is very important to you because you've been wondering whether she was just seeing the negative in your work, and now you
feel much more encouraged that she is appreciating you." Ask the speaker if
the listener really "got it?" Switch roles. Repeat steps two and three until the
couple is able to do them with no coaching.

*Step 4: Have the couple reflect on what they have learned through the dis-
cussion.* How did it feel to share their triumphs and have the partner keep
asking for more information and expressing positive and encouraging
feelings? Did they feel supported? Did they feel like their partner was listening and really valuing them? Is there a way to do this at home that would
work for the two of them? How might they maintain a healthy relationship
by staying connected to each others' life dreams, triumphs and positive experiences?

*Step 5: Talk with the couple about repeating PAR daily at home with 5-10
minute discussions (see the five-minute date, intervention 12-1), with a longer
discussion perhaps once a week.* The repetition of the practice is important.

Virtues: courage, compassion, temperance, love, prudence/wisdom

Principle: Use communication to help the couple stay connected with
each other, improve attachment, and be more sensitive to each other's life
struggles, triumphs and needs.

HOPE INTERVENTION 18-10: GRATITUDE

This intervention coaches couples to use gratitude as an effective method of
increasing positivity in their relationship. It offers a practical way to use the
virtue of gratitude to strengthen their relationship.

Gratitude is being thankful or appreciative. There is considerable research that gratitude is a powerful intervention in relationship maintenance
(Gordon, Impett, Kogan, Oveis & Keltner, 2012). Partners that feel appreciated tend to show more appreciation and be more committed, cooperative
and positive in their relationship. All of this increases the bond between
partners, which is the end goal of couple counseling. There is less direct
research to support gratitude as a relationship intervention, but the general
research on gratitude as an intervention is supportive. Hope and gratitude
in particular help to link the past and the future in the minds of partners
(Harvey & Pauwels, 2004).

In contrast, people who are depressed are stuck in negative attribution cycles and tend to observe and remember negative things much more than positive things (Lee, Hermens, Porter & Redoblado-Hodge, 2012). There is a feedback loop in depression, where depressed partners are more negative, and even have difficulty noticing something positive that their partner might do (Jones, Beach & Fincham, 2006). Gratitude interventions are like an antacid to this caustic negative cycle. They redirect the cognition toward positive behaviors and attributions.

Counselors and partners together can be creative in how to implement gratitude interventions that fit their context. Things we have tried include:

- Partners express appreciation and gratitude in session toward each other and reflect on that experience
- Space in the room can be used as a sculpting technique together with gratitude (for more on sculpting, see BOND 19-11; Hernandez, 1998)
- Partners can keep a daily gratitude journal listing things about their partner or relationship that they are grateful for
- Partners can send each other notes, emails or texts of gratitude during the week
- Christian partners can express gratitude to God for their partner during worship or prayer
- Partners who are parents can say appreciative things about their partner to their children

There are endless creative possibilities.

Virtues: Gratitude, generosity

Principle: Use of the virtue of gratitude can help increase valuing, positive observations and decrease selective negative behavior observations and negative attributions in couples.

HOPE INTERVENTION 18-11: A COKE AND A SMILE

This intervention communicates how self-control is a "muscle" that can be depleted when glucose levels are low or stress is high. Couples identify times in their weekly routine when they are more likely to have negative interactions due to lack of self-control. Couples then identify skills and strategies to manage their high-risk times.

The research on the virtue of self-control has blossomed in the last ten years. There is now detailed psychological information on how people use, or do not use, their self-control. The research supports the theory that self-control is like a muscle (Cacioppo, Bianchi-Demicheli, Frum, Pfaus & Lewis, 2012). If you do not use self-control and never exercise it, then it will atrophy and you will not have it when needed. On the other hand, if self-control is taxed too much in a short period of time, then it becomes exhausted (or ego-depleted) and there will not be much energy for self-control later. If we are tired, feel stressed or are fatigued, then our usual self-control might fail us. At the least, when we are ego-depleted, exerting self-control will be even more exhausting. There is actually research indicating that a little bit of sugar (like a Coca-Cola or a fruit) can help a person with self-control tasks (Gailliot & Baumeister, 2007).

Anyone on a diet understands this. Early in the day (or the first week of a diet), when self-control is higher, it is easy to turn down a sweet or fatty snack. It feels good to beat the temptation. However, if the self-control muscle is fatigued after a day of turning down yummy, sweet snacks, then in the evening the person is more likely to give in to their desire for an ice cream cone.

The application of this psychological finding is to help the couple identify times that are best to address difficult issues, make big decisions or solve a problem together. Many couples have very little regulation of their disagreements. They seem to "bleed out" in the relationship at any time. Part of what makes for a wise couple is that they find a way to contain their disagreements. They do not tackle the mother-in-law issue on an empty stomach or when exhausted. So help couples find their sweet spot for productive discussions.

Step 1: Use psychoeducation about self-control and about being wise or judicious in selecting when to discuss difficult topics or make important decisions as a couple.

Step 2: Ask the couple to discuss times that are good—and not so good—to talk about difficult things. The counselor can list these for the couple using a two-column method.

Step 3: Ask the couple how they might implement this two-column discussion in their life even this week. (If it is appropriate, this might also be a good time to discuss whether their counseling is most effective if they come to sessions depleted.) This is also a good time to discuss general self-care as one avenue for improving their stress. This can have a spillover effect into their relationship. For couples with high levels of stress, this optional add-on can help make a big difference in reaching their goals more efficiently.

Virtues: self-control, wisdom/prudence

Principle: Couples can identify times when they are depleted of resources for self-control and avoid complex and difficult conversations or conflicts during that time.

HOPE INTERVENTION 18-12: LOVE BANK (hf)

This classic couple intervention promulgated by Willard Harley (2008) is described as an effective skills-based intervention to increase positivity in a couple's relationship, thus warming the "home fires" for the possibility of increased bond. The couple's relationship is described as a love bank where each positive loving and valuing action is a deposit, but each negative action is a withdrawal. The cumulative effect of too few deposits and too many withdrawals is emphasized with the easily remembered metaphor. This intervention is particularly good for couples who need to increase the work in their relationship.

Over the years in both our labs, we have used the love bank in a variety of ways. The simplest version of the intervention has each partner list things the other does that they appreciate. They can put monetary amounts on the love-bank deposit to further communicate the value of various deposits. Then they decide what things they could do that week and attempt five to seven positive "love bank deposits" during the week.

Given Gottman's (Gottman, Ryan, Carrére & Erley, 2002) research indicating that negative interactions are more powerful than positive interactions, we have coupled teaching this concept with the instructions on love-bank intervention as well. In fact, Roy Baumeister and his colleagues have found six different literatures that indicate that negative events do about four to five times as much damage as a positive event does good. So, to keep a positive balance in the love bank, couples can count each negative as five love units that are withdrawn from the love bank and each positive act as one unit deposited. So we encourage partners to use as many positive love bank contributions as they can considering that negative interactions are inevitable in every relationship.

Other versions of applying the love-bank concept for enrichment or counseling include:

- Creating a love bank "jar" with positive deposits written on the list

- Having the couple keep a log or journal of love-bank deposits (but not withdrawals) during the week to focus them on positive interactions

- Using a computer or smartphone to keep lists and reminders to make specific love-bank deposits in an electronic calendar

- Discussing attributions for love-bank deposits can illustrate the negative attributions that have developed in the relationship and help the couple reflect on them

Virtues: love, perseverance, generosity, compassion

Principle: This intervention helps increase the positives in the relationship. This is often an important early step in a treatment plan to help the couple gain enough ground and experience counseling in a positive light so that they can take on more difficult aspects of their relationship in subsequent sessions. This intervention is also appropriate for relationship enrichment in a group or dyadic format.

HOPE INTERVENTION 18-13: REATTRIBUTIONS FOR NEUTRAL (OR NEGATIVE) BEHAVIORS

Attributions in a romantic relationship are powerful. For over 25 years, research has repeatedly shown that global, stable negative attributions predict relationship distress, dysfunction and dissolution (Fincham, Harold & Gano-Phillips, 2000). The antecedents, moderators and underlying mechanisms of the negative attribution-distress connection are still being investigated. Researchers who study attributions advise that they are effective targets for clinical intervention in couple counseling (Fincham et al., 2000). In particular, attributions reflecting perceived criticism (Peterson & Smith, 2011), threat and neglect (Sanford, 2010) are particularly harmful to partnerships.

This intervention is better implemented with some basic understanding of cognitive behavioral therapy. However, the basic ideas are easily understood. The new positivity can begin to allow more flexibility in attributions. Attributions may also be "softened" by reminding the couple that they have noted positive character traits in each other, which might assist them in changing the negative attributions. This is an exercise best done when both partners are relatively calm and able to retain perspective.

Step 1: Introduce the idea to the couple that how they think about their relationship, whether accurate or not, affects their relationship and their personal happiness. Explore whether each person accepts that they sometimes see the relationship through "dark glasses." Ask whether they have ever felt that way, perhaps when tired, after an argument, on a particularly bad day or perhaps (for couples in more distress) most of the time.

Step 2: Introduce an "experiment" to see whether how they feel and see their partner and relationship is true, or is seen through dark glasses. This is a type of reality-testing experiment. Use the Couple's Attribution Worksheet to help each one explore his or her cognition and attributions. The goal of this part of the exercise is to articulate negative attributions. Doing the first part of the exercise with partners separately might be necessary.

Step 3: Allow partners to respond to the beliefs and attributions that they both have. Watch for discouragement. This may indicate the couple is not ready for this intervention or need considerable support to know that perception is not reality. The counselor needs to be very active in this step in supporting both partners.

Step 4: Complete Theory A and Theory B Attribution Intervention Worksheet. This worksheet can be used with both partners to consider whether there may be soft, vulnerable and more positive reasons for the behaviors they are concerned about. At the bottom of the worksheet, the partners have the opportunity to reframe the negative attributions they have been carrying for their partner's behavior into something more benevolent. Partner's intent can actually be "mixed." Sometimes people are just plain mean and selfish in a relationship, but they also may have more understandable reasons for their behavior. Helping the couple remain optimistic and positive in attributions will improve a relationship.

Step 5: Process the intervention with the couple for their response. Elicit how helpful they feel it is. Discuss how they might repeat this exercise or the principles from the exercise in their everyday life as a couple.

Virtues: gentleness, ability to retain perspective, optimism

Principle: Attributions contribute either positively or negatively to a relationship. Partners identify and evaluate whether their attributions about their partner's behavior (positive or negative) add or subtract quality from their relationship.

Couple's Attribution Worksheet

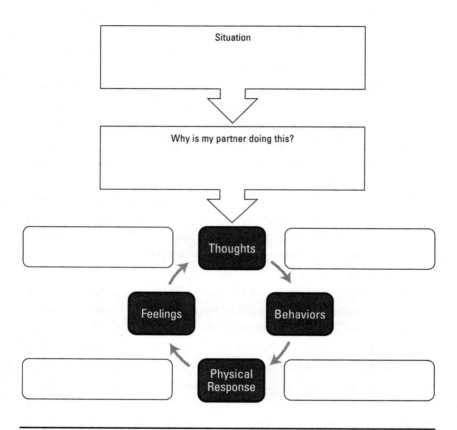

Figure 18.3

Theory A and Theory B Attribution Intervention Worksheet

Compare two theories. Consider two possible reasons why your partner might be acting negatively. Positive examples might be fear, stress or wanting something better for us. The second theory tests if the partner is acting this way out of negative intent.

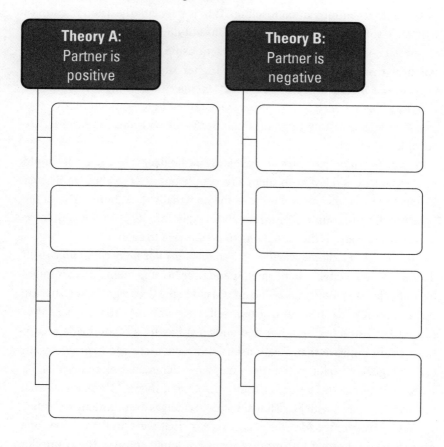

Theory A:
Partner is positive

Theory B:
Partner is negative

Figure 18.4

How might the behavior you are concerned with be reframed?

HOPE INTERVENTION 18-14: VIDEOS OF COMMUNICATION

In this intervention, couples create videotapes of themselves communicating positively as part of counseling or homework. They then watch and evaluate their own communication and create interventions to improve their communication.

In our experience, some couples find this intervention is one of the most positive interventions in counseling. This is particularly true for couples who have some negative communications but do not seem to comprehend the impact of their behavior on their relationship. This will often move the partners from precontemplation to a higher stage of change. This intervention was included in *Hope-Focused Marriage Counseling* (Worthington, 2005) with some description. What is described here is an alternative way to use videos in counseling, although both this way and the original are considered effective.

Step 1: The counselor helps the couple decide on a topic to discuss. It should be a topic that is relevant to them as a couple but not too "hot" to discuss. Instruct them to discuss the topic as they normally do at home. This is the "baseline" for the couple. Record for about eight minutes. Do not stop them unless you are afraid they are going to do damage to each other.

Step 2: Ask the couple whether this is how they normally communicate. If they say it went better than normal, spend time helping them see what might have affected that. Factors may include (1) not being tired right now so having more resources to speak and listen well, (2) being in a space where they cannot be distracted by other demands, (3) having already made a commitment to improve their relationship may have increased their efforts, or (4) having a counselor in the room may have dampened some negative behaviors. If things did go better than normal, tell them, "That's great! That means it is possible with just a few situational changes to communicate better!"

Step 3: Watch the video together. Discuss what went well and what one area they could target for improvement. For some couples, the counselor will have to firmly direct them to frame improvements positively.

If the partners are persistently critical of each other's behaviors, redirect them to focus instead on their own behavior, over which they have some control. Ask them to trust that things will get better between them over time. Any putdowns and criticisms of their partner are moving them away from better communication. If one partner continues to be stuck on focusing on his or her partner's negative behavior, consider stopping and implementing one of the resistance interventions described in chapter 23.

Step 4: Ask the couple to videotape the communication of the same topic again. This time they should use their ideas for more positive communication and listening. Review their ideas with them before beginning. Ask them whether they feel they can do those things more often in the next eight minute video. Then record. Repeat this cycle as time allows. Even in one cycle the couple will often see vast improvement because they are trying to be more positive.

Step 5: Review the exercise with the couple. Discuss what they learned. Ask the couple to repeat this exercise at home with a ten minute video (most cameras, computers and smartphones have video recording capabilities). Help them decide when to create the positive communication video, so that they do so when they have little ego depletion. They should write notes on what they did well, and bring those to the next session.

Virtues: love, perseverance, humility, temperance, self-control

Principle: Video review allows for third-person perspective on communication. Focusing on positive communication uses positive psychology principles to encourage more positive communication. Because the couple is creating their own ideas (instead of using the counselor's ideas) for more improved communication, they might feel cognitive dissonance if they break their own rules.

HOPE INTERVENTION 18-15: STOPPING NEGATIVE RECIPROCITY

Negative reciprocity is a common relationship stressor. One partner is perceived as negative, followed by a negative reaction, which fuels a negative cycle of reactions with increasing fury. In the field of anthropology negative reciprocity is when one person tries to get something for nothing from the other person in a bargain. Social psychologists have studied positive and negative reciprocity in relationships as maintaining social norms.

Negative reciprocity can explain brutal behaviors. Perceived hostile actions are often responded to with even more hostile

> Take the first step in faith. You don't have to see the whole staircase, just take the first step.
>
> MARTIN LUTHER KING JR.

actions, thus escalating conflict. Couples with high conflict often have a pattern of engaging in hostility quickly over relatively minor offenses or even neutral behaviors. Some traits predict more negative reciprocity—hostile personality patterns, machismo attitudes, tendency toward violence, brain injury, poor emotional regulation and antisocial personality traits (O'Leary, 2008). It is important to assess these traits to help determine prognosis, pace and expectations for change. If there is violence in the couple, then counselors should be cautious. Negative reciprocity cycles are often characteristic of male to female violence patterns (Cordova, Jacobson, Gottman, Rushe & Cox, 1993). The present intervention might be helpful if there has been mild violence, but it is necessary to ensure the couple is stable enough to address the cycle.

Use character strengths. Particularly with partners who have traits that make negative reciprocity likely, it is important to bring out their character strengths and virtues as the avenues for change. For example, while a male may have a high sensitivity to perceived criticism and hostility, he may also have strengths in forgiveness, courage and generosity. If changing negative reciprocity can be framed as a courageous response to a stressful situation where a generous response is needed, then the client may have a much easier time seeing an avenue of change.

Step 1: Use the Couple's Negative Reciprocity Cycle Worksheet to articulate the facts of what happened in a recent negative escalation. It is important in the worksheet not to allow for elaboration, blaming, criticism or attacks. The counselor should maintain the expectation of civil and kind actions in his or her office.

Step 2: The counselor and couple should explore how negative reciprocity works and discuss whether it is a pattern in the couple's relationship. The enemy in this situation is the process of negative reciprocity, not the partner.

Step 3: The counselor asks the couple for ideas about how they might stop the negative reciprocity. Some couples may need to have this intervention coupled with the self-care interventions (see intervention 3-8), self-soothing interventions (intervention 14-3), a negative attributions intervention (HOPE 18-13), time-out (intervention 14-2), or a simple positive communication intervention (HOPE 18-1; 18-2; 18-4). However, if the couple is able to come up with some ideas on their own about how they might short-circuit the cycle, then those ideas should be strongly encouraged. Key words of their ideas can be written in the right column of the worksheet to aid memory.

Step 4: The counselor tells the couple that the real trick is for them to practice and then to use their ideas in the heat of the moment. Use role play or attempt simple behavioral rehearsal during a session. Most couples in counseling will have difficulty stopping a negative reciprocity cycle without much practice. Knowledge is not usually enough. Couples seeking enrichment or prevention, or engaged or more well-regulated couples may be able to implement the idea without much rehearsal. The less emotionally regulated the partners, the more support will be needed.

Virtues: kindness, temperance, wisdom/prudence, gentleness, love, self-control

Principle: The purposes of this intervention are for the couple to (1) identify negative cycles in their relationship and (2) begin to create strategies for stopping the negative cycle. This intervention is intended to be part of a process of change to include learning skills for emotional regulation, more positive communication and conflict resolution.

INTERVENTION 18-16: THE CONFIRMATION BIAS EXPERIMENT

This intervention would be useful for a couple who are locked in a struggle over an offense or set of offenses. It can be difficult to find forgiveness and work through resistance to change characterized by partners dedicated to a narrative of events around an offense that diffuses their responsibility. This experiment can help partners reevaluate whether they might need to use different cognitive strategies in their relationship, with an attitude of humility around their memories and beliefs regarding offenses. This intervention could be implemented in the office or as homework, but the counselor must be careful to help the partners see personal bias as an understandable human error, not as a personal failure. Partners with fragile egos, very low in perspective-taking, or those with a weak connection with the counselor may not be a good match for this intervention.

Step 1: Search for information. Give each partner two envelopes. The first envelope has a paper that asks each partner to think of an instance in which their partner was unkind in their relationship. The event should be something relevant to their lives today, but not a "bomb" in the room if they were to discuss it later. They should give as many details of the events as they can remember: who was there, what was said, what happened before and after the event and so on. Ask them to time how long they spent on the description. Then they are to take the description and seal it in the envelope and write the number 1 on the outside. A second envelope is opened and this one asks them to describe a time when they were unkind in their relationship. The rest of the instructions are the same. When the couple returns to therapy, the counselor can almost be assured that there will be more words, details, time spent and negative description of their partner's offense than their own. Have them count the words and circle especially negative words or descriptions. This creates cognitive dissonance that should assist in breaking up their deadlock.

Step 2: Biased memory and interpretation. Have each partner discuss the content of the envelopes. They will then write down their interpretations of why they each acted as they did in those situations. The counselor asks them to describe what they remember of their own two stories, and what they remember of their partners' stories. The original stories are used to look for details that were changed, or missed in their memories. The stronger their feelings about the events selected, the more likely an effect will be seen here with differentials in memories of the events and in positive to negative attributions. The counselor emphasizes that all people have a tendency to remember offenses self-protectively, whether they were offended or were the offender. Have them reflect on how that might contribute to a negative pattern in a relationship.

Step 3: Psychoeducation. Have each partner learn about issues of attribution bias and confirmation bias. A Google search should be sufficient to help them see the research that is accessible to most clients with some science education in high school or college. The counselor can discuss with them whether negative events in their relationship might fall victim to self-confirming biases at times. Discuss their reactions and the possibility that their views of the offense may be polarized due to these normal human cognitive errors. The good news is that if they can be aware of this error, then they can find new ways of handling the offense based on what is true, good and noble in their relationship.

Step 4: Plan of action. After completing this "experiment" in their relationship, the couple is given time to discuss how they might do things differently based on what they have learned. The new learning is highly encouraged and praised by the counselor. The wisdom learned from the experiment is applicable to other relationships in their lives too such as those with coworkers, friends or family members.

Virtues: wisdom, humility

Principle: Normal human cognitive errors and biases can create vulnerabilities in intimate relationships. By identifying and understanding these errors couples can improve their relationship.

Couple's Negative Reciprocity Cycle Worksheet

Use the graphic below to help identify negative reciprocity cycles in your relationship. Notice that a negative event could begin at any point around the circle.

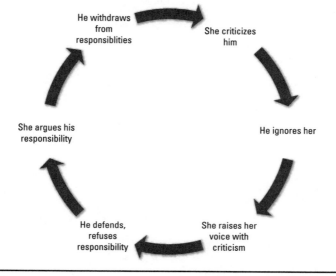

He withdraws from responsiblities

She criticizes him

She argues his responsibility

He ignores her

He defends, refuses responsibility

She raises her voice with criticism

Figure 18.5

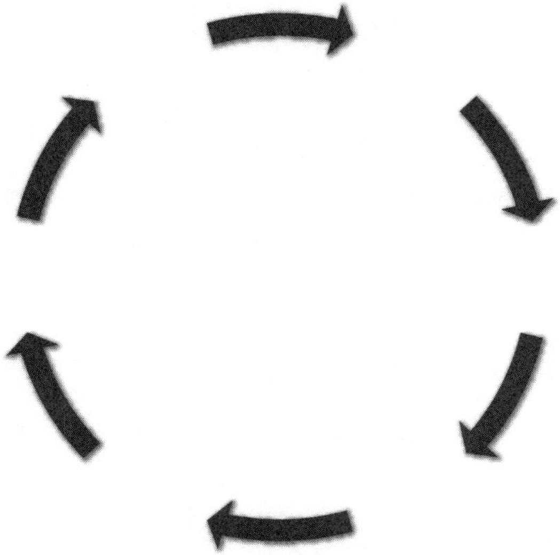

Figure 18.6a

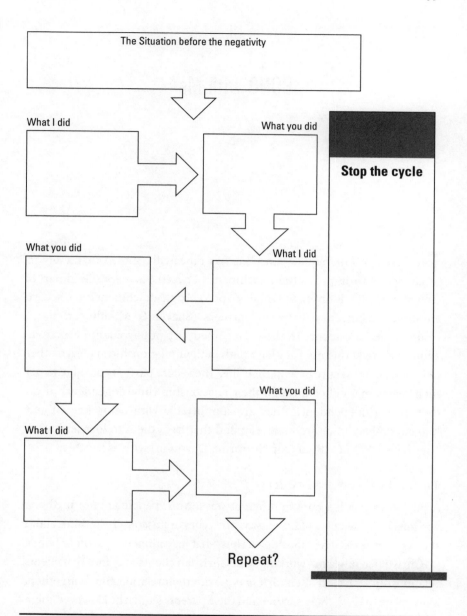

The Situation before the negativity

What I did

What you did

Stop the cycle

What you did

What I did

What you did

What I did

Repeat?

Figure 18.6b

19

BOND with Me

᠀

The research on couple counseling has repeatedly shown that a key to change is to improve the attachment between partners (Goldman & Greenberg, 2010; Johnson & Woolley, 2008). Adult attachment is the secure emotional connection between partners (Shaver & Mikulincer, 2010). Couples who are secure in their attachment are not avoidant or anxious about their relationship. They have faith in their relationship and each other to be a safe and secure base in their life. The secure partners are able to get their needs met either through their relationship (interdependent) or on their own (independent). They are comfortable with being known and knowing others in an intimate way, and that frees them to love and work. They have a BOND (Bind Our Nurturing Devotion) with each other.

THREE TYPES OF INSECURITY

A person can be insecure in different ways. Most people are not textbook versions of these types of insecurity. The types are used to help think about the experiences and relationship "scripts" that may influence partners' bonds.

Christian counselors working with Christian clients may find that clients' relationship with God often *corresponds* with their relationships with others. They relate to God, their partner and their parents similarly. However, there is also evidence that some people can create a more secure relationship with God than with people. They *compensate* for inadequacies in human relationships in their relationship with God (Granqvist, 2005). People who have insecure relationships with their parents or other important attachment figures can become more secure by creating a healthy secure relationship with God. If clients are religious and interested in adding this exploration to counseling, they may find it enriching.

Preoccupied-anxious attachment. People in this category may feel insecure and anxious about relationships. Anxious people feel unsure whether their partner is going to be there in the future; may do things that push others away; worry that they are not loved; and seem to have a strong need for closeness. They look to others to "fix" their anxiety and do not look to themselves to meet interpersonal needs like security. They are often pursuers in an emotional pursuer-distancer relationship. They may sometimes become overwhelmed because their needs are rarely ever fully met. They have an interpersonal "script" that they follow in which they seek out others in romantic relationships, often quickly wanting to bond and repeatedly feeling disappointed in relationships. In times of disappointment, they often stop attempting to bond with others and are depressed.

Fearful-avoidant attachment. These people may fear intimacy, feel anxious in relationships and resolve that anxiety by avoiding intimacy. However, everyone needs people and intimacy. So they will often be in a relationship, but they make it difficult for others to know them deeply, and they are not able to know others deeply either. They keep their partner at arm's length. Avoidant people have difficulty trusting, feel uncomfortable with closeness, and find that others often want to be more intimate than they would like to be. They may hide weaknesses or keep information or secrets from their partner out of fear of losing their partner. Because intimacy is difficult, affairs, internet sexuality or distancing during sex with their partner may be a problem. In counseling, fearful-avoidant clients may feel like a "cloud"—it is hard to understand or pin down what is going on for this person. The saying, "It is complicated," fits these people to a T.

Dismissing-avoidant attachment. These people have had repeated relational disappointments. They have usually decided that they simply do not need close relationships. Interpersonal interactions are characterized by a laissez-faire, take-it-or-leave-it attitude about relationships. They have good self-esteem (at least on the surface) but have no faith that other people will provide the bond, warmth or nurturing that they need. They need a bond with others, so they will sometimes be in a relationship (although less often than other types). However, they do not expect a good bond nor understand what one could be.

THE SOURCE OF THE STRUGGLE

There are two sources of these struggles in adult relationship attachment. One is an anxious or avoidant personality disposition. This is thought to be influenced by family of origin experiences (Dinero, Conger, Shaver, Widaman & Larsen-Rife, 2011). There is growing evidence that the disposition is influenced by neurobiology (Cacioppo, Bianchi-Demicheli, Hatfield & Rapson, 2012; Cozolino, 2006). Repeated parenting experiences appear to create "scripts" for thinking, which are reflected in mirror neurons (which activate people's ability to copy others' behavior) and thus shape their behavior in relationships.

Once developed in childhood, the attachment is further influenced by adult attachments (Dinero et al., 2011), the second source of struggle. Repeated experiences in rules or scripts can be reinforced or revised in experiences of adult relationships. Therefore, positive or negative adult attachment experiences, such as a previous marriage or long-term relationship, can strongly influence one's present relationship. A positive adult attachment can heal wounds experienced in childhood. A hurtful adult attachment can shift people toward becoming more anxious or more avoidant.

This present chapter focuses on interventions that work to increase the strength and security of the bond between the partners. While all good interventions in couple therapy should increase the couple's bond, these interventions seek *directly* to strengthen attachment.

When directly working on creating bonds between partners, stay aware of their level of anxiety. Remember that when you see a couple who have weak emotional bonds there are usually long-standing reasons why partners have put on their armor and defended against intimacy in their relationship. Some stretch back to childhood or to a previous toxic relationship, and some are simply the product of the current relationship's toxicity. Repeated experiences of hurts, putdowns, contempt and offenses create a situation where it is not safe to bond with one's partner. It can take a great deal of courage and gentleness to be vulnerable in some relationships. Here are a couple important questions to ask.

Are both partners ready to be vulnerable and cooperative with each other almost all the time? If one of them is sabotaging the safety and vulnerability in the relationship, then it is advisable to stick with behavioral interventions. This is true if there is any recent history of violence or verbally abusive behaviors.

Do attempts to strengthen or repair the bond between the partners go poorly? If so, then it is important to discuss this in some depth with the couple. If a goal of counseling is to become closer to each other—as is displayed in the space-in-the-room technique (BOND 19-11) where partners move in steps toward each other—then what is keeping them apart? Anxiety of some sort is typically the reason. If they can softly share their fears of being hurt, this can help strengthen or repair their bond. Some anxiety-reducing types of cognitive interventions can be helpful adjuncts here to help the couple take risks in the relationship. If the couple repeatedly cannot overcome their anxiety, they may not be ready for interventions that promote closeness directly. Some of the less vulnerable or more psychoeducational types of interventions for closeness include BOND interventions 19-5 (Perfect Relationship), 19-10 (Graphing Their History of Closeness), 19-11 (Sculpting Intimacy) and 19-12 (CLEAVE).

BOND INTERVENTION 19-1: REFLECTIVE PROCESSING WORKSHEET

An emphasis of the hope-focused couple approach is to make interventions memorable and demonstrable. Several bond-focused interventions are emotionally evocative and thus can lead to memory loss and distortions. The Reflective Processing Worksheet is recommended for these types of interventions. At least five minutes of the session is spent with the couple and counselor writing down "what just happened" in the session and whether it is meeting the couple's needs and goals for counseling. The worksheets are then shared and discussed in session. Some clients, either those early in treatment or those with limited experience and motivation for treatment, may need the counselor to work through the worksheet with them. More experienced clients may be able to do the worksheet as homework and discuss it the following week.

BOND INTERVENTION 19-2: EMPTY CHAIR FOR RELATIONAL HURTS OUTSIDE OF THE RELATIONSHIP (hf)

This intervention was inspired by an article by Les Greenberg (Greenberg, Warwar & Malcolm, 2008). The counselor has the partner assist in reexperiencing and understanding the hurts within other relationships. This is not to involve a hurt by one's partner. The classic Gestalt technique of the empty chair is used to evoke an emotional response from the one working on the

---

Reflective Processing Worksheet

It can be very easy in counseling to lose track of where you have been and where you are going in your journey toward your goals. This worksheet is designed to help you consider where you are in your journey.

From your perspective, what happened today in your session?

What is something you want to remember from this session?

How can you connect what you learned in this session to what you are learning overall and how you are changing overall (whether through counseling or in life)?

What can you do at home this week to make this experience in counseling help you toward your goals for counseling?

Make a commitment and share it with your counselor and partner. This week I will:

---

remembered hurt, and it also allows the observing partner to empathize. This allows the partners to build a closer attachment to each other. The hurt partner may spontaneously choose to forgive the offender, but even if that does not occur, the partners have shared the hurt and emotional reaction to it with each other in counseling. Special attention is given to understanding the effects of the past hurt on relationship sensitivities in the current relationship. Each partner should imagine that their offender (e.g., a parent or other important offender) has walked into the session today.

> This is not to involve a hurt by one's partner. . . . It is used to evoke an emotional response from the one working on the remembered hurt, and it also allows the observing partner to empathize. This allows the partners to build a closer attachment to each other.

We recommend that counselors select the spouse who is most able to access and express emotions first to engage in the empty chair technique. Partners can share a brief description of what offense they are about to discuss. You can help them gauge whether they are ready for this conversation today. Traumas (e.g., incest, rape, severe abuse) would not be addressed this way. Traumas should be addressed with a comprehensive trauma therapy approach (which the hope-focused couple approach is not) to effectively reduce potential harm to the traumatized client.

Christian or other religious couples may resonate with imagining a perfect sanctuary or holy space where nothing bad can happen. It is a spiritual place that has been blessed by God as peaceful and safe. They would describe this place and then have their partner come join them in the imagined space as they talk with their offender.

Step 1: For a few minutes, talk with the partner who is going to work with the empty chair (called the worker) about the offense and what that experience was like. Ask whether the observing partner knows about this offense, and ask the observing partner if he or she feels willing and able to support the worker in addressing the offense.

Step 2: Ask the worker whether he or she would like to hold hands with the observer while talking with the empty chair. Then have the worker tell the imagined offender in the empty chair how he or she has been affected (e.g., hurt, angered, damaged, made vulnerable) by the offender's actions. Coach the worker through this and encourage him or her to access emotions, not run from them. Encourage the worker to express how the offense has made his or her life more difficult in the past or present.

Step 3: The worker should turn toward the partner and tell the partner how fears affect him or her and the relationship—talking to the partner, not the counselor. Keep coaching the speaker's communication. Then ask the observing partner to reflect back what was heard. The partner just wants to express understanding (but tears and other signs of empathy are good too).

Then switch partners.

Do not rush this session. Take the time to unpack some of the fears, hurts or offenses from their past in other relationships. If you have to add a session here to address the offense at a deliberate pace, then do so with the couple's permission.

Emotion is necessary for this part of the intervention to work. Attending closely to emotions and empathic reflection are likely the most important skills needed to assist the couple. If clients move away from emotions, the counselor should refocus them to stay with the feelings. Stay focused on the present. Metaphors can be helpful to keep clients in the moment and intensify their experience.

Note patterns of withdrawal or attack. If clients appear to be withdrawing into a protective shell, you can use a turtle or armadillo metaphor. Clients feel the need to protect themselves, and it is not safe out here. If clients throw barbs at the empty chair, you can note that they must feel unsafe because they are throwing "porcupine quills." Then help them explore where in their life that pattern of armadillo or porcupine came from. Did it exist before marriage? Or has it just emerged since marriage?

Watch for your own discomfort with strong emotions or offense. Many new counselors can feel overwhelmed with some stories of offense, and the counselor can collaborate with the partners to pull away from the strong feelings. It is important for the counselor to develop the ability to stay with strong feelings.

Virtues: wisdom, creativity, listening

Principle: Partners can improve their bond by supporting each other in the offenses and hurts they encounter. Done in an emotionally evocative way, an empty chair technique can allow partners to process outside hurts, bond with their partner, and increase insight into the effects of past hurts on their current relationship.

BOND INTERVENTION 19-3: DREAMS

This intervention helps couples discuss their dreams for their relationship (Gottman, Ryan, Carrére & Erley, 2002). The focus is the underlying deeper dreams that may be threatened due to relationship distress such as safety, security, avoiding loneliness or being loved.

The counselor asks the couple to remember back to their childhood. What did they used to think that a romantic relationship or marriage would be like? What did they hope to find in a relationship as an adult?

The counselor then asks the couple to remember back to the origin of their relationship. What first attracted them to each other? What was the first moment when they realized that the other person loved them, and they loved that person? What is the narrative of their relationship? These types of questions are intended to elicit the underlying dreams for the relationship.

The counselor's role. The counselor actively seeks themes such as being loved, finding security, being respected, feeling valued, not being alone, belonging, being safe, experiencing compassion, getting attention, being helpful, finding trust, or being understood or understanding. There may be others but the counselor should look for underlying themes of needs and help each partner identify at least one that was part of their dream for a healthy romantic relationship. The counselor also assesses the partners' hope for an improved relationship. Partners with little hope often have a difficult time remembering their dreams or might not remember ever having dreams for their relationship. An inability to do so may indicate that a person has already given up on the relationship.

Once identified, the relationship needs can be used to help the partners make intentional decisions to meet each other's needs more effectively. The partners can discuss how they might meet each other's needs healthily. This can be discussed as part of the session or attempted as homework.

Unrealistic dreams. Some partners need to adjust their dreams for their relationship to something more realistic to their relationship strengths and abilities. This intervention can help identify unrealistic dreams. If partners have unrealistic dreams, the counselor should redirect the couple to see ways to accept each other at the place in their life journey where they are, to embrace healthy dreams, or to look to whether they might get some needs met elsewhere. For example, if someone has a strong need for belonging but their partner cannot create a sense of belonging, then finding belonging through a local church, club, workplace or volunteer organization can help meet that need and relieve some pressure from the relationship. Marriages or romantic relationships cannot meet every psychological need.

Virtues: creativity, love, grace, courage

Principle: Exploring life dreams can bring a couple closer together. They can identify and capture a sense of shared purpose and meaning in life.

BOND INTERVENTION 19-4: PERSONAL RELATIONSHIP VISION STATEMENTS

In this intervention the couple explores their vision for their relationship. By clarifying their positive values, they affirm each other. This intervention works well as a relationship enrichment intervention but may also be useful to couples who are mildly to moderately distressed. Use it early in treatment to help couples focus on their shared bond and to increase hope and work.

It also works well as a homework assignment. Prompts or questions to help the couple create a vision statement include:

- Reflect on your individual life purposes and goals
- Reflect on your personal faith journeys and histories, and how they relate to relationship vision and goals
- Search the internet for information on writing vision statements
- Reflect as a couple on the questions: Why do we exist as a couple? Do we have a ministry as a couple apart from our individual ministries?
- Create a common vision statement for yourselves as a couple
- Consider yourselves 5, 10 and 20 years in the future. What does your relationship look like?
- What things will it take to get to your vision of your future together?

   Virtues: creativity, generosity, writing ability
   Principle: Creating a vision statement together can help couples develop a sense of common purpose and meaning.

BOND INTERVENTION 19-5: PERFECT RELATIONSHIP

Here the couple create a narrative of their future as a "perfect" couple with an eye toward what their ideal future would be like. This explores personal dreams, vision and hope, and it motivates partners for work. The counselor helps the couple identify underlying dreams within their narrative of a perfect future. He or she can also explore threats to their dream and potential responses they can make. This intervention is very similar to 19-4 but is simpler so it could be used with couples with less available time, or less need to focus on relationship goals and vision. The Reflective Processing Worksheet (see BOND 19-1) would be coupled with this intervention.

   Virtues: hope, optimism
   Principle: Discussing a perfect relationship can help couples come together with common purpose and meaning.

BOND INTERVENTION 19-6: SHARING PSYCHOLOGICAL NEEDS CARD SORT

The counselor works with the couple to explore what they need in their relationship. Couples use an assessment of their personal relationship needs by completing a card-sort activity. Each partner receives a set of cards with various psychological needs on them. They sort the cards into three categories. The first category is *absolutely essential, this defines what our relationship is all about.* The second category is *very important to me* and the third category is *somewhat important to not important.* After the partners have each sorted the cards, they can look at each other's card sorts and discuss them. Finally, the counselor asks the partners to select a few of the needs that they would like to focus on as part of their goals in working on their relationship.

Processing. This type of exercise is intended to be grist for the mill as they discuss their relationship needs and how to meet them. Similar to previous interventions, the counselor coaches the couple to consider whether their needs can be met within the relationship or whether they need to, at least partially, be met elsewhere. For example, the need for approval is normal and healthy but can be met at work or through hobbies as well as in their relationship. This exercise brings the couple closer together as they understand each other more. It is particularly good for couples who are newer in their relationship, or for those who have begun to lose touch and need to reconnect.

One of the counselor's jobs is to help make the experience a "soft" one. Partners should not feel criticized or put down during the card sort. Needs should be discussed as normal and natural parts of relationships. It should be considered normal that not all of their needs will be able to be met by their partner.

This card sort is a springboard for discussing the meaning behind their expression of their needs in the relationship. By doing the activity as a card sort the session is more active and memorable for couples. The card sort activity is one that has proven effective and interesting to engaged couples. This intervention may also be helpful for clients who have difficulty articulating their needs because the card sort gives them various relationship needs and they simply sort the cards by level of perceived need.

How to create the card sort. Counselors can create their own cards by printing the needs on labels and then attaching the labels to blank index cards. Table 9.1 shows a list of needs often used for this exercise, divided by groups or categories of needs. Each card should have one need. The category of need would not be on the card itself but could be communicated later if it is helpful to the couple. The categories allow the counselor to be aware of the overarching need that the card is pointing to.

Virtues: honesty, courage

Principle: Sharing needs can increase insight and understanding of the partner. It can help partners articulate their needs clearly. Identifying key needs can also help partners to efficiently focus on highest-impact improvements in their relationship.

Table 19.1

Acceptance, the need for approval • My partner to approve of me • My friends to approve of our relationship • My family to approve of our relationship *Family,* the need to raise children • To raise current or future children with my partner *Romance,* the need for romantic fulfillment and sex • To have passion in my life • To have sex *Social contact,* the need for friends (peer relationships) • A lifelong friend through our relationship • To have friends or a community we spend time with *Tranquility,* the need to be safe • To know I am safe with my partner • For us to have a peaceful relationship *Honor,* the need to be loyal to the traditional values of marriage of one's reference group (religious, ethnic, community, etc.) • To honor the values of marriage passed on through my religion • To honor the values of marriage passed on through my family (if same values as religion, you can "clip" these two cards together; if not religious, remove religion card) *Social status,* the need for social standing/importance • To have the social position of being a married person/in a relationship	*Order,* the need for organized, stable, predictable environments • To have the stability found in a long-term relationship • To be able to predict the future because I know who my partner will be *Power,* the need for influence of will • To have some control over what happens in our lives *Vengeance,* the need to strike back/to win • To be right about things in our relationship • To give a good argument in a disagreement *Independence,* the need for individuality • To have autonomy/independence • To be an individual, apart from our relationship *Idealism,* the need for social justice • To have fairness in our relationship • To have the two of us address issues or problems with our relationship *Eating,* the need for food • To provide for basic needs (food, shelter, essentials) *Saving,* the need to collect • To save for the future

BOND INTERVENTION 19-7: EXPLORING HURTS
FROM FAMILY OF ORIGIN

The couple spends time exploring patterns of hurt from their families of origin and how those patterns might affect their current relationship. This shift in understanding creates a space where the couple can better connect with each other, reduce defensiveness and increase understanding.

Counselor's role. The counselor actively seeks ways to connect the stories of hurt between the partners. While the content of the stories may be different, the process is often the same. There is often one or both parents that failed to meet needs. The parent might have been harsh, punitive and negative. Or the parent might have been neglecting, distracted and preoccupied. As a result, children and adolescents may feel insecure, unloved or unimportant. This feeling can carry over into adult attachments. If the counselor understands the partners' attachment styles, then some expected patterns will emerge. Most people blend more than one attachment style in their adult relationships, but they tend to have one predominant type.

Attachment style applied to family of origin. Avoidant type. People high in avoidance may believe that their needs will not be met regardless of what they do. Typically, only a few childhood needs were met, and parents may have overemphasized the avoidant child's independence. Avoidant people often long to have someone interested in their inner needs and desires but are afraid to take risks to meet that longing.

Anxious type. Anxious people may seem unpredictable. Sometimes it seems impossible to meet their needs. As soon as it seems that needs are being met, these people become anxious about ever getting their needs met or new needs arise. It is helpful for anxious people to reflect on unmet needs from childhood and move toward accepting the losses of living in an unpredictable or chaotic household.

Disorganized, neglected and abuse backgrounds. Adults with these backgrounds often have difficulty coping. They lacked mirroring experiences in childhood and so often have difficulty understanding their own interior needs. They might have difficulty understanding that their partner, children, counselor or others have an interior life and needs. Not everyone who had an abused or neglected childhood has a disorganized attachment style. Many people are resilient, and many parents at times provide some nurture even though they abuse or neglect their children at other times.

A word of caution. Some partners tend to dismiss their partner's childhood wounds and needs. Before engaging in this intervention, be aware of this possibility and assess whether this is an issue for the current case. If a partner is likely to be dismissing, then this intervention may harm the relationship.

Virtues: wisdom, patience, love

Principle: By understanding unmet childhood needs and wounds, the couple can support each other and improve their emotional bond.

BOND INTERVENTION 19-8: BONDING THROUGH SPIRITUAL INTIMACY CONVERSATIONS

To encourage partners to grow closer and more intimate, ask them to share their spiritual journey and experiences. This intervention could be used as homework or within a session. Conversation starters help the couple to share with each other. Adjust these prompts to fit the style and faith experience of the partners.

- What is the time in your life when you were closest to God? What happened?
- Talk about a time in your life when you experienced God's grace.
- What does the sacrifice of Christ on the cross mean in your life?
- Why do you think that marriage is considered holy?
- What is God doing in your life right now?
- What aspects of worship services most encourage your spiritual life?
- If Jesus were to sit down with you, what would you like to hear? What would you say?
- When you have done something wrong, what do you imagine God thinking?
- What spiritual song or hymn is your favorite? Why?
- Talk about something you have read that changed the way you think about your faith, God or yourself (either in the Bible or other books).
- When you are forgiven by God, how do you experience that?
- What character in the Bible do you most appreciate and why?

Seeking to improve their bond, partners may also enjoy creating their own spiritual intimacy questions and discussing them on a date with each other. However, partners who tend to dismiss spiritual issues or their partner's spiritual life may not be ready for this intervention. For example, if a wife thinks that her husband is "not spiritual enough," then she may listen to his answers to questions with the presupposition that he is not spiritual enough. An assessment of the spiritual life of the couple and each one's understanding of his or her partner's spiritual life is an important precursor to this intervention.

Virtues: faith, listening, honesty

Principle: Sharing spiritual experiences that have not been shared previously will improve the couple's bond with each other.

BOND INTERVENTION 19-9: WRITING HOT LOVE LETTERS

This intervention seeks to increase the couple's romantic passion. The couple is asked to write hot, passionate and sexy love letters to each other during the week and exchange them. For some couples who have been avoiding sex or general intimacy, this might be a difficult intervention to do early in the course of treatment. Partners might need to work up to it. For example, if a couple has not had sex in months, then they may not be ready to write hot love letters. The counselor might not wish to do this with unmarried couples who have traditional values about sexuality. Generally, the letter is not shared with the counselor, but they can discuss in the next meeting how the homework went, what was good about it, and whether it can be used in the future to increase intimacy.

Virtues: love, courage

Principle: The couple will increase the relationship bond by increasing passion in the relationship.

BOND INTERVENTION 19-10: GRAPHING THEIR HISTORY OF CLOSENESS (hf)

The couple reviews points in their history as a couple when they felt closest to each other and when they felt most distant. This allows a couple to increase self-efficacy in improving their bond by emphasizing factors that they can improve. This intervention can be especially helpful for couples who have experienced the natural ebb and flow of intimacy within a long-term relationship but perceive that to be a problem. This is a key intervention updated from *Hope-Focused Marriage Counseling* (Worthington, 2005).

Robert Sternberg's triangular theory of love (Hsia & Schweinle, 2012) is helpful in describing romantic relationships. Love has three parts—passion, commitment and intimacy. Passion can change quickly, even within a single day. Commitment is the glue that holds the relationship together through the long-term with dedication and constraints on leaving the relationship. Intimacy takes a long time to build, or to erode. For this intervention, the couple reflects on key points in their relationship and the level of passion, commitment and intimacy during pivotal moments. They might also benefit from expressing gratitude for different moments throughout their history.

Times in the couple's history that are commonly discussed include when they met, got engaged, moved in together, married, returned from their honeymoon, had their one-year anniversary, and had other key anniversaries or important life events (like births, deaths, moves or job changes). If the couple has children, they can discuss developmental milestones of their family such as the birth of their first child (after which passion drops for the

Figure 19.1

vast majority of couples), when their children were in elementary school, when their children were adolescents, and when they became empty nesters. We have provided a rough chart of a young couple (see figure 19.1).

Virtues: wisdom/prudence, honesty, gratitude, love

Principle: The couple should see demonstrated the changes in love across time, including when things improved or went south in the past. They should also see how the three aspects of their love can ebb and flow over time.

BOND Intervention 19-11: Sculpting Intimacy/Space in Office (hf)

In this exercise, the couple use space in the room and sculpting techniques (Hernandez, 1998) to create a memorable demonstration of the effects of communication on a sense of intimacy. This is one of the classic hope-focused interventions (Worthington & Ripley, 2009) tested and often used in our couple labs. There is a demonstration of a couple in counseling with Ev using sculpting with a forgiveness issue at hopecouples.com. This intervention strongly demonstrates that partners have the power through their communication to create closeness or distance between them emotionally.

Couples who are younger, less conventional in their style and more "artsy" tend to step into this intervention with both feet (so to speak). Yet sometimes conventional couples will surprise you with the creativity of their sculptures. Sculpting is shaping their bodies in a way that physically demonstrates the ideas they are discussing. Using space in the room is a physical demonstration of the closeness or nearness partners feel toward each other. They represent intimacy through placing themselves close or far apart.

This can be done a variety of ways. Ideas for use of sculpture or space as a metaphor for the relationship are as follows.

- Each partner can have a turn sculpting their bodies to demonstrate the intimacy or emotions of their relationship at the time or the events of counseling.

- The couple can create a compromise sculpture as a task of working together and practicing compromise with each other. (For couples who like to play, you could write the names of six animals on index cards, folding them to hide the writing. Each partner draws one, and the compromise sculpture must contain each animal.)

- The couple can create an ideal sculpture, either together or as individuals.

- The couple can create a sculpture to model something like the way they see their relationship that day. The counselor can ask questions like: What would help to improve this sculpture to something happier [or with less tension, healthier, less in-your-face, etc.]? What is the difference between this goal for the session that you just illustrated and your overall goal for counseling as a couple? What should we do in session today to help shift and change this sculpture to be more what you would like it to be?

- Sculpting or space in the room is generally done repeatedly to help demonstrate whether the interventions that the couple have engaged in during counseling are helping improve the relationship.

- If the couple is interested, then use a camera (or the camera on their phone) to take a picture of their sculpture so they can see their ideas and progress in the future. In fact, couples who shot a series of pictures of their sculptures have sometimes used the prints to make their Joshua memorial (see intervention 28-1) at the end of counseling. Be careful not to violate privacy laws or ethics when taking pictures in sessions.

Virtues: creativity, wisdom/prudence, open-mindedness, honesty

Principle: Use sculpting or space metaphors to help make the work of counseling obvious, clearly communicated and verifiable.

BOND *INTERVENTION 19-12 CLEAVE* (hf)

CLEAVE— *for building intimacy*

- **Change actions to positive**—*increase interactions that are valuing and encouraging.*
- **Loving romance**—*what can you do to be romantic this week?*
- **Employ a calendar**—*plan specific times to spend time together.*
- **Adjust intimacy elsewhere**—*de-emphasize or end other intimacies that are taking away from your marital intimacy.*
- **Value your partner**—*what do you love about your partner? Tell them!*
- **Enjoy yourselves sexually**—*develop your sexual bond.*

Figure 19.2

CLEAVE allows for discussion with the couple of various ways of improving their bond. It works well with couples in enrichment or with those who need some education about intimacy. There is a take-home index card for couples (see figure 19.2) available at hopecouples.com that is useful for reinforcing the ideas from this intervention. CLEAVE stands for:

C: Change actions to positive. Increasing small everyday positive interactions will increase closeness and the bond between partners. Partners can reflect on previous positive interventions they might have done such as the love bank (HOPE 18-12). Partners can discuss what small everyday things they do that are perceived as positive and how those things affect their intimacy.

L: Loving romance. Partners can put work into creating romantic experiences. They might go on a date together pretending that they are back in their original dating time period and reflect on how they are different now. Generally couples in counseling were kinder, gentler and more forgiving of each other earlier in their history. They can discuss whether that is possible today.

E: Employ a calendar. For some couples this is one of the most important interventions they engage in. Many couples have such busy calendars that there is no time for intimacy or bonding. They may need to plan positive events, dates, time together, weekend getaways—even if there is some level of cost to other activities in their life. Couples who have arranged their lives to be fairly independent of each other may want to reflect on whether that is working for them now.

A: Adjust intimacy elsewhere. If one partner has more need for intimacy while the other is more independent, then the partners can discuss how the person with the higher need will get those needs met. The needs may be met through other friendships, family relationships, shared hobbies with other people and group spiritual activities. The more independent partner may need to cut back on intimate friendship time elsewhere (such as at work) in order not to feel stifled in the relationship.

V: Value my partner. This concept is repeated throughout counseling because it is so central to a healthy relationship. People must feel loved and valued in order to feel close to someone. Partners can discuss how they value each other observably and tangibly.

E: Enjoy ourselves physically (sexually if sexually active). Partners can learn more about lovemaking by reading books on sexual intimacy or by communicating more about and during sex. Partners may need to set aside uninterrupted time to increase their understanding of what is pleasurable to their partner. They can take on the goal of becoming a tailor-made lover to their mate. For this particular part of the intervention, it is especially important to take developmental and health considerations into account.

Virtues: generosity, honesty, love, gentleness, forbearance, compassion, humility

Principle: There are multiple ways to increase the intimacy between romantic partners. This intervention focuses on six of them, which the couple then attempt to tailor to their own needs and life-stage.

BOND INTERVENTION 19-13: INSIGHT INTO THE DISTANCER-PURSUER PATTERN

The distancer-pursuer pattern is very common in couples but becomes more entrenched and extreme with couples who are dysfunctional or have a fear of intimacy. The counselor helps couples see each person's contribution to the pattern. The couple learn how fear of intimacy tends to be the cause of this pattern and discusses personal fears that might occur when one is being close and undefended. The Distancer-Pursuer Worksheet is used to structure the conversation around this issue. The Reflective Processing Worksheet (see BOND 19-1) would generally be coupled with this intervention.

Virtues: courage, gentleness, love, compassion

Principle: Increasing insight into the distancer-pursuer relationship helps to change patterns of behavior. Offering practical ways to break the pattern helps with behavioral change.

BOND INTERVENTION 19-14: HEALTHY WAYS TO GET NEEDS FOR INTIMACY AND INDEPENDENCE MET (hf)

The couple discuss unhealthy and healthy ways that they might attempt to get their needs for intimacy and independence met. Both needs are characterized as normal and healthy. Partners who have engaged the Distancer-Pursuer Worksheet (see BOND 19-13) might find a discussion paired with that in sequence to be helpful. Differences in needs can be due to many things including personality differences. There are also sometimes gender differences. Women tend to request more closeness from males in a relationship than vice versa. For couples who are more egalitarian, they might find it interesting to reflect on whether there is power inequality in the relationship where the male is the person with less needs in the relationship. The person with more needs (often the female) is going to be in the one-down position, which would put the female more often in the role of making requests for intimacy or other bonding types of activities. Some researchers

Distancer-Pursuer Worksheet

Consider each of these areas of the relationship where someone might want something from the other person. Which one of you tends to be the one to request these from your partner? Write "me" if you usually request this, and write "you" if your partner does. If you both seem to request the item equally, write "both." If this is not really something that is ever requested, write "NA." There are some blank spots at the bottom for you to consider what additional things you might request from your partner.

Table 19.2

Requests for household help (kitchen, vacuuming, etc.)		Requests for home improvement help (repairs, yard work, etc.)		Requests for sex	
Requests for help with children		Requests for friendship types of conversations		Requests to listen as a person talks about the events of their day	
Requests to help with spiritual needs		Requests to help with extended family needs		Requests for money management/budget needs	
Requests for time together		Requests to repair the relationship after a hurt		Requests for romance (other than sex)	
Requests for gifts/ presents		Requests for more commitment		Bids for recognition, supporting and valuing	

What do you notice from this list of requests or bids for things from each other? Research has demonstrated that whoever has a need in a relationship tends to be the pursuer. The other person, who needs less or requests less, is the distancer.

Some couples who have problems with a distance-pursuer pattern will have the following happen when there are requests for something. Circle if any of these are *often true* for your relationship?

Table 19.3

Emotionally blocked	Defensive	Criticisms
Make the other person feel guilty	Make demands instead of requests	Use coercion/"play games"
Use hostility or verbal aggression	Put the partner down	Whining or complaining

These responses create a negative cycle of pursuit from the person requesting something paired with negativity and then distancing from the other partner who defends against the negativity. Both partners are participating in a hurtful and angry dance.

Breaking Up the Distancer-Pursuer Pattern

The reason why many people use these tactics is because they are afraid they will not be able to handle intimacy or vulnerability and closeness in the relationship. The relationship is in a negative place. It does not feel safe to ask vulnerably for something, so requests and bids and the responses to those requests and bids are made defensively or angrily. Yet there is a strong desire to request something, either for pragmatic or psychological reasons. So the request and response are not valuing, loving or gentle. That cycle is repeated over and over so it becomes expected. It is like you both have put on suits of armor and taken up arms in order to make a request or respond to a request because you are afraid to be soft and vulnerable and so get hurt.

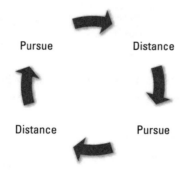

Pursue   Distance

Distance   Pursue

Figure 19.3

How can you break up the pattern of emotional distance-pursuer?

Determine to drop your armor and arms. Value your partner. Determine to speak with respect, love and gentleness. Think about how to request something softly and gently. If a request is made and you must say "not now," then say it in a gentle and caring tone paired with a valuing statement. Practice doing this in counseling or at home.

- A request might be made like this with a gentle tone "I know you have a lot going on today, but I could use some help with dinner. Would you be willing to cook the pasta?"

- A gentle denial for a request might sound like this, "I would really like to help you with the pasta. I have to return two phone calls for work or else I'll be in trouble there. I really want to help you. Can I assist with clean up instead? Oh, and honey, thanks for making dinner. I love you very much."

The idea of this is very simple, but doing it can be difficult. It can be especially difficult to maintain the valuing gentleness if your partner is having a bad day and does not do *his or her* part. The challenge is to be responsible for yourself to do what is best, even if your partner does not. This might feel awkward, vulnerable and risky if there has been negative interaction in recent history. It will require a strong dose of courage not to take up your armor or attack. However, if you do this consistently, it breaks up the negative cycle. To help think about how to say things, pretend that your partner is someone else, perhaps someone at work, at church or in the community without the history of negativity. How would you make or respond to that request from that person?

Accept intimacy from your partner. Requests for things are often really about requests to be close to you, to understand you and be understood, and to cooperate. These are the everyday things that create intimacy in a relationship. If your partner is requesting something from you, then consider whether the "real" request is for intimacy. Even if you must say "not now" for the request, you may still be able to offer intimacy. For example, if your partner requests sex but you are feeling very tired, then you might be able to offer to substitute emotional intimacy such as to listen to his or her day. Or you might be able to plan to have sex at a later appointed time, to just kiss, or for "quickie" sex that requires less energy. This meets the real need for intimacy that every relationship needs.

have postulated that this is the reason for the predictable gender roles of female as pursuer and male as distancer.

Excellent corresponding homework for this intervention is a classic from *Hope-Focused Marriage Counseling* (Worthington, 2005)—breaking up the emotional distancer-pursuer pattern through "sealed orders."

The Reflective Processing Worksheet (see BOND 19-1) would generally be coupled with this intervention.

Virtues: wisdom, humility, love

Principle: As partners become more aware of the distancer-pursuer pattern and of each partner's contribution to the pattern, they can make more intentional and healthy decisions about how to handle varied needs in their relationship.

BOND INTERVENTION 19-15: IMPROVING SEXUAL INTIMACY

Simple sensate-focus interventions are used, usually as homework for couples with uncomplicated poor sexual intimacy. Counselors should be humble when doing sensate-focus interventions and not take on more than the couple can do. Counselors need to fully assess for sexual trauma history as well as fear or disgust responses to sexuality. Such experiences often require a referral to a specialist in sexual issues in couple therapy. If there are sexual problems, then an appointment with a physician is recommended to rule out the possibility of physical causes. Counselors should be aware of and investigate whether medications or medical conditions of either partner might affect sexual functioning.

We draw from Doug Rosenau's work on sexuality to help couples. If this is going to be an area of focus for treatment, then his workbook *A Celebration of Sex* (2002), which is especially tailored for Christian couples, would blend nicely with the hope-focused couple approach. Doug recommends three things for counselors to do.

1. *Education.* Many couples need education on what is considered normal, human and true. It is common for younger couples, couples from conservative backgrounds or those with little sexual experience to need more education. However, it is not unusual in many couples for sexual problems to be due to a lack of information on specific aspects of sexuality.

2. *Dialogue.* For couples who are not openly discussing their sexual desires,

needs or cognition, then a dialogue is often helpful. Sometimes other problems, such as a passive partner, will affect the couple's sex life. When one or both partners will not talk with each other about what they enjoy or do not enjoy in their sexual experiences, finding satisfying sexual patterns can be difficult. A counselor can help the couple discuss their sexual needs, preferences and desires in session and during homework.

3. *Coaching.* There are some simple sexual therapy techniques, such as sensate focus, that can be helpful with couples who have sexual problems. Sensate focus is built on the premise that the couple will focus on giving and receiving pleasure instead of orgasms for a time to learn pleasure responses. Removing the objective of an orgasm takes the pressure off the couple and redirects their energy in lovemaking toward pleasure. The sensate focus times increase slowly from nongenital touching to genital touching and caressing. After a few weeks of practicing this several times a week, the couple is generally ready for sexual intercourse and orgasm.

We recommend the following for counselors seeking to learn more about helping couples with sexual problems. As mentioned, a good Christian sex therapy book and workbook is *A Celebration of Sex* by Doug Rosenau (2002). A standard secular sex therapy textbook is *Principles and Practice of Sex Therapy* by Sandra Leiblum (2006). A standard secular sex therapy workbook is *Enhancing Sexuality: A Problem Solving Approach to Treating Dysfunction* by John Wincze (2009).

BOND INTERVENTION 19-16: VOW MAKING

Couples with a covenantal view of their relationship may benefit from interventions that make use of vows. The vows are used to help the couple bond around a common set of values and purposes for their relationship. This exercise works well as a group enrichment activity. It is often used as part of termination and can be an alternative to the Joshua memorial (intervention 28-1).

Malachi 2:14-15 can be used as a Scripture reference for the use of vows in marriage. This passage speaks to the unfaithful children of God about why God has turned away from them: "It is because the LORD is the witness between you and the wife of your youth. You have been unfaithful to her, though she is your partner, the wife of your *marriage covenant*. Has not the one God made you? You belong to him in body and spirit."

As homework, ask the partners to write down the vows they would make today for their relationship. They should be creative and talk about things relevant to their marriage today or their sense of God's plan for their marriage in the future. The couple then should say the vows out loud to each other, either in an enrichment group, in counseling, or perhaps within their church. Some couples have created an event for the renewal of vows like a party or gathering of friends. A social media posting (like on Facebook) might be an option for people who are reluctant or unable to have an in-person announcement of their vows.

Virtues: commitment, loyalty, creativity

Principle: Rewriting vows for the couple's relationship today will increase their relationship bond.

BOND INTERVENTION 19-17: SOJOURNING TOGETHER

Some couples respond to the idea of sojourning in personal life changes. Sojourning is an ancient concept of travel, often with a spiritual or meaningful purpose. This intervention allows for a partner's experiences to be set within a narrative of personal growth and change. This is also a good intervention to use late in counseling or as a termination activity, although it can be used to help create goals for counseling early in treatment as well.

This intervention involves the couple writing a narrative of their life experience with a prospective ending that involves growth and transformation. Time in counseling is spent developing the major concepts of their narrative of personal changes and growth over time. The counselor might write down major concepts they discussed in previous life-history types of interventions or in their intake information. As the partners discuss their life journeys before meeting each other and then together as a couple, they are encouraged to gain perspective of where they have been and where they are going. The narrative has three parts: (1) my journey before you, (2) our journey together and (3) our future. Interventions that reflect on past hurt (BOND 19-7), cast vision (BOND 19-4) and graph the history of their closeness (BOND 19-10) are natural pairings with this intervention.

For homework the partners' task is the third part of the narrative. They are to take their story from the present time into the future by writing their future together. This future would be focused especially on how they will move past hurts or patterns of hurt into a better relationship together. They should be specific about what will work for them, what will be indicators that they are moving past the hurts, how they will become more loving and caring toward each other. Some couples can construct this narrative without much support from a counselor while others may need to work on the narrative more within counseling sessions to process roadblocks.

Virtues: creativity, openness

Principle: Creating a transformative narrative of a preferred future helps partners "move on" from the problems they are facing today.

20

Addressing Hurts in Relationships

ॐ

This chapter introduces interventions relevant to addressing HURTs (Handling Unacceptable Relationship Tears) without bringing in forgiveness. Some couples may need to address hurts, and yet they are not able or willing to use forgiveness. For the Christian counselor, this may be difficult because forgiveness is highly valued in the Christian tradition. However, many clients have had negative experiences with forgiveness. They are wary of it. Yet they have deep hurts that need to be repaired. Forgiveness is not the only avenue to repairing hurts. It is common for couples to use many strategies. The present chapter sets the stage for creative ways to repair hurts.

Other ways of handling hurts can include:

- Forbearance, or choosing to suppress all signs of upset toward the other for the sake of harmony in the relationship of a group
- Making different attributions about what caused the offense that excuse or justify what the offender did
- Reconciliation without forgiveness
- Reducing the intensity of negative emotions
- Obtaining restitution
- Stress management
- Giving up on revenge
- Empathizing with the offender
- Looking honestly at one's own contributions to a hurtful situation

- Creating personal meaning out of the offense
- Seeking appropriate justice for the offense
- Simply accepting that bad things happen and moving on with life

None of these is forgiveness, but they are good actions to take in response to an offense. Some clients may need these additional ways to address hurts in their relationship, while some may use forgiveness. We will address forgiveness separately in chapter 21.

In intimate relationships the distinction between forgiveness, other ways of handling hurts, and reconciliation can lack clarity. We believe this is even more the case for intimate partners where the decision regarding reconciliation is ever present. Some couples are unsure whether their relationship can be repaired, making it difficult to address hurts. In other types of relationships, it is easy and often appropriate to decide not to reconcile. If an employer were to offend by refusing to pay an employee, then the employee does not have to reconcile with the untrustworthy employer. He or she can leave the company and never see the employer again. However, in romantic relationships there are often commitments, attachments and vows that keep the partners from leaving despite major offenses.

> *If you judge people, you have no time to love them.*
> MOTHER TERESA

In contrast, for couples who stay together, it is impossible to avoid the question of reconciliation on some level. For minor to moderate offenses, this may be relatively easy; yet for severe offenses, the question of whether to attempt reconciliation is considerable. Couples can engage in revenge, unforgiveness and separation for a time. Some couples will maintain a new level of separation in their relationship after a severe offense. They may be emotionally guarded or live in separate bedrooms. Yet the nature of sharing a home, life and other family members tends to draw a couple together over time if they do not legally separate. The counselor's role in these situations is to help the couple make intentional and healthy steps toward repairing hurts in their relationship.

CUMULATIVE EFFECTS OF HURTS

Hurts are a part of life as a couple. The cooperation that is needed for many aspects of living—such as sex or bills—the fallen nature of humans, and the emotional attachment in intimate relationships all create a situation where hurts are inevitable. Many couples seeking couple counseling have a "build-up" of many offenses. Research indicates that the climate of the couple's relationship is predictive of how well they handle offenses (Fincham, Hall & Beach, 2005). It is a situation where the poor get poorer in relationship health. If a couple has a build-up of offenses, then they have fewer resources and less motivation to repair new offenses leading to a downward trend. It is like ego-depletion, couple style.

This "cumulative effect" has a significant effect on how hurts should be addressed in counseling. Some couples will need to work to increase the positivity in their relationship before they can begin to address healing the hurts that have occurred between them. Some couples will have considerable resistance and fear of extending benevolence and repairing hurts out of fear that they are vulnerable to future hurts. Other couples will be ready to address hurts early in counseling. This aspect of dysfunctional relationships requires good assessment, wisdom and courage on the part of the counselor and couple.

Cognitive Reaction to a Partner's Offenses

Not all partners are created equally. Some people struggle more with their thoughts and reactions to offenses. This may be due to disposition, personality or past. Research indicates that certain types of cognition make repair of offenses more difficult (Fincham et al., 2005). This toxic cognition includes negative rumination, resentment, avoidance, revenge seeking and blame. Other relationship dynamics also make repair of offenses more troublesome: lack of emotional empathy for the partner, perceived lack of relationship support, low self-esteem and general depressive mood. Partners with hostile or narcissistic personalities also tend to be intolerant of offenses, making it more difficult to repair them (Brown, 2004). These factors can help predict the prognosis that partners will not likely address their hurts positively. Motivation levels can vary widely. Some partners with considerable negative cognitive reactions to a partner's offenses may be ready to change habitual cognitive patterns in favor of repairing their relationship.

Here are some questions to ask as you enter the domain of addressing hurts in relationships.

What stage of change is each partner in? Baucom, Snyder and Gordon

(Baucom, Snyder & Gordon, 2009) have proposed that partners move through three stages as they address moderate to severe offenses. First they react to the offense and attempt to take stock of the *impact* of the offense. They essentially stop and look around and see what has happened, what's been lost, what are the threats as a result of the offense. Second, they try to understand the *meaning* of the offense. Why did it happen? What could have predicted it or prevented it? What will this mean in their life personally and as a couple? Third, they work to *move on* from the offense by attempting to repair the relationship, leave the relationship, or create a new standard for the relationship. Understanding where each partner is in terms of either a severe offense or an accumulation of offenses is important in knowing how to address their needs.

Is either partner moving to a quick but false repair? While grace, mercy and forgiveness are certainly valued as virtues, some partners quickly seek to repair a rather large offense without consideration of justice, restitution or the impact of the offense on their relationship. This is like breaking one's foot, and in an eagerness to resume athletic activities pronouncing it healed, throwing off the cast and pretending that all is normal. By not giving the wound a chance to heal, reinjury or incurring additional injuries in attempt to compensate might beset the overeager person. Partners need to be fully aware of the impact of the offense on themselves and their relationship. Rushing to repair may be an indicator of someone who is anxious about losing the relationship and subjugating the needs of the relationship and themselves for the needs of the other. Rush to repair may also be a sign of an aggression cycle in the relationship. Even if there is not physical violence, a good assessment of the relationship offense and repair cycle history should help the counselor and couple determine what is going on.

How open is the couple to working toward repair of their relationship? Let's face it. For some people, it can be rewarding to nurse a grudge or hold on to an offense. It gives the offended partner some power in the relationship as they can "pull out" the offense whenever they want something. They may even use the manipulation as revenge. If the partners are holding grudges, it is important to discuss restitution as something that is healthy for the relationship overall. The partners will need to have some conversation about how much repair and restitution will be needed before the relationship can return to normal, benevolent and gentle interactions. Relationships do not sustain themselves well with long-term or permanent grudges.

HURT INTERVENTION 20-1: FORBEARANCE

If a partner is not ready to address forgiveness and reconciliation, then the focus of intervention can be forbearing. This can prevent revenge seeking. Defining what revenge behaviors are, identifying the temptations to seek revenge and contracting to engage in alternatives to revenge are some of the sub-goals within counseling. This intervention teaches the concept of forbearance as a relational virtue.

> Smooth seas do not
> make skillful sailors.
>
> ETHIOPIAN PROVERB

Step 1: Discuss with the couple that there are many options for addressing hurts in relationship, even if they are not interested in forgiveness or full reconciliation work at this time. With a slight alteration (i.e., discussing fictional offenses), you could use this intervention with enrichment couples to prevent future grudge holding.

Define forbearance. *Forbearance* is the decision to restrain emotionally driven negative expressions of hurt or anger for the sake of the relationship or family. Forbearance involves acting kindly toward the other person. It does not show anger, anxiety or distress over the other person's wrongdoing. It involves patience and acceptance in difficult circumstances. Ask the partners whether they are interested in increasing their forbearance.

Step 2: Partners engage in thinking about, reflecting on and reading about forbearance during the week. They might find that Scripture recommends forbearing at times (e.g., Eph 4:2; Col 3:13). In collectivistic cultures (such as that of the New Testament) forbearance is normative. That is, if someone were as confrontative as the typical person in the United States, the personal anxiety and social rejection would have been extreme. In the United States, we can think of forbearance as being restrictive, but it is advocated by Scripture. Partners can journal about forbearance as a strategy for handling hurts. They can engage in acceptance-oriented cognition such as, "This offense has already happened. We cannot go back in time and undo it. It is important to accept that it has happened." The serenity prayer may be helpful for some people. Accepting that the partner is human with faults may be helpful in forbearing also. Focusing on one's own faults or contributions to the offensive situation may be helpful. Some partners might find it helpful to work on increasing their distress tolerance in general through cognitive or relaxation exercises. Interventions relevant to "radical acceptance" from the dialectical behavior therapy tradition (Koerner, 2012) may also be useful for this step. There are numerous radical acceptance worksheets or interventions available through therapy textbooks or online. See below for one example.

Step 3: Process the experience of forbearance with the partners. Discuss how this might be like building a muscle where practice will increase their strength in virtue, but extreme circumstances or stress might wear out the "muscle" of forbearance and cause it to fail. Partners can identify stressful situations in which they might be likely to give up on forbearance and end up in a less healthy place in their relationship.

Radical Acceptance of Relationship Offense Worksheet

What offense are you focusing on?

What specifically about the offense is hard for you to accept?

What part of you makes it hard to accept the offense?

Practice accepting that the offense happened without overwhelming negativity. You can do things like:

- Relaxation, meditation or prayer
- Use the parts of yourself that find it easier to accept the offense to persuade the part that is having the hard time accepting it not to split yourself into separate parts but to be a unified whole person
- Write out some alternatives to not accepting the offense. For example, you could write, *It just is what it is.*
- Read inspiring writings such as positive quotes, encouraging stories or Scriptures.
- If you start to feel strong anger, resentment or other negativity, tell yourself, *This is not good for you, your relationship or others in your life who depend on you.* Replace the negativity with something positive to think about.

What did you do this week to work on accepting what has happened?

0

Virtues: forbearance, mercy, self-control, perseverance

Principle: Partners can learn to bear with each other's faults and offenses by increasing the virtue of forbearance. This decreases rumination, revenge and negativity in the relationship overall and increases individual virtue.

HURT Intervention 20-2: Stopping Rumination

Ruminating about an offense causes further damage to the relationship and individual. In this intervention couples are encouraged to use distraction, self-care, acceptance of each partner's sinful nature, grace for the partner and other principles to stop the ongoing effects of rumination over offenses.

We've all seen it. We've all done it to some degree. Rumination is the mind's attempt to understand and gain a sense of control over an offense or distressing situation. It involves replaying the event, the argument or the offense over and over in the mind. It can become obsessive. A person might spend time ruminating when he or she should be doing other things. The brain is "stuck" on the event. Ruminating is related to depression, helplessness, anxiety and even binge-drinking and binge-eating (Nolen-Hoeksema, 2011; Paleari, Regalia & Fincham, 2009). It can cause people to lose support from family or friends who lose patience with listening to the ruminations.

> Although the world is full of suffering, it is also full of the overcoming of it.
>
> HELEN KELLER

Intervening with partners stuck in ruminations may be difficult. It may require some individual types of intervention, although keeping the partner in the room is recommended if possible without causing damage to their relationship.

Step 1: Define the problem. Sometimes when people ruminate they do not see it as a problem. Their mind is so busy attempting to gain understanding and control of the situation that they do not consider the price they are paying for their preoccupation. If the client appears to be precontemplative or contemplative about the problems with rumination, then an education approach may be helpful. This can be done by:

- Having the client identify the positive and negative consequences of ruminating

- Having the client ask important friends and family about whether they think they are ruminating or obsessing about the problem

- Telling the client that depression, helplessness, anxiety, health problems, distancing from supportive others, pessimism, problems with sleeping or eating can be consequences of ruminating, then asking the client to determine whether any of those is a consequence for him or her

- Having the client read information on the internet or in readings that you provide about the rumination-depression cycle

Step 2: Engage the client in healthier thought patterns and situations. The client can list positive activities and thinking that would be helpful. Examples include watching a positive movie, reading a positive book, surfing the internet for something other than the rumination, praying, exercising hard enough that the mind cannot ruminate, playing games or doing a hobby that distracts from obsessive rumination.

Step 3: Encourage the client to consider whether there is anything within his or her power to improve the situation. This might include using forbearance, considering one's own contribution to the hurtful situation, employing positive self-care, using step 2 (above) often, or considering starting depression-specific psychotherapy or medications to improve the depression side of the rumination cycle.

Step 4: Review and process the rumination cycle with the client and partner. Assess where there are continued problems with ruminations and solutions to the problem of rumination. Examine whether either partner continues to engage in anything that tolerates or encourages rumination. The partners may also consider if there is a friend or family member who encourages rumination by often discussing or complaining about the relationship problems. Even if counseling must move forward into other types of interventions, this problem may require a counseling checkup for a number of weeks to encourage lasting change.

Virtues: forbearance, self-control, honesty, fidelity

Principle: By reducing rumination about offenses or relationship problems, there is increased opportunity for change and growth beyond the problems the couple is facing.

HURT INTERVENTION 20-3: MAKING RESTITUTION

There is a good record of research indicating that making restitution after an offense can help repair the relationship (Worthington, Mazzeo & Canter,

2005). After an offense there is an injustice gap in a relationship. One partner (the offender) "owes" the other due to the offense. If both partners have wholeheartedly engaged in offenses, then they are both "in the hole" in the relationship and need some digging out. Some partners naturally engage in making restitution for offenses in their relationship. Other partners have little experience with this. Restitution is generally considered more for severe offenses but smaller offers of restitution can be used for small to moderate offenses.

Step 1: The counselor can introduce the concept of making restitution by the offender to short-circuit the temptation to seek revenge by the victim. Restitution can also serve as an antidote to a victim's revenge seeking that may already be going on in the relationship. Or an offended party can politely request restitution in response to an offense instead of being tempted to seek revenge.

Step 2: The counselor helps the couple discuss what restitution seems appropriate for a current offense. If this is a prevention intervention, then the couple might discuss imagined offenses, past offenses or common offenses in relationships. Some couples can easily create a restitution plan. Others will find that difficult. If the couple struggles, explore with them what the source of the struggle might be. It might be fear, loss or anger.

Ideas for restitution: Offer to take a responsibility (or chore) from the partner, sell a personal item to make up for a financial offense, buy a gift, take an extra job to earn money to purchase a gift, offer public words of apology, give to the poor or charity, or perhaps build or create something of value to the partner.

Step 3: Create a specific plan and timeline for the restitution. Discuss possible barriers to implementing the plan. Ask for a commitment to complete it. State that you will follow up on how it went with them at your next meeting.

Step 4: Follow up on the restitution. Assess the effects on the relationship. Problem solve and explore with the couple if there were barriers to implementing the restitution. Evaluate the extent and fallout of any effects on the relationship that implementing the restitution strategy might cause. Some partners have a difficult time accepting an offer of restitution from an offending partner. They might fear that they will be harmed again, discount the offender's restitution as "buying your way out of trouble," not consider such a justice-shaped transaction legitimate (especially for grace-oriented Christians), or think that the restitution is too little too late. If an offender makes restitution in good faith and that restitution is rejected after the fact by the victim, this can be discouraging to the offender. The counselor can help the partners process the dynamic they are stuck in, which prevents them from moving on from the offense. More time may be necessary for the effects of the offense to erode. At other times, partners need to consider what is needed to move forward in their goals of repairing their relationship.

Virtues: generosity, courage

Principle: Use restitution as a means of reducing the injustice gap in the relationship when there has been an offense.

HURT INTERVENTION 20-4: DECISIONS TO GET NEEDS MET ELSEWHERE WHILE THE RELATIONSHIP IS IN THE "RELATIONSHIP HOSPITAL"

Couples who have experienced hurts that are more difficult to repair may need to look to alternative healthy ways to meet needs during a difficult time in the relationship. When there has been a significant offense, partners will retreat from their relationship. They often are unable to meet each other's needs. This intervention has the couple discuss their personal needs such as friendship, support and security. They discuss how relationship distress causes a depletion of a couple's resources to meet those needs. For the immediate future, the couple is encouraged to find ways to meet personal needs from a variety of resources, not just their relationship.

Using virtues like self-control or patience requires some emotional energy. If partners are ego-depleted, they will be strapped to find the energy to work on repairing their relationship. For partners who are struggling to improve their relationship, some focus on self-care and personal wellness may be helpful.

Step 1: Have partners rate on a scale of 1 to 100 how much relationship distress they feel. The counselor should help them softly share the effects of the distress on the sleeping, eating, work, relationships with others, health, mood and mental state. The nature of the discussion must be soft and caring, not accusing or blaming. For couples that need a more memorable and concrete intervention, it might be helpful for them to write down their distress on one side of a paper. At the bottom of the paper, they might add other external stressors from work, family, health or other things that add to their distress in living.

Step 2: Identify things that help them cope with the distress in their life.
Often partners have a hard time articulating their natural coping methods.
Some partners have few coping methods and so are repeatedly flooded with
their distress. Others have coping methods but are not thinking about them
as potential resources for handling their current problems. Examples of
coping include using distraction, eating well, sleeping enough, exercising,
going to therapy, making effective attempts to improve the situation, being
grateful, staying optimistic, praying, attending worship services, and engaging supportive friends or family. Partners also might be using risky or
self-sabotaging coping strategies, like binge drinking, binge eating, procras-
tinating or withdrawing from others. Partners who struggle with ideas about
how they might be coping well or poorly might benefit from searching the
internet during the week to increase their understanding of coping and
various coping strategies.

Step 3: Create plans for positive coping strategies during the week. One's own
preferred coping strategies tend to be more effective than ones suggested by
the counselor or partner. Partners can help each other think of things they
have done in the past that help them to relax, appreciate life, be healthy and
feel more fulfilled as a person. It is helpful if the plans for coping can include
things they can do at no cost, things they can do alone or with others, and
things that can be readily available if their distress were to rise quickly.

HURT INTERVENTION 20-5: GRACE

Credit goes to Camden Morgante for the development of this grace intervention drawn from the relational grace theory of James Sells (Sells & Yarhouse, 2011).

This intervention introduces to couples the idea that grace is not merely
a theological concept but can be applied within their relationship. The intervention can be conducted within two or more separate sessions or con-
densed to one session. Grace can often seem like a vague concept. Grace has
been defined in many ways even by Christian psychologists we know and
trust. Sells and Yarhouse (2011) define grace as an undeserved gift while the
Balswicks (Balswick & Balswick, 2006) define grace as to forgive and be
forgiven. We define grace as an altruistic action of undeserved love. These
sessions involve *psychoeducation* to help explain myths or misunderstandings about how grace applies to the couple's relationship. A *metaphor*

and activity for grace makes the concept more understandable. An *imagery exercise*, with both a religious-themed and standard version, is included as a powerful way to commemorate relational grace. Finally, open-ended *discussion* questions can help elicit specific, concrete examples of behaviors that communicate grace in the relationship, with *homework* assignments to implement the behaviors.

> We define grace as an altruistic action of undeserved love.

Step 1: Psychoeducation about grace. Because the concept of grace is not familiar to everyone, information can be given to a couple with information about relational grace. The counselor must judge the best way to transmit the information to each couple. See the Grace Psychoeducational Worksheet below.

Step 2: Inspirational narrative. The therapist can use stories and examples to illustrate grace to the couple. Some examples for Christian couples include the parables of the prodigal son or the Good Samaritan. Scriptures to discuss include Galatians 6:2, "Carry each other's burdens, and in this way you will fulfill the law of Christ." For the standard version, O. Henry's fable "The Gift of the Magi" gives an example of grace. A movie clip pertaining to grace, such as the priest and the soldier carrying a burden up a mountain in *The Mission,* would also make a good illustration although not likely as well-received by those who are not interested in Christianity. The therapist can use his or her own clinical judgment to decide which illustration would resonate most with the couple. Whichever illustration the therapist chooses, a discussion with personal application questions relevant to the couple's relationship should follow.

Step 3: Discussion and application. The discussion and application are essential for this intervention to have impact. Without a personal application to their relationship, it will do little good for the couple to merely understand the concept of grace. The tone should be conversational, with a practical eye to how the couple can apply this knowledge to their relationship.

1. Who are people in your life that consistently exhibit these qualities of grace? What do they look like?

2. Tell me your understanding and experience of unmerited gift-giving in your relationship. When have you shown these capacities toward each other? How did you know your partner was showing grace? How did you know your grace was received?

3. Identify something you think would be an area of tension for your partner in your relationship. When considering this discussion about grace, what might you now decide to extend to your partner when this tension comes up? What are some practical ways you can show grace to each other? How can you build a "grace-full relationship"?

The Reflective Processing Worksheet (see BOND 19-1) can be useful to help make this discussion concrete for the couple and to give them a memorable record of their discussion and any decisions they reach about making their relationship more gracious.

Step 4: Homework. You can use the grace handout and discuss their assignment.

Virtues: grace, mercy, kindness

Principle: Learning about grace and considering how to improve in graciousness is healthy for the relationship.

HURT INTERVENTION 20-6: PREVENTING HURTS THROUGH SOFT START-UP

John Gottman has developed an intervention that he calls the "soft start-up." It is described fully in *The Relationship Cure* (2002). This intervention combines Gottman's soft start-up idea with the emotional connection metaphor of a porcupine often used in emotion-focused couple therapy (Johnson & Woolley, 2008). This is a brief introduction to the idea with application.

Couples often hurt each other by starting difficult conversations harshly. Partners may be harsh because they anticipate an argument will ensue on the topic. They are often right! However, a harsh start-up is a self-fulfilling prophecy. A prickly porcupine approach is highly unlikely to have a good outcome for the conversation.

In contrast, if the person is able to start a difficult conversation softly, then a better outcome is more likely. At least the person can know he or she is innocent of negativity in the discussion.

Counselors can teach the concept to partners for enrichment, prevention or relationship repair. A good metaphor that is helpful for this concept is that of porcupines mating. If a porcupine wants to mate, would he or she come to the partner with all their quills up and ready to throw darts? If it begins to throw darts, is mating likely to happen? However, if it shows its soft underbelly, a positive response is likely. Difficult conversations are similar.

Grace Psychoeducational Worksheet

You may have heard of the concept of grace, but perhaps you are unsure of how it relates to your relationship. Grace is an altruistic action of undeserved love from one person to another. It is given without expecting anything in return. It is similar to offering kindness, goodness or mercy to another person who does not necessarily deserve it. Sometimes grace allows your partner to make mistakes, without the demand for change. Grace is acceptance of your partner for how he or she is made. It does not matter who offers the gift of grace first, but once it is given, it must be respected and protected or it will be hard to offer again. In fact, offering grace can be an act of trusting. Receiving grace requires trust as well. A grace-full relationship encourages trust to develop, and trust in return encourages more acts of grace.

Is not grace just like forgiveness? Grace has some role in the forgiveness process. Grace is giving people good things they do not deserve, and mercy is not giving people consequences they do deserve. When a person offends, he or she legitimately deserves condemnation. So forgiving involves mercy—not giving the deserved condemnation. However, forgiveness also gives something the person does not deserve (grace)— a gift of restored value. So forgiveness involves both grace and mercy. A spirit of grace may motivate the couple to forgive offenses more easily.

Does not grace just apply to Christians? Grace is something that can apply to all couples. McMinn et al. (2006; 2008) distinguishes between common grace, which is grace to all creation, and special grace, which is God's grace revealed through Jesus to Christians. So all people have received (common) grace.

Does grace mean you should accept mistreatment? It is important to recognize that giving one's partner grace is not an excuse for accepting ongoing offenses without considering the consequences of sin, which would be what Dietrich Bonheoffer (2011) called "cheap grace." Giving grace does not require you to be morally neutral. Rather, receiving grace should produce a sense of remorse and sorrow for one's misdoings, which can be constructive (McMinn, Ruiz, Marx, Wright & Gilbert, 2006). Also, grace is not sufficient alone. Couples must give grace in the context of justice, which is a mutual commitment to fairness and equality in the marriage (Sells & Yarhouse, 2011). All relationships should provide a balance of both loving acts of grace and obligations (justice).

Grace Homework Worksheet

Grace is an unmerited or undeserved gift offered from one person to
another. It is given without expecting anything in return. It is similar to
offering kindness, goodness, or
mercy to another person who does
not necessarily deserve it. Sometimes grace allows your partner to
make mistakes, without the demand
that he or she change. Grace is acceptance of your partner for who he
or she is. It does not matter who

*Like any other gift, the gift
of grace can be yours only if
you'll reach out and take it.
Maybe being able to reach out
and take it is a gift too.*

UNKNOWN

offers the gift of grace first, but once it is given, it must be respected
and protected or it will be hard to offer again. In fact, offering grace
can be an act of trusting and receiving grace requires you to trust as
well. A grace-full relationship encourages trust to develop, and trust,
in return, encourages more acts of grace.

1. Think of your recurring conflict themes in your relationship and about
   your contribution to them. These are things *you* need grace for. These
   can be perpetual problems you introduce into your relationship that
   come up repeatedly, such as being messy, forgetful, having high expectations, any unpleasant personal habits, or personality issues.

2. Think about your recurrent conflict themes of your relationship in
   terms of what your partner needs grace for.

3. What are the mutual, reciprocating gifts that can be given to your
   partner around those themes? Write your ideas on the picture of the
   gift that follows.

4. During the week share what you wrote down with your partner. This
   is not a time to discuss the problems or place blame, but simply communicate grace with each other.

5. Look for ways to give this gift of grace in your relationship.

Give the couple the Principles for Couples for a Soft Start-Up Worksheet (below). Discuss how to use the principles at least a few times during the course of a week as homework.

Virtues: gentleness, long-term perspective, wisdom/prudence

Principle: The use of softness and gentleness in beginning a difficult conversation or making a request will prevent hurts and bring the couple closer together.

PRINCIPLES FOR COUPLES FOR A SOFT START-UP WORKSHEET

"A soft answer turns away wrath, but a harsh word stirs up anger" (Prov 15:1 ESV).

Soft start-up is a way of starting a difficult conversation or making a request in a way that is soft and gentle. It treats your relationship and partner as valuable, with respect.

1. Remember that the relationship is important. Protect it by treating your partner with gentleness and grace whenever possible. Your relationship is more important than being "right" or "one-upping" your partner.

2. Stop and think about how to start a difficult conversation. If you have difficulty thinking about how to talk, think about what you would say to someone else in your life that you care about—perhaps a close friend, employer or your minister. You would likely speak carefully about a difficult topic with such people. Does not the person you have invested the most in throughout the time you've been together deserve at least as much consideration?

3. Choose times when you and your partner are likely to have good self-control. When people are tired, stressed or distracted—ego depleted—they tend to lose self-control more easily.

4. Start with a loving, caring and gentle statement about your relationship or partner. Consider that most of your communication is nonverbal, so use tender touch, good eye contact, soft voice tone and a relaxed body.

5. Use an "I" statement. Say something like, "I would like for us to spend more time together. I miss being together." In contrast, if you use "you" statements, you can sound accusatory.

6. Close by giving the other person a sense of control and freedom about the topic. You might say something like, "Are you able to have a conver-

sation (or help with this now) or do we need to find another time?" Have faith in each other that if you cannot engage in the conversation at that time that there will be another opportunity soon.

7. Observe the effect of your soft start-up attempt. If it did not go well, bring that observation to counseling so you might discern why.

Table 20.1

A topic	A soft start-up example
Help with housework	"I love how you take out the trash. Could I ask you to help with cleaning up dinner more often? Are you up for that conversation?"
Increased passion in sexual relationship	"I love how we are in bed together. It is so much fun. I was thinking we might discuss making things even more passionate. When could we talk about that?"
Reducing criticism	"What you say about me is really important to me. I am affected by what you say because I love you. Could we talk about how to reduce negative words in our relationship? Can we talk about that together?"

HURT INTERVENTION 20-7: TRANSFORMING EMOTION WITH EMOTION

Sometimes a partner becomes "stuck" in an emotional experience around offense or hurt. This intervention helps partners understand the purpose behind their emotions and then access underlying alternative emotions. If further information is needed, emotion-focused couple therapy (Johnson & Woolley, 2008) often uses this technique.

Emotions have layers to them. Strong emotions can have many layers. People can feel more than one emotion at a time, even about the same situation. It is not uncommon for people who are angry to discover that sadness, loss or vulnerability are associated with unrealized emotions. The opposite can be true. If people are feeling vulnerable, they can further explore their experience and find they are also angry, sad and feel a sense of loss. By fully experiencing all emotions about their relationship, the couple can "unstick" emotions that might be blocking them from obtaining emotional forgiveness. In particular, this intervention can often help people who feel harsh negative emotions to access softer emotions that their partner can better attach to.

For example, say a woman named Jamie feels a sense of righteous indignation toward her husband for a recent pattern of withdrawal and unhelpfulness. She may be expressing primarily anger-related emotions like frustration. The counselor wonders with Jamie whether she might also be feeling a sense of loss of closeness with her husband. With some noncoercive suggestions and encouragement, people will often access softer emotions. The counselor would also want to explore her husband's feelings as well.

The Reflective Processing Worksheet (see BOND 19-1) is a helpful adjunct to this intervention, which is less concrete and more process oriented.

Virtues: gentleness, mercy, grace, wisdom/prudence

Principle: Accessing softer, more vulnerable emotions can help transform hard angry emotions to a more complex and authentic experience for partners. This can allow partners to better attach to each other and move on from offenses.

21

Forgiving and Reconciling Through
Experiencing Empathy (FREE)

ॐ

Forgiveness-based interventions have been used with the hope-focused couple approach for 20 years. Some of the earliest experiences with forgiveness in couple therapy happened on the campus of Virginia Commonwealth University in the 1980s. The counselors and I (Ev) were amazed at how dramatically effective it could be. I began to think we might be on to something.

Since those early studies about 30 years ago, we have learned much about forgiveness with couples. There have now been many reviews of the research on forgiveness. For example, Fehr, Gelfand and Nag (2010) reviewed a vast amount of research in the *Psychological Bulletin,* the largest psychology journal that publishes general reviews. In the *American Psychologist,* the flagship journal for the field of psychology, McNulty and Fincham (2012) reviewed the studies on forgiveness with couples. In the *Journal of Psychology and Theology,* Worthington, Jennings and DiBlasio (2010) reviewed forgiveness interventions with adolescents. In the *Journal of Consulting and Clinical Psychology,* Wade, Hoyt and Worthington (2014) reviewed all of the treatments to help people forgive. Finally, in *Psychology of Religion and Spirituality,* Davis and his colleagues reviewed research on forgiveness and the role of religion and spirituality (2013).

Our goal in this chapter is to apply the research to clinical intervention that will help couples to forgive. While some of these interventions were described in *Hope-Focused Marriage Counseling* (Worthington, 2005), it was first published (1999) before many forgiveness studies had gotten underway. In fact, in 1998 there were only 58 studies (reviewed by McCullough, Exline & Baumeister); by 2013, there were over 2500 studies! In the present chapter, we will include up-to-date interventions for couple enrichment or counseling. Let's start with a few things we know.

- Forgiveness interventions produce forgiveness, and they do so with a straight-line dose-response relationship. That is, more time spent trying to forgive translates directly into more forgiving.

- Forgiveness interventions work with couples, but sometimes there are negative effects. This is especially true if people take advantage of the partner and continue to offend after being forgiven.

- Religious people tend to say they are more forgiving than people who are not religious. (This is not true for self-forgiveness; they are about the same on that.)

- Forgiveness interventions also work with individual adults, parents and adolescents but not (reliably) with children under 11 or 12. Teaching children about how to apologize and how to say, "I forgive you" lays a foundation for later learning about adult forgiveness.

THE FREE INTERVENTION

The FREE intervention is a complex intervention that helps couples both forgive and reconcile. The reconciliation occurs in four steps:

1. Decision: Should we reconcile, and if so, when and how?

2. Discussion: How do we ask the other person to explain something that seems to have been a wrongdoing, and how do we make a good confession?

3. Detoxification: How do we remove the poison from a period of estrangement that might have gone on for years?

4. Devotion: How do we build positive love and devotion into the relationship?

Ev Worthington has laid these out in detail in his popular Christian self-help book *Forgiving and Reconciling: Bridges to Wholeness and Hope* (2003) and in a similarly named but higher-level book for professional counselors, *For-*

giveness and Reconciliation: Theory and Application (2006).

REACH forgiveness. Within the second step of FREE, we talk about the offended partner making a good reproach (a soft request of "I do not understand what happened—that hurt me") and the wrongdoer making a good confession. Part of the confession is a good apology. Once the apology is made, however, the person whose feelings were hurt must consider forgiving. We teach the REACH forgiveness model to walk people through a five-step method of forgiving. That five-step model has been investigated in over 20 published studies from our own labs and from the labs of others. It has been effective with groups, individuals and couples.

Stress-and-coping theory of forgiveness. The FREE and REACH forgiveness methods are based on a stress-and-coping theory of forgiveness. The theory has four parts: stressors, appraisals, stress reactions and coping mechanisms.

Stressors. Injustices and hurts are stressors. Stressors can be more or less severe. More important than the absolute severity is the way people evaluate or appraise them.

Appraisals. People appraise those stressors for (a) the degree of threat or challenge they bring and (b) the size of the injustice gap that must be dealt with. The strength of a person's response to a stressor depends on whether it is seen as a threat—that is, whether it has inflicted or has the potential to inflict physical or psychological harm.

Stress reactions. On the basis of a threat appraisal and a fairly large injustice gap, the person might experience a stress reaction of freezing, fleeing or fighting. Furthermore, negative emotions of fear, anger and sadness can attend the stress reaction. People might be motivated to be vengeful or avoidant if they are threatened.

Coping responses. The person tries to cope with the injustice, adjust the appraisals or deal with the stress reaction using the coping skills and support system that he or she has available. The person might reduce the injustice gap by seeking an apology or restitution, justice, or revenge. The efforts are aimed mostly at restoring a balance of justice. If he or she is able to deal with the stress reaction effectively, the person returns to a normal state. Sadly, that is not always the case.

Unforgiveness and its effects. If coping is unsuccessful, then negative emotions might begin to be salient—resentment, bitterness, hostility, hate, anger and fear. The body wraps those emotions into a jumbled ball labeled *unforgiveness*. Unforgiveness has many bad effects on the person, especially if it is chronic or long-lasting. It creates problems for physical health (heart, stroke, high blood pressure and immune system malfunction) as well as mental health (depression, anxiety, anger and PTSD), usually as a result of rumination. It also creates problems for relational and spiritual health.

Coping mechanisms to deal with unforgiveness. There are many biblical ways of dealing with unforgiveness. For example, one could turn the matter over to God for divine justice. Or a person could choose to forbear, or accept that life simply is unfair and move on. But a person might also forgive.

Two types of forgiveness: Decisional and emotional. There are two separate types of forgiveness. They are related to each other but can occur separately. One is a *decision* to forgive, to treat the person as a valued human and not to seek retaliation. Decisional forgiveness might be made in all sincerity and yet the person might still *feel* unforgiving. The decision to forgive is genuine and is what God really wants of us—a volitional resolution about how we will behave. We cannot always control our emotions. We have much more ability to control our behavioral intentions. The second type of forgiveness is *emotional* forgiveness, which is usually slower to develop and occurs when a person replaces the unforgiveness by forgiving emotions like empathy, sympathy, compassion and love for the other person.

The intervention to help REACH forgiveness teaches people to make a decision to forgive the offender, and then it works on the more stubborn emotional reactions. The emotional work usually takes a lot longer, so most of the treatment focuses there. When we deal with couples, we teach the REACH forgiveness model with each one working on a transgression that occurred before the couple met. The partner is present, and he or she acts as a support and empathizes with the other. Only after each has practiced forgiving an early hurt and empathizing with his or her partner do we tackle forgiveness of a transgression within the couple. Even then, we usually deal with two—with each partner identifying a specific issue. We try to keep things well balanced in couple counseling.

Emotional replacement hypothesis. The fundamental hypothesis on which the REACH forgiveness method is built is that negative emotions like unforgiveness can be replaced by positive emotions like empathy, sympathy, compassion and love if the positive emotions are stronger at the time. Thus if couples can discuss their past hurts in counseling or at home during times when their highest negativity is not at the fore, and if they can have experiences empathizing with their partner or feeling sympathy, compassion, or love for their partner, the positive emotions will work to neutralize the negative. There is a wide array of evidence supporting this, as I (Ev) have summarized in an entire chapter of my book *Forgiveness and Reconciliation* (Worthington, 2006).

It does not matter how the positive emotional experiences are instigated. It might be through simple interaction between the partners that develops in their normal interactions. But counselors can also use virtually any kind of method to bring those positive emotions into play: cognitive-behavioral methods, emotionally evocative methods (like emotionally focused couple therapy), behavioral methods (like communication training), acceptance methods, interpersonal methods, or even insight-based methods (like those from the psychoanalytic tradition). In the following pages, we share interventions that have worked well with couples we have helped.[1]

FREE INTERVENTION 21-1: PREPARING FOR FORGIVENESS

Proper preparation can be half of the work in forgiveness. It is important to soften the ground and prepare the couple to forgive each other. Some couples may come to counseling feeling ready to offer forgiveness for an offense or a collection of offenses, but most couples will not be ready. If they were ready, they would unlikely need counseling. This is one of the reasons why forgiveness is often in the second half of a treatment plan. Many couples need to increase their positive interactions, improve their attributions and increase their bond before they can apologize and forgive offenses effectively. We believe forgiveness is often the climax of the couple's relationship improvement story, but the other interventions (HOPE, BOND, HURT) are necessary parts of the story of forgiveness.

Increasing empathy. One method for preparing a couple to forgive is to

---

[1] If you would like more interventions beyond what we provide here, you can get no-cost downloadable Word documents with my (Ev's) explicit permission to duplicate and modify them to your own needs for running groups or counseling couples at www.people.vcu.edu/~eworth. See also www.evworthington.com. For other resources especially about self-forgiveness see www .forgiveself.com. I also offer free DVDs that show you how to lead Christian groups or secular groups. Our department asks only for postage and handling fees ($5.00 for each set). Checks can be mailed to the VCU Department of Psychology, P.O. Box 842018, Richmond, VA 23284-2018.

increase their empathy for each other in situations other than the current offense. Discussing the history of their hurts (BOND 19-7), an empty chair technique (BOND 19-2) or encouraging good understanding of current life stressors with simple listening (HOPE 18-1) can all help to increase empathy with the end goal of being able to forgive.

Emotional softening. Emotional softening is an intervention drawn from emotion-focused psychotherapy. Emotional softening is considered a critical event in emotion-focused therapy (Furrow & Bradley, 2011; Furrow, Edwards, Choi & Bradley, 2012). It happens when the counselor and couple explore their attachment fears together and move toward each other in vulnerability. The softening occurs when the partners move from blaming, negativity or defensiveness to a softer and more vulnerable position in the relationship. The partners might talk about feeling helpless, alone or afraid of losing their partner. By helping partners access soft and vulnerable emotions together, they increase their attachment and open up avenues for healthy forgiveness.

Emotional regulation. Another way to help prepare couples for forgiveness is to assist partners with emotional regulation skills. Partners who are ruminating about the offense might need to decrease rumination (HURT 20-2). Some partners have an interpersonal stance to overexpress while others underexpress their emotions. The counselor can help partners with emotional regulation by integrating dialectical-behavior therapy skills into counseling (Koerner, 2012; Scheel, 2000). Cognitive interventions that question the assumptions and thoughts that coexist with the over- or underexpression of emotion can be effective in learning to regulate emotions (Koerner, 2012). Simple physiological interventions can also help partners who are feeling flooded with emotion: counting to 20, taking deep breaths for a minute, taking a brief time-out walk or exercise, or controlling facial expressions to influence emotions. Partners can consider what situations to be cautious in *before* they occur to prevent emotional dysregulation. Finally, if one partner struggles with dysregulation more than the other, then sometimes that partner can "borrow" emotional calm from the other in times of distress.

Be aware, however, that the underexpression of emotion is typically due to a numbing response to the flooding of emotions rather than proper emotional regulation. Sometimes the counselor can assist dysregulated partners in the moment by focusing them and modeling a response for them. There are numerous traditions to draw from in counseling that can help prepare couples for forgiveness when emotional regulation is a barrier to change.

Seeking wisdom from God. Partners can draw from their faith tradition and spiritual practice to help prepare them for forgiveness. The counselor can follow the lead of the partners in terms of their spiritual experiences with forgiveness. Common ways to seek wisdom when struggling with forgiveness include:

- Remembering one's own forgiveness from God
- Reading Scriptures or inspirational writings on forgiveness
- Prayer (alone or together as a couple)
- Fasting
- *Lectio divina*
- Meditation
- Time of spiritual retreat or isolation
- Seeking spiritual discipleship or mentoring from a leader
- Spiritual act of service
- Worship

Given a counselor's role and ethics surrounding the use of religion or spirituality in counseling, it is important that clients either self-select their spiritual practices or seek guidance from a spiritual leader. Counselors who take the role of spiritual leaders (unless they are pastoral counselors as well) can cause confusion in clients and impose on the role of the couple's spiritual leader within their church group.

FREE INTERVENTION 21-2: DEALING WITH RESISTANCES, FUZZY DEFINITIONS AND FEARS

In *Mere Christianity* C. S. Lewis said, "Everyone says forgiveness is a lovely idea, until they have something to forgive. . . . And then, to mention the subject at all is to be greeted with howls of anger" (Lewis, 1952). People often have painful experiences with forgiveness from their past. They sometimes think that forgiveness makes them more vulnerable to attack or that they will never see justice. This intervention uses discussion and "experimentation" to explore what forgiveness will actually mean for the couple and to address resistances and fears about forgiveness.

Step 1: Assess the reason for the resistance or fear. Sometimes couples are unaware of why they feel hesitant or downright fearful of dealing directly with apologies and forgiveness. You can encourage each partner to tell a story of a time growing up when there was forgiveness in their family. If they cannot remember any specific times, it is possible that the family members did not forgive each other, or that they rarely did. Forgiveness might be a new experience for them. For others, forgiveness was forced by dogmatic and authoritarian parents. Clients may feel angry, controlled or even spiritually abused when they think of forgiveness experiences with family, church or previous partners. Helping clients articulate their experiences with forgiveness can help with the overall goal of a better relationship and individual health.

Step 2: Redefine what forgiveness, apologies and reconciliation will mean in their relationship. As they begin this journey of definition, encourage the couple to seek input from sources or people they trust. They can search the internet for inspirational quotes, ask their minister, read Scripture or books on forgiveness. The preparation for step two is generally done as homework. It is helpful to discuss the definitions in session, though, because research has shown that regardless of what approach counselors take to promoting forgiveness, the time spent arriving at a consensus working definition for counseling is highly related to success. (Correlations are about .6, which is high for any counseling intervention.) We recommend that couples work from the understanding we laid out earlier—that forgiveness is internal and that there are two separate types, decisional and emotional, which are often related but do not have to be.

Step 3: Discuss what the new definition of forgiveness means in terms of everyday living in their relationship. Allowing the couple to make some decisions about how they want to incorporate apologies, forgiveness and reconciliation in their relationship teaches them to discuss positive goals and helps them create some goals for their relationship. Couples with fewer psychological resources may need more coaching from the counselor while psychologically minded or enrichment-type couples may need little coaching.

Virtues: forgiveness, courage, forbearance

Principle: Addressing emotional barriers to forgiveness is an important step in addressing offenses in a relationship. Arriving at an agreed on working definition is just as important. Without removing barriers and agreeing on the direction of work in counseling, each partner and the counselor can be working at cross purposes and have very different motivations. There are a wide variety of psychological and spiritual interventions from various traditions that can assist a couple who struggles with forgiving, but the basics have to come first.

FREE INTERVENTION 21-3: LETTER OF APOLOGY (hf)

This intervention has been found to be powerful for couples who are ready to apologize. Before attempting this intervention, it is recommended that you have done a good assessment of readiness to change. Your hope is that the partners are generally soft and caring toward each other around the issue. If an apology is offered and the offended partner is not ready to receive it, then the interchange can be discouraging for the couple. So check to see if everyone is ready for the apology.

In couple relationships, it is rare that one partner is completely innocent in a hurtful event. Even if one partner is clearly at fault for a major offense (say, gambling away a large amount of money without consulting the partner, or initiating or participating in an affair), it is common for the offended partner to have said or done things afterward that were hurtful. Partners often will belittle, malign and talk negatively about the partner to others, or even take revenge in response to an offense. Both partners are often focused on the injustice gap between them, so the retaliatory offenses can be deemphasized. Partners easily get stuck in "all or nothing" thinking where one or the other of them is completely at fault. Certainly few relationship hurts come out of the blue. There are almost always things one partner has done that the offending partner points to in order to justify his or her wrongdoing. Because couple relationships are complex, it is helpful for partners to think more complexly about the process of negativity that has led to their problems in their relationship. You should take the position that each partner is responsible for his or her own behavior. No offense by one's partner justifies a wrong done. People do not have to return evil for evil. Thus each wrong must be treated as separate rather than as dependent on the other person's provocation.

The principle of the letter of apology is for partners to set clear boundaries of their own responsibilities in the relationship and lovingly to express regret for their own actions. Both partners are encouraged to write letters of apology for their own part in the hurtfulness in the relationship.

Step 1: Introduce the intervention as a possibility to reach their relationship goals. Help the couple gauge whether they are both ready to make a heartfelt and sincere apology for their own negative actions. For some couples there is a long history of small to moderate offenses that have formed a negative pattern in their relationship. They need to apologize for the whole pattern rather than hundreds of small events. For others there is a specific larger offense they might want to address. This intervention is not designed for events like abuse or affairs, which will need additional interventions to assist the couple in addressing that level of offense.

Step 2: Discuss the principles of a good apology with the couple. There is considerable research on this that can help inform them. For instance, the following actions help partners to receive a good apology: apologizing before one is "caught," taking full responsibility for one's own contributions to the offense, offering a clear and direct apology, not using the circumstances and situational factors that contributed to the offense as excuses for one's actions (at least until asked for them), using soft tenderness and touch if it can be accepted, and stating that one hopes to be forgiven for one's actions without pressuring the partner.

Step 3: Have the partners write letters of apology. Generally this is done as homework. Partners do not show the other person the letters until the next session. There is a worksheet with the principles of a good apology at the top of the page to help partners remember the principles.

Step 4: Read the letters of apology in session. The counselor helps partners process how they experienced giving and hearing the apologies.

Step 5: Process the partners' responses to the apologies. Sometimes partners will want to offer forgiveness. As counselor, you can treat this like decisional forgiveness. However, even a sincerely forgiven offense hurts. It will take time for the partner to experience changed emotions (i.e., emotional forgiveness). Partners who have worked themselves up to give an emotional apology often expect full emotional forgiveness, not just decisional forgiveness, immediately. When that event has been sprung on the partner as a new offense, though, this is not likely. In fact, even willingness to grant decisional forgiveness immediately is heroic. As counselor, you must explain these responses—preferably even before the partners read their letters of apology so that you keep expectations modest.

Sometimes partners dealing with a new, or at least a not previously con-fessed or apologized-for offense, will want to ask for the reasons why the other person offended. This is fine, but coach them to do so without accu-sation and blame in their voice. At other times they might ask for additional time to work toward resolving the offense before they are willing to make a decision to forgive, and certainly they need time to report that they have emotionally forgiven. Again, this actually is to be expected, and partners should know that ahead of time. If an apology is responded to passively or negatively, then the counselor can process that with both partners. It can be discouraging to the one making the apology if this happens, so counselors should be cautious in using apologies with partners who are still in the "impact" stage of offense and not ready to move forward at all.

Sometimes the disappointment is on the side of the people receiving the apology. Perhaps they hoped that something else would be apologized for, and the other person did not do so. Sometimes this is an oversight. Some-times it is due to offenders not taking responsibility for their actions. Other times it is a move in a deadly power struggle, an attempt to publicly coerce the other person to admit defeat. These conversations are difficult, but coun-selors must be able to set such issues on the table and deal with the power struggle explicitly. Usually it is best to identify the issue and mark it for later discussion rather than sidetrack the apology intervention.

Step 6: Preparing for "one step back." If the apology intervention goes well, the partners might be feeling more positive toward each other than they have in a while. The counselor should predict for the couple that the feelings may ebb and flow during the week. The counselor might wonder whether they feel a little raw or vulnerable as they say and hear the apologies. The counselor might also wonder whether they might want to retreat from that feeling of vulnerability. It is helpful if partners can predict how they think they might retreat from vulnerability during the week.

As reader, you might have wondered why we make such negative predic-tions. Some people have said to us, "I thought you were trying to work in more principles of positive psychology to this approach. This just seems like you are being a wet blanket that takes away the partners' enjoyment or sa-voring of a positive experience. That does not sound much like positive psychology." We do agree that predicting the possibility of a reaction does not sound like the happy-smiley-face caricature of positive psychology. But we see positive psychology as more about character strength and virtue than about happy-smiley happiness. Deep happiness will emerge through sensitive, loving truth-telling. By predicting the retreat, the counselor does douse the flames of immediate happiness, but this prediction lines up with clinical truth, and telling that truth sensitively to clients can help lessen the negative impact on the couple if the reaction does occur. And sometimes it will stop the reaction from happening by directing the reaction toward the counselor and "showing" him or her that they are *not* going to relapse.

Virtues: courage, gentleness, love, honesty, humility

Principle: Offering a direct, sincere and heartfelt apology is healthy for the relationship. Both partners can offer apologies, whether they have many small offenses or a large one or two. Processing the responses is just as important as the apologies.

FREE INTERVENTION 21-4 REACH FORGIVENESS (hf)

REACH forgiveness is actually a whole set of interventions drawn from previous articles and books by Ev and others (Ripley, Worthington & Maclin, 2011; Wade, Worthington & Haake, 2009; Worthington, 2001, 2003, 2006, 2013; Worthington, Hook, et al., 2010). Here we will describe the model and highlight a few of the best of these interventions repackaged for use with couples in this updated version of the approach. We refer readers to the other books for additional ideas on using the REACH theory to help partners forgive.

REACH forgiveness is based on a stress-and-coping theory of forgiveness. It has been supported by over 20 published randomized clinical trials—the highest standard of evidence supporting an evidence-based treatment. REACH forgiveness has been tested with individuals, couples and families as a group intervention. Groups have been conducted with university students, members of the adult community and members of local churches. It has been tested in the United States and other countries, with both couples and individuals meeting with a counselor, and in both secular and Christian formats. It has been written into books, and studies have tested its efficacy as a self-directed workbook for both Christian and secular use. Furthermore, groups using the REACH forgiveness model have worked equally well regardless of whether they were run by trained counselors with at least a master's degree in counseling or by people who had not yet received a bachelor's degree. This, simply put, is an intervention you can have confidence in.

REACH is an acrostic to aid people's memory of the five steps. The letters in REACH are explained below. We recommend teaching the model to each partner using hurts he or she experienced prior to meeting the other. The other partner empathizes and is drawn into the session as the counselor solicits statements of empathy, sympathy, compassion and love for the partner's difficult hurt and how he or she deals with it in applying the REACH steps. Below we describe each step and suggest some methods of helping each partner go through each step individually.

R: Recall the event. It is important for people to accurately and honestly remember the offense. For couples working on an offense within their relationship, this can be difficult because their perceptions of the offense may differ widely. But if each spouse deals separately with an event prior to their meeting, then that eliminates the perception difference. Ask about the offense, but also solicit the person's feelings and the impact that the event might have had on later life. When the partners finally deal with an event in their relationship, it is good not to get caught up in the details of the offense. Rather, accept each partner's emotional experience of the offense as a genuine expression of his or her perception. As you describe and reflect what is occurring, you will continually say, "So, your perception is . . ." and "So you see this as . . ." or "Although she sees this as [x], you see this as [y]." Stay focused on the recollection.

E: Empathize with the offender. To forgive, recall that positive emotions must replace the negative unforgiveness. Thus, when partners are learning REACH forgiveness, they work with an early hurt. We often use a couple of methods of promoting empathy with the person who hurt the partner. We might say, "Few people really want to destroy another person's life. Think back. You have probably hurt someone in the past. You probably did not get up in the morning and say, 'Today, I plan to ruin a life.' Rather, you probably intended to do good for the person, but it blew up in the process. So if you were the person who long ago hurt you, and you were going to write a letter from his or her point of view, then what do you think he or she would have said? Perhaps he or she was trying to help. See if you can just compose a letter out loud to give the other person's point of view."

Another intervention that works well is an empty-chair conversation between a partner and the long-ago offender (BOND 19-2). Stage this intervention and then, after you have processed it with the one working in the empty-chair exercise, you can ask the observing partner to comment.

When you deal with a hot issue within the couple, things are a bit different. For couple relationships empathy is a two-edged sword. It is easier to empathize with someone one is bonded to and loves. There is usually a long history together, so it is easier to accurately understand factors that influenced the person to fall into the offense. Ideally, couples have a history of empathizing with each other. On the other hand, offenses in close relationships also hurt more because the relationship is so important. Couples often feel that because they empathize with each other their partner "should have known" the impact of the offense on the relationship and on the partner. The "E" part of the model is to help partners increase their empathy for each other within the offense. We often ask the partners to speculate about what they think the other person was thinking and feeling, again under the assumption that people usually are not intent on hurting the other person but that things can go badly once the interaction begins. After the partner has given (we hope) an empathic speculation, we ask the offending partner how accurate that was. This helps the offended partner build and exercise empathy, but it also helps the offending partner know that the other person can understand their point of view and might think the best of them rather than think nothing but accusation.

A: Altruistic gift. Forgiveness is characterized as an altruistic gift. Humility is one of the parts of this principle. When learning the method, partners will reflect on when they have needed to be forgiven in the past, either in their relationship or (preferably) other relationships. They are to find a time when they did not expect or deserve forgiveness but the person— perhaps a parent, a school teacher, a Scout leader—simply forgave them. Christian clients can reflect on God's forgiveness of their sins, but we ask that they also recall a time when a person has forgiven them. This is because it is easy for them to disqualify the experience by thinking, "Of course God forgives me; God is God. But humans cannot do that."

The important part of recalling the experience of having been unexpectedly forgiven by a person is to get the person to reflect on how receiving that forgiveness felt. People typically say, "I felt free. I felt unburdened. A weight was removed from my shoulders." That memory is followed with this crucial question: "Now that you have empathized with your offender and you know how good it feels to receive that undeserved gift of forgiveness, would you like to forgive?" Usually, the person can experience some forgiveness. We ask that the person turn it into a number. "If you started learning the REACH forgiveness method with a certain amount of unforgiveness toward that offender from your past, then what percent of the unforgiveness have you replaced with forgiveness to this point?" By stating a number—80% or whatever they say—they have helped shape their internal experience of forgiveness of that offender. When the partners are discussing their own relationship offenses, a lot of this can be shortened because they have already each thought of a time they were forgiven even though they did not deserve it, and they have extended that forgiveness to the person in their past. It becomes easier to do so with the partner.

C: Commit to Forgive. It solidifies the experience and also helps people maintain the forgiveness if the partners make some kind of commitment to forgiveness. If the commitment can be made relatively public (that is, not just a silent experience in their heart but at minimum written down), the forgiveness is more memorable and persuasive. When the partners are working individually through the past offense, they can state aloud to the counselor or each other that they have forgiven the person whatever percentage reflected their experience.

They also can do any of a number of commitment exercises. Common interventions for this step in forgiveness include creating a certificate or writing a letter of forgiveness. The principles of writing this letter include making a clear and direct statement of forgiveness without justifications. The forgiveness letter can communicate a decision and also share how they commit to reducing negativity in the relationship and replacing it with positive emotions. They also could create a certificate of forgiveness, write a shorthand account in ink on their hand (like "abused") and then wash it off, or do a number of other symbolic gestures, like burning a note with the offense written on it. Also the couple might tell their minister, some close friends or family, or a church small group of their commitment to forgive. They should gauge if these people are safe to share with and likely to keep confidences as requested. Some partners are quite creative in creating a touchstone for committing to forgiveness, similar to the Joshua memorial (intervention 28-1), with art work, poems, music or other things.

H: Hold on to Forgiveness. Forgiveness is an emotional event in an ongoing relationship. Once offered and committed to, then it is highly likely that events will ensue in the future that will cause strong feelings to recur. New offenses can cause this, of course, so if the offender offends again, that is a new offense that must be dealt with. But many times, seeing a forgiven offender or even thinking about the forgiven offense will cause feelings of anger and anxiety to arise.

These feelings of anger and anxiety are often misinterpreted. People think that the forgiveness must have failed. Not at all! Life stress, being tired or even reminders of the offense by a TV show can cause the old feelings to resurface. But instead of being unforgiveness, these feelings are merely conditioned responses to something that harmed us in the past. They do not indicate unforgiveness. We use an example from cooking. Suppose a person burns his or her hand on a hot stove burner. After it heals, the person unawares gets his or her hand near to a burner again. As the heat touches the skin, the person responds with automatic anger and fear. That is not an indication that he or she has not "forgiven" the stove. Rather, those emotions are attached to that old experience. "That is the way God made us," says the counselor. "If we got hurt in one situation previously, we are hard-wired so that strong emotions warn us to be careful in that situation again."

The *H* (Hold on to forgiveness) part of the model teaches couples:

1. Expect feelings of unforgiveness to surface. Especially if the offense was moderate to severe, then this is highly likely. It is important to ensure there is no "catastrophizing" type of thinking when either remembering the hurt or being hurt in the same way in the future. For mild to moderate offenses it is likely that the offense will happen again. It is hard for most couples to go through a month without saying *something* hurtful. They can draw on their courage to face these kinds of regular struggles.

2. Forgiveness is both emotional and decisional (Worthington, Witvliet, Pietrini & Miller, 2007). While holding on to emotional forgiveness will require time and effort, this does not diminish the decision to forgive.

3. Repeating the REACH forgiveness steps can help increase emotional forgiveness. Particularly empathy and altruism can help partners return to a feeling of being forgiving.

4. Emotional forgiveness can be assisted with all sorts of emotional regulation activities and interventions (see FREE 21-1), self-care, and al-

lowing the negative emotions to naturally fade with some time. The key is not to act on negative feelings in a knee-jerk reaction, seek revenge, and say or do something hurtful to the partner. For example, if a partner is reminded of a financial offense by watching a TV show about a similar event, then it might be a good idea not to bring up the TV show, not to remind the partner of his or her offense, and not to criticize the partner's offense. Instead, the partner can tell the other person that he or she is feeling negative right now and would like to increase the positives between them, softly requesting the partner's help in deciding how to do that (HURT 20-6 or HOPE 18-12 might be helpful).

Group couple forgiveness is not a good idea. One thing we learned early on is that group interventions for couples that focus on forgiveness do not work well (Ripley & Worthington, 2002). It is too easy to cause partners to feel embarrassed and ashamed in group forgiveness interventions when the offending partner is in the room. Even if instructed not to share their partner's offense, the group situation pulls for open sharing. All that has to happen is for one person to "spill the beans" on their partner's offense and suddenly no one feels safe in the room. Stirring up memories of offenses without being able to openly discuss them in the group is also not helpful. So we recommend that forgiveness interventions happen either as individuals attending a group (not couples) or as couples in counseling. In group settings, other related interventions can be helpful, such as how to give a good apology (FREE 21-3).

FREE INTERVENTION 21-5: REDUCING THE INJUSTICE GAP BY MAKING AMENDS

An important step in the forgiveness process in a romantic relationship is finding ways to reduce the injustice gap. An injustice gap occurs whenever there has been an offense. For example, if a partner shares something private and embarrassing with a family member causing offense and even perhaps a loss of face with the family, this creates an injustice gap. The offending partner is in a "one-down" position where they owe their partner due to the unjust offense.

Step 1: Talk about the injustice gap. Talk with the partners about how much of an injustice gap they sense from the offense or series of offenses. Expect there to be differences in perception here. A counselor might even predict that the couple will have differences in perception. The couple can use space in the room as a metaphor of the injustice gap, rating it on a scale of 0 to 100. Or they can use their hands to show large gaps (hands separated by, say, ten inches) or small ones (less separation). The counselor should honor both partners' perceptions of the injustice gap and allow for differences. It is not necessary for them to agree. Yet they both need to be satisfied with the resolution of an injustice gap.

Step 2: Discuss amends. Discuss how amends might be made for the offense that will reduce the injustice gap and allow them to reach their goal of returning to a peaceful and healthy relationship (see FREE 21-5). Specific ideas for making amends are important. Talking about the degree of amends needed to reduce the injustice gap is also important. Sometimes an offender feels as though no amount of amends will return the relationship to peace and health. He or she might have made some attempts in the past that were rejected. The offended partner often needs to make a commitment to allowing the injustice gap to reduce. The good news is that the injustice gap does not have to be completely closed. Forgiveness can leap the gap!

Amends making can include grand romantic gestures. It can also increase work on the relationship, and it can lead to activity that will reduce negative effects. For example, if one person publicly embarrassed the partner, then he or she might apologize or say something honoring (or both) to the same people. The counselor helps the couple find ways to reduce their injustice gap.

Step 3: Gauge efforts. After the partners have attempted to reduce their injustice gap during the week, the counselor helps them gauge response to the efforts. The most common problem here is the offended partner having difficulty letting go of hostility or negative affect to accept the attempts to repair the relationship. The counselor may need to process that response with the offended partner. A variety of approaches could be used. For example, the counselor might explore the history of offenses in their relationship or past relationships (see BOND 19-2, 19-7) that might make them fearful of letting go of negative feelings. There might be personality issues that make it harder to let go, and partners can develop insight about themselves from that. There could be other people in their life that were affected by the offense and carry some of the injustice gap (for example, a child that got caught up in an argument). In that case the offended partner may feel solidarity and the need to protect the third party. If this is the case, then the response to the injustice gap would need to include the other injured party.

For some partners a history of power struggles makes maintaining the injustice gap rewarding for the offended party. If the offended party has been disempowered in the past, then the offense may have actually helped to balance the power toward a healthier relationship. In that case, the partners may need to work on how to reduce general power imbalances in the relationship overall in order to fully trust that amends will work for them toward healthy goals.

Virtues: humility, courage, perseverance, love, gentleness

Principle: Making amends in a relationship with offenses can help to reduce the injustice gap and improve relationship health.

FREE INTERVENTION 21-6: FORGIVING THE SELF

One of the unique characteristics of forgiveness work with couples is that the offender and offended are in the counseling session together. This means that in any offense, one partner might be trying to forgive the other, while at the same time the offender is trying to forgive himself or herself. Self-condemnation occurs when people do wrong or fail to live up to their standards or their expectations for themselves.

If partners struggle with feelings of guilt, then some activities may be helpful. This intervention may be protracted or difficult if the client has narcissistic features making it difficult to take responsibility for weaknesses or failures, short-circuiting the receiving of forgiveness. The less that clients are able to take responsibility for their own failures, the less likely they will be able to fully forgive others, receive forgiveness from others, or forgive themselves. For those clients treatments that focus more on behavioral interventions to improve the relationship are recommended until there is some softening and acceptance of responsibility.

The essence of the self-forgiveness intervention is a six-step procedure. Here are the steps, as conveyed in my (Ev's) *Moving Forward: Six Steps to Forgiving Yourself and Breaking Free from the Past* (Worthington, 2013). If a partner is struggling with self-forgiveness, reading this book would be helpful as homework.

Preliminary step. Michael Jordan said in a Nike commercial, "I have missed more than 9,000 shots in my career. I have lost almost 300 games. On 26 occasions, I have been entrusted to take the game winning shot, and I missed. I have failed over and over and over again in my life. And that is why I succeed." For homework some partners might benefit by searching out famous people who have failed. Accepting failure as part of living in a relationship is an important cognitive step to forgiving the self. For Christian clients, they may find it helpful to reflect on their experience of God's forgiveness and explore what makes it hard to accept forgiveness.

Step 1: Receive God's forgiveness. One cannot simply forgive oneself for all wrongs. That is simply letting oneself off of the hook. It is morally, socially and personally irresponsible. Imagine Hitler thinking, I'll just forgive myself for committing or approving of six million murders. Everyone can see that such an act would be irresponsible. When we do wrong, there are consequences. King David found that out. After the prophet Nathan confronted him about his adultery with Bathsheba and murder of her husband Uriah, David confessed and Nathan pronounced that God had forgiven David. Yet there were consequences for his wrongdoing that he and his family had to bear.

God's forgiveness takes away our moral guilt. As Christians believe, Jesus came to die so that through his death our moral guilt could be taken care of in God the Father's sight. Relief of our moral guilt is the first step. Even people who do not embrace this good news of Jesus' sacrificial death usually believe that serious wrongdoing is a "crime against nature" or a "wrong done to humanity." They must seek to do something to make restoration to whatever is beyond human comprehension.

In couple counseling we typically are not witnessing to the Christian message and leading people to Christ. While that is of supreme importance, as counselors we are in a position of power and trust, in which clients who are vulnerable and highly open to influence come to seek our help. Usually direct proselytization is avoided, and the person can be referred to a minister for spiritual witnessing and evangelization. What we can do as counselors is to make sure that the person is well aware that he or she needs to do something to restore the balance between God (or the sacred) and the person. Of course, if the person comes for explicitly Christian counseling and has agreed to this emphasis in the informed consent, then the Christian counselor would be remiss in not mentioning Christ's work explicitly.

Step 2: Repair relationships. Wrongs have social consequences. Thus, for dealing with self-condemnation, especially through self-forgiveness, making amends (FREE 21-5) is a crucial preliminary step. There are many harms, though, that simply cannot be put right. Damage has been done, and it is irreparable. However, amends making is still good if the person "pays it forward." Paying it forward is aimed at blessing someone else who does not deserve it because one cannot restore the damage done in a relationship.

Step 3: Rethink ruminations. Wrongs have psychological consequences too. Rumination about one's wrongdoing can keep people in depressed and anxious moods. Many CBT methods have been developed to help people manage and reduce ruminations (see HURT 20-2). Other psychological damage occurs when people have unrealistic expectations of themselves or hold standards for themselves that are impossibly high. Again, to deal with unrealistic expectations or standards, CBT methods have proven to be effective, and many evidence-based interventions are available.

Step 4: REACH emotional self-forgiveness. The person who has done his or her best to make up for the spiritual, social and psychological consequences, self-forgiveness now becomes a responsible act. Decisional self-forgiveness is choosing to treat oneself as a valued person, parallel to decisional forgiveness of others. Emotional self-forgiveness might also occur by replacing negative emotions toward the self—which in the case of self-condemnation are regret, remorse, guilt, shame, anger, anxiety, resentment, bitterness and self-hatred—with more positive emotions like empathy, sympathy, compassion and love. Many of the exercises in the REACH forgiveness intervention (FREE 21-4) can easily be adapted to self-forgiveness.

Step 5: Rebuild self-acceptance. While people often struggle with emotional self-forgiveness, many times self-acceptance is even more difficult. A person might be able to move through the first four steps and REACH emotional self-forgiveness, but still think, "How could I have done such a terrible thing?" That is, when we do wrong, we often come up against our fallen nature in force. We discover that we are more deeply flawed than we ever would have thought or admitted to ourselves. For the Christian, knowing and deeply experiencing that Jesus died for people while they were yet sinners can help them know that they might be terribly flawed but are indeed precious to God. Partners also can help convey to the other person, "I know you and I know your flaws. Yet despite your flaws I love you and think you are a precious person." As a counselor you too are in the position to really know clients in sometimes deeper ways than people in their own families who have interacted with them for a lifetime, yet relatively unreflectively. So when we can give assurance that a client is known, warts and all (as they say), and yet we still think they are precious, this can have healing effects.

Step 6: Resolve to live virtuously. Responsible self-forgiveness involves not just getting rid of troublesome regret, remorse, shame and guilt. It also involves a commitment to not doing wrong in the future. While no one can promise not to do wrong (we are all fallen), we can recommit ourselves to try to live virtuously.

FREE INTERVENTION 21-7: HUMILITY IN SELF

One intervention helpful for all parties in offensive situations is the use of the virtue of humility. This intervention introduces the virtue of humility with discussion of how partners might practice humility in their current situation.

Humility is hard to define, but we like how the former archbishop of Canterbury, William Temple, put it: "Humility does not mean thinking less of yourself than of other people, nor does it mean having a low opinion of your gifts. It means freedom from having to think about yourself at all." In this definition, we see that humility is not thinking of oneself as a worm, but is having an accurate self-assessment. But it also is about thinking of and serving others. If we are other-oriented, Temple observes, while we might think of ourselves at times out of necessity, we do not have to do so. We are free to follow God's will. We believe, then, that often we can discern the most about humility by not reflecting on whether we ourselves are humble. Rather we can learn by thinking about those who are in our hall of fame of humility. In addition, humility is all about (1) seeing the goal, (2) practicing humility repeatedly, (3) meeting the tests that life throws at us while remaining humble, and then (4) finding happiness in a right relationship with others and God.

People can develop the virtue of humility in their life. They can also do so within a partnership. The acid test is then applying humility to offense situations in the relationship. Here are some examples of exercises partners can do to promote humility.

- Identify as a couple some people who might be in your hall of fame of humility. Talk about the characteristics that make the people humble.

- At home read the New Testament book of James together or separately. Try to see this as a reflection of a humility exercise, which advocates seeing the goal to which people are called, meeting the tests along the way, and experiencing humble happiness in helping others and serving God. Discuss it as guidelines for humility.

- Begin something that is difficult to learn. If the skill is something that one of you is more proficient at, that can help further with being humble within the relationship. This forces the other to become a learner. It might be a new hobby, musical instrument, new area of study, new sport or new spiritual discipline. Taking on the role of novice will develop humility.

- Spend time with someone or learn more about someone who is truly great at something. If people do not have personal contact with someone who is truly great at something, they can attend sports events and watch great athletes, go to lectures and expose themselves to great ideas, watch Ted-talks online to see some amazing communicators, read books by great authors or biographies of great leaders.

- Spend time in worship of God. The worship of God places a person in the position of worshiper of a far greater personal being, such as the Trinity (in Christian worship). In particular, building gratitude to God for undeserved gifts and blessings is recommended. This practice builds the character of humility.

- Serve those that are less fortunate than you are and focus on how similar you are to the person you are serving. It is possible to develop pride from serving others by feeling better than those one serves. This is a risk of serving others, but if clients are interested in doing so, they can develop humility by focusing on similarities.

- Examine areas of life that are self-centered or in which there are traces of narcissism—this is the opposite of humility. Explore where this self-centeredness comes from and what it means, and then concentrate on reducing it.

- Practice honest (but loving) feedback on strengths and personal weaknesses. Work on "taking the edge" off personal weaknesses but accepting one's weaknesses as a part of living in the fallen world.

- Read books or websites, or listen to sermons or other resources on the topic of humility (Harvey & Pauwels, 2004; Worthington, 2008).

Virtue: humility

Principle: Personal development of the virtue of humility will yield benefits in the couple's relationship.

22

Reconciliation and Rebuilding
Trust with Couples

ॐ

Bill and Keisha had forgiven the offenses involved in Keisha's alcohol binging last year. Keisha's mother had died and Keisha had turned from an occasional drinker to a binge drinker in response. She had several friends who would go to the bar and drink heavily on the weekends, and Keisha increased her time with those friends. She felt she "needed" the drinking and the socializing to cope with the loss. During those months of drinking and grieving, she had flirted with and kissed another man at the bar, had neglected housework that she normally took care of and had ignored her husband. Bill was tolerant for several months, trying to be understanding of her grief. However, Bill's father was an abusive alcoholic. Bill had responded to this childhood experience by avoiding alcohol, so he did not want to join her at the bar. He became increasingly afraid she was becoming an alcoholic like his father. He would criticize her drinking and withdraw from her in attempts to improve things. This relationship was "on the brink."

After the kissing incident, Keisha had become fearful she was changing as a person. One of her friends began an affair and another friend moved away. She took a long look in the mirror, had a long talk with her grandmother who had been praying for her, and decided to stop going to the bar with her friends. She asked Bill whether they could go away together for a weekend. There

> *Have enough courage to trust love one more time and always one more time.*
> MAYA ANGELOU

she told him about the flirting and kiss with tears of regret. Keisha had made a heartfelt apology, and Bill had communicated his (decisional) forgiveness for her hurts. Bill was still finding it hard to trust Keisha again. They sought counseling with Mark to help them move forward.

While reconciliation and rebuilding TRUST (Trusting Response United with Shared Trustworthiness) may be related to forgiveness to some degree, there are interventions that are specific to helping couples rebuild trust after a significant offense. *Reconciliation is reestablishing a good (trusting) relationship between the partners.* It is characterized by the story of the prodigal son who on returning to his father's home is greeted with open arms and acceptance. In modern terms, the word reconciliation is used often for resolution of political differences, such as when Nelson Mandela called for reconciliation during early rebuilding of South African society after apartheid (Worthington et al., 2000). *Rebuilding trust is couples acting in mutually trustworthy ways across a period of time such that they feel a relaxation of tension and a tendency toward trust.* Actions that rebuild trust are the mechanism for a full reconciliation to a good relationship, or sometimes even a better relationship than prior to the hurts.

Couples like Bill and Keisha are not unusual in counseling. The couple has made much improvement in their relationship already. Keisha has stopped the negative behaviors and openly confessed, and Bill has been understanding and has forgiven her. What is difficult for couples is holding on to that forgiveness, reconciling and rebuilding deeper levels of trust in the relationship. Their counselor, Mark, worked with the couple for interventions to help them with these goals.

Many of the interventions throughout this book can build trust. Couples who come to counseling looking to build trust may find it helpful to improve communication skills, improve their bond, address hurts in a more healthy way and learn to explicitly forgive. We offer a few ideas of interventions specific to improving trust. Trust-building is often a waiting game. It can take time to build up a bank of mutually trustworthy behaviors. These interventions are intended to put energy toward that goal.

TRUST INTERVENTION 22-1: INCREASING POSITIVE EMOTIONS THROUGH GRATITUDE

Gratitude is a powerful emotion to help increase positivity in the relationship and thus increase motivation for trust-building. For couples who need to increase the positive momentum in their relationship, then a gratitude experience can be important. Part of what is needed when there has been a hurt, or series of hurts, is to replace the negative emotions that have become prevalent during the hurtful time with more positive emotions. Gratitude is a powerful positive emotion. Gratitude can be expressed in numerous ways. Here are some examples:

- Both partners can write letters of gratitude explaining what about their partner they are thankful for (for religious couples the letter can be written to God as a prayer).

- Partners can read letters of gratitude, or lists of things they are grateful for to each other in counseling. They can discuss their response to receiving positive emotions from their partner. For couples who have been in a "negative space" for a long time, it can feel awkward to receive positive emotions. It can be helpful for them to reflect on that and discuss the patience that will be needed for positive feelings to feel natural again in their relationship.

- Partners can create a work of art or some other expression of their gratitude for their partner. The creativity expressed here is only limited by the couple's imagination. If the couple want ideas, suggest planting a tree at their home, painting a picture, creating a mosaic, or adopting a pet and giving it a name that means "grateful," like the African name Shakira.

- Public expressions of gratitude can be powerful positive experiences for couples. Couples can express gratitude by hosting an anniversary party or renewal of vows. They can express gratitude for their partner to leaders in their church, family members, close friends or important mentors in their life. If the Thanksgiving holiday is near, the partners may want to focus on gratitude for their relationship as part of their celebration.

Virtues: gratitude, humility, compassion, honesty, patience

Principle: Couples can engage in activities that express gratitude for their relationship to infuse positive emotions into it for reconciliation.

TRUST INTERVENTION 22-2: CREATING POSITIVE SHIFTS FOR CHANGE THROUGH SMALL TRUSTWORTHY ACTIONS

"Whoever can be trusted with very little can also be trusted with much" (Lk 16:10).

Rebuilding trust in a relationship involves demonstrating trust in small everyday actions. Couples have many opportunities to demonstrate small trustworthy actions—and also to undermine them. The counselor's role is to help frame their task of rebuilding trust as attention to small everyday interactions that build a relationship.

Partners can discuss between them what will make them feel like they are demonstrating good intentions and working toward a trusting relationship. These can be small positive acts—things that are said or done for each other as attempts to build a stronger foundation. This could be similar to the love bank intervention (HOPE 18-12) or something creative the couple and counselor do or make together.

Some small trustworthy actions can be directly relevant to the violation of trust. For example, in the case of Keisha and Bill, the violation of trust was due to binge drinking. Therefore, Keisha's refraining from binge drinking and even from going to the bar would be a relevant change in behavior that should quell some of Bill's fears. Another example would be a couple in which one partner had made a financial offense. In that case, the offending partner would make the couple's finances transparent and discuss them regularly with the other partner. In addition, the offending partner might also offer to increase his or her income or sell personal assets to compensate for losing money. Another example would be a partner who had a problem with an inappropriate internet relationship or unacceptable pornography use. That partner might make choices about using the computer that help build trust with the partner, like using it in public areas of the home, putting a pornography website monitoring service on the computer, or stopping use of the computer for some time if possible.

Often the offended partner might have difficulty taking a risk to rebuild trust. The offended partner wants to self-protect. He or she will need to focus on the courage to be vulnerable in the relationship again. It can be helpful to offer this partner some language or scripts to use when discussing the difficulty with trusting the partner again.

Virtues: generosity, patience, perseverance, love, mercy

Principle: The work of rebuilding trust in a relationship requires attention to small trustworthy behaviors and to exercising the courage to trust again after offense.

TRUST INTERVENTION 22-3: DEALING WITH REINJURY

Reinjury after an offense is highly likely in a relationship that is struggling or has a history of offense. As in the case of Keisha and Bill, it is likely that Keisha may drink too much again, or she may give too much attention to another man (or Bill might think she is). Some types of offenses are highly likely to reoccur due to the nature of the behavior. They are either very common or have been a long-standing struggle for the individual. If a counselor can help to protect and shield the couple from some of the negative effects of reinjury, this can be helpful in the reconciliation process.

Step 1: Assess for likelihood of reinjury and beliefs about reinjury. When the likelihood of reinjury is high (e.g., he will yell again someday) and the beliefs about reinjury are negative (e.g., if he yells again, I'm out of here), the partners have a problem. There is virtually no chance of perfection, so the partner making the ultimatum has set up an almost impossible situation. Help the couple assess whether their situation has a possible future or whether they have doomed it to an inevitable breakup. The partner making the ultimatum has set things up so that it appears that failure of the relationship will be completely due to the other person, when in fact the ultimatum, and the rejection of any grace or mercy inherent in it, is itself the major reason for the failure of the relationship.

Beliefs can also play a pivotal role. Partners may be in a cycle of apology followed by fantasies of never having negativity again. This is similar to many cycles involving domestic violence. It is possible for a nonviolent couple to have a cycle of negative-hurtful events, followed by a strong showing of contrition, then a "honeymoon" time, followed by a build-up of negativity and tension and another negative-hurtful event. In this case, they need to explore the meaning and the rewards inherent in that cycle for them. This type of couple often has high conflict and an overexpression of emotions.

Step 2: Cognitive interventions for beliefs about trust. If it is found that there are unhealthy beliefs about reinjury and trust, then various cognitive interventions can be used to address those beliefs. In particular, addressing catastrophic thinking about offenses can help address partners' fears. Couples can be told that if there is a minor event or misunderstanding that causes reinjury, this is a great test of their relationship instead of a catastrophic event.

Step 3: Plan for two steps forward, one step back. In the event of reinjury, partners can be prepared for response. They can make decisions not to respond to the injury by being hurtful. They can plan for a time-out or cool-down period after the offense to allow for emotional flooding to recede. Response to the injury should primarily be created by the couple. Common approaches include use of an effective and heartfelt apology and efforts to bring the relationship back to work toward health. Couples can also clearly but firmly communicate how they expect to respond to a significant reinjury by their partner—perhaps seeking counseling again or considering a separation (such as in the case of violence or infidelity).

Step 4: Discuss a new relationship norm of "gratitude and latitude." Partners can talk about the long-term vision for their relationship. Having a sense of gratitude means that the partners work on having a relationship they can be thankful for. Thus they try to act in ways that are healthy, loving and honoring of their partner. They then express their gratitude to the partner as they achieve success. Latitude involves offering grace and mercy to the partner for small hurts and negligence as a fellow fallen human. Some injuries should have no latitude (violence or infidelity, for instance) and those can be discussed if there is any relevant history. However, for other injuries, such as saying something hurtful, forgetting a responsibility or misunderstandings, partners should cultivate an attitude of latitude. The counselor helps the couple to flesh out a vision of a relationship that is characterized by these principles and everyday actions that can help them achieve that vision.

Virtues: forgiveness, gratitude, love

Principle: Reinjury for minor or moderate injuries is unavoidable in a long-term relationship. Partners can prepare for injuries by having a plan to address them positively and return the relationship to a healthy trajectory.

TRUST INTERVENTION 22-4: PSYCHOEDUCATION ON TIME AND TRUST PROCESS

For couples who are rebuilding trust, sometimes a little bit of information can go a long way. So we created a psychoeducational intervention for couples who are rebuilding trust to help normalize some of their experiences. We recommend that you consider some conversation about the topic with the couple, and then have the couple read over the material as homework and discuss it the following week. This allows the counselor to apply the principles in the psychoeducational materials to the couple's situation.

Worksheet for Partners Having Difficulty Trusting Again

One of the most courageous things that a person does in an intimate relationship is trust. Trust is easily broken, and difficult to rebuild. Both partners must work together to build a relationship where trust is normal and rarely threatened. Yet sometimes people have difficulty trusting again after an offense despite their partner's efforts to improve things.

1. Ask yourself whether your partner is doing a reasonable job trying to rebuild trust? Is he or she acting in small trustworthy ways? Has he or she apologized and understood the effects of the loss of trust on you? If these things have not happened yet, it may be too early to trust again. Consider bringing this up in counseling. However, if these things are happening and you still are not able to trust, you might ask yourself whether you might have difficulty trusting others in general? Perhaps other important people in your life (past relationship partners, parents or trusted friends) have violated your trust, making it harder for you to trust your partner again.

2. Communicate your desired efforts toward trusting and reconciling in your relationship. You can do this by using the following principles:

   - **Use "I" statements.** It is helpful when discussing trust if you are able to use "I" statements like "I feel unsafe when you go to the bar with your friends, as if I'm not desirable to you anymore."

   - **Do not throw in everything but the kitchen sink.** It can be tempting to remind your partner of earlier offenses when you are stressed. Do all you can to stay in the "here and now" of the discussion about what is making it hard to trust right now.

   - **Say that you are committed to learning to trust.** Offended partners can tell their partner that they are working toward trusting again. Talk about the progress that is being made to rebuild trust in the relationship and what is helpful in that process.

   - **Distinguish decisions from emotions.** You and your partner can express that you have *decided* to trust but do not always *feel* trusting. Distinguishing decisions from emotions can help some partners as they work toward replacing negative skeptical feelings with more trusting feelings over time.

- **Share a secret.** People develop trusting relationships by sharing personal information. Both partners can share personal things about their life in areas other than the offense, which will improve the couple's bond and trust.

Psychoeducational Worksheet on Trust-busting and Trust-building

You have experienced a breach of trust in your relationship. Perhaps there has been a financial secret, gossip, or flirting with someone else. Many hurts can lead you to feel that you can't trust your partner. Repeated hurts over time can especially be difficult. We want you to have some information on what causes trust to be lost in a relationship and how most couples tend to rebuild trust.

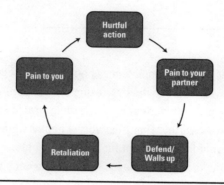

Figure 22.1

This cycle is inspired by the conflict-reconciliation model (Sells, Beckenbach & Patrick, 2009) which points out that in a relationship pain is often responded to with defenses, which can spiral out of control and cause more retaliation, pain and suffering. Everyone knows this cycle can happen, but it can be hard to see in the moment. Sometimes partners keep secrets of their hurtful actions because they don't want to start this cycle of pain and struggle. Yet the hurt still "leaks out" into the relationship, either directly by uncovering the secret, or indirectly by the way we act when keeping a secret. The relationship undergoes a downward spiral of conflict, pain and heartache.

The courage to trust one's partner. Building trust requires a new approach to pain. Instead of responding to pain with defensiveness, retaliation and further hurt, the partner needs to take a risk and have courage. It is scary! Sometimes the risk to trust and treat your partner with grace and kindness receives a positive and rewarding response. Sometimes it can cause more pain. You don't know what the response will be.

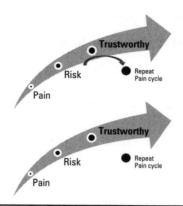

Figure 22.2

For the offender (which sometimes is both of you, depending on the situation) the key is to notice the risk-taking of your partner to trust you again and respond to your partner in a rewarding, gracious and kind way. You have to be trustworthy. That trustworthy behavior needs to be consistent. If you avoid flirting except for Saturday nights, then you aren't being trustworthy. Your partner needs to be able to depend on you.

For the offended (which also is sometimes both of you) it's important to let go of the power to retaliate and withdraw. It can appear to be protective and comforting to defend yourself with high emotional walls or retaliate with small or large acts of revenge. Yet it's like protecting a wound by not letting it get medicine. It will not allow the relationship to get healthy again.

A special note: Sometimes the loss of trust in a relationship has been so egregious and damaging that reengaging in trusting again is not appropriate. Sometimes one's partner has a problem that causes him or her to repeatedly hurt his or her partner or family. Going back to trust when the person's problem has not been fully addressed and healed is not healthy. In fact, it minimizes the problem which keeps the person from full healing. For example, suppose a wife has a shopping addiction so that she spends money and causes financial crisis in the family. The husband should not minimize the problem and forgive it without addressing the underlying problem of shopping addiction. Once the problem is addressed and improving, then the couple can begin to build trust again. Before that, it's not wise to trust around the problem issue.

Sometimes a partner (or both partners) have had repeated experiences of broken trust in their life. Anyone who has repeatedly experienced people as deceptive, undependable and untrustworthy will transfer that experience to their spouse. So if one partner is finding it difficult to trust the other, without any breach of trust, then it would be important to seek healing around the issue of trust in general. Some self-help reading, professional counseling and spiritual guidance can help bring healing to breeches of trust from childhood or other important relationships.

See if this cycle sounds familiar: Kobie lost his job due to layoffs. He didn't want to hurt his wife Madison, so he didn't tell her. He just pretended he still had a job. His goal to protect his wife was noble, but his method was not trustworthy. He broke trust with Madison by lying to her. Eventually Madison found out when she tried to contact him at work. She was livid!

- Kobie's hurtful action was to keep a secret about losing his job.
- Madison's response was pain.
- Madison tried to defend herself against that pain by focusing on her anger and yelling at Kobie. She then stormed off and drove to her sister's house. Kobie tried to call but she refused to answer her phone. She threw up a wall.
- Madison's retaliation of yelling and refusing to answer the phone was hurtful to Kobie.
- Kobie was hurt and in pain.

Everyone is in a bad place in this situation. How do they rebuild trust?

1. The emotional flood will need to come down. Sometimes it's not a bad idea to take a bit of a time-out in a relationship for some hours when there's been a breach of trust. The flood of emotions can make you say and do things that just feed the negative cycle. No one wins that game. Madison can tell Kobie that she needs to take a break because she doesn't want to say or do anything that will hurt them more.

2. Kobie can take a risk and make a sincere, heartfelt apology for his hurtful actions. She may receive his apology, and she may not be ready yet. Kobie may have to wait to be forgiven.

3. Madison's risk is to accept Kobie's apology and trust him again. She may need to see some trustworthy actions on Kobie's part.

4. Kobie can show his trustworthiness by sharing the soft and vulnerable hurt he felt about being laid off. He can state that he won't keep a secret from Madison in the future. He can ask Madison if there is anything else he can do to show himself trustworthy to her.

5. Madison can decide to extend forgiveness to Kobie. She can decide to try to put the offense behind them. She can empathize with his hurt over being laid off and not wanting to extend that hurt to her. She might even explore what about Kobie's past experiences in life cause him to keep his pain and struggles to himself instead of sharing them with her.

6. Kobie will need to maintain the trust. Madison is taking a risk to trust Kobie again out of her love and care for him. It's important that he respect that trust and earn it again by avoiding secrets in the future. If he finds himself struggling with that, he may need to seek some counseling to understand why he feels he can't share things with his wife. That may be part of long-standing family patterns from his family of origin, or unrealistic beliefs he has about his role as a husband or about what Madison can handle.

Now it's your turn. Consider something you have to rebuild trust for in your relationship. If trust hasn't been broken for you yet and you are early in your relationship, you might consider common trust-busters as described in this worksheet. If the topic you choose is still hurtful and tender for either of you, then you should discuss it with your counselor.

1. What is your role in the hurtful cycle of pain and defenses?

2. Where are you in terms of your flooded emotions receding so you can consider how to respond to this situation? Is there an underlying problem that is preventing you from rebuilding trust?

3. What personal strengths or faith experiences can you draw on to take the risk to be trustworthy or trust again?

4. What is your role in repairing your relationship?

5. What is something you feel you are able to do this week to take a step toward building trust again in your relationship?

Part Five

CONQUERING THE DIFFICULTIES YOU'LL FACE

We have come a long way. We have considered the theory and begun to walk you through counseling, beginning with the early sessions, which included initial assessments. Then, we provided many interventions from which you can choose during the "meat" of counseling—the times when most of the work is going on. Before we get to the end of counseling, though, we need to step back a moment and consider some of the difficulties that you will face throughout counseling. These are topics that our supervisees and those that have given us feedback on the hope-focused approach have raised across the years. Counseling rarely is a linear straight-shot toward glory. It involves many fits and starts, roadblocks and resistances. We want to share some of our practices in addressing these issues. This is the purpose of the next several chapters.

23

Assessing Change Throughout Treatment

૨૧

Linda is a well-trained and respected young psychologist in her community. She specializes in parenting evaluations and forensic psychology, but she sees some couples and families as part of her practice. She has six couple cases on her load right now. Two seem to be doing poorly. They are not doing homework, seem stuck in negative patterns during their sessions, and appear to lack motivation or ability to empathize with their partner's hurts and needs. Two couples are doing well. They hit roadblocks and problems now and then, but they persevere and are making slow but steady progress. One is an uncomplicated premarital couple. They are gaining knowledge and skills quickly. The final couple came to counseling with significant problems. However, they have completely thrown themselves into the process, are doing homework, reading books on relationship problems on their own, and making fast progress. Linda observes all of this in her office. What she does not know is how each client thinks he or she is doing. She has facts to base her prognosis and evaluation of their progress on, but she lacks a measureable unbiased review of change.

One of the more interesting areas of research in the last decade examines how we assess whether clients are improving. Virtually every clinician feels like his or her clients are improving. In fact, generally clinicians rate the clients as experiencing more positive change than clients rate themselves, objective measures reveal, or impartial observers estimate. This is not surprising. We are, after all, really invested in our clients succeeding, and we also only have the behavior in session—when we are ever-present to control their more negative behaviors—on which to base our own observations.

Research shows that couple therapy in general does work (Owen, Duncan, Anker & Sparks, 2012). Yet each individual clinician has a full range of outcomes among his or her clients, and within any clinic there are clinicians who have better outcomes than others. The fields of medicine and education have both taken steps toward patient or student ratings as a normal part of doing business. We believe it is only a matter of time before meaningful client ratings are an expected part of the counseling business. Perhaps you are a new clinician and often wonder whether all the work you are putting into your clients is actually helping them. Or perhaps you are an experienced but humble clinician who is willing to examine new materials and ideas for assessing change in your clients.

PROCESS TYPES OF ASSESSMENTS

We think all couple counseling could use some assessment of working alliance, partner alliance, hope, work, love and progress toward goals. We provide these ideas for your consideration.

Working alliance. Working alliance has three parts: tasks, goals and bond (Bordin, 1979). A good working alliance is characterized by counselor and client who agree on the tasks of counseling, concur on the goals for outcome and also have a warm bond between partners and the counselor. Working alliance is one of the most well-studied transtheoretical constructs in mental health (Orlinsky, Ronnestad & Willutski, 2004). It has been shown to account for 30-40% of the variance in outcomes in psychotherapy research.

Partner alliance. In a couple relationship, there is also an alliance of the partners with each other. That alliance might be more important than the alliance with the counselor (Bartle-Haring et al., 2012). The research in this area is less robust than for the working alliance, but for couple therapy the partner alliance appears to be an important predictor of outcome. Therefore, for couple therapy it is important to understand how much the partners feel like they are working together on tasks and goals, and how warm their bond is with each other.

Hope. Change relies on hope. Nineteenth-century French writer Stendhal is quoted as saying, "A very small degree of hope is sufficient to cause the birth of love." It is important to stay aware of the couple's degree of hope. This is why our approach is called the hope-focused couple approach to counseling. We work to maximize the effects of hope in counseling. Snyder (Irving et al., 2004) defined hope as *willpower* (motivation) and *waypower* (agency for change)—and we have added *wait power* (patience to wait for change). If partners seem to be losing or not maintaining hope that their love will improve, you would do well to assess these components of hope.

Work. It is common in therapy for people to want to change, to trust in the counselor, to have hoped that change is possible. Yet when it is time to work, expend effort, take risks or put in time to make the relationship change, they falter. A regular assessment of the work they are putting into their relationship can help motivate partners to invest more work. It can also help explain why there has not been expected change or why change has been slow in coming. This is similar to tracking exercise and calories during a diet so that you are able to determine why there has or has not been change in weight.

Love. Because improving the love in the relationship is a major goal of couple counseling, then assessing the partners' relationship is an important measure of progress. Partners may have more specific goals for treatment, such as increasing emotional forgiveness or learning communication skills, but you can safely bet that the partners' underlying assumption is that as a result of counseling the love between them will grow stronger and deeper. So we believe it is important to assess regularly the partners' perceptions of their love.

Progress toward goals. Partners have goals for their relationship. They hope couple counseling will help them move closer to those goals. It is good for partners to periodically assess how well they are doing in terms of progress toward their goals for counseling. The goals could change across the course of counseling. A regular check-in on the goals will help to make these changes explicit and allow for discussion and intentional decisions in changing goals.

The purpose of periodic case assessment is to induce clinical change. Each of these things can be a therapeutic intervention for increasing motivation and reevaluating progress toward goals. The discussion that happens in response to the assessment can make a real difference in marking progress.

How to Present Process Assessment to Clients

Some clients have been asked by their counselor how helpful counseling was to them. This is not a common experience for the public, however. People are used to going to the counselor, the doctor, the dentist or other healthcare professionals and assuming that the knowledgeable doctor will be able to understand what needs to be done. Thus they can passively comply with the doctor's orders. Even if you ask, "How is counseling going, and what do you still need from counseling?" many clients will not state any concerns that they are not making progress. Asking in an offhand or informal way is not the best way to get the information you need from clients. It is important to give a strong message that *this information is* crucial *to their improvement in counseling*. Therefore, you take their feedback very seriously. You need to closely listen to the client's voice.

If you give clients a more active role in their counseling process, they will improve more in objective outcomes (Owen et al., 2012). Therefore it is crucial that the regular assessment process of counseling clearly communicate how important it is. Let us say it again. Tell the clients how it is helpful to them, the clients, not just to the counselor.

Your demeanor and nonverbal style are centrally important here. If this script is said to a client in a way that seems like the counselor is not highly interested in the answers, the client will think that it is just pro forma or perhaps that it is just something required by your boss. The client must hear that you are deeply interested in his or her experience of therapy. To make this point, you might say something like this at the beginning of counseling:

> It is important to me that we both stay fully aware of how we think counseling is going. Sometimes we will try things and they will work very well for the two of you. You might get excited about that and tell your friends. Other times, things we try will fizzle. Hopefully nothing will harm your relationship. But it is impossible for every intervention to be a perfect match for your needs. This is where you come in. I need constant input from both of you on how your relationship is doing, and how helpful the work we are doing is for you to meet your goals. Every week I'm going to ask how things are going in counseling and in your relationship overall. I have this form to track our progress each week. From your answers I'm going to create a graph and show it to you regularly to help us track how you are doing on these things: working alliance, partner alliance, hope, love, work and progress toward your goals.

You may have to explain some of these terms—like *working alliance* and *partner alliance*—so that they can understand, depending on their background and exposure to counseling ideas.

The first time that the questionnaire is given to the client, you as counselor should be the one giving it to them. This way questions can be answered and attention given to fully understanding the concepts. After that initial assessment, though, the form could be given and the responses even graphed by a staff member. Generally the form is given weekly to ensure that these factors stay in focus during the course of counseling, and plateaus of treatment, or regression, are caught early and addressed.

AFTER THE QUESTIONNAIRE IS GRAPHED

It is amazing how many counselors administer feedback forms, patient surveys and other ways of collecting information from their clients, but then they do not use the results to help improve counseling for those clients. We do not think that's the best way to use client feedback. It is important to take the time in counseling to look at the results of a weekly survey and graph the results, then discuss the progress briefly with the client.

What if they are doing well? If both partners are reporting that they are improving, then the counselor should give the couple encouragement and praise for their hard work. Process with the couple what they have been doing differently that has caused the changes in their relationship. Discuss obstacles to maintaining the positive momentum. If the couple is beginning to indicate that their goals are being met, then you can begin to discuss when they want to finish counseling.

What if they disagree about how they are doing? It is not unusual for one partner to perceive the relationship to be more positive than the other partner does. There are a number of reasons why there might be differences in perception between the partners. You'll want to explore the differences. It is possible that there is a *power struggle* going on between the partners that they might want to explore. Sometimes *interpersonal patterns* of relationships with intimate partners, or people in helping roles in their life (such as parents, medical caregivers or teachers), will be replayed in counseling situations. For example, if a client had a distant and conflictual relationship with his or her family of origin, he or she might replay that with the counselor. There are also levels of *motivation* that can influence how partners might respond to a questionnaire with different evaluations. You might ask yourself whether different levels of motivation might explain the different ratings. *Personality differences* can also explain the results. One person might simply be more optimistic than the other. Finally, a *psychological disorder* or mood swings could explain the difference. Depressed clients tend to see things more negatively. Discuss with the couple what they believe to be the reason for different ratings. That discussion can be a therapeutic intervention for the couple. It is possible that seeing things differently is one of the problems they face. Discussing it gives them an opportunity to address the disagreement in a healthy way.

What if they have hit a plateau? If your clients are like most who come for counseling, then there will be obvious gains in self-report data for the first four to seven sessions (Bartle-Haring et al., 2012). The results will improve in general and rise fairly quickly to a noticeably better place. This can be surprising for counselors who feel that they have really just begun to dig into the problems the couple is facing and learn new ways to address them. The couple's experience of change can be rather different than the counselor's perspective. The couple can essentially be saying, "This is so much better than things used to be! So we have hope that we are changing."

Most couples will plateau around session four to seven. It is good to discuss with the couple what they think is going on when a plateau occurs. Then a counselor has a perfect opportunity to explain the process of counseling to the couple. At first they are distressed and unhappy and simply seeking help. So any change that happens early on is a breath of fresh air and brings hope that more change can happen. It is like the early stages of learning a new hobby or skill like piano. At first you know nothing about playing the piano and your ability to play increases very quickly by just learning a few small things. But then it is time to dig deeper and work harder at learning to play so you can get to the next level. The same thing happens in counseling after the "joining" period of counseling at the beginning. The couple has set goals, and they have a better understanding of their relationship and each other. Now it is time to work toward *being* different in the relationship. They will be in the working phase of counseling for as long as they decide they are willing to work. Eventually they will be ready to stop counseling and continue working on their relationship on their own. The couple and counselor can discuss together what that timeline will look like now that they are in the working phase.

What if they do not seem to be improving enough? If the partners are indicating that they (1) are continuing to be dissatisfied, (2) lack a working alliance with the counselor, or (3) lack a good bond with each other, then it is good to have a conversation about that. The counselor might not be aware of the lack of progress in cases where a regular assessment is not being conducted. But lack of improvement is very common in couple counseling. It is better to be aware of this and be able to address it than just to have clients continue to suffer or to drop out early from treatment. Clients will often not bring up their dissatisfactions. The regular assessment is an invitation to discuss a lack of progress.

It is important to bring a lack of improvement to the attention of the couple and collaboratively discuss how to address the problem. Sometimes the clients are communicating a discouragement and lack of hope for their relationship. Sometimes one or both partners are stuck in negative patterns, and they are communicating that they are not seeing changes yet. At times the counselor-client match is not ideal. Not every counselor can help every couple who are seeking help. If the working alliance with the counselor is strained, then it is very important to process that with the partners. Anything below a very high level (top 20% of the scale) of working alliance is an indicator that the client may not feel understood. Or it might indicate that the couple feel that your goals for counseling do not match theirs. There may be a hundred reasons why couples feel dissatisfied or unbonded with each other or with you. It is good to help the partners explore why they might feel like the working alliance is less than high. The counselor should spend a good amount of time and energy exploring this openly and nondefensively.

It is equally important to have a discussion when the partners rate low partner alliance. Even if partners have two different goals for counseling, they should feel like their partner is supportive of both partners' goals. For example, if the counselor finds that the wife is seeking a more emotionally close relationship while the husband is seeking a more peaceful relationship, then both partners should be able to value both closeness and peace as good for their relationship. The counselor can offer this solution to the couple and discuss whether they are able to support multiple goals in counseling.

If the ratings of improvement continue to stay low even after good processing, attempting to address concerns and spending adequate time in counseling, then it might be time to discuss referral. Clients will often not bring this up out of respect for the role of the counselor as a provider. However, if the couple has engaged in a number of weeks of counseling without much improvement, then the counselor should discuss whether another venue of counseling might be more helpful for them. They might need individual counseling for some time to address a psychopathology that is interfering with change. They might need to delay couple counseling until after an important life event such as the birth of a child, a deployment or surgery. Couple counseling requires energy and focus in order to fully realize the goals. At times the couple might benefit from working with a different counselor. Helping clients with a referral will often assist them to continue to seek treatment from a qualified provider instead of dropping out.

The HOPE Weekly Couples Assessment

Make an X on the line indicating how you feel about each of these areas of your relationship and counseling *this week*.

Table 23.1

	None— Could not be worse	100%— Could not be better
Love. How much do you feel like you were valuing each other and not devaluing each other this week?	_____	
Hope. How much do you feel like you have hope that things are going to change in your relationship for the better?	_____	
Working Alliance. This week how much do you feel like you and the counselor are working well together for your relationship goals?	_____	
Partner Alliance. This week how much do you feel like you and your partner are working well together for your relationship goals?	_____	
Work. This week how much time and effort did you put into improving your relationship (doing homework, doing something positive/healthy)?	_____	
How much progress have you made in reaching this goal since counseling started? Goal 1 _____ Goal 2 _____ Goal 3 _____	_____ 1 _____ 2 _____ 3	

This form can be downloaded from hopecouples.com.

24

Resistances, Roadblocks and Rabbit Trails

ॐ

Not surprisingly, we both (Jen and Ev) love to read counseling books. There is a sense of excitement when encountering one, wading through the concepts, and being lured into the world of clients seen through the lens of the authors. But one of the things that always frustrated us when reading books on counseling is that the ideas in the book often did not work with the cases we were actually seeing like they did in the book. Books seemed to explain things like a linear equation, working straight ahead for the improvement of the clinical problem with hardly a hiccup. The clients that we saw in our offices had incredible cases of the hiccups. And when they were not hiccupping, they were running headlong into roadblocks or blasting full-speed off into tangential rabbit trails. It felt like all we did was address resistances, roadblocks and rabbit trails. The challenge in translating book-learning into the clinic was to balance time addressing those resistances, roadblocks and rabbit trails with the delicious ideas we had learned from the book.

RESISTANCE VERSUS ROADBLOCK

We distinguish between a resistance and a roadblock. A *resistance* is an inner psychological barrier to change. It may be expressed practically or psychologically, but the reason counseling is blocked is that partners are afraid of something. They may be afraid of changing their relationship or themselves. They may be afraid that something is wrong with them and that counseling will confirm their insecurities. Sometimes they are afraid that they will lose autonomy and control if they have a better bond with their partner.

In contrast, a *roadblock* is something external that impedes counseling. It may be a busy lifestyle, low income, a chronic illness, rotating work schedules or car trouble. It is possible for a resistance to be expressed as a roadblock or a tangential rabbit trail. This means that a fear causes a couple to keep a busy schedule which makes attending counseling regularly difficult or distracts them from focusing on their goal of a better relationship. Clients will often point to roadblocks to counseling. They rarely want to discuss fears and resistances. Both resistances and roadblocks can be expressed in behavior that slows down counseling, such as not doing homework.

It is important when addressing resistances and roadblocks not to get stuck in either-or thinking about a case. The wise counselor will simultaneously address resistances, roadblocks and rabbit trails while also bringing delicious ideas of intervention to sessions with clients. This is especially important in brief strategic types of counseling where the agreement with the couple is that counseling will last from 5 to 20 sessions.

UNDERSTAND THE RESISTANCE OR ROADBLOCK

Couples can grow considerably by understanding what is going on when they slow down in counseling. If the issue has little to do with internal psychological problems but is an external roadblock, then a problem-solving discussion can be helpful. The couple might need to consolidate their resources and reduce their effort in other areas of their life in order to get what they want from counseling. Or they might need to extend their plans for the duration of counseling if rotating work schedules will lead to missed sessions. The couple has to decide how to prioritize the limited resources in their life. Counseling requires much time, money and energy. The couple may have underestimated the amount of resources they would need, so they need to rethink how to address roadblocks.

If the reason counseling is slowed down is due to resistance and internal psychological fears, then a more therapeutic approach is needed. Couples can often find their way through resistances by asking whether they have ever felt this way in the past. By exploring common fears in their life they can often identify the ones that are making change difficult for them. Counselors find it helpful to assume that couples probably have some fears of counseling and of changing their relationship. In much of life it is often true that "better the devil you know, than the one you do not know." So people will maintain unhealthy but familiar patterns rather than create a new pattern with unknown consequences. This fear is logical and reasonable. Couples often rely heavily on their counselor to reassure them that the new patterns they are creating will not first make them hopeful for change and then dash those hopes on the rocks of daily life. Confronting resistances as well as roadblocks can be made a common and expected experience in counseling. Doing so can help many couples who do not want to name their fears. One cannot slay dragons that one cannot see or name.

USE COURAGE

Many clients have incredible reserves of courage that they can use to address fears. They might need to be reminded of their ability to address problems, but most people have displayed courage many times. People are also capable of being quite cowardly as well, but focusing on fears and cowardice is more likely to increase resistances. Couples often benefit from asking them what they need to summon up the nerve to move forward in their relationship. They may need reassurance from their partner or encouragement from the counselor or their minister, or they may just need to make a decision to jump into the situation. You can ask the couple to consider what other times in the past they have done things that required courage. By drawing on virtues and personal strengths, you can equip clients toward a positive view of their abilities and increase the likelihood that they will face their fears.

MAKE OVERCOMING RESISTANCES AND ROADBLOCKS A THERAPEUTIC GOAL

Resistances and roadblocks are concerns for everyone who has a stake in couple therapy being successful. You can help clients by making overcoming resistances or roadblocks a therapy goal. For example, perhaps a client fears confronting his or her partner. That fear is making it difficult to engage in interventions that address conflict resolution. Once that fear is identified, then both partners and the counselor can help address that fear and create success experiences with confrontations or challenges. Often the fears are unwarranted and are actually more relevant to past relationships with parents or previous partners. So partners can invite challenge or confrontation and state that it is acceptable. One partner can calmly listen to a complaint or request with an openness to hearing what the defensive other is saying. The counselor can coach the partners through this in an effort to learn new skills in the relationship that will open doors for future interventions. By having a corrective emotional experience, the partners can open new possibilities for their relationship.

By making overcoming resistances or roadblocks a therapeutic goal, you can also ask for permission to note when the resistance or roadblock might appear again in counseling. So if the partner seems to be holding back on a request or complaint about something in a later session, then the counselor already has permission to bring it up and confront the behavior collaboratively. For example, the counselor might say, "As I look at your nonverbal behavior, you seem to be upset about something, John, but you are holding it in. You had asked for me to say something when it looked like you were holding back in asking for what you need in the relationship. Is that what is going on for you inside now, John?" Having established an agreement about this goal earlier gives the counselor more leeway to intervene when the resistance or roadblock arises in the future to accomplish "in the moment" change.

RESISTANCES AND ROADBLOCKS CAN BE WORN DOWN
ONCE THE WATERS RECEDE

Often there are strong feelings associated with resistances in particular and sometimes with roadblocks. Clients will feel flooded with feelings of vulnerability, fear, sadness, or anger and frustration. When people are flooded with emotion, they are going to remain defended. They are in an emotional survival frame of mind in which their brain's emotion structures are in control of the self and the reasoning or self-control centers are just hanging on and trying to stay alive. If a partner appears to be emotionally flooded in session or at home, then the old saying "safety first" is the guide. Nothing good is likely to happen until partners feel a sense of safety from the flood of emotions. You may say something like, "It feels like things just got overwhelming or unsafe. Is that what is going on?" This metacognitive statement can help refocus the conversation from whatever was flooding it to the effects of the conversation on the partners. By observing the effects of the conversation, the couple attempt to gain perspective and stem the flood.

However, for many situations just observing the effects will not be enough to lower the flood water. As counselor, you should be ready to help partners manage their emotions. You can do this by helping them shift the mood in the room to a calmer tone. The partners may need to practice either time-out or calming techniques in the office. You can try using a sculpting technique (BOND 19-11) to help the partners get perspective. It might be helpful to have them sculpt where they would like to be as a couple around the issue they are discussing. Then have them discuss what it would be like if that were the case and what they need to do to get there. Also you can teach them to use emotion to transform emotion (HURT 20-7) or to engage in emotional soothing (intervention 14-3). Those interventions can assist partners in learning emotional regulation skills to help with resistances and floods.

CONCLUSIONS

Whatever the reason for the resistance or roadblock, it is important to be not only warm with the couple and also unwavering in your commitment to their improvement. You must retain hope that the relationship can improve meaningfully even if the partners encounter many obstacles to improvements. You need to hold on to empathy for the clients' fears and the roadblocks that inevitably happen. Counselors who are able to understand and empathize with clients' fears and obstacles and yet encourage forward movement toward their goals can be a powerful force for their good.

25

Counselors' Negative Reactions to Couples

૨**

ouple counseling is emotionally charged for the counselor, not just for the couple. Counselors are influenced by their own personal attachment experiences and other experiences in past and present relationships. Negative reactions or countertransference issues—and even positive countertransference reactions—can make it difficult to navigate in any case, but couple counseling adds more layers of complexity than individual counseling (if for no other reason than there are twice as many clients to react to). Counselors often have strong reactions to a spouse within a client couple who is reluctant to attend therapy, is narcissistic, or mistreats his or her spouse. Couple counseling is full of strong emotions, attachments and conflict. It is all about love after all. A counselor's own gender biases or beliefs are often activated in couple counseling. Couple relationships have a high degree of diversity in values and style in modern cultures, which requires diversity of expertise for counselors. And the potential is always present for the counselor to take sides with one partner and get caught right between the desires of each partner.

Ah, these are the challenges—and the joys—of counseling couples. They are never dull. But there is a downside. The strong emotions, attachments and conflicts of couple counseling make it likely that counselors will have negative feelings about some clients or individual partners who seek couple counseling. A primary skill for an effective couple counselor is to understand and manage negative feelings of countertransference helpfully and effectively for the couple.

There is a great deal of clinical discussion, particularly from psychoanalytic theorists, about the importance of understanding negative reactions to couples or negative countertransference. Case studies are common, and the issue is included in most psychotherapy training books. However, there is little actual research on counselor's negative reactions to clients. Moyers and Rollnick (2002) conceptualized client resistance as the client's ambivalence about change and the counselor's response to that ambivalence. There is an interaction taking place among the individuals, and it involves the relationship of couple and counselor and also each member of the couple and the counselor. Client resistance and diagnosis is a significant predictor of dropout and poor outcomes of psychotherapy in general (Swift & Greenberg, 2012). However, the counselor's negative reactions, or even resistances, to the client are not fully understood in the research. Therefore, we provide support for couple counselors by drawing from clinical experience and the limited research to help counselors who are feeling negatively about a client or couple.

COUNSELOR'S NEGATIVE REACTION IS USEFUL INFORMATION

One of the classic teachings about countertransference from the psychoanalytic tradition is that once you can sort out what part of the counselor's reaction is due to the counselor himself or herself and his or her background, the counselor's reaction to a client provides significant information about the client. If it is difficult for a counselor to care about or empathize with the client, then it is important to ask what information this might be providing. Perhaps the client tends to have a reserved or standoffish relationship with others in general. The client may tend to be globally hostile, or have negative reactions to authority figures or caregivers. It may be difficult for the client to trust others. Even in the first session the counselor's feelings about the client can be important grist for the mill of counseling.

This information should be used judiciously in counseling. After all, it might be harsh for a client to enter the second session of counseling and hear from his or her counselor, "You know, I do not really like you. I wonder why that is?" Most clinical relationships could not handle a challenge that direct. However, counselors can explore with the couple each partner's feelings about the therapist-client relationship while the counselor looks for interpersonal patterns. It is often helpful to talk with the couple about whether the counseling situation feels safe to them, and why or why not. Issues of trust are often accessible early in treatment when couples are settling into the relationship with the counselor who is trying to create a safe "container" of couple counseling.

What is unique to their relationship? Countertransference within couple counseling has some unique aspects to it. It is important to assess in the intake both partners' interpersonal stance with regard to each other and others in their life. Sometimes the couple's attachment or interpersonal stance with each other is unique. If their relationship has deteriorated or if they have few other important relationships, you may find that the couple's relationship with each other does not predict their relationship with others or with you as their counselor. The wife might be hostile toward her husband, but not hostile in any other relationship.

In other cases their attachment style or interpersonal stance might be similar across relationships. For example, E. J. has a negative relationship with his wife, Princella. He tries to control her, and he often speaks down to her. Princella also has a tendency to respond to E. J. in ways that are emotionally dysregulated and immature. Their relationship often reminds their counselor of a parent-child relationship. However, in the workplace Princella is a successful bank executive with dozens of people working for her. She has high expectations of employees, and the immature and dysregulated behaviors that exist in her marriage do not characterize other relationships. E. J., however, has negative relationships with virtually all of the women in his life. His relationship with his mother is emotionally distant. He often fights with his sister. The woman who serves as secretary for his group at a software company has complained about him often to their boss. He has been sent to sensitivity trainings at work to decrease the conflict between E. J. and women in the workplace. In this case E. J.'s interpersonal stance with women tends to be conflictual and combative, which is consistent across relationships. A female counselor might find herself feeling negatively toward both partners because E. J. is likely to be argumentative and resistant with the counselor and Princella displays immature behaviors with E. J. in sessions.

Counselors need to assess the interpersonal stance and patterns of the couple with each other, with the counselor, and as reported with significant others in their life. In particular, reports on relationships with parents, previous partners, children, siblings, coworkers and bosses can help provide a bigger picture of whether the interpersonal stance apparent in the couple's relationship with each other is pervasive to all relationships. The more specific the problem is to their relationship the more likely they will be able to make shifts and changes in their interpersonal stance with each other.

What does the client "pull" from me? A client's interpersonal stance will pull for the counselor to feel and behave in certain ways. I (Jen) find that, if I review my feelings about a client at the end of the intake session, I often discover important interpersonal patterns already developing. Some clients are complimentary, submissive and deferring, which pulls for me to take the role of expert or parent in the relationship. I like this—and that is just as much a cue for me to be careful as not liking a client. Other clients withhold information, have difficulty trusting or even "tease" with information they are obviously withholding. This makes me feel frustrated, ineffective or incompetent. I do not like that, and I know to be just as careful in those cases.

For example, if Leo tends to be shy and avoidant and has difficulty trusting in relationships in general, then that characterizes his interpersonal stance. He may be defensive and guarded in the intake session, giving little information about himself and the relationship. This is frustrating to his wife, Kate, who would like more emotional intimacy than Leo will be comfortable with. This also may be frustrating to the counselor. However, if the counselor understands and empathizes with how that interpersonal stance developed for Leo then it is easier to be compassionate and develop a working alliance with both partners. The information from the counselor may be useful in helping Leo increase his understanding of his effects on others, including his wife.

What if the interpersonal relationship is about me? Whenever there is an interpersonal relationship in counseling, whether with individuals or couples, the role of the counselor in the relationship should be fully understood. While clients may not fully understand their impact on others and their interpersonal stance, the counselor should have a good understanding of his or her own interpersonal stance. For example, many new counselors feel insecure about their role as authority figures and about their competency. Some respond by attempting to be more authoritarian and defensive than they need to be. They "puff up" in the relationship. If the client tends to have an interpersonal stance that lacks trust or questions authority, then the counselor's issues can be activated with significant negative feelings toward the client or couple. Those negative feelings can further an interpersonal pattern that harms the outcomes of counseling. These negative feelings do not happen just with neophyte counselors. Counselors are more vulnerable to having negative feelings that are due to their own issues when they are stressed or when stretched into new areas of practice, or when clients touch on unexplored and painful parts of the counselor's life. It is the ethical obligation for counselors to be fully aware of these issues and to manage them with self-care, supervision or seeking counseling themselves. That said, I (Ev) am continually amazed at finding new aspects of my own defensiveness that I never before realized—even in my mid-sixties. So we probably are never going to "arrive" at perfect self-awareness. (Or perhaps that is just projection on my part. Yikes! Another defense.)

COUNTERTRANSFERENCE PUTS COUPLE COUNSELORS AT RISK FOR IMBALANCED ALLIANCES

There are few things that a counselor can do that can damage a client. (There are some, of course. For instance we would discourage romantic relationships with your clients. That is harmful to clients.) However, creating a stronger alliance with one of the partners in a couple is predictive of poor psychotherapy outcomes and relationship dissolution. A counselor who consistently takes sides with one partner increases the chances of further relationship dysfunction and dissolution—the opposite of the stated goals of most couple counseling. Counselors must not take sides consistently in couple counseling, although on particular issues, side-taking may occur as long as it is kept balanced. The only exception for this rule is when safety is an issue, such as in domestic violence situations. In those cases in which one partner is more vulnerable to harm, it is necessary to protect the vulnerable person.

Counselors need to be fully aware of imbalanced alliance and constantly vigilant for cases where one partner is more likeable and easier for the counselor to work with. This may be due to the counselor's personal issues, but more often is due to the client's issues. Within some couples there is an imbalance in ability to be likeable and interpersonally connect with the counselor. Sometimes one partner is more hostile, negative and mistrusting than the other. Often one partner is more invested in the counseling process, making for a natural alliance with the counselor. At other times demographic similarities with the counselor create an imbalance such as gender, religion, age, race or disability. Some couples that are in power struggles will vie for the primary alliance with the counselor, making a balanced alliance more difficult. The ways that an imbalanced alliance can occur are numerous.

The counselor needs to constantly stay aware of his or her feelings about each partner. When the counselor sympathizes with one partner and agrees more often with that partner, there is a real risk of harming the couple's relationship. It is often a good idea to have some open discussion about how each partner feels regarding the balance of alliance. Some couples are not aware that the counselor's role is usually not to take sides in their arguments. The stated goal is that the couple's counselor is loyal to the health of the relationship primarily, not to individuals. This can help if the couple is engaged in a power struggle or conflict. The counselor can restate that his or her loyalty is to what is healthy for the relationship and discuss with the couple what avenue would help promote that health.

TURNING THE TIDE ON NEGATIVE FEELINGS TOWARD PARTNERS

I (Jen) have seen negative feelings develop in my own cases and in those I have supervised so often that it seems to be almost as common as resistance. Sometimes the negative feelings sneak up on the counselor over several sessions. Other times they are clearly happening in the first twenty minutes of the first session. Given that negative feelings toward clients are so common and that they run the risk of harming the relationship, it is important to have some strategies for handling those feelings.

Compassion. One of the best avenues for changing negative feelings toward a client is to develop compassion for the person. This may require creating a conceptualization of why the partner (or couple) has developed the frustrating or difficult behavior. For example, in the case of Leo and Kate earlier in this chapter, Leo is emotionally withdrawn and defensive. It is common for people with this problem to have been criticized, belittled or devalued repeatedly. In his past Leo might have struggled with low self-esteem and been bullied or even abused. His emotional distance and defensiveness serve a function in his life to avoid further hurt. He is guarding what little bit of self-esteem he has left in a way that demonstrates his desperation.

Humility. Another avenue for helping counselors handle negative feelings toward clients is to work with an attitude of humility. Everyone has behaviors or habits that are difficult on others. Even one's personal strengths have inherent limitations within them. For example, if counselors are level-headed and calm in the face of difficult situations, then they are often also slow to change when needed and emotionally cool. If counselors can understand and accept their own personal limitations and weaknesses, then it is easier to accept the limits of others.

Weekly assessment. Counselors can find it helpful to use the weekly assessments (as discussed in chapter 23) to address problems in counseling. If the counselor is having negative feelings toward a client, then it is likely that the client will report a weaker working alliance with the counselor. This provides an opportunity to talk about how to improve the warm and supportive relationship between clients and counselor that is needed for positive change to occur.

Remembering the goal. Another avenue for handling negative feelings toward clients is to orient toward the end goals of counseling. Negative feelings are often part of rabbit trails or resistances in counseling. While negative feelings may provide information about a couple's relationship or individual needs, they can also easily distract the counselor from the goals of counseling. It can be easy to focus for weeks on some negative behavior that clients are displaying in counseling, like incomplete homework. However, focusing on the negative can discourage partners and slow down change for a couple. Once the negative behavior or attitude is identified, at least minimally, then it is important to create opportunities for change to occur more positively. The experience of counseling needs to be one of encouragement and positive change.

Remembering the client's strengths. Positive psychology principles indicate that clients often reach goals by using their strengths to help them with their weaknesses (Harvey & Pauwels, 2004). If Leo comes to counseling each week to hear from his counselor (and perhaps his wife) that he is defensive and has been damaged by childhood bullying, and the counselor asks him to dig deeper into this pain, he may find it hard to change. However, Leo's strengths can be used to help overcome his defensiveness. Perhaps he can also be gentle and thoughtful with his wife. These positive behaviors can receive attention and be further explored and encouraged so that they will increase. The focus on Leo's strengths provides momentum to decrease the negative defensive behaviors. Clients need to perceive and practice the positive behaviors that will pull them toward their goals. By focusing counseling and homework on positive change and on developing positive interactions and traits, there is a better chance for healthy relationship change across time.

Conclusions

Counselors' negative reactions to couples are common, and they predict problems in couple counseling. Assessing the negative reaction in terms of the couple's relationship, their interpersonal stance and the counselor's own personal issues is an important step. Counselors can also supportively increase the couple's understanding of any difficult interpersonal stances or behavior patterns. Then counselors will need to find ways to handle their own negative reactions so that they can help the couple move forward toward their goal of a healthier relationship.

26

Working with Partners Who Have a Trauma History

❧

There is increased awareness of the effects of trauma on families and relationships, whether from childhood abuse, combat exposure or even accidents.[1] Trauma has been a substantial new area of development in mental healthcare in the past decade and the treatment of couples with trauma history has significantly improved (Hecker, 2011). Often traumas happen in the family and they certainly have an impact on families. Because family trauma has become increasingly frequent, we include this chapter about how to deal with couples who have experienced trauma.

Andre and Joy have had chronic problems with trust and intimacy. Joy has had difficulty with sexual intimacy since the couple began having sex when they were engaged. She tells the counselor that she can only have sex with Andre if she is drunk and that this was true with two past boyfriends as well. Andre, who enjoys drinking fairly heavily himself, had no problem with this at first but now is feeling the strain on their new marriage. Joy often accuses Andre of being attracted to other women, and she makes disparaging remarks about herself. She also often becomes upset if Andre attempts to influence her to improve their sexual relationship or decrease her own obvious distress. When Andre tries to encourage her, she rejects his attempts. He has stopped trying for the last several months. When they were

---

[1]Some material in this chapter is taken from the writings of Tabitha Sierra, Abrielle Conway, Amy Smith and Heather Kemp, previously published at www.hopecouples.com.

engaged, Joy told him that she was molested by a teacher when she was ten, but the two had not made the connection that her childhood experience is affecting their relationship on multiple levels.

TYPES OF FAMILY TRAUMA

Childhood sexual abuse. Research identifies a host of negative long-term sequelae for childhood sexual abuse survivors. These include decreased emotional intimacy, sexual dysfunction and dissatisfaction, lack of trust, feelings of betrayal, low self-esteem, depression, anxiety, and fear of retraumatization (Anderson-Jacob & McCarthy-Veach, 2005). In particular, flashbacks and intrusive memories of sexual abuse may interfere with the survivor's quality of sexual intimacy or even deter the survivor from engaging in sexual activity with a partner (Nelson-Goff et al., 2006). In contrast, some survivors report experiencing sexual promiscuity and preoccupation with sexual encounters following childhood sexual abuse (Anderson-Jacob & McCarthy-Veach, 2005).

Combat exposure. Couples where one partner has been exposed to trauma through combat have similar types of issues. This may include problems with alcohol, violence in the relationship or PTSD symptoms, which are difficult on a relationship. Combat exposure symptoms can include hypervigilence, mistrust, aggression, depression, hopelessness, nightmares, physical symptoms or isolation. Ev and psychotherapist Diane Langberg (Worthington & Langberg, 2012) recently explored the difficulties of complex combat trauma especially regarding self-condemnation and self-forgiveness. Partners are often sympathetic to the veteran's experiences of combat at first. However, when symptoms continue, the relationship is at risk. This can lead to further problems within the military service, depression and sometimes suicidality. Research indicates a correlation between combat exposure and marital distress (Gimbel & Booth, 1994). However, there is some research that if the couple can persevere for the approximate 6 to 12 months of readjustment, their functioning tends to return to precombat levels (Solomon et al., 1992). This research was not done on military members with multiple deployments. So the counselor's role in many ways is to help couples traverse *at least* that first year after combat exposure—perhaps even longer—and to assist couples that are not recovering well. Two problems in particular that should be assessed with combat exposure are suicidality and domestic violence. Whereas most people with combat exposure will not have these symptoms, the symptoms are threats to safety and they occur with much higher prevalence than in the general client population.

ADDRESSING TRAUMA ISSUES IN COUPLE COUNSELING

Step 1: Assessment. A counselor will need to assess for trauma history as a regular part of working with couples. This can be part of the intake paperwork which might ask whether the person was abused in childhood in any way, has been in a severe accident, or has been in a combat situation. Those three situations capture the most common traumas. If partners indicate a trauma history, then a further assessment is recommended. The Trauma Symptom Inventory (Arbisi, Erbes, Polusny & Nelson, 2010) published by Psychological Assessment Resources is commonly used to capture a broad assessment of trauma. The Combat Exposure Scale (Keane et al., 1989) can help the counselor screen for possible PTSD symptoms due to combat.

Regardless of the type of trauma, counselors should ensure that they assess the impact of the trauma on the partners (Nelson et al., 2002). Do not assume that a history of trauma necessarily means that there are negative effects on the relationship. Many people with trauma history recover with little impact on their relationship functioning (Lamoureux, Palmieri, Jackson & Hobfoll, 2012). If a couple report that there have not been effects in their relationship and there is no evidence to the contrary, it is important to believe them and not go digging for symptoms.

It is helpful to assess for secondary trauma as well. In secondary trauma the partner without the trauma has trauma-type symptoms due to his or her strong attachment (Compton & Follette, 2002). This may be surprising to both partners because there is little information communicated to the public about secondary trauma.

Step 2: Discuss confidentiality with the partners individually. In some cases one partner is unaware of the trauma or its details. It is important to communicate clearly how information will be shared between partners. Counselors should tread cautiously when partners are not aware of trauma. It is important for relationships to be open and honest. However, it is also important that clients are not retraumatized. Sometimes partners have a sense that their mate will not be able to handle the information, so they keep it to themselves. Some relationships are new and lack the commitment level needed to address the trauma jointly. At other times, refusing to tell their partner is part of trust problems or an avoidance pattern of symptoms. It is not necessary for partners to share every detail of their trauma history with each other. If a traumatized partner with symptoms requests not to have his or her trauma shared in the course of treatment, then individual psychotherapy to address the trauma is likely the best course of treatment. It will be difficult to make much progress in couple treatment with a trauma diagnosis that cannot be discussed with one partner due to a client's request.

Step 3: Consider psychoeducation and individual psychotherapy if those treatment modalities have not been used in the past. Some psychoeducation about their particular trauma and the common effects of the trauma on relationships can normalize the partners' experiences and bring relief. Discuss with the couple whether simultaneous individual psychotherapy with a clinician who is experienced in working with trauma would be helpful, preferably with an empirically supported treatment like trauma-focused cognitive behavioral therapy (TF-CBT). Generally TF-CBT would be the primary treatment for PTSD symptoms, with couple counseling as adjunctive to address relevant relationship issues. Any type of alternative treatment should include informed consent to the clients about the alternatives for treatment, along with the research support for validated interventions like TF-CBT. This is especially true if an alternative treatment is selected instead of an evidence-based treatment. Just because a client is requesting couple counseling does not mean that is the best course of treatment. Informed consent should clearly state this information to the couple. At times, a counselor may refuse couple counseling out of a conviction that a more relevant form of treatment is necessary.

Step 4: Couple therapy that addresses the effects of trauma on the relationship should promote a collaborative approach that builds trust. Partners that can effectively engage in improving their relationship broadly can often find relief. This is especially true for couples where the primary outlet of the trauma symptoms is within their relationship. Partners often need to use self-care, externalize the problem and learn to increase empathy for each other in the process of counseling. There are often incidents, or patterns of negative behavior, that need forgiveness. Partners can benefit from identifying triggers to the trauma experience. Partners who have not been traumatized will often need to share their own struggles, such as feeling rejected or not trusted. In moving through treatment, both partners should take joint credit for advances or resistance in treatment. The power for change resides in both partners, not just the traumatized partner. Counselors with little experience in treating traumas or couples in general should seek supervision for trauma cases.

Step 5: The counselor should use good self-care, assess for his or her own secondary trauma and seek consultative supervision as needed. Cases with trauma history often tax the counselor. To be fully effective for the couple's needs, it is important that the counselor stay present with the couple and not withdraw from the trauma. There are two common experiences for counselors treating traumas—especially those inexperienced in trauma counseling: withdrawal from trauma and overconfidence. Because withdrawal and avoidance are common responses to trauma, it is important for counselors to be fully aware of their own responses and to find resources that enable them to face the trauma courageously.

INTERVENTION 26-1: IDENTIFYING TRIGGERS IN THEIR RELATIONSHIP

After the assessment phase is complete it can be helpful for partners to work collaboratively to identify what events seem to trigger PTSD symptoms such as flashbacks or nightmares. If partners with a history of trauma have been identifying triggers in individual psychotherapy, then they can often share with their partner what they have been learning. The primary goal in this case is for their partner to extend compassion and empathy for the experience of being triggered. The counselor may need to empathize with the experience of the partner without trauma without amplifying it. The counselor may say something like, "Neither one of you went looking for these symptoms or trauma experiences, yet here they are, and they are affecting your relationship. If we identify triggers for the symptoms, I think that will help both of you with the goal of a better relationship."

Counselors must be vigilant not to actually trigger a trauma response in counseling when identifying triggers. Effective treatment involves being able to break down the traumatic sensory input into details that are unpacked but not emotionally flooding. By moving slowly, piece by piece, through the senses, clients can remember the triggering experience without retraumatization. In addressing triggers with couples, it is often helpful to start with a recent trigger experience that has brought about anxiety in order to make the partners aware of the trauma response. When feeling anxious, the client will need to learn to bring down the feelings of anxiety while talking about the trauma or the trigger. This can be done through a variety of techniques but commonly by removing the flood of emotions and discussing them as an external process. The client with trauma can be taught to focus repetitively on sensory information that communicates safety. The client should be simultaneously learning how to handle the anxiety associated with trauma more healthily.

For example, suppose a couple came to the session and explained they were having sex and a certain smell triggered anxiety in the wife, who had a history of childhood sexual abuse experiences. She can review that trigger with her partner. The partner will need to offer empathy and kindness for the triggering experience. An emotional softening between the partners should occur if they are to move forward. Then she can focus her attention on any indicators at that moment, before that moment or after that moment that demonstrated that she is safe with her partner. This process not only helps the client to refocus her attention, but it should bring down her anxiety. If her anxiety is not returning to a lower level in the session, then the counselor may need to coach the client in an anxiety management technique. If effective, this conversation also gives many clues to the husband about what behaviors during sex help his partner feel more safe and secure.

This type of intervention should always involve a good assessment at the first step, checking in with the couple before the intervention to ensure they are up for it that day as a couple, stopping to check in on their experience throughout the intervention, and processing their experience at the end of the session. Counselors should also follow up on the effects of the intervention at the next session. This kind of close collaboration with the couple will bring about trust, which is typically a goal of treatment. In addition, it will help to redirect the session quickly should the discussion of triggers actually trigger a partner and flood him or her with negative emotion.

Virtues: courage, compassion, kindness

Principle: The goal of this intervention is to increase awareness of triggers by both partners, and for the partner with a trauma history to be able to focus on cues of safety in the relationship so that both partners can increase the sense of safety.

27

Pornography Use and Internet Sexuality

ﻬ

D oug and Trish have been married for 25 years, and Doug has had an interest in pornography most of his life. The interest was relatively minor in his life until he decided to become a minister around the same time the internet entered their home. At that point Doug became overwhelmed and isolated in ministry. His teenage sons were in constant conflict with his wife. He dealt with his stress by isolating himself and seeking pornography. Due to his moral beliefs, this was a great conflict for him. It caused intense distress and some depression. He confessed his struggle to the lead minister at the large church in which he served. That pastor prayed for him and asked how he was doing with the problem a few times after that. Doug experienced temporary relief. However, when the church went through a downturn and his job was threatened, Doug returned to viewing pornography almost every night. Trish found out about the problem when she was searching for something on their computer. Trish was a no-nonsense, down-to-earth daughter of a farmer who confronted Doug with what she found. She demanded they enter couple counseling. So Doug made a call to Mark, a local Christian psychologist known to work with sexual issues.

According to research, 12% of all websites are dedicated to internet pornography, with 42.7% of the world population willingly or unwillingly accessing internet pornography. An estimated 72 million people visit pornography sites monthly (Ropelato, 2014; see also http://internet-filter-review .toptenreviews.com/internet-pornography-statistics-pg4.html). The impact of the increase in viewing pornography on intimate partners is unknown. A survey of marriage and family counselors found that pornography use was a common concern for couples (Goldberg, Peterson & Rosen, 2008). This new area of concern in couple treatment is growing while the treatment guidelines for counselors are lacking. Although there is little research to draw from in this area, we felt it was important to include this topic to help equip counselors when this problem arises.

Pornography addiction has been defined as the viewing of pornography such that it causes problems in everyday living—such as work, legal or relationship problems (Poulsen, Busby & Galovan, 2013). Several concerns regarding the use of pornography have been identified. Typically these should be considered warning signs that suggest that treatment might be sought. It is concerning when pornography is used to deal with stress, when there are increased risk-taking behaviors due to pornography (such as engaging in sexual voyeurism or moving toward forms of sexual expression that might injure sexual partners or oneself), when increased tolerance of pornography has occurred due to extensive use, or when the client is spending extensive time viewing pornography (Cooper, Morahan-Martin, Mathy & Maheu, 2002). Additionally relationship partners can feel demeaned and inadequate relative to the attractive models who often are involved in pornographic sites, so pornography might be involved in injuring one's partner's self-esteem in addition to injuring the romantic relationship. Pornography use seems to be correlated with depression (Levin, Lillis & Hayes, 2012), sleep problems (Carnes, Delmonico, Griffin & Moriarty, 2001) and other family problems.

There appears to be a neurobiological basis for viewing pornography as a type of addiction, similar to gambling addiction. Pornography activates pleasure pathways in the brain, which can cause motivational pursuit of other pornographic stimuli or real-life sexual objects (Struthers, 2010). This can be troublesome especially if used to cope with stress because it might derail other more productive problem-focused or emotion-focused coping (Hundt, Williams, Mendelson & Nelson-Gray, 2013). The client might have anxiety or depressive symptoms and cope by activating pleasure through pornography. This pattern is self-reinforcing, but it does not help alleviate the psychological symptoms.

For couple treatment, there is especially a concern if pornography becomes a barrier to a meaningful relationship, either sexually or emotionally. If one or both partners are seeking relief from anxiety or sexual outlet other than their partner, this can create a pattern that undermines authentic intimacy.

INTERNET INTIMATE RELATIONSHIPS

The research on internet-based intimate relationships is even sparser. However there are many opportunities for internet-based intimate relationships to develop, whether through social media or seeking an internet affair through websites that promote affairs. This type of infidelity seems to have a similar complex etiology as other types of affairs. Partners seek other relationships due to dissatisfaction with the current relationship, sensation-seeking, impulse, revenge, or sometimes as a "cry for help." Some partners appear to want to be caught. Others do not. Experimenting with internet intimate relationships can be a sign that a partner is seriously considering divorce and is "trying out" other relationships (Previti & Amato, 2004). The impact of the internet relationship can vary widely by couple. The negative impact can range from none to severe depending on the perception of the threat of the internet relationship. Internet relationships sometimes develop into sexual infidelity as well, and the movement down that path should be assessed.

COUNSELOR SELF-ASSESSMENT AND ETHICS

Ideally a counselor has some training and self-exploration before seeing a case with pornography or internet sexuality. Sexual issues are accompanied by strong emotions and sense of morality. For conservative Christians, there may be many boundaries on sexual behaviors such that the use of pornography or internet sexual relationships would be considered sinful and thought to be separating the person from God. Others view these behaviors as completely acceptable and even healthy sexual outlets. Counselors should ask themselves many questions when entering into this arena of counseling.

What is my view of pornography and internet sexual relationships? This may be well-defined or shifting. Yet it is important to have some sense of definition to be fully aware of one's own views in order to decrease the chances of countertransference or negative counselor behaviors.

What is my level of tolerance for people with varied moral views of sexuality? What can I do for clients without compromising my ability to be helpful? If there are limits on what you feel you are able to do, then it is your obligation to inform relevant clients of your limits in counseling. If your tolerance is very slim and accompanied with feelings of disgust or disdain for those that struggle with this problem (or do not view it as a problem), then we recommend that you discuss this with a confidential supervisor or peer. This topic is relatively common and likely to increase in the future as internet social media increases.

It is important to be able to respect and have some level of compassion for clients in all areas of struggle. In addition, it is important to respect client autonomy in issues of sexual morality as all mental health ethics guidelines promote. If a couple use pornography or have internet romantic relationships without any moral or relational concerns, then the counselor will need to move on and not make it a concern for the couple. Depending on the nature of the couple's use of the internet, counselors may need to refer the case if they think that they cannot agree with the couple's goals for treatment. For example, if the couple has an open relationship and are engaging in internet romantic relationships, and if counselors feel they cannot work around that issue, then a referral might be best for the couple.

What is my experience with pornography and internet sexuality? Few adults have no experience with this. Some feel drawn to this, others have been hurt by important people in their life. For the counselor with a history of personal struggle with pornography or sexuality in general, there may be a need to seek care for healing. If there have been offenses in the counselor's own past, then seeking or granting forgiveness may be helpful for the counselor. Countertransference is likely. Some counselors find there is a tendency to expect clients with a similar struggle to have similar experiences. Some counselors get stuck in a rescuer mode with clients who have similar experiences. If this is a tender area for the counselor, then consultative supervision is recommended to ensure that the counselor is providing effective care without damage to the counselor or client.

ASSESSMENT

We recommend that a simple screening for problems with pornography or internet sexuality be a part of all couple screenings. A single-item question such as, "Pornography or internet relationships have been a problem in our relationship" with answer options of (a) never, (b) not in the last year, (c) in the last year, or (d) this is one of our primary problems. This can help to alert the counselor to the problem and may warrant a more extensive assessment.

Some written assessments can assist in screening or assessing for cyber sexuality. The Cyber Pornography Use Inventory (Grubbs, Sessoms, Wheeler & Volk, 2010) is a 39-item measure that helps to detail three types of use including compulsivity, social or interpersonal use, and isolation. The scale was created with a primarily Christian sample, so it is expected to be more useful for that population.

To further assess in the dyadic intake, it can be helpful to observe how the couple discuss it together. The counselor can watch for how comfortable the couple is discussing sexuality in general, and internet sexuality specifically. Other issues to observe include who takes responsibility for the conversation, how the couple discusses the problem in terms of their relationship and their sense of morality, and their emotional reactions during the discussion. The counselor should assess whether children have been exposed to sexual images or ideas and, if so, whether they have become part of the couple's conflict pattern. Partners can be in different "stages" of addressing the problem, although it is unclear whether these are truly stages. The "stages" might include denial, shock, grief, shame, feelings of competition with the pornography, repair and growth patterns (Carnes et al., 2001). Within individual intakes, it can be helpful to further explore the extent, context and impact of use on both partners and their stage of change in dealing with the issue. In the end it is important for the couple to decide whether addressing cyber sexuality issues is a goal of treatment for them.

TREATMENT PLANNING WITH COUPLES WHO WISH TREATMENT

If addressing internet sexuality is a goal of treatment, then the counselor needs to frame the problem in terms of the type of issue they are facing.

Internet addiction and compulsion treatment. At times, the problem is a compulsion that would likely need additional treatment to address compulsive sexual behaviors and the underlying needs that drive the compulsion. This would be the classic pornography addiction type of case. Treatments similar to gambling addiction are often helpful. Some Christian community resources exist such as pornography support groups through the "Recovery for the City" movement. The couple counselor's role is to provide psychoeducation and support for the couple, and to work through issues of trust and forgiveness common to this type of problem. For partners with extensive addiction or compulsion types of problems, it can be helpful for the couple to view this as a chronic issue, given that the research indicates many individuals struggle with pornography addiction and compulsions for extended periods of time. If partners were expecting that a brief couple counseling treatment would "cure" the addiction, they will need some education about the *process* of recovery.

Internet pornography use offense. For some couples, there is not extensive addiction or compulsion. Instead they are grappling with a particular offense or less severe series of offenses relevant to internet pornography use. This is a difficult situation in counseling because the assessment of internet pornography use is based on trusting the report of the user, who may be motivated to limit revealing the extent of use particularly in couple treatment. However, if the counselor feels confident that there is not an addiction-level of problem, then forgiveness-based interventions coupled with improving the warm bond and intimacy of the couple is recommended as the course of treatment. In working through the definition of the hurt, or remembering the hurt, it is important not to allow for specificity of offense in a way that will further damage the relationship. For example, it is not necessary for the offender to describe details of his or her use of pornography or internet romance that might be upsetting to the partner.

One of the more difficult aspects of pornography offenses is that the offended partner often feels disgust and a sense of inferiority due to the offense. These can be very difficult emotions to overcome. In addition, they can often be activated during the lead-up to sexual intimacy with their partner, which is an emotionally charged time. These disgust and inferiority feelings can become attached to the couple's lovemaking, and they might be triggered whenever lovemaking is initiated. However, if the offended partner is expressing disgust or degradation of the pornography-using partner, it is important to help the partner reduce this disgust because it will only prolong their problems (Bergner & Bridges, 2002). The offended partner will need to address whether the offense has taken a toll on self-esteem or feeling desirable by their partner. The counselor can address this cognition by reframing the issue as an individual problem or general relationship problem, not something due to the person's own deficit.

Internet infidelity. If there has been internet-based infidelity that the couple want to address, then we recommend treatment that blends classic couple interventions such as those found in the hope-focused couple approach with infidelity-specific counseling such as the approach developed by Baucom, Snyder & Gordon (2009). If the offense has been less severe, or if the couple is authentically ready to move forward, then forgiveness-oriented treatment may be most helpful.

Further information and references about internet sexuality and pornography can be found at hopecouples.com.

INTERVENTION 27-1: PORNOGRAPHY USE INTERNET APPLICATION

For couples where a partner has difficulty with pornography use, there is an application that can assist with addressing the problem at home. The application was created by two Christian psychologists, Jim Sells and Mark Yarhouse, at Regent University. The approach uses a stress model for change by helping users understand pornography as a response to stress. The application helps users identify stressors and times of the week with more stress vulnerability, and helps find alternative responses to stress besides pornography use. While created by Christians, it is useful for people of all religious belief systems. Counselors can recommend that couples look into the app as a support for their goals. More information can be found at www.privateintegrity.org.

Part Six

CONCLUDING TREATMENT

In this final part of the book, we talk about ending well. "All's well that ends well," says Shakespeare. But actual couple counseling does not always end well in terms of the couple reaching their goal. Still, we can end counseling well and send the couple off with a good experience in counseling, making it more likely that they will seek counseling in the future.

28

Termination

ò❧

If you want to be humbled as a counselor, then follow up with a couple who had a successful course of treatment and ask them what they perceive was helpful to them. We have found in the early research within the hope-focused labs that many either focused on one thing they were looking for in counseling or gave global positive responses. They often said it was just the relationship with you. (Aw, shucks. Thanks.) Or they appreciated the chance to talk things out. What was missing in their reports? All the conceptualizations, techniques and theories used in the session. Clients do not remember everything that happened in counseling or why it helped them improve their relationship. They often do not have the vocabulary or understanding specifically to discuss what made counseling helpful to them. We think that one of the reasons why specific memories about the effects different parts of counseling had can fade is that clients do not have an adequate understanding of what is causing the growth or improved health in their relationship. Memories fade easily. New (and more positive) attachment experiences with their partner overwhelm many of the experiences before counseling and most of those during couple counseling. There is a real risk that the effects of couple counseling will not persist. In fact, there is some research to indicate that recidivism is relatively high in couple counseling (Owen, Duncan, Anker & Sparks, 2012).

Given these conditions, we believe it is crucial that the termination phase of counseling be effective, memorable and clear for the couple. That is what we aim for now. There are three important things that we believe need to happen in the termination phase:

1. Review the maintenance of change and risks to recidivism.

2. Create a memorable attachment event between the couple.

3. Have a meaningful goodbye with the counselor.

These three things need to be "sticky." That is, they need to stick to the couple as they leave counseling to help maintain the effects of counseling across time.

WHAT WORKED?

The discussion in the termination session or sessions should focus on the few key aspects of counseling that seemed to mean the most to the couple. The counselor may ask, "What about the experience of counseling together do you most value?" It is important for the counselor to focus on what the couple did in counseling that is creating positive change for them. The couple will often want to be appreciative and thankful to the counselor. Counselors should graciously accept their appreciation and extend words of appreciation to them as a couple as well. However, something is far more important. The couple needs to *extend words of appreciation to each other* and in doing so, they need to focus on what they were doing together *that helped them*. They may want to talk about how they have grown individually with insight, changed their attitude or increased attention to their relationship. If each of them can reinforce their partner's changes positively, this is a good sign for their future. Some counselors take notes of these discussions for the couple and give the notes to them. To structure the notes, you could write two questions: (1) What do you appreciate that your partner did during counseling that really helped? (2) What activities did you do together in counseling that helped you?

The counselor's message during termination can be one of, "You improved things during counseling, and that means you know how to make improvements, so you could do it again if needed." This increases their sense of efficacy in repairing their relationship, which increases hope and motivation for change in the future. The subtext too is that if they can remember some of the activities that really helped them, they can use those in the future as well.

What Still Needs Work?

In every counseling situation there are areas that were not attended to, opportunities passed over for something else, or time and life situations that limited change. It is not uncommon to see a couple like Joe and Maria Gomez. They enter counseling with five years of extensive relationship damage, which included mild violence, retaliations for perceived offenses, and dysfunctional relationships with Maria's family of origin. They had just had their third child and that adjustment was causing increased stress. The family was scheduled to relocate with the military in four months. While they agreed to meet twice a week some weeks, there were other times that they cancelled due to a sick child or a sudden change in Joe's duty roster. In four months, they were able to complete 13 sessions, which is more than many couples receive, but less than their counselor Carissa thought they needed. In the final four sessions they were beginning to make real changes to their offend-attack-retaliate cycle of conflict and improve their vulnerability and safety with each other. But the changes were new and ripe to unravel with the next "blow out" argument. Yet the time was up. The relocation was set in military stone. So counseling had to end.

It is important in every case to discuss with the couple a wrap-up self-assessment. They need to identify what other areas of change they would like to address on their own now that counseling is ending. They should discuss what signs might cause them to reenter counseling in the future and what they might hope to get from that experience to make it even better than this time.

Final Attachment Event

As counseling comes to a close, it is important to end the experience for the couple with a memorable event that turns them toward each other and makes final improvements on their attachment. One of the interventions most commonly used in the hope-focused couple approach, and used in each of the counseling interventions in past research (Worthington & Ripley, 2009) is the Joshua memorial. You are no doubt familiar with this intervention by now because we have talked about it in several cases throughout this book, but see intervention 28-1 where we describe it in more detail. In this book we add some new ideas for this intervention, but the original was described in *Hope-Focused Marriage Counseling* (Worthington, 2005). Because the couple is creating their own memorial, they have high autonomy. Maximum autonomy in this intervention is developmentally appropriate for the end of counseling but also helps to increase the couple's attachment. By creating a memorial object together the couple has a tangible reminder of the work they have done in counseling and the project they created together.

WARM ENCOURAGEMENT AND HEALTHY FAREWELL

The relationship with the couple counselor can be an authentic and important one for most partners. Hopefully they have been able to trust the counselor with their vulnerabilities and receive warm encouragement throughout their time in counseling. The termination session or sessions are a good time to reminisce about the experience in terms of its meaning to each person. At times issues of trust will resurface at the termination phase. Some clients will emotionally pull away from the counselor to protect against feelings of loss. Other clients will become more dependent and needy out of a fear that they will not be able to handle their problems without the counselor's involvement. It is important for the counselor to address those fears directly and warmly encourage the couple. Clients can often learn about themselves through the process of saying goodbye, though this may have less of an effect in couple counseling than individual counseling because the partners leave together as a unit. However, counselors should not be surprised if issues of loss or fear arise at termination.

We encourage a healthy farewell for the couple. It is important to talk about the relationship and reminisce about what it has meant to each person. Counselors can say they will miss the couple and offer well wishes. Many Christian counselors will end counseling with prayer for Christian couples as a part of a healthy farewell, symbolically and spiritually releasing the counselor from the role in supporting the couple. This reminds the couple they are always in the hands of God throughout their lives together.

IF THINGS END BADLY FOR THE COUPLE

The most common number of sessions in psychotherapy is one. And the dropout rate for couple therapy is somewhat higher than individual therapy. After all, there are two people who can end the counseling relationship, two who have life circumstances that might require stopping counseling. In the hope-focused research with hundreds of couples we have seen couples withdraw at every stage of treatment and for almost every possible reason. Any experienced counselor understands this. Couple counseling does at times end badly. This is a common enough experience that counselors need to be ready for the effects that it has on them.

Early dropout. If the couple drops out very early in treatment, it is usually due to a poor fit between couple and type of counseling. Or it might be that at least one partner was too early in the stage of change to engage in counseling at this time. It is important to follow up, at least with a phone call or letter, for the sake of practice building and maintaining contact with clients. In that contact, it can be helpful to encourage the couple to assess for themselves what they need right now in their relationship and what might indicate they should seek couple counseling again in the future.

Chronic issues that do not change. Some couples stick with counseling for at least six or seven sessions, but by then find that they are not making good progress. It is important to use the tools we have described in this book, such as the Hope Weekly Couples Assessment, to identify when progress is poor and help the couple to discuss their roadblocks or resistances. The couple should be asked whether they believe increased attention or a refocus in counseling will help them to move through the roadblock or resistance. For other couples, there might be few options to create change in their life due to financial survival situations, chronic mental health problems, or other chronic life stressors. It is common to find couples who are living with relatives due to financial constraints, have significant stressors caring for a dependent family member, or encounter a personal health crisis that is causing strain and is unlikely to change. If a chronic and serious condition exists, it is most helpful for the counselor to shift focus toward acceptance of situations that are not going to change, increase emphasis on the couple's self-care and increase their willingness to act in gentleness and grace toward each other.

Too little, too late. Sometimes couples will enter counseling already having decided that they have no hope for counseling to repair their relationship. They may not be forthright with their partner about this, and thus not forthright with the counselor. Counseling is seen simply as an exit visa that will support their narrative that, "We tried everything—even counseling—and nothing worked." Or they may see counseling as a last-ditch effort with little hope that the relationship can be resurrected. So they just go through the motions with zero expectation of help. It is helpful to assess for this during the intake period to see if one partner has already decided to exit the relationship, but even if they are ambivalent it is not uncommon for a couple to decide to break up weeks or months into the trial counseling. We believe that counselors should always leave that decision to terminate up to the couple for ethical reasons. However, once a couple decides to stop counseling, the counselor can offer referrals for individual counseling or connect the partners with other community resources.

We recommend that if couple counseling ends, clients start over with a new counselor (or return to an old one) when there is a breakup, instead of one partner "keeping" the couple counselor for individual work. The reasons for this are numerous and often discussed in couple counseling training. They include the fact that some couples will break up and then reunite some weeks or months later. If one partner has been meeting with the couple counselor during the breakup time, then complex issues of confidentiality and imbalance of relationship between the partners can damage counseling from that point on. It makes it almost impossible to restart couple counseling for the couple, leaving them without that important resource. It is strongly recommended that the couple counselor does not see both partners on an individual basis due to the complex relationships possibly compromising the counselor's efficacy.

A crisis. On occasion a couple will have a crisis, perhaps discovering a relationship infidelity or other major offense during the course of treatment. These crises will often derail counseling for couples. Just in the time when they most need counseling, they disengage while they are considering whether to continue in the relationship. If the crisis is external to their relationship like a health problem, then they may stop counseling to put energy to managing the crisis. It is most important in those cases to consider remaining as a resource to the couple with a checkup scheduled for weeks ahead when they can come together (if remaining in their relationship) or ask for a referral for individual counseling (if they decide to split up). Once the flood waters of the crisis abate, they may decide to restart counseling. This is more likely to happen if the counselor was diligent in ending the counseling relationship as well as possible.

CONCLUSION

It is important for the counselor to utilize the principles from the treatment authentically, living them out to the end of counseling. If virtues have been a focus of treatment, then the counselor can focus on virtues relevant to ending relationship well, with honesty, integrity and compassion.

INTERVENTION 28-1: THE JOSHUA MEMORIAL (hf)

The Joshua memorial was originally described in *Hope-Focused Marriage Counseling* (Worthington, 2005). The intervention allows the couple to create some kind of memorial object that will help them remember this time when they invested in improving their relationship through couple counseling. Across time this has been one of the most well-liked and rewarding interventions we have found in our labs. The couples who put significant thought into the project appear to appreciate the outcome most. Couples commonly create something with symbolic meaning for their Joshua memorials. Some of the more memorable memorials have included:

- Writing a song about their experience in counseling and singing it for the counselor

- Creating a craft or artwork with words and concepts from their counseling

- Getting a professional picture made of them as a couple

- Brewing their own beer and naming it "Hope Beer" with ingredients symbolic of their experience in counseling

- Creating a mosaic tile mirror with colors that symbolize things they have learned in counseling

- Finding and decorating a box and putting homework sheets, Scriptures they have focused on, and information they received in counseling in it

The creativity of couples in the Joshua memorial appears to be limitless.

The Joshua memorial intervention can go awry if one partner has little involvement in the creation. If just one of the two partners creates the memorial, then there is not a sense of shared meaning. In fact, some partners might take this to indicate that their couple bond is still not strong. Others might be offended that they were left with doing the couple's homework while both get "credit" for it. This is not an ideal way to end the course of counseling. The counselor can help avoid a one-sided Joshua memorial by encouraging the couple in the next-to-last session to understand the importance of the work of creation together. Some couples become distracted by creating a high quality product, making the object more important than the relationship or the symbolism of working together on a project, regardless of its aesthetic value. Warning the couple of these potential difficulties and explaining that this final task is an exercise in making a memorial for their relationship together should decrease the chances of a poor outcome.

For couples who are not religious, we alter the name to "graduation memorial." The same principles are used, but instead of pointing the couple toward religious figures like Joshua, they are encouraged to find the memorable experiences from counseling they want to remember as part of "graduating."

Virtues: perseverance, commitment, cooperativeness

Principle: Creating a final memorial of their relationship increases the bond of the couple as they finish counseling. It creates a memory marker to help maintain the gains made in treatment.

INTERVENTION 28-2: COMMUNITY FOLLOW-UP

As couples finish counseling, they are often still on a trajectory toward change without having solidified the changes in their relationship. There are opportunities in most communities to maintain gains and continue to grow after counseling ends through relationship enhancement. If a counselor is aware of these opportunities, then the couple can be encouraged to engage in these psychoeducation opportunities. They are often found through government healthy marriage initiatives (see http://archive.acf.hhs.gov/healthy-marriage), local churches, and community groups like the YMCA or Jewish community center, universities and some local clinicians. Online options include marriage mentoring offered by Les and Leslie Parrott at marriage-mentoring.com, e-PREP (currently under development by the group that developed the PREP program) and the Prepare-Enrich program, which has started online psychoeducation. There are also many self-help relationship books that can assist with relationship maintenance. If there are no couple maintenance classes or groups in a local area, a group of counselors may want to consider working together to offer occasional classes to local couples.

INTERVENTION 28-3: A FINAL TERMINATION REPORT (hf)

A final termination report can be used to help make treatment more memorable and review what happened in counseling. It can help focus the final session or sessions as the counselor and couple review where they have been in the course of counseling. Final reports tend to be brief, less than a page single-spaced. If the counselor used a written treatment plan early in counseling, then this plan can be useful by pairing it with a general brief discussion of which portions of the intervention the clinician believes were effective for the couple and which portions are areas that the couple should continue growth in. The couple can read the termination report in their final session (or it can be sent securely to them ahead of the final session, although this can create a disincentive to attend the final session). An example of a termination report integrated with results of a final assessment measure is found at the end of this chapter.

Virtues for the counselor: perseverance, industry, dependability

INTERVENTION 28-4: FINAL ASSESSMENT

The couple can benefit in their relationship from making a relationship assessment at the termination stage of counseling. In the second to last meeting, the couple would take the same measures that were taken at the intake stage of counseling. Counselors who give measures repeatedly can report change over time. The important thing about the final assessment is that the counselor does the work of comparing the original assessment with the final assessment. This digest of the comparison is a powerful intervention for many couples in several ways. For couples where both partners have improved, there is confirmation that their relationship has improved. The use of charts or graphs (easily created in Microsoft Word or other word processing programs) helps the couple visualize the changes in the relationship in different areas of functioning. It is important to tailor any charts or graphs for the education level of the couple. While counselors may be familiar with working with graphs, many people never use charts or graphs in their everyday life unless they come across a nice visual on television or in a news magazine or online article. It is better to use simple graphics that are easily understood than to give every detail of movement in assessment (see figure 28.1).

One model of the Hope-Focused research at Regent University has been to give the average score on a scaled questionnaire (for instance, average score of 4.2 on a scale of 1 to 7), which is more readily understood by the partners and easy to graph, either by hand or with a computer program. If there are multiple measures, it is best to review them each individually. For example, if the couple took a general relationship satisfaction measure, a measure of relationship trust, the Relationship Efficacy Measure (Fincham, Harold & Gano-Phillips, 2000) or sense of efficacy in the relationship, and an efficacy of psychotherapy (weekly) measure then it is best to give each of

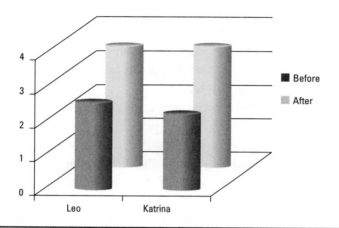

Figure 28.1

these results on its own graph. Most of the time individual results are given for each partner (see figure 28.1, which depicts relationship satisfaction for Leo and Katrina individually), instead of added or average results for the couple. We want to be able to call attention to differences in perceptions if they exist.

The benefits of the effort involved in reviewing change graphically should not be underestimated. While it is common to have a qualitative type of discussion about changes that have happened while the couple was in counseling, the quantitative measure of those changes is important for the couple and the counselor. The couple's ability to see the changes that have come about as a result of their hard work is an important boost as they enter a future without regular counseling available to them. A final assessment is an opportunity to encourage a couple who still has a good deal of learning and growing to do in their relationship with specific written suggestions. In times of difficulty the chances of them reading the final report and other information you gave to them is much greater than them remembering what you say.

EXAMPLE FINAL ASSESSMENT REPORT

Couple: Joe and Maria Gomez

Joe and Maria, over the thirteen sessions of the hope-focused couple approach to counseling, you focused on your relationship in terms of faith working through love. You seemed to find that faith working through love produced hope for a better and stronger relationship. You had the opportunity to learn skills and grow in the following areas: examining your strengths and vision, improving communication and conflict resolution, improving your relationship bond, and increasing your ability to apologize and forgive when offended.

In week one, you were encouraged to grow by noticing the positives in your marriage. Noticing the positives in each other is like making deposits in each of your love banks. We focused some time and attention on several positives such as your hopes for participating; the story of your dating, engagement and marriage; what is already good about your marriage; and what your marriage would be like if a miracle occurred and any problems disappeared. You completed homework to reinforce this.

In session two, you were encouraged to grow by a marriage covenant and to continue to look for and affirm the positives traits and virtues in your partner. You discussed your core vision for your marriage ten years from now and what that would look like to each of you. You completed homework to make deposits in each other's love banks.

In sessions three to five, you were encouraged to grow by becoming good listeners. You learned the Communication TANGO as a technique for discussing issues, including unsolvable ones. The TANGO dance card you were given summarizes the steps in the process and the floor tiles help facilitate those steps. You completed homework to practice the TANGO technique for communication. While you do not plan to use the TANGO technique regularly, you learned principles that can be used in difficult conversations to increase your understanding of each other, like slowing down and taking turns listening.

In sessions six and seven, you were encouraged to grow by using good principles of problem solving. You learned that many issues in marriage are unsolvable. You also learned how to manage conflict with unsolvable problems. You learned the LOVE acrostic as a process for solving those issues that are solvable. You received a card with the LOVE process on it and completed homework to practice it.

In sessions eight and nine, you were encouraged to grow by deeply connecting with each other. You explored how past relationships can affect your present relationship and that vulnerability and expressing soft emotions such as fear to each other can result in more empathy, intimacy and oneness, while hard emotions such as anger tend to reduce closeness and intimacy. You completed homework to write a letter of vulnerability to each other sharing how past relationships may be affecting your marriage today.

In session ten, you were encouraged to grow by empathy and apology. You learned and practiced the process of expressing empathy and the components of an effective apology. You each completed homework to write a journal entry apologizing to your spouse for some past marital offense.

In sessions eleven and twelve, you were encouraged to grow by forgiving. You learned the REACH model of forgiveness for healing from past hurts and received a card with the REACH principles on it. You completed homework that focused on furthering forgiveness in your relationship.

In your commencement (this session), you were encouraged to grow by graduating into a new future together. We will discuss your Joshua memorial and review your experience of counseling together this week.

This is your current relationship graph for Joe (see figure 28.2). [Maria's graph would be shown also.] This graph is based on the CARE measure (see intervention 5-3).

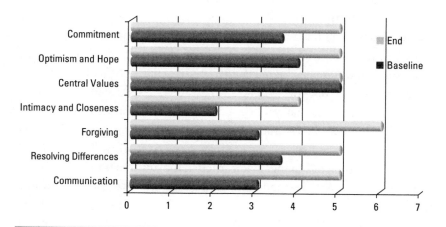

Figure 28.2

Overall, you entered counseling with some strengths and some areas to improve. I've seen improvement in *communication* and *forgiving* and so have you both. [Add this type of message for a struggling couple: There still are areas of your relationship where it is difficult to find peaceful solutions.] However, I believe at this time if you continue down the path you started in counseling and use the tools you learned here consistently, then over time your relationship will become even healthier. If, however, after six months, when we have our follow-up visit, the gains have been lost or things have not improved, then another course of counseling may be needed to reach your goals.

I hope that you both continue to use the methods you learned to grow deeper in faith, hope and love as you work together on your relationship!

[Counselor's full name and today's date]

29

Post-counseling Checkups

ès

One of the most challenging things about couple counseling is the high rate of recidivism. Couples can easily return to old habits and dysfunctional patterns once their energy and attention has shifted away from counseling. Some of the research has tried to establish whether couple counseling has significant long-term effects (Owen, Duncan, Anker & Sparks, 2012). Poor one-, two- or five-year outcomes are realities of caring for intimate partner relationships. We think providing couple counseling is similar to providing nutritional counseling or exercise coaching for weight problems. Researchers at UCLA summarized the research on people who regain weight after a diet finding that over 65% regain the weight they had lost within four or five years (Voss, 2010). The interventions that people are using for weight loss appear to lack staying power. However, just because it is difficult to keep a healthy weight does not mean that healthcare providers should stop their efforts toward healthy weight for their patients. The same is true for couple counseling.

INTERVENTION 29-1: THE SIX-MONTH CHECKUP

Given the realities of recidivism in couple counseling, it is important for this subfield to be creative in helping couples with their goals. One of the ways we have worked in our labs to assist with this goal is to use the six-month checkup. Everyone is familiar with checkups from the medical and dental professions. Similarly, for relationship problems we find that it is helpful to schedule an appointment with a couple for approximately six months after finishing counseling to assess how well they are maintaining their gains.

Some counselors plan these checkups as assessment-focused events with only 15-20 minute meeting time with the couple and 30 minutes spent completing simple questionnaires. Ideally those measures are completed prior to the meeting, so they can be scored and used in the final meeting.

The counselor is one of the beneficiaries of a follow-up session with a couple. The couple benefits as well in accountability and in a service to help prevent recidivism. However, the follow-up session is a gold mine of information about what couples are finding most effective in the counseling they have received. Several months after counseling has ended the couple will be able to communicate what has "stuck" from their experience of counseling. This feedback is valuable as counselors decide what interventions, personal style and theoretical principles to apply to similar couples in the future. This is a case study analysis on one's own personal efficacy. Repeated case study is an effective method for personal growth and improvement as a clinician. If done ethically, it also provides hard data to use in marketing to future couples and interested parties.

Pragmatics for scheduling. We have found that the most effective way to ensure that this becomes a regular part of your practice is to include it in pre-therapy information, discuss it during the intake period as a regular part of practice, and build in the cost so that the six-month checkup has been paid for as part of the regular course of counseling. (Unless, of course, the couple is able to use their insurance. Prepaying is not an acceptable practice for most insurance companies.)

At the end of counseling, the counselor reintroduces the follow-up meeting. There is nothing magical about the six-month time period. Some couples may do better with a three-month time period, especially if they have increased concerns that the gains they made in counseling will not persist. If travel or deployment interferes with meeting, then varied follow-up times may be needed.

If the couple has gotten worse. Sometimes circumstances, situations and traits cause a couple to decline in their relationship. There was a couple seen in our lab that improved in all their measures from prior to treatment to the point where they finished. They seemed ready to finish treatment. However, after the counseling had ended they seemed to be exhausted from the effort they were putting into their relationship. They stopped the date nights. They stopped checking in daily on how the other person was doing at work or with individual things in their life. They stopped using apologies for minor types of offenses. They were more irritable with each other. Added to that, the couple experienced the loss of a sibling in war and had difficulty supporting each other through the grief.

At first, they did not want to come back for their follow-up visit because they felt embarrassed about how much their relationship had deteriorated in the five months since they finished counseling. Their counselor strongly encouraged them to come in, especially *because* things had gone downhill. The counselor appealed to them that this might be a good session to talk about what they wanted to do to get things back on track. Once in the office they were able to identify what they had stopped doing, and they gained a better understanding of how important these small actions were (i.e., date nights, apologies, daily check-ins, speaking with kindness). The couple decided not to reengage in counseling at that time, although they did return to counseling for a short time several months later.

Some couples are like the case described here but others are more difficult. Sometimes an affair is revealed after counseling has finished, or a similar severe offense occurs that precipitates a breakup. We have found that couples who have extensive and long-standing relationship problems across the spectrum of their life often have difficulty with a short-term model of counseling. They might require longer-term types of counseling with relatively frequent checkups.

If the couple has stayed the same. Maintenance of gains made in couple counseling is generally a good outcome in the research on clinical outcomes of couple interventions (Anker, Sparks, Duncan, Owen & Stapnes, 2011; Baucom, Sevier, Eldridge, Doss & Christensen, 2011). If the scores for the couple have remained relatively stable since the end of counseling, and this was an improvement compared to prior to counseling, then the couple may be happy with those results. The important discussion to have with the couple is whether they had hoped to further improve their relationship, or whether they were satisfied with the state of their relationship as it was at that point. If they hoped for further improvement, then they may need to address whether they are putting the necessary work into the relationship to expect improvements.

If, however, the couple made small progress in counseling and has not made progress after counseling, then a more difficult conversation is needed.

It is possible that situational, trait or circumstantial factors are making change unlikely to happen. Change requires the right combination of variables in their life in order to expend the energy to see changes in the relationship. They might not be using the right skills at the right time. They might not have garnered the resources to change. They might be getting their needs met within a dysfunctional dynamic. An honest discussion either accepting the situation or deciding to double down and put increased work into the relationship is important to have. Counselors should be cautious about encouraging the couple to double down to improve their relationship. If the course of treatment was adequate and time has passed with continued lack of change, then there are likely factors in play making change very difficult. Some clients will have a sudden burst of motivation when they come for a follow-up visit, similar to someone who vows to their doctor that *now* they will start exercising regularly. They might keep it up for two days or a week. Then they fade back to normal. This is discouraging to the couple. The couple is better served by asking what factors would be needed for them to make small but noticeable changes in their relationship.

If the couple has improved. While not typical, there are couples who continue to improve after they complete counseling. It is good to process with the couple their attribution of that change. If they believe that the change is due to situational factors, such as a new job or decreased workloads, then the change may not be lasting. All relationships go through ups and downs across time. What is important is for the couple to feel a sense of efficacy. They need to know that no matter what difficult times they face, they are equipped to face them together, to support each other and know how to improve their bond. It is good if the couple feels like they were able to use the counseling situation to help themselves. They can be reminded that they can use counseling again in the future if they need it. It is most helpful to have them identify what specific actions, behaviors or attitudes they took on at what specific times that enabled them to reach their relationship goals.

30

It Works, but Is It True?

❧

Each clinical case we see is an opportunity for reflection. To conclude this book we want to promote reflection. First, in keeping with our consistent urging of clients to self-reflect on what is important to them, we will ask you to think back over this book and reflect on where you were when you picked it up and where you are now. Second, we will share three important reflections on what we've discovered in our own work as couple counselors. Those three truths are about faith, work and love—just like the three principles of the hope-focused couple approach.

Where Were You When We Started? Where Are You Now?
You might have begun this book never having seen a couple for counseling, not being married yourself, and knowing few couples well enough to have a sense of how couples can live with each other. Or you might have begun the book with 1,000 cases behind you, looking for some new wrinkles. Wherever you began, if you have hung in there this long, you must have gotten something from the experience. What are those things?

Let us pose a series of questions. Try to think of your honest answer to each.

- What was your confidence level about being able to help couples when you began reading relative to what it is now?
- Did your view of couples problems change? Do you think of couples now as having more difficult, yet more intriguing problems? Do you look

forward to helping couples unravel the knots more now than when you began reading?

- Do you have many more interventions that you think you could do than you did when you started? Thinking back through all of the interventions, which ones are you able to recall? Think group by group. Perhaps to begin the counseling with assessment and a report to the couple? To promote communication and conflict-resolution HOPE? To build BONDs? To deal with HURT? To promote forgiveness (FREE, REACH, Six Steps to Self-Forgiveness)? To build reconciliation through TRUST? To terminate well?

- Did you increase your motivation to work with couples through reading the book? (If not, how does that motivation compare now with the beginning of the book—less motivation now, or the same?)

- To what degree do you think you'll be able to integrate the hope-focused couple approach with other couple therapy theories?

As you ponder these questions, we hope you believe that the time we have spent together has been worthwhile to your career goals. We also hope that it will have inspired you to feel much better about the joy and privilege of helping couples repair those emotional bonds that have become strained. We also hope that this book has actually helped your own relationship, or if you have not established a long-term relationship yet, we hope this will help you develop a healthy and happy one when the time is right.

Do You Have Faith in the Truths Within the Hope-Focused Couple Approach?

Wisdom can be found in psychotherapy theory and approaches. Faith in what you cannot see is a profound concept. Valuing love, regardless of situation, is weighty. Using God-given strengths and virtues to handle weaknesses or sins is glorious. The requirement of work in relationships provides an opportunity for us to share in our own future, and the futures of those around us, by where we invest our energies. This investment is God's gift to us. Repeated forgiveness in a lifetime relationship is a high calling. These and many other concepts that we have included in the hope-focused couple approach are wise ideas brought together from a wide variety of sources for the sake of couple relationships.

The real test of whether these ideas are true is answered in a question: *Are the principles of the approach apparent in my own life?* Am I valuing of others? Is there hidden unforgiveness in my heart? What transformation is God doing in my life now so that I will be more like Christ? What strengths and gifts has God given me and how am I using them? We ask these questions of our couples and should be willing to ask them of ourselves.

The hope-focused approach to couple counseling is much more than using good ideas with couples for an hour a week. In our own lives, fear can be so much stronger than faith. Past hurts can create veritable grooves of behavior that detract from God's plan. Our own faith in prayer and God's work in this world can be called into question. Situations can be heartbreaking, and struggles are often chronic. Yet if God is the King of the flood and able to redeem any situation with the right truths applied to life's problems, then the ideas we have discovered and share are true. We pray you will find the qualities apparent in your own relationships, work and life.

Work is not sexy. Being a couple counselor requires learning information, building skills and experiencing internal change. It requires accessing emotional states and tolerating strong feelings. It is not an easy job, and it will not offer great recognition or reward. One of the gifts of being a counselor is that trying to be "great" will only make you self-centered and thus a poor counselor. Just humbly working hard with perseverance for the good of others will make one a great counselor. And if you work, you will live consistently with what you are teaching and demonstrating to your clients. How can we ask them to work hard on their relationship if we're not living that out? We encourage you to be excellent in all you do for the couples that seek your services. Memorize treatment steps, read supplementary materials, seek honest supervision, review training before meetings and scoring assessments. It is hard work without immediate reward. Delayed gratification will pay off though so that you will be a skilled, wise and capable couple counselor who feels the reward of operating at your best as God intended.

Real love is not a wish-dream. It is important for us to know the difference between really loving others and a wish-dream. Martyred theologian Dietrich Bonhoeffer (2012) talks about wish-dreams in his book *Life Together*. He challenges readers that God will not give us our wish-dreams, because they are poor substitutes for God's perfect will. They seem good, but God has something better. This book was written in the midst of Nazis taking over Germany and the church that Bonhoeffer loved being torn apart over the response to the rapidly shifting sands of their time. Wishing for something different than their lot would have been understandable. In our work today, our wishes for couples in counseling may seem good but actually be a wish-dream, not God's plan. Things may seem dark and the couple may despair. Yet there may be an opportunity for patient love to triumph in the most difficult circumstances. It does not mean the spouse will stop using drugs and be able to move back in. It does not mean that an affair or pornography problem will not leave scars on the relationship. Yet redemption is sweet if it can be obtained, together or individually.

Many people who become couple counselors have their own reasons for wanting to "save" marriages. Those reasons may include religious passion or personal experiences. But few people are always discerning about God's plans for the individuals and relationships in front of them. Handling each case with humility and love for the work that God will do in even the most difficult circumstances will sustain a counselor across a lifetime of walking alongside couples. Wish-dreams will cause burnout.

Tony Snow, the White House press secretary who died of cancer in 2008, said, "God places us in predicaments that seem to defy our endurance and comprehension—and yet do not. By His love and grace, we persevere. The challenges that make our hearts leap and stomachs churn invariably strengthen our faith and grant measures of wisdom and joy we would not experience otherwise." Marriage and intimate relationships are full of heart-leaping and stomach-churning experiences. Some of the couple's goals for a smooth, peaceful and easy marriage need to be sacrificed on the altar as wish-dreams. Some of our goals for them are wish-dreams too. It is far better to face the fallen nature apparent in this world and garner grace for the sin present in everyone's life. It brings humility and deeper love. Hope must be in what is true, authentic and God's plan for this time in order for real love to surround your work. We pray that this will be your experience.

References

Ainsworth, M. D. S. (1991). Attachments and other affectional bonds across the life cycle. In C. M. Parkes, J. Stevenson-Hinde & P. Marris (Eds.), *Attachment across the life cycle*. New York: Tavistock/Routledge.

Alicke, M. D., & Sedikides, C. (2011). *The handbook of self-enhancement and self-protection*. New York: Guilford Press.

Anderson-Jacob, C. M., & McCarthy-Veach, P. (2005). Intrapersonal and familial effects of child sexual abuse on female partners of male survivors. *Journal of Counseling Psychology, 52*, 284-97.

Anker, M. G., Sparks, J. A., Duncan, B. L., Owen, J. J., & Stapnes, A. K. (2011). Footprints of couple therapy: Client reflections at follow-up. *Journal of Family Psychotherapy, 22*(1), 22-45. doi:10.1080/08975353.2011.551098

Arbisi, P. A., Erbes, C. R., Polusny, M. A., & Nelson, N. W. (2010). The concurrent and incremental validity of the Trauma Symptom Inventory in women reporting histories of sexual maltreatment. *Assessment, 17*(3), 406-18. doi:10.1177/1073191110376163

Balswick, J., & Balswick, J. (2006). *A model for marriage*. Downers Grove, IL: InterVarsity Press.

Barlow, D. H. (2010). Negative effects from psychological treatments: A perspective. *American Psychologist, 65*(1), 13-20.

Bartle-Haring, S., Knerr, M., Adkins, K., Delaney, R. O., Gangamma, R., Glebova, T. . . . Meyer, K. (2012). Trajectories of therapeutic alliance in couple versus individual therapy: Three-level models. *Journal of Sex & Marital Therapy, 38*(1), 79-107. doi:10.1080/0092623X.2011.569635

Baucom, D. H., Snyder, D. K., & Gordon, K. C. (2009). *Helping couples get past the affair: A clinician's guide* (pp. xvi, 351). New York: Guilford Press.

Baucom, K. J. W., Sevier, M., Eldridge, K., Doss, B. D., & Christensen, A. (2011).

Observed communication in couples two years after integrative and traditional behavioral couple therapy: Outcome and link with five-year follow-up.
Journal of Consulting and Clinical Psychology, 79(5), 565-76. doi:10.1037/
a0025121

Baumeister, R. F., & Tierney, J. (2011). *Willpower: Rediscovering the greatest
human strength.* New York: Penguin.

Beach, S. R. H., & Gupta, M. (2003). Depression. In D. K. Snyder & M. A.
Whisman (Eds.), *Treating difficult couples: Helping clients with coexisting
mental and relationship disorders* (pp. 88-113). New York: Guilford Press.

Beach, S. R. H., Hurt, T. R., Fincham, F. D., Kameron, J., Franklin, K. J., McNair,
L. M., & Stanley, S. M. (2011). Enhancing marital enrichment through spirituality: Efficacy data for prayer focused relationship enhancement. *Psychology of Religion and Spirituality, 3*, 201-16.

Bergner, R. M., & Bridges, A. J. (2002). The significance of heavy pornography
involvement for romantic partners: Research and clinical implications.
Journal of Sex & Marital Therapy, 28(3), 193-206.

Blow, A. J., Sprenkle, D. H., & Davis, S. D. (2007). Is who delivers the treatment
more important than the treatment itself? The role of the therapist in
common factors. *Journal of Marital and Family Therapy, 33*(3), 298-317.
doi:10.1111/j.1752-0606.2007.00029.x

Bonhoeffer, D. (2011). *The cost of discipleship.* Norwich, UK: SCM Press.

Bonhoeffer, D. (2012). *Life together.* Norwich, UK: SCM Press.

Bordin, E. S. (1979). The generalizability of the psychoanalytic concept of
the working alliance. *Psychotherapy: Theory, Research & Practice, 16*(3),
252-60.

Bradford, K. (2012). Assessing readiness for couple therapy: The Stages of Relationship Change Questionnaire. *Journal of Marital and Family Therapy, 38*(3),
486-501. doi:10.1111/j.1752-0606.2010.00211.x

Braithwaite, S. R., & Fincham, F. D. (2009). A randomized clinical trial of a
computer based preventive intervention: Replication and extension of ePREP.
Journal of Family Psychology, 23(1), 32-38. doi:10.1037/a0014061

Brown, R. P. (2004). Vengeance is mine: Narcissism, vengeance, and the tendency to forgive. *Journal of Research in Personality, 38*(6), 576-84. doi:10.1016/j
.jrp.2003.10.003

Burchard, G. A., Yarhouse, M. A., Worthington, E. L., Jr., Berry, J. W., Killian,
M., & Canter, D. E. (2003). A study of two marital enrichment programs and
couples' quality of life. *Journal of Psychology and Theology, 31*, 240-52.

Cacioppo, S., Bianchi-Demicheli, F., Frum, C., Pfaus, J. G., & Lewis, J. W. (2012). The common neural bases between sexual desire and love: A multilevel kernel density fMRI analysis. *Journal of Sexual Medicine, 9*(4), 1048-54. doi:10.1111/j.1743-6109.2012.02651.x

Cacioppo, S., Bianchi-Demicheli, F., Hatfield, E., & Rapson, R. L. (2012). Social neuroscience of love. *Clinical Neuropsychiatry: Journal of Treatment Evaluation, 9*(1), 3-13.

Cahill, L., Gorski, L., & Le, K. (2003). Enhanced human memory consolidation with post-learning stress: Interaction with the degree of arousal at encoding. *Learning and Memory, 10,* 270-74.

Carey, M. P., Spector, I. P., Lantinga, L. J., & Krauss, D. J. (1993). Reliability of the Dyadic Adjustment Scale. *Psychological Assessment, 5*(2), 238-40. doi:10.1037/1040-3590.5.2.238

Carnes, P., Delmonico, D., Griffin, E., & Moriarty, J. (2001). *In the shadows of the net: Breaking free of online sexual behavior.* Center City, MN: Hazelden.

Carter, R., Aldridge, S., Page, M., Parker, S., & Frith, C. (2009). *The human brain book.* New York: DK Adult.

Chesterton, G. K. (1905). *Heretics.* Rockville, MD: Serenity Publishing.

Church, U. S. C. (2003). *Catechism of the Catholic Church* (2nd ed.). New York: Doubleday.

Coan, J. A. (2008). Toward a neuroscience of attachment. In J. C. P. R. Shaver (Ed.), *Handbook of attachment: Theory, research, and clinical applications* (2nd ed.) (pp. 241-65). New York: Guilford Press.

Compton, J. S., & Follette, V. M. (2002). Couple therapy when a partner has a history of child sexual abuse. In A. S. Gurman & N. S. Jacobson (Eds.), *Clinical handbook of couple therapy* (3rd ed.) (pp. 466-87). New York: Guilford Press.

Cooper, A., Morahan-Martin, J., Mathy, R., & Maheu, M. (2002). Toward an increased understanding of user demographics in online sexual activities. *Journal of Sex & Marital Therapy, 28*(2), 105-29.

Cordova, J. V., Jacobson, N. S., Gottman, J. M., Rushe, R., & Cox, G. (1993). Negative reciprocity and communication in couples with a violent husband. *Journal of Abnormal Psychology, 102*(4), 559-64.

Cozolino, L. (2006). *The neuroscience of human relationships: Attachment and the developing social brain.* New York: Norton.

Dalenberg, C. J., Brand, B. L., Gleaves, D. H., Dorahy, M. J., Loewenstein, R. J., Cardeña, E., Frewen, P. A., Carlson, E. B., & Spiegel, D. (2012). Evaluation of the evidence for the trauma and fantasy models of dissociation. *Psychological Bulletin, 138,* 550-88.

Davis, D. E., Hook, J. N., & Worthington, E. L., Jr. (2008). Relational spirituality and forgiveness: The roles of attachment to God, religious coping, and viewing the transgression as a desecration. *Journal of Psychology and Christianity, 27*(4), 293-301.

Davis, D. E., Worthington, E. L., Jr., Hook, J. N., & Hill, P. C. (2013). Research on religion/spirituality and forgiveness: A meta-analytic review. *Psychology of Religion and Spirituality, 5*(4), 233-41.

De Ayala, R. J., Vonderharr-Carlson, D. J., & Kim, D. (2005). Assessing the reliability of the Beck Anxiety Inventory scores. *Educational and Psychological Measurement, 65*(5), 742-56. doi:10.1177/0013164405278557

Demaris, A., Mahoney, A., & Pargament, K. I. (2010). Sanctification of marriage and general religiousness as buffers of the effects of marital inequity. *Journal of Family Issues, 31,* 1255-78.

Diamantopoulou, A., Oitzl, M. S., & Grauer, E. (2012). Fear memory for cue and context: Opposite and time-dependent effects of a physiological dose of corticosterone in male BALB/c and C57BL/6J mice. *Brain Research, 1466,* 112-18.

Diamond, L. M., & Fagundes, C. P. (2010). Psychobiological research on attachment. *Journal of Social and Personal Relationships, 27*(2), 218-25. doi:10.1177/0265407509360906.

Dinero, R. E., Conger, R. D., Shaver, P. R., Widaman, K. F., & Larsen-Rife, D. (2011). Influence of family of origin and adult romantic partners on romantic attachment security. *Couple and Family Psychology: Research and Practice, 1*(S), 16-30. doi:10.1037/2160-4096.1.S.16

Dinkmeyer, D., Sr., McKay, G. D., & Dinkmeyer, D., Jr. (2007). *The parents' handbook: Systematic training for effective parenting.* Fredericksburg, VA: STEP Publishers.

Dozois, D. J. A., Dobson, K. S., & Ahnberg, J. L. (1998). A psychometric evaluation of the Beck Depression Inventory–II. *Psychological Assessment, 10*(2), 83-89. doi:10.1037/1040-3590.10.2.83

Epstein, N. B., & Baucom, D. H. (2003). Couple therapy. In R. L. Leahy (Ed.), *Roadblocks in cognitive-behavioral therapy: Transforming challenges into opportunities for change* (pp. 217-35). New York: Guilford.

Fagbemi, K. (2011). Q: What is the best questionnaire to screen for alcohol use disorder in an office practice? *Cleveland Clinic Journal of Medicine, 78*(10), 649-51. doi:10.3949/ccjm.78a.10186

Fehr, R., Gelfand, M. J., & Nag, M. (2010). The road to forgiveness: A meta-analytic synthesis of its situational and dispositional correlates. *Psychological Bulletin, 136*(5), 894-914.

Fincham, F. D., Beach, S. R. H., & Davila, J. (2007). Longitudinal relations between forgiveness and conflict resolution in marriage. *Journal of Family Psychology, 21*(3), 542-45. doi:10.1037/0893-3200.21.3.542

Fincham, F. D., Hall, J. H., & Beach, S. R. H. (2005). 'Til lack of forgiveness doth us part: Forgiveness in marriage. In E. L. Worthington (Ed.), *Handbook of forgiveness* (pp. 207-26). New York: Routledge.

Fincham, F. D., Harold, G. T., & Gano-Phillips, S. (2000). The longitudinal association between attributions and marital satisfaction: Direction of effects and role of efficacy expectations. *Journal of Family Psychology, 14*(2), 267-85. doi:10.1037//0893-3200.14.2.267

Fisher, R., Ury, W. L., & Patton, B. (2011). *Getting to yes: Negotiating agreement without giving in.* New York: Penguin.

Friedlander, M. L., Escudero, V., Heatherington, L., & Diamond, G. M. (2011). Alliance in couple and family therapy. *Psychotherapy, 48*(1), 25-33. doi:10.1037/a0022060

Funder, D. C. (1987). Errors and mistakes: Evaluating the accuracy of social judgment. *Psychological Bulletin, 101,* 75-90.

Furnham, A., & Lester, D. (2012). The development of a short measure of character strength. *European Journal of Psychological Assessment, 28*(2), 95-101. doi:10.1027/1015-5759/a000096

Furrow, J. L., & Bradley, B. (2011). Emotionally focused couple therapy: Making the case for effective couple therapy. In J. L. Furrow, S. M. Johnson & B. A. Bradley (Eds.), *The emotionally focused casebook: New directions in treating couples* (pp. 3-29). New York: Routledge.

Furrow, J. L., Edwards, S., Choi, Y., & Bradley, B. (2012). Therapist presence in emotionally focused couple therapy blamer softening events: Promoting change through emotional experience. *Journal of Marital and Family Therapy, 38 Suppl 1*(June), 39-49. doi:10.1111/j.1752-0606.2012.00293.x

Gailliot, M. T., & Baumeister, R. F. (2007). The physiology of willpower: Linking blood glucose to self-control. *Personality and Social Psychology Review, 11*(4), 303-27. doi:10.1177/1088868307303030

Gimbel, C., & Booth, A. (1994). Why does military combat experience adversely affect marital relations? *Journal of Marriage and the Family, 56,* 691-703.

Goldberg, P. D., Peterson, B. D., & Rosen, K. H. (2008). Cybersex: The impact of a contemporary problem on the practices of marriage and family therapists. *Journal of Marriage and Family Therapy, 34,* 469-80.

Goldman, R. N., & Greenberg, L. S. (2010). Self-soothing and other-soothing in emotion-focused therapy for couples. In A. S. Gurman (Ed.), *Clinical casebook of couple therapy* (pp. 255-80). New York: Guilford.

Gordon, A. M., Impett, E., Kogan, A., Oveis, C., & Keltner, D. (2012). To have and to hold: Gratitude promotes relationship maintenance in intimate bonds. *Journal of Personality and Social Psychology, 103*(2), 257-74. doi:10.1037/a0028723

Gordon, K. C., & Baucom, D. H. (2003). Forgiveness and marriage: Preliminary support for a measure based on a model of recovery from a marital betrayal. *American Journal of Family Therapy, 31*(3), 179-99. doi:10.1080/0192618030115

Gordon, K. C., & Christman, J. A. (2008). Integrating social information processing and attachment style research with cognitive-behavioral couple therapy. *Journal of Contemporary Psychotherapy, 38*(3), 129-38. doi:10.1007/s10879-008-9084-2

Gottman, J. M. (1999). *The marriage clinic: A scientifically based marital therapy.* New York: Norton Professional Books.

Gottman, J. M. (2002). *The relationship cure: A 5-step guide to strengthening your marriage, family, and friendships.* New York: Three Rivers.

Gottman, J. M., Ryan, K. D., Carrère, S., & Erley, A. M. (2002). Toward a scientifically based marital therapy. In H. A. Liddle, D. A. Santisteban, R. F. Levant, & J. H. Bray (Eds.), *Family psychology: Science-based interventions* (pp. 147-74). Washington, DC: American Psychological Association. doi:10.1037/10438-008

Granqvist, P. (2005). Building a bridge between attachment and religious coping: Tests of moderators and mediators. *Mental Health, Religion & Culture, 8*(1), 35-47. doi:10.1080/13674670410001666598

Greenberg, L. J., Warwar, S. H., & Malcolm, W. M. (2008). Differential effects of emotion-focused therapy and psychoeducation in facilitating forgiveness and letting go of emotional injuries. *Journal of Counseling Psychology, 55*(2), 185-96. doi:10.1037/0022-0167.55.2.185

Grubbs, J. B., Sessoms, J., Wheeler, D. M., & Volk, F. (2010). The Cyber-Pornography Use Inventory: The development of a new assessment instrument. *Sexual Addiction & Compulsivity, 17*(2), 106-26. doi:10.1080/10720161003776166

Haley, J. (1976). *Problem solving therapy.* San Francisco: Jossey-Bass.

Harley, W. (2001). *His needs, her needs.* New York: Revell.

Harley, W. F., Jr. (2008). *Love busters: Protecting your marriage from habits that destroy romantic love.* Ada, MI: Revell.

Hart, A. D., & May, S. M. (2003). *Safe haven marriage: Building a relationship you want to come home to.* Nashville, TN: Nelson.

Harvey, J. H., & Pauwels, B. G. (2004). Modesty, humility, character strength, and positive psychology. *Journal of Social and Clinical Psychology, 23*(5), 620-23. doi:10.1521/jscp.23.5.620.50753

Hayes, S., Strosahl, K. D., & Wilson, K. G. (2011). *Acceptance and commitment therapy: The process and practice of mindful change* (2nd ed.). New York: Guilford.

Hecker, L. (2011). Trauma and recovery in couple therapy. In Wetchler, J. L. (Ed.), *Handbook of clinical issues in couple therapy* (2nd ed., pp. 129-44). New York: Routledge.

Hernandez, S. L. (1998). The emotional thermometer: Using family sculpting for emotional assessment. *Family Therapy, 25*(2), 121-28.

Hirst, W., Phelps, E. A., Buckner, R. L., Budson, A. E., Cuc, A., Gabrieli, J. D. E. . . . Vaidya, C. J. (2009). Long-term memory for the terrorist attack of September 11: Flashbulb memories, event memories, and the factors that influence their retention. *Journal of Experimental Psychology: General, 138*(2), 161-76. doi:10.1037/a0015527

Hook, J. N., Davis, D. E., Owen, J., Worthington, E. L., Jr., & Utsey, S. O. (2013). Cultural humility: Acknowledging limitations in one's multicultural competencies. *Journal of Counseling Psychology 60*(3), 353-60.

Hook, J. N., Worthington, E. L., Jr., Ripley, J. S., & Davis, D. E. (2011). Christian approaches for helping couples: Review of empirical research and recommendations for clinicians. *Journal of Psychology and Christianity, 30*(3), 213-22.

Hsia, J. F., & Schweinle, W. E. (2012). Psychological definitions of love. In M. Paludi (Ed.), *The psychology of love* (pp. 15-17). Santa Barbara, CA: Praeger.

Hubble, M. A., Duncan, B. L., & Miller, S. D. (1999). *The heart and soul of change: What works in therapy.* Washington, D.C.: American Psychological Association.

Hugo, Victor. (1994). *Les misérables.* Hertfordshire, UK: Wordsworth Editions.

Hundt, N. E., Williams, A. M., Mendelson, J., & Nelson-Gray, R. O. (2013). Coping mediates relationships between reinforcement sensitivity and symptoms of psychopathology. *Personality and Individual Differences, 54*(6), 726-31. doi:10.1016/j.paid.2012.11.028

Irving, L. M., Snyder, C. R., Cheavens, J., Gravel, L., Hanke, J., Hilberg, P., & Nelson, N. (2004). The relationships between hope and outcomes at the pretreatment, beginning, and later phases of psychotherapy. *Journal of Psycho-*

therapy Integration, 14(4), 419-43. doi:10.1037/1053-0479.14.4.419

Jacobson, N. S., and Margolin, G. (1979). *Marital therapy: Strategies based on social learning and behavior exchange principles.* New York: Brunner/Mazel.

Jacobson, N. S., & Addis, M. E. (1993). Couple therapy: What do we know and where are we going? *Journal of Consulting and Clinical Psychology, 61*(1), 85-93.

Jakubowski, S. F., Milne, E. P., Brunner, H., & Miller, R. B. (2004). A review of empirically supported marital enrichment programs. *Family Relations, 53*(5), 528-36. doi:10.1111/j.0197-6664.2004.00062.x

Johnson, S., & Woolley, S. R. (2008). Emotionally focused couples therapy: An attachment-based treatment. In G. O. Gabbard (Ed.), *Textbook of psychotherapeutic treatments* (pp. 553-79). Arlington, VA: American Psychiatric Publishing.

Jones, D. J., Beach, S. R. H., & Fincham, F. D. (2006). Family relationships and depression. In A. L. Vangelisti & D. Perlman (Eds.), *The Cambridge handbook of personal relationships* (pp. 313-27). New York: Cambridge University Press.

Kahneman, D. (2013). *Thinking, fast and slow.* New York: Farrar, Straus and Giroux.

Keane, T. M., Fairbank, J. A., Caddell, J. M., Zimering, R. T., Taylor, K. L., & Mora, C. A. (1989). Clinical evaluation of a measure to assess combat exposure. *Psychological Assessments: A Journal of Consulting & Clinical Psychology, 1,* 53-55.

Knaus, W. J., & Ellis, A. (2012). *The cognitive behavioral workbook for depression: A step by step program.* New York: New Harbinger.

Koerner, K. (2012). *Doing dialectical behavior therapy: A practical guide.* New York: Guilford.

Kohout, F. J., Berkman, L. F., Evans, D. A., & Cornoni-Huntley, J. (1993). Two shorter forms of the CES-D Depression Symptoms Index. *Journal of Aging and Health, 5*(2), 179-93. doi:10.1177/089826439300500202

Lambert, N. M., Fincham, F. D., LaVallee, D. C., & Brantley, C. W. (2012). Praying together and staying together: Couple prayer and trust. *Psychology of Religion and Spirituality, 4*(1), 1-9. doi:10.1037/a0023060

Lamoureux, B. E., Palmieri, P., Jackson, A. P., & Hobfoll, S. E. (2012). Child sexual abuse and adulthood-interpersonal outcomes: Examining pathways for intervention. *Psychological Trauma, 4*(6), 605-13. doi:10.1037/a0026079

Lawrence, E., Eldridge, K., Christensen, A., & Jacobson, N. S. (1999). Integrative couple therapy: The dyadic relationship of acceptance and change. In J. M. Donovan (Ed.), *Short-term couple therapy* (pp. 226-61). New York: Guilford.

Lee, R. S. C., Hermens, D. F., Porter, M. A., & Redoblado-Hodge, M. A. (2012). A meta-analysis of cognitive deficits in first-episode major depressive disorder. *Journal of Affective Disorders, 140*(2), 113-24. doi:10.1016/j.jad.2011.10.023

Leiblum, S. R. (2006). *Principles and practice of sex therapy.* New York: Guilford Press.

Levin, M. E., Lillis, J., & Hayes, S. C. (2012). When is online pornography viewing problematic among college males? Examining the moderating role of experiential avoidance. *Sexual Addiction & Compulsivity, 19*(3), 168-80.

Lewis, C. S. (1952). *Mere Christianity.* New York: Macmillan.

Madigan, S. (2010). *Narrative therapy.* Washington, DC: American Psychological Association.

McCullough, M. E., Exline, J. J., & Baumeister, T. F. (1998). An annotated bibliography of research on forgiveness and related topics. In Evertt L. Worthington Jr. (Ed.), *Dimensions of forgiveness: Psychological research and theological speculations* (pp. 193-317). Philadelphia: The Templeton Foundation Press.

McGoldrick, M., Giordano, J., & Garcia-Preto, N. (Eds.). (2005). *Ethnicity and family therapy* (3rd ed.). New York: Guilford.

McMinn, M. R., Fervida, H., Louwerse, K. A., Pop, J. L., Thompson, R. D., Trihub, B. L., & McLeod-Harrison, S. (2008). Forgiveness and prayer. *Journal of Psychology and Christianity, 27*(2), 101-9.

McMinn, M. R., Ruiz, J. N., Marx, D., Wright, J. B., & Gilbert, N. B. (2006). Professional psychology and the doctrines of sin and grace: Christian leaders' perspectives. *Professional Psychology: Research and Practice, 37*(3), 295-302.

McNulty, J. K., & Fincham, F. D. (2012). Beyond positive psychology? Toward a contextual view of psychological processes and well-being. *American Psychologist, 67*(2), 101-10.

Miller, S., Wackman, D. B., & Nunnally, E. W. (1983). Couple communication: Equipping couples to be their own best problem solvers. *The Counseling Psychologist, 11*(3), 73-77. doi:10.1177/0011000083113007

Minuchin, S., Lee, W.-Y., & Simon, G. M. (2006). *Mastering family therapy: Journeys of growth and transformation* (2nd ed.). Hoboken, NJ: Wiley & Sons.

Minuchin, S., Reiter, M. D., & Borda, C. (2014). *The craft of family therapy: Challenging certainties.* New York: Routledge.

Moyers, T. B., & Rollnick, S. (2002). A motivational interviewing perspective on resistance in psychotherapy. *Journal of Clinical Psychology, 58*(2), 185-93.

Nelson, B. S., Wangsgaard, S., Yorgason, J., Kessler, M. H., & Carter-Vassol, E. (2002). Single- and dual-trauma couples: Clinical observations of relational characteristics and dynamics. *American Journal of Orthopsychiatry, 72*(1), 58-69.

Nelson Goff, B. S., Reisbig, A. M. J., Bole, A., Scheer, T., Hayes, E., Archuleta, K. L., Henry, S. B., Hoheisel, C. B., Nye, B., Osby, J., Sanders-Hahs, E., Schwerdt-feger, K. L., & Smith, D. B. (2006). The effects of trauma on intimate relation-ships: A qualitative study with clinical couples. *American Journal of Ortho-psychiatry, 76*, 451-60.

Newton, R. R., Connelly, C. D., & Landsverk, J. A. (2001). An examination of measurement characteristics and factorial validity of the Revised Conflict Tactics Scale. *Educational and Psychological Measurement, 61*(2), 317-35. doi:10.1177/00131640121971130

Nolen-Hoeksema, S. (2011). Lost in thought: The perils of rumination. In M. A. Gernsbacher, R. W. Pew, L. M. Hough & J. R. Pomerantz (Eds.), *Psychology and the real world: Essays illustrating fundamental contributions to society* (pp. 189-95). New York: Worth.

Norcross, J. C., Krebs, P. M., & Prochaska, J. O. (2011). Stages of change. *Journal of Clinical Psychology, 67*(2), 143-54. doi:10.1002/jclp.20758

O'Farrell, T. J., & Schein, A. Z. (2011). Behavioral couples therapy for alcoholism and drug abuse. *Journal of Family Psychotherapy, 22*(3), 193-215. doi:10.1080/08975353.2011.602615

O'Leary, K. D. (2008). Couple therapy and physical aggression. In A. S. Gurman (Ed.), *Clinical handbook of couple therapy* (4th ed., pp. 478-98). New York: Guilford.

Olino, T. M., Yu, L., Klein, D. N., Rohde, P., Seeley, J. R., Pilkonis, P. A., & Lew-insohn, P. M. (2012). Measuring depression using item response theory: An examination of three measures of depressive symptomatology. *International Journal of Methods in Psychiatric Research, 21*(1), 76-85. doi:10.1002/mpr.1348

Orlinsky, D. E., Ronnestad, M. H., Willutski, U. (2004). Fifty years of psychotherapy process-outcome research: Continuity and change. In M. J. Lambert (Ed.), *Handbook of psychotherapy and behavior change* (5th ed.). New York: Wiley.

Owen, J., Duncan, B., Anker, M., & Sparks, J. (2012). Initial relationship goal and couple therapy outcomes at post and six-month follow-up. *Journal of family psychology, 26*(2), 179-86. doi:10.1037/a0026998

Paleari, F. G., Regalia, C., & Fincham, F. D. (2009). Measuring offence-specific forgiveness in marriage: The Marital Offence-Specific Forgiveness Scale (MOFS). *Psychological Assessment, 21*(2), 194-209. doi:10.1037/a0016068

Pargament, K. I., Magyar, G. M., Benore, E., & Mahoney, A. (2005). Sacrilege: A study of sacred loss and desecration and their implications for health and well-being in a community sample. *Journal for the Scientific Study of Religion,* *44,* 59-78.

Peterson, K. M., & Smith, D. A. (2011). Attributions for spousal behavior in relation to criticism and perceived criticism. *Behavior Therapy, 42*(4), 655-66.

Poulsen, F. O., Busby, D. M., & Galovan, A. M. (2013). Pornography use: Who uses it and how it is associated with couple outcomes. *Journal of Sex Research, 50*(1), 72-83. doi:10.1080/00224499.2011.648027

Previti, D., & Amato, P. R. (2004). Is infidelity a cause or a consequence of poor marital quality? *Journal of Social and Personal Relationships, 21*(2), 217-30. doi:10.1177/0265407504041384

Reis, H. T., & Shaver, P. R. (1988). Intimacy as an interpersonal process. In S. Duck (Ed.), *Handbook of research in personal relationships* (pp. 367-89). London: Wiley.

Rhoades, G. K., Stanley, S. M., & Markman, H. J. (2012). The impact of the transition to cohabitation on relationship functioning: Cross-sectional and longitudinal findings. *Journal of Family Psychology, 26*(3), 348-58. doi:10.1037/a0028316

Ripley, J. S., Leon, C., Worthington, E. L., Jr., Berry, J. W., Davis, E. B., Smith, A., Atkinson, A., & Sierra, T. (Forthcoming, 2014). Efficacy of religion accommodative strategic hope-focused theory applied to couples therapy. *Couple and Family Psychology: Research and Practice.*

Ripley, J. S., Maclin, V., Hook, J. N., Worthington, E. L., Jr. (2013). The hope-focused couples approach to counseling and enrichment. In E. L. Worthington Jr., E. L. Johnson, J. N. Hook & J. D. Aten (Eds.), *Evidence-based practices for Christian counseling and psychotherapy* (pp. 189-208). Downers Grove, IL: InterVarsity Press.

Ripley, J. S., & Worthington, E. L., Jr. (2002). Hope-focused and forgiveness-based group interventions to promote marital enrichment. *Journal of Counseling & Development, 80*(4), 452-63. doi:10.1002/j.1556-6678.2002.tb00212.x

Ripley, J. S., Worthington, E. L., Jr., Bromley, D. G., & Kemper, S. D. (2005). Covenantal and contractual values in marriage: Marital Values Orientation towards Wedlock or Self-actualization: (Marital VOWS) Scale. *Personal Relationships, 12,* 317-36.

Ripley, J. S., Worthington, E. L., Jr., & Maclin, V. L. (2011). The hope-focused approach to couple enrichment and counseling. In D. K. Carson & M. Casado-Kehoe (Eds.), *Case studies in couples therapy: Theory-based approaches* (pp. 369-81). New York: Routledge.

Ropelato, J. (2014, January). Internet pornography statistics. Retrieved from

http://internet-filter-review.toptenreviews.com/internet-pornography-sta
tistics-pg4.html.

Rosenau, D. (2002). *A celebration of sex: A guide to enjoying God's gift of sexual intimacy*. New York: HarperCollins.

Sanford, K. (2010). Perceived threat and perceived neglect: Couples' underlying concerns during conflict. *Psychological Assessment, 22*(2), 288-97.

Scheel, K. R. (2000). The empirical basis of dialectical behavior therapy: Summary, critique, and implications. *Clinical Psychology: Science and Practice, 7*(1), 68-86. doi:10.1093/clipsy/7.1.68

Scheel, M. J. (2010). Client common factors represented by client motivation and autonomy. *The Counseling Psychologist, 39*(2), 276-85. doi:10.1177/0011000010375309

Seligman, M. E. P. (1995). The effectiveness of psychotherapy: The *Consumer Reports* study, *American Psychologist, 50*(12), 965-74.

Seligman, M. E. P. (2012). *Flourish: Positive psychology and positive interventions*. The Tanner lectures on human values, 31. Salt Lake City: University of Utah Press.

Sells, J. N., Beckenbach, J., & Patrick, S. (2009). Pain and defense versus grace and justice: The relational conflict and restoration model. *The Family Journal, 17*(3), 203-12. doi:10.1177/1066480709337802

Sells, J. N., & Yarhouse, M. A. (2011). *Counseling couples in conflict: A relational restoration model*. Downers Grove, IL: InterVarsity Press.

Shaver, P. R., & Mikulincer, M. (2010). New directions in attachment theory and research. *Journal of Social and Personal Relationships, 27*(2), 163-72. doi:10.1177/0265407509360899

Snyder, D. K., Castellani, A. M., & Whisman, M. A. (2006). Current status and future directions in couple therapy. *Annual Review of Psychology, 57*, 317-44. doi:10.1146/annurev.psych.56.091103.070154

Snyder, D. K., & Whisman, M. A. (Eds.). (2003). *Treating difficult couples: Helping clients with coexisting mental and relationship disorders*. New York: Guilford Press.

Solomon, Z., Waysman, M., Levy, G., Fried, B., Mikulincer, M., Benbenishty, R., Florian, V., & Bleich, A. (1992). From front line to home front: A study of secondary traumatization. *Family Process, 31*(3), 289-302.

Sprenkle, D. H., Davis, S. D., & Lebow, J. L. (2009). *Common factors in couple and family therapy: The overlooked foundation for effective practice*. New York: Guilford Press.

Stith, S. M., McCollum, E. E., & Rosen, K. H. (2011). *Couples therapy for domestic violence: Finding safe solutions*. Washington, DC: American Psychological Association. doi:10.1037/12329-000

Struthers, W. M. (2010). *Wired for intimacy: How pornography hijacks the male brain*. Downers Grove, IL: InterVarsity Press.

Swift, J. K., & Greenberg, R. P. (2012). Premature discontinuation in adult psychotherapy: A meta-analysis. *Journal of consulting and clinical psychology, 80*(4), 547-59. doi:10.1037/a0028226

Talarico, J. M., & Rubin, D. C. (2003). Confidence, not consistency, characterizes flashbulb memories. *Psychological Science, 14*(5), 455-61. doi:10.1111/1467-9280.02453

Tervalon, M., & Murray-Garcia, J. (1998). Cultural humility versus cultural competence: A critical distinction in defining physician training outcomes. *Journal of Health Care for the Poor and Underserved, 9*(2), 117-25. Reproduced with permission of the copyright owner. Further reproduction prohibited without permission.

Voss., G. (2010). When you lose weight, and gain it all back. *Women's Health*, online edition. Retrieved from http://www.nbcnews.com/id/36716808/ns/health-diet_and_nutrition/t/when-you-lose-weight-gain-it-all-back/#.UvL9-fldWgY.

Wade, N. G., Hoyt, W. T., Kidwell, J. E. M., & Worthington, E. L., Jr. (2014). Efficacy of psychotherapeutic interventions to promote forgiveness: A meta-analysis. *Journal of Consulting and Clinical Psychology, 82*(1), 154-70.

Wade, N. G., Worthington, E. L., Jr., & Haake, S. (2009). Comparison of explicit forgiveness interventions with an alternative treatment: A randomized clinical trial. *Journal of Counseling and Development, 87*(2), 143-51.

Wincze, J. (2009). *Enhancing sexuality: A problem-solving approach to treating dysfunction, workbook*. New York: Oxford University Press.

Worthington, E. L., Jr. (2001). *Five steps to forgiveness: The art and science of forgiving*. New York: Crown.

Worthington, E. L., Jr. (2003). *Forgiving and reconciling: Bridges to wholeness and hope*. Downers Grove, IL: InterVarsity Press.

Worthington, E. L., Jr. (2005). *Hope-focused marriage counseling: A guide to brief therapy* (2nd ed.). Downers Gove, IL: InterVarsity Press.

Worthington, E. L., Jr. (2006). *Forgiveness and reconciliation: Theory and application*. New York: Routledge.

Worthington, E. L., Jr. (2008). Humility: The quiet virtue. *Journal of Psychology and Christianity, 27*(3), 270-73.

Worthington, E. L., Jr. (2013). A Christian psychologist looks at virtue. *Bibliotheca Sacra, 170*, 3-16.

Worthington, E. L., Jr. (2013). *Moving forward: Six steps to forgiving yourself and breaking free from the past.* Colorado Springs, CO: Waterbrook.

Worthington, E. L., Jr. & Berry, J. W. (2005). Virtues, vices, and character education. In W. R. Miller & H. D. Delaney (Eds.), *Judeo-Christian perspectives on psychology: Human nature, motivation, and change* (pp. 145-64). Washington, DC: American Psychological Association. doi:10.1037/10859-008

Worthington, E. L., Jr., Hight, T. L., Ripley, J. S., Perrone, K. M., Kurusu, T. A., & Jones, D. R. (1997). Strategic hope-focused relationship-enrichment counseling with individual couples. *Journal of Counseling Psychology, 44*(4), 381-89.

Worthington, E. L, Jr., Hook, J. N., Davis, D. E., & McDaniel, M. A. (2010). Religion and spirituality. *Journal of Clinical Psychology, 67*, 204-14.

Worthington, E. L., Jr., Jennings, D. J., & DiBlasio, F. A. (2010). Interventions to promote forgiveness in couple and family context: Conceptualization, review, and analysis. *Journal of Psychology and Theology, 38*(4), 231-45.

Worthington, E. L., Jr., Johnson, E. L., Hook, J. N., & Aten, J. D. (2013). *Evidence-based practices in Christian counseling and psychotherapy.* Downers Grove, IL: InterVarsity Press.

Worthington, E. L., Jr., Kurusu, T. A., Collins, W., Berry, J. W., Ripley, J. S., & Baier, S. N. (2000). Forgiving usually takes time: A lesson learned by studying interventions to promote forgiveness. *Journal of Psychology and Theology, 28*(1), 3-20.

Worthington, E. L., Jr., & Langberg, D. (2012). Religious considerations and self-forgiveness in treating complex trauma and moral injury in present and former soldiers. *Journal of Psychology and Theology, 40*(4), 274-88.

Worthington, E. L., Jr., Mazzeo, S. E., & Canter, D. E. (2005). Forgiveness-promoting approach: Helping clients REACH forgiveness through using a longer model that teaches reconciliation. In L. Sperry & E. P. Shafranske (Eds.), *Spiritually-oriented psychotherapy* (pp. 235-57). Washington, DC: American Psychological Association.

Worthington, E. L., Jr., & Ripley, J. S. (2009). Advances in clinical research on the hope-focused couple approach. Paper presented at the American Psychological Association Conference, San Francisco, CA.

Worthington, E. L., Jr., Ripley, J. S., Hook, J. N., & Miller, A. J. (2007). The hope-focused approach to couple therapy and enrichment. *Journal of Psychology and Christianity, 26*(2), 132-39.

Worthington, E. L., Jr., Sandage, S. J., Davis, D. E., Hook, J. N., Miller, A., Hall, M. E. L., & Hall, T. W. (2008). Training therapists to address spiritual concerns in clinical practice and research. In J. D. Aten & M. Leach (Eds.), *Integrating spirituality across the therapeutic process: A comprehensive resource from intake to termination* (pp. 267–91). Washington, DC: American Psychological Association.

Worthington, E. L., Jr., Witvliet, C. V. O., Pietrini, P., & Miller, A. J. (2007). Forgiveness, health, and well-being: A review of evidence for emotional versus decisional forgiveness, dispositional forgivingness, and reduced unforgiveness. *Journal of Behavioral Medicine, 30*(4), 291-302. doi:10.1007/s10865-007-9105-8

Wright, N. T. (2010). *After you believe: Why Christian character matters.* New York: HarperCollins.

Zuckerman, M. (1979). Attribution of success and failure revisited, or: The motivational bias is alive and well in attribution theory. *Journal of Personality, 47*(2), 245-87. doi:10.1111/j.1467-6494.1979.tb00202.x

Acknowledgments

I (Jen) am grateful to so many people for their influence on me in this book. First, my husband Jeff has journeyed through 21 years of marriage with me and loved me since I was 13. He brings me the security and safety of a loving home that he has co-created with me for our two daughters. In his quiet way, he has taught me what it means to develop a secure love that can be counted on for a lifetime.

My family has been an inspiration of loving marriages. I'm grateful for my parents and parents-in-law who had loving and dedicated marriages until they were parted in this life. Their patterns of caring marriages are a legacy for generations. I'm grateful also for my three brothers, four sisters-in-law and two brothers-in-law. I couldn't imagine going through this life without them and their children in this adventure of marriage and family.

I have many friends and colleagues who have encouraged me in this work and taught me about marriage from their own lives and expertise: Rhonda Tatum Ladd, Donna Julian, Jim Sells, Bill Hathaway and Mark Yarhouse. I am especially indebted to the long walks with Rhonda and the long Starbucks "meetings" with Donna.

A special thanks to my colleague and friend Ev Worthington, who taught me what it means to be a couple therapist with devotion, integrity and virtue. All of the ideas in this book were inspired by his great ideas. I am privileged to have had the opportunity to join him in this endeavor of training great couple therapists through this approach to treatment for the last 20 years. Since I met Ev on a snowy day in 1993, my life has been enriched and blessed by him. I am grateful also to his wife Kirby, a passionate follower of God, who took several long and encouraging walks with me while I was writing this book.

I am grateful to Regent University for granting me several faculty senate grants and a sabbatical semester primarily for the completion of this book. Regent is an inspiring place to work alongside others who are in service to God each day. The students at Regent University who have been on the Hope team for the last seven years have been a tireless force of work to test, retest, create and research the interventions from this book. Those who have led the Regent Hope team include: Cynthia Leon, Ward Davis, Patrice Turner, Amy Smith, April Lambes, Seth and Brittany Rainwater, Tabitha Sierra, Elizabeth Pearce, Audrey Atkinson, Tiffany Erspamer, Camden Morgante, Anastasia Teng, Stacey Villanueva, Justin Hopkins, Elizabeth Wine, Candace Lassiter, Carolyn Bridges, Anna Ord and Aleksandra Wantke.

In a book on couple counseling, I (Ev) must acknowledge Kirby and bless her for our 44 years of happy marriage. She was instrumental in my becoming a follower of Jesus and in my growth in the faith. I owe her more than anyone could ever repay. Studying faith, work and love, especially as it shows up in forgiveness and reconciliation, has been a blessing from God. God has also blessed me with so many colleagues, many of whom I was privileged to work alongside of during their doctoral education. My own children and church home have continually kept me grounded. I also am grateful to both Virginia Commonwealth University and funding agencies that have supported my research over the years—most prominently the John Templeton Foundation, the Fetzer Institute, and the National Institutes of Health via VCU's General Clinical Research Center.

We are grateful to David Congdon of InterVarsity Press, the editor who stepped into his role as this book was beginning. He has been the ultimate professional and encourager of this work.

The hundreds of couples who have benefitted from the hope-focused approach research teams at VCU and Regent University are quiet contributors to the ideas we share here. We have learned more from them than anyone.

All of these people, and others we have not been able to mention, are gifts from God and a great support for this book and our lives. We are deeply grateful to God for them and grateful to God for the lives he has given us that allow us the opportunity to share these ideas with readers.

Subject Index

Finding the Textbook You Need

The IVP Academic Textbook Selector
is an online tool for instantly finding the IVP books
suitable for over 250 courses across 24 disciplines.

ivpacademic.com

IVP Academic Instructor Resources

Using this or other IVP Academic books as a classroom text?
Find resources for instructors at:

ivpacademic.com/resources

IVP Academic
An imprint of InterVarsity Press
Downers Grove, Illinois

An Association for Christian Psychologists,
Therapists, Counselors and Academicians

CAPS is a vibrant Christian organization with a rich tradition. Founded in 1956 by a small group of Christian mental health professionals, chaplains and pastors, CAPS has grown to more than 2,100 members in the U.S., Canada and more than 25 other countries.

CAPS encourages in-depth consideration of therapeutic, research, theoretical and theological issues. The association is a forum for creative new ideas. In fact, their publications and conferences are the birthplace for many of the formative concepts in our field today.

CAPS members represent a variety of denominations, professional groups and theoretical orientations; yet all are united in their commitment to Christ and to professional excellence.

CAPS is a non-profit, member-supported organization. It is led by a fully functioning board of directors, and the membership has a voice in the direction of CAPS.

CAPS is more than a professional association. It is a fellowship, and in addition to national and international activities, the organization strongly encourages regional, local and area activities which provide networking and fellowship opportunities as well as professional enrichment.

To learn more about CAPS, visit www.caps.net.

The joint publishing venture between IVP Academic and CAPS aims to promote the understanding of the relationship between Christianity and the behavioral sciences at both the clinical/counseling and the theoretical/research levels. These books will be of particular value for students and practitioners, teachers and researchers.

For more information about CAPS Books, visit InterVarsity Press's website at www.ivpress.com/cgi-ivpress/book.pl/code=2801.